TURTLE ISLAND

B
A

"I've been completely seduced by Sean Sherman's new book—the only thing that could get me to put it down is the invitation to go harvest dandelion capers from the field. This is so much more than enticing recipes and gorgeous photos. Each imagined bite is a story, of the people and places that nourish us, of a history of resilience and ingenuity. These pages are an expression of Indigenous identity and a pathway for reconnection to the land. Gḅekte ne?"
—**ROBIN WALL KIMMERER, author of *Braiding Sweetgrass* and *The Serviceberry***

"So many of us in the industry look up to Sean for his dedication to sharing the foods and stories of the Indigenous peoples of North America. This cookbook is a collection of the stories that tell deeper truths about our country and the people who have always been here."
—**JOSÉ ANDRÉS, chef and founder of World Central Kitchen**

"Chef Sean takes us on a journey across North America to honor and appreciate the food traditions of its original people. At a time when perspectives like his are being minimized, this book is a must-read for a true understanding of the beauty of the Indigenous culture and history of this land."
—**LEVAR BURTON, actor, author, and advocate for readers**

"The great Sean Sherman has done more than anyone of his generation to showcase and popularize the Indigenous, pre-colonial foods of this land. In *Turtle Island,* he delivers more in-depth research and fabulous recipes; it's a book that belongs in the kitchen of anyone who's serious about some of the most important roots of 'American' cooking."
—**MARK BITTMAN, author of *How to Cook Everything* and founder of The Bittman Project**

"Chef Sean Sherman is a true pioneer, both in preserving and advancing the rich culinary history of Indigenous people. With *Turtle Island,* he brings his talent and passion to the page, sharing recipes, beautiful photos, and his thoughts on what it means to honor and promote Indigenous food systems. This is a book to cook from and also to simply read and enjoy for anyone interested in food and what it means to our human history."
—**JACQUES PÉPIN, chef and television host**

"*Turtle Island* is so much more than a cookbook—it's a powerful act of storytelling, rooted in tradition and shaped by the land that surrounds it. Through the voice of Sean Sherman, we're reminded that nature is our first teacher, our deepest pantry, and our enduring inspiration. Indigenous food traditions carry knowledge not just of ingredients and techniques, but of place, season, spirit—of who we are. This book is a celebration of connection, a map of how cuisine can reflect the soul of a place—and how, in returning to these roots, we might find ourselves again."
—**RENÉ REDZEPI, chef of Noma**

"Sean has galvanized a new generation of Indigenous chefs to honor their culinary heritage and to decolonize their diets. Sean brings a deep sense of pride and identity to the Indigenous community, the importance of which can't be overstated. Sean has inspired many people, myself included, to become more curious about Native communities, the beauty of their dishes, and the importance of eating harmoniously with Mother Nature."
—**from the *Time* 100 Most Influential People entry by PADMA LAKSHMI, author of *Padma's All American***

"Indigenous food is a complex and rich cuisine that has been overlooked for far too long. Sean's book shines a welcomed light on the rich history of Indigenous food and its continued place in our growing communities."
—**STERLIN HARJO, showrunner, *Reservation Dogs***

"Native perspectives are a crucial part of the American story. Chef Sean Sherman shares his rich, delicious take on storytelling through food, and I've been fortunate enough to experience it firsthand. Now, he is shining a light on Indigenous foodways and cultures to paint a beautiful, complex picture of our intersecting histories and connections with the natural world around us. This book serves as a testament to the powerful resilience of Native peoples across North America."
—**DEB HAALAND, 54th secretary of the interior**

FOODS AND TRADITIONS OF THE INDIGENOUS PEOPLES OF NORTH AMERICA

TURTLE ISLAND

SEAN SHERMAN

WITH KATE NELSON AND KRISTIN DONNELLY

PHOTOGRAPHS BY DAVID ALVARADO, WITH JAIDA GREY EAGLE

CLARKSON POTTER/PUBLISHERS *NEW YORK*

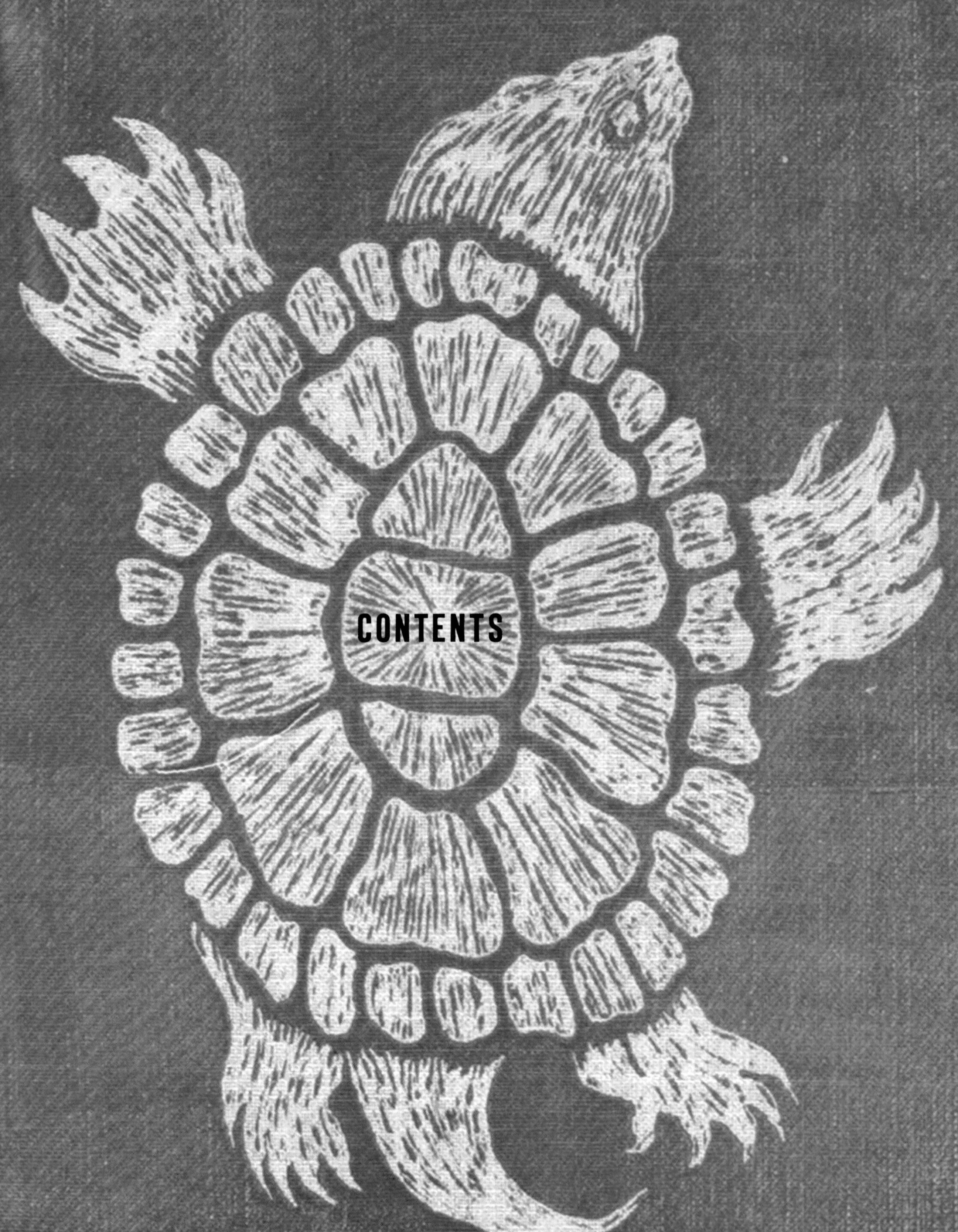

CONTENTS

INTRODUCTION

I do not think the measure of a civilization is how tall its buildings of concrete are, but rather how well its people have learned to relate to their environment and fellow man. —SUN BEAR, ANISHINAABE

"YOU ARE ON NATIVE LAND." WALKING into the entrance of my restaurant in Minneapolis, Minnesota, you're welcomed with a glowing red neon sign with those words. Inside the restaurant, you're drawn to the beautiful view of the Mississippi River, the location of a once-mighty waterfall that in the Dakota language was called *Owamniyomni,* roughly translating to "place of the falling swirling waters." The waterfall is long gone, replaced by concrete skirting and a lock and dam, but the importance of the location still holds for those who know the history.

We named the restaurant Owamni to take back the original namesake of this special place, which has held significance for the Dakota community for centuries, long before the arrival of European colonists in the early 1800s. This restaurant was years in the making, and we couldn't be prouder of creating something that not only showcases culturally important foods from Indigenous producers but also normalizes these health-sustaining foods. That was the early driving force behind my work—to help address the health issues plaguing our tribal communities, including high rates of diabetes, obesity, and heart disease. I realized we needed to return to a diet of the nourishing foods we ate before contact, which helped solidify my philosophy on decolonized cuisine. Reflecting that credo, our menu at Owamni is totally devoid of Eurocentric ingredients, such as dairy, wheat, cane sugar, beef, pork, and chicken. Eliminating these elements introduced during colonialism also meant that we would highlight the amazing and diverse Native foods of North America, and encourage guests to embrace their beauty as well.

But we aren't cooking like it's 1491. With dishes like cedar-braised duck tacos, antelope tartare with aronia berries, grilled sweet potatoes with maple chili crisp, and wild foraged teas, our team serves up delicious, nutritious, modern Indigenous food, proving to the world that it's possible to run a successful restaurant without soda and ranch dressing. I've been told time and again how ambitious and innovative this mission is in the American restaurant world, but in my mind, we're just doing what Indigenous peoples the world over have been doing since time immemorial.

When I look back on the journey that got me here, I understand I was always on this path. It just took me time in life to realize it. I was born on the Pine Ridge Reservation in South Dakota and am an enrolled member of the Oglala Lakota. When I was young, running wild across the grasslands with my sister and cousins, we had so much freedom. Like most kids in the '80s, we had sparse parental supervision and were often left to our own mischief. I remember walking along miles of barbed-wire fence lines, dogs at our sides, darting redwing blackbirds on the fence posts. The occasional curlew flew overhead, making their presence known with their shrilling high-pitched calls, and curious prairie dogs ducked into their holes that dotted the landscape. We would spend hours outside in dusty cowboy boots, our imaginations the main source of our entertainment. The prairies smelled of dust, white sage, and nearby alfalfa fields. We rode horses, wandered through shelter belts of overgrown trees, and crossed wide open grasslands on foot, always coming up with ways to keep ourselves busy.

Because we lived on a ranch, dinner consisted of lots of beef, and we eventually ate our way through the whole animal. It was normal to have tongue, kidneys, and intestines in rotation for meals. There were no restaurants on Pine Ridge during those days. My grandparents had a cabin just off the Needles Highway in the Black Hills, where we spent many a summer playing in the creek, free-climbing rock walls, and just wandering. Growing up feral had its perks. We didn't have a lot of money, but I wouldn't change my childhood for anything.

After my folks split up and my mom moved us off the reservation, a new path started. Spearfish was a town of some seven thousand people in the northern Black Hills, about fifteen miles from the Wyoming border off I-90. My mom was going back to school at Black Hills State University (where I would later attend), and I was totally outside my comfort zone. I eventually found some friends and began the transition of living in a "big city."

My life in restaurant kitchens started in Spearfish, where I got my first kitchen job at thirteen. The Sluice, as it was called, was a mining-themed American steakhouse with a mining cart salad bar. I learned quickly and continued to work in restaurants all through high school. When I was nineteen, I worked in Deadwood, South Dakota, where legalized gambling had brought hordes of tourists. I would start my day breaking down cases of whole beef tenderloins, cleaning the silver skins, portioning and bacon-wrapping them to an exact weight of five ounces. The restaurant had a $4.99 filet mignon special that came with a baked potato and a piece of Texas toast. After making a few hundred filet mignons, I would prep for dinner service.

I'd organize my station for the fury to come and pick out my music: the Black Sabbath album *Paranoid* was my usual choice to get through the rush. Right before we opened, the seventeen-year-old dishwasher and I would step outside and take a couple hits off a one-hitter usually packed with low-grade Mexican brick weed that was always in my pocket back then. We went through about four hundred steak dinners a night, more on the weekends, and I was the only one running the flattop. I had a natural ability to move and learn fast, but at that point in life, I really didn't have much exposure to good food. That would change with my next journey. After a bad truck accident that three of my friends and I were in, I got a settlement of $7,000, bought a crappy 1981 GMC pickup with mismatched doors, packed up everything I owned, and left South Dakota behind.

My first couple years in Minneapolis I lived paycheck to paycheck, leaning on cash from pawn shops to pay for food, gas, and beer. The only items I owned that had any value (and barely any at that) were a Yamaha acoustic guitar, a TV/VCR combo, and a Samsung boom box. I could usually borrow about $25 for one of those at the pawn shop down the street, whose owners I got to know pretty well. It would cost me about $35 to get them out, which I'd do on payday only to have them back in hock the next week. After a failed attempt at getting into art school (because I had no financial resources), I continued working in restaurants. Again, I wouldn't change anything.

The scene in Minneapolis back in the late '90s was really big for me at the time, with so many great musicians constantly coming through and artists having the freedom to be however weird they wanted to be. As I adjusted and started to find more friends, I got my first chance to be an executive chef at a small Spanish tapas restaurant (the first one in Minneapolis). I didn't know anything about Spanish food, but I jumped on the opportunity. Because this was still before widespread Internet access, books were my main source of education. I began devouring cookbooks, but I couldn't afford them so I would just sit at a bookstore in Uptown for hours learning about techniques, flipping through photos of dishes, and reading essays from the chefs in their own words. Rarely would I write anything down; mostly I just logged it in my memory to attempt later at work if the opportunity came up.

This hands-on self-education approach to the culinary arts was valuable, and I still love cookbooks to this day. That's why after years of study and practice with Indigenous foods, I see it's so necessary to create more resources about a topic that just didn't exist in those days. I learned a lot about European foods back then, but never even had a notion to think about Native American foods.

FORGING MY PATH

My outlook on food had begun to change as I grew more curious about Native foods, and one late spring day around 2012, I hosted my first Indigenous-focused dinner in Bemidji, Minnesota. I wasn't sure what our guests—paying customers who had seen my Facebook posts or the flyers I had posted around town—would think of a multicourse meal made sans European ingredients, but I felt confident in my conviction to introduce them to the rich Native foods all around them. To prepare, I spent a day foraging with my friend Simone Senogles, a member of the Red Lake Nation. We ventured deep into the woods to harvest seasonal ingredients. The buzzing of mosquitoes surrounded us as we navigated along the trails, our eyes scanning the underbrush in search of ramps, mushrooms, and the final fiddleheads of spring. As we collected ramps, known for their pungent flavor, Simone shared stories about their traditional uses in her community, both as food and medicine. Foraging in the woods that day became more than a culinary exercise; it was a reconnection with the land and its bounty. Each plant we gathered had a story, a purpose, and a role in the ecosystem. These experiences deepened my understanding of the interconnectedness of plants, animals, and humans in Native food systems and the profound importance of getting these ideas out there.

Emerging from the woods, I returned to a rented kitchen on the backside of a local food co-op. I was preparing a four-course meal for twenty-five people, many of whom had never tasted these foods that are the backdrop of everyday landscapes, hiding under the trees, dotting the lake shores, and popping up in random spots around town. The meal was an important stepping stone, both for me and for those who partook. One guest had me sign their menu, saying they wanted to have it for when I got famous. It was not just the flavors that resonated with diners but also the stories behind the ingredients and the irony of savoring foods that are right underfoot but seemed so foreign, since Eurocentric cuisines were the norm. Each dish was an educational experience, offering insights into a modern take on the ancient traditions and values of Indigenous cultures. That meal underscored the importance of storytelling in food—how each bite can carry centuries of history and cultural significance.

A key part of this journey started a few years before then, during a year spent in the state of Nayarit, Mexico, in the quaint village of San Pancho, where I ended up by chance to take a break from the grind of restaurant life. There, I encountered the Huichol community and started learning about their ancestral foodways. The experience of living in small-town Mexico—where hand-grinding masa for tortillas, making nixtamal for pozole, and harvesting local ingredients like hoja santa was the norm—awakened me to the disconnection I had with my own Lakota heritage. In Mexico, I saw the commonalities between our Native communities even though we were thousands of miles apart. I began to question why there weren't any Native American restaurants and why I knew so little about Indigenous foods even though I grew up with Lakota family.

Upon returning to the United States, it became clear to me that reclaiming our food traditions was more than just cooking—it was a quest for identity. It became a way to connect with our ancestors and a mission to educate a broader audience about the rich potential of Indigenous cuisine. The experience in Mexico inspired me to delve deeper into the culinary traditions of my own people and to explore how we could revitalize these practices in contemporary settings.

My work has brought me full circle to the foods of my Lakota heritage, trying to raise awareness about the amazing beauty of our many, many Native communities across North America—or Turtle Island as it's known within Indigenous circles. In the years since that initial epiphany, I have dedicated myself to learning about the rich Native foodways on this continent (and around the world). I have had the rare opportunity to visit countless tribal nations and learn from culture bearers in those communities—from the arid desert of the Southwest to the brisk waters of Southeast Alaska. All of these experiences have reaffirmed my vision and broadened my understanding of the diverse richness of Indigenous life; they also serve as the inspiration for this book.

At its heart, this book is a cookbook; I hope you will make these dishes and feed yourself and your loved ones delicious, nurturing meals. They're meant for home cooks, any night of the week, and while some recipes require very specific ingredients, many of the dishes can be made with ingredients you already know—a testament to the enduring prevalence of foods that are Indigenous, even if they're not always seen as such.

But this is not meant to be *simply* a cookbook; rather, I hope it serves as an Indigenous lens to view our past while also highlighting a pathway toward a better future. I hope it stands as a vital resource to reintroduce everyone to the diverse tapestry of Native peoples and their foodways, which have largely been overlooked in the past and present. Until very recently, food world luminaries have ignored Indigenous food to the point that they will sit on panels and declare there is no such thing as American cuisine. Dan Barber, a chef I very much admire, has gone so far as to say that, as a young nation, America has not yet developed its quintessential food culture. That couldn't be further from the truth.

This misconception is all too common and is an unfortunate consequence of the US educational system, which has long neglected true American histories, especially from non-Eurocentric perspectives. Many schools focus on uplifting one-sided, incomplete, or altogether false narratives about the great deeds of the colonizers while erasing the centuries of violent trauma they inflicted on Black and Indigenous communities.

Many of today's politicians continue to push schools to ignore or bury Black and Indigenous histories. They insist that telling this history in its fullness, bringing forth the stories of historically underprivileged and underrepresented communities is somehow "racist" against nonmelanated citizens.

This is a harmful act that will only deepen future generations' ignorance and perpetuate the racial inequalities embedded in America.

History is not always pleasant, but it is essential we learn from it and apply its lessons to our current state of affairs. Otherwise, we are doomed to repeat past atrocities, and progress will remain out of reach.

Although I can only scratch the surface of this history and the cultures and stories of North America's many tribal nations, I hope this book sheds light on the connection between food, culture, and land, and challenges the false narratives that have persisted. The culinary traditions of Turtle Island are as varied and rich as the landscapes from which they arise. Native foodways can teach us all how to connect with the natural world around us, to embrace our diversities, and to strive for a world that centers around humanity and respect.

GETTING TO KNOW TURTLE ISLAND

Many cultures have mythology about the world being created on the back of an ancient turtle, like the Haudenosaunee (Iroquois) creation stories. The term represents a world where humans live in harmony with nature. This understanding shifts how we perceive the land, moving away from arbitrary colonial borders and recognizing the vast interconnectedness of our countless Indigenous communities across what is now the United States, Mexico, and Canada. (There are so many stories to tell beyond these places, but we'll save those for a future book.) In many Native stories, a turtle typically has 13 scales on its shell, representing the 13 moons. To reflect that, this book is divided into 13 chapters, each representing a different region across the continent. While we do our very best to honor all the tribal nations, our Indigenous stories are evolving and unfolding in real time, and it's impossible to capture all that information in a single book.

The concept of Turtle Island transcends mere geography; it embodies a worldview that emphasizes balance, respect, and unity. The Haudenosaunee creation story tells of Sky Woman falling from the sky world, landing on a giant turtle's back, and creating the Earth with soil brought up by animals from the water below. This narrative symbolizes a deep reverence for the Earth, which is seen as a living entity deserving of care and respect. This perspective influences Indigenous foodways, where sustainable practices and seasonal cycles are integral to the cultivation, harvest, and preparation of food.

Each Native community has unique traditions related to their respective environments—from the icy shores of Alaska to the deserts of the Southwest to the forests of the Pacific Northwest to the rolling arid hills of Central Mexico to the Great Plains, where I grew up. Every region across Turtle Island offers a unique culinary heritage that reflects the environmental, spiritual, and social intricacies of its people. The Inuit and Iñupiat of the Arctic, for example, have developed intricate knowledge of marine life. Their diets are rich in omega-3 fatty acids, a necessity for surviving the harsh, cold climate. In contrast, the desert-dwelling tribes of the Southwest such as the Diné (Navajo), Hopi, and Apache have mastered dry-farming techniques, growing corn, beans, squash, and chiles—all staples of their ancestral diets. These variations tell stories of resourcefulness, resilience, and reverence for the ecosystem that supports them.

The Anishinaabe of the Great Lakes celebrate the harvest of wild rice that comes in late summer. This sacred grain is not only a dietary staple but also a spiritual symbol, embodying a covenant between the people and the Creator. The harvesting process involves ceremonies and practices passed down through generations, reinforcing communal ties and cultural continuity. The Coast Salish peoples of the Pacific Northwest, meanwhile, engage in the First Salmon Ceremony, an annual ritual that honors the return of the salmon and the interconnectedness of all life. This custom involves catching the first salmon of the season, sharing it with the community, and returning its remains to the river, symbolizing respect for the fish and gratitude for its role in their survival. The foodways of each region hold generations of wisdom that address not only nutrition but also spirituality and community well-being.

STARTING AN INDIGENOUS (R)EVOLUTION

Traditional foodways are innately tied to our identities as Indigenous peoples. The meals we prepare nourish not just our bodies but also our spirits and our connections to our heritage. In Native cultures, food practices are imbued with stories of creation, determination, and survival. They express joy and sorrow that connect us to our legacies. Generations of colonization have disconnected many Native peoples from their food sources, contributing to health issues and an erosion of traditional practices. European contact also introduced new ingredients that overshadowed our ancestral ones. As I explored my culinary roots, it became evident how colonial tactics and policies tried to systematically erase many Indigenous lifeways.

Recognizing this loss motivated me to launch The Sioux Chef in 2014. Creating pop-up dinners and catering events gave me the opportunity to educate people about Indigenous cuisine. I began sharing the stories behind the food and reclaiming our culinary narrative. The response was overwhelmingly positive, revealing a deep hunger not just for the food itself but also for the cultural context that accompanied it. The process of reclaiming Native food traditions involves more than just sourcing traditional ingredients; it requires a holistic approach that considers the ecological, social, and spiritual dimensions of food.

In 2018, I founded the nonprofit North American Traditional Indigenous Food Systems (NATIFS), which aims to support food sovereignty initiatives across Indian Country. This effort culminated in the opening of the Indigenous Food Lab in early 2020. However, as with many businesses, the COVID pandemic drastically shifted our operations. Then in late May, George Floyd was murdered by a Minneapolis police officer just blocks from our kitchen, and we had to adapt quickly as food deserts popped up all around us amid the unrest. The Indigenous Food Lab became a hub of activity, providing ten thousand healthy Indigenous meals a week to tribal communities across Minnesota.

The Indigenous Food Lab's mission is to promote Native foodways and provide education on how to incorporate traditional ingredients and cooking methods into modern diets. Through workshops, cooking demonstrations, and community outreach, we aim to revitalize these ancient practices and make them accessible to a broader audience. This educational component is crucial, as it helps dispel myths about our foods and highlights their nutritional and cultural value.

The resurgence of Native food traditions is not just a culinary movement; it's a reclamation of identity and culture. It's about recognizing the value of Indigenous knowledge systems and integrating them into contemporary life. This movement also addresses issues of food sovereignty, highlighting the importance of access to healthy, culturally appropriate foods. Many tribal communities face food insecurity due to historical and ongoing injustices, and reclaiming traditional foodways is a step toward self-sufficiency and self-determination.

WALKING INTO A NEW WORLD, HOLDING THE HANDS OF OUR ANCESTORS

This book aims to begin to showcase the rich diversity of Indigenous foodways, emphasizing the importance of place. By organizing the book by regions—such as the Great Lakes, the Southeastern Woodlands, and the Mesoamerican Highlands—we highlight the unique foods and culinary practices of each area and the peoples who sustain them. Each of the thirteen chapters shares the remarkable stories of ingenuity and adaptation that reflect the resilience of tribal communities. Along the way, we also highlight Indigenous chefs and community leaders who are contributing to the revival of our food systems. Their stories illustrate the ongoing movement toward food sovereignty.

Throughout this book, we followed the philosophy I developed from the beginning: In order to fully showcase the Indigenous foods of Turtle Island, we had to remove Eurocentric influences. So you'll find no dairy, wheat, cane sugar, beef, pork, or chicken, and we'll use in their place heirloom Native agricultural products, foraged wild foods, game meat and birds, fish and shellfish.

The modern Indigenous culinary movement is not about nostalgia for a past that can never be fully reclaimed. It's about stepping into the future, holding the hands of our ancestors, and creating a vibrant, living culture that honors the past while innovating for future generations. Native chefs are reimagining traditional dishes with contemporary techniques and ingredients, making them accessible to a broader audience while staying true to their roots. This fusion of old and new is a testament to the creativity of Indigenous cultures.

TAKING RESPONSIBILITY FOR OUR OWN FUTURES

One of the key messages of this book is the importance of food sovereignty. More than food security, which focuses on the availability of food, food sovereignty emphasizes the right of people to define their own food systems, to have access to healthy and culturally appropriate foods, and to control the methods of food production and distribution. This is especially important for Indigenous communities, who have often been marginalized in mainstream food systems.

By reclaiming traditional foodways, Native communities are not only preserving their cultural heritage but also addressing contemporary issues such as health disparities, social injustice, and environmental degradation. Traditional food practices often embody sustainable principles—such as community well-being, biodiversity, and respect for natural resources—that offer valuable lessons for addressing the global challenges we face as a planet.

Writing this book gave me an opportunity to reflect on my journey, the lessons learned, the connections forged, and the path toward reclamation. *Turtle Island* goes so far beyond just recipes; it's a tapestry woven with stories of healing and hope. It recognizes the voices of Indigenous peoples, a narrative long silenced in our culinary history, now revived through our food traditions. This book emerges as a beacon for those eager to explore the original flavors of this land. Through these foods, we tell the stories of who we are, where we come from, and where we can go from here.

I invite you to embark on a culinary journey that honors the rich diversity and resilience of Indigenous cultures while paying homage to the land where you currently live. As you read it, I hope you better understand and respect those who came before us, whose stories have been historically removed and are still being dismantled today. This is a celebration of the past, a recognition of the present, and a hopeful vision for the future. By exploring and embracing Native foodways, we can all participate in a broader movement toward food sovereignty, cultural respect, and environmental stewardship. Let us savor each bite as a step toward healing, connection, and understanding—a tribute to the enduring spirit of what we call Turtle Island.

THE INDIGENOUS PANTRY

> We need acts of restoration, not only for polluted waters and degraded lands, but also for our relationship to the world.
>
> —ROBIN WALL KIMMERER

INDIGENOUS PEOPLES TRADITIONALLY sourced, preserved, and cooked food before colonization in ways that varied immensely depending on where they lived. Some were skilled farmers, often using methods we now call permaculture and regenerative agriculture, while others ate diets composed almost exclusively of wild foods. Many tribes actively traded with others, too: In fact, that's how corn, the seed of a grass from Mexico, became one of the most important foods in many Indigenous peoples' diets all across much of North America.

The recipes in this book are not about re-creating the past. Some are traditional, but many are contemporary uses of traditional methods or ingredients. I encourage you to make as many of them as you can, and you'll find that many feature readily available ingredients. But in truth, a fair number of them are not dishes you can whip up easily with ingredients from the grocery store. Some of the foods in this book are hyperregional or wild and are not commercially available outside of a few sellers online or within a local community. There are also some recipes in this book you might not be able to make unless you live in the region. All of that's by design. I want to help document those foods for the present and the future. And one of my goals with this book is to help you look at where you live through an Indigenous lens and see the bounty that exists around you.

While each chapter in this book delves deeper into the foods of each region, certain foods and techniques are common throughout much of Turtle Island, so I've detailed them here.

THE INGREDIENTS

Corn

Corn, also known as maize or maíz, evolved from a wild grass known as teosinte, which is native to Mexico and Central America. Ancient farmers domesticated it over thousands of years from skinny ears holding just a few hard kernels into a high-yield, easy-to-harvest food. Corn allowed civilizations to flourish, providing complex carbohydrates in a form that stores easily without the need to leave home. Through trade, corn made its way from what is now Mexico up to the Great Lakes and Canada as well as over to the Atlantic Coast and down to the Gulf of Mexico.

For many Indigenous peoples, corn is a sacred food, and tribes have ceremonies to celebrate different parts of its season. The spiritual connection to corn makes sense: Just as people rely on corn for sustenance, corn needs humans to propagate. Without people to open the husks, most of the seeds would stay tightly locked inside. (Teosinte, on the other hand, has a husk that eventually opens, allowing birds and other animals to easily spread the seed.)

Corn is also prone to regular spontaneous mutation, which accounts for the countless varieties in the world. Over time, humans have selected corn for different qualities: its color, its plump kernels, its ability to be ground into flour or eaten when sweet, right off the cob. It also adapts over time to different climates, which is why you can find varieties suited to the desert, which grow deep roots to access water.

Another discovery Indigenous peoples made: When they cooked corn in water containing hardwood ash or other alkaline substances like lime (as in slaked lime, not the citrus), it softened the kernels enough to be made into a malleable dough. This process, known as nixtamalization, also makes more of the nutrients in corn bioavailable. Now, people nixtamalize corn using many different methods (see On Nixtamalization, page 24). The secret is to lower the pH of the water and cook the corn in that liquid for hours.

In this book, I include many different types of corn, including dried corn, sweet corn, cornmeal, hominy (which is nixtamalized and cooked whole kernels), and green corn, which is harvested midseason. At the Indigenous Food Lab in Minneapolis, we nixtamalize corn to make masa for tortillas. At home, I'll often reach for high-quality masa harina, which is a flour made from already nixtamalized corn.

Beans

Several species of beans are native to the Americas, including some of the most common ones we eat today, like black beans, pinto beans, and cranberry beans as well as lima beans and runner beans. In the three or four sisters garden (see facing page), they provide nitrogen for the soil and a source of plant-based protein.

Beans, like corn, have evolved into thousands of varieties in different sizes and colors. Many of them were unique to a single tribe or region. Over time, some of these seeds were lost or nearly lost, but many Indigenous seed savers are working to revive these heirloom varieties and reunite them with their ancestral lands and people. I write recipes that include many of the lesser-known varieties. You can often substitute a more widely available variety if needed.

Beans can be harvested at a few different stages. Green beans, which we sometimes call string beans, are simply underripe beans, harvested early and while the pods are tender enough to eat whole. When they are ripe and dried, the beans can be stored for at least a year if not longer. You can also harvest them at an in-between phase—when the pods are tough and the beans are ripe but still fresh. In the South, these are often called shelling beans (or shelly beans), and they cook much faster than fully dried beans.

When I'm cooking with dried beans, I like to soak them overnight. I find they cook more evenly this way. They also cook more quickly when they're already plumped with water.

Squash

The fruit of a vining plant, squash grows in a kaleidoscopic array of shapes and colors. Like beans and corn, some thicker-skinned varieties of squash and pumpkins (which are essentially just round versions of winter squash) are able to be stored for many months, providing sustenance for long, hard winters. Others are typically harvested early, when they have milder flavors; these are the varieties we now often refer to as summer squash.

Traditionally, some tribes preserved squash by burying them in the ground or cutting them into strips to air-dry or smoke over an open fire.

In the recipes in the book, I call for many different heirloom varieties of squash and pumpkin that are local to the region. You can often substitute with different varieties and have similar results.

I also frequently use squash seeds. Sometimes, I call for you to roast the seeds from the squash itself. But if the recipe only uses the seeds and not the fruit, I call for pepitas, which are the green hulless pumpkin seeds.

Sunflowers

Not only are they beautiful, but sunflowers provide nutrient-rich seeds that can be pulverized for flour, pureed into butter, pressed for oil, or blended into a milky liquid. Some varieties grow sweet nubby tubers known as sunchokes (sometimes called Jerusalem artichokes).

If you grow your own sunflowers, collect them when the heads are droopy, the center petals are

THE THREE (OR FOUR) SISTERS

"I hold in my hand the genius of Indigenous agriculture, the three sisters. Together these plants—corn, beans, and squash—feed the people, feed the land, and feed our imaginations, telling us how we might live," writes Robin Wall Kimmerer in her glorious book *Braiding Sweetgrass.* "For millennia, from Mexico to Montana, women have mounded up the earth and laid these three seeds in the ground, all in the same square foot of soil."

Stories vary about how these plants came to be called the three sisters, but it's clear these plants are mutually beneficial when grown together. Corn provides the tall structure on which vining beans can grow, while squash shades the ground to crowd out weeds. Bean roots work with microscopic bacteria in the soil to create a nitrogen fertilizer so all the plants thrive. Sometimes, there's also a fourth sister: the sunflower, which attracts the pollinators needed to fertilize the squash and distracts the birds from eating the corn.

It was the colonizers who brought the notion of growing crops in rows and who, as the industrialization of agriculture flourished, planted acres upon acres of single crops, a prelude to the environmentally degrading monocropping that is the standard of industrial agriculture today. Many organic gardeners and some farmers have embraced more Indigenous farming practices, often known as permaculture because they find their gardens are more productive and less prone to pest destruction when there's diversity. And that's really the bigger lesson, isn't it?

Again, as Kimmerer writes, "The way of the Three Sisters reminds me of one of the basic teachings of our people. The most important thing each can know is our unique gift and how to use it in the world. Individuality is cherished and nurtured, because in order for the whole to flourish, each of us has to be strong in who we are and carry our gifts with conviction, so they can be shared with others."

dry, and the seeds are visible. To harvest, cut the flower's head from the stalk and place it face down on a flat surface. Rub the center to shake the seeds from the flower.

I pulverize hulled sunflower seeds to make a dough of sorts for desserts, blend them with water to make a dairy substitute, or toast them to add some delicious crunch to dishes. When I call for oil, it's almost always sunflower seed oil.

Chiles

Indigenous to South America and Mesoamerica, chiles made their way over time through Mexico into the southern United States, before colonization. The word *chile* comes from a Nahuatl word. I tend to avoid using the word pepper to describe these vegetables as much as possible, since that term for them came about after colonization. (Columbus and others confused chiles with the peppercorns from South Asia.)

Originally, all chiles were spicy—to all animals except birds, that is, who devoured them without competition and spread the chiles' seeds far and wide. But it turns out that many humans also enjoyed the slightly painful sensation their heat can cause; they've been cultivated for at least five thousand years. Sweet chiles (more often known as sweet peppers) came along as the plants spontaneously mutated and humans selected them for this trait.

I use chiles both dried and fresh as vegetables and seasonings.

Tomatoes

Tomatoes are originally from South America and they made their way north into what is now Mexico well before colonization. They were not a widespread crop in most of what is now the United States and Canada until after European colonization. While I do use tomatoes in my cooking, I have mostly included them here in the chapters focused on the southern United States and Mesoamerica.

Wild plants

Indigenous peoples were expert gatherers and many still grow up today intimately knowing the plants that surround them. Not all wild plants we harvest are native to this land, but many have been folded into our diets. Wild plants—which can include trees, shrubs, and herbaceous plants—often provide us with more nutrition than cultivated ones. These plants can be used for food, medicine, seasonings, or all of the above, and many parts of the plant—whether the leaves, fruits, barks, flowers, seeds, roots, or stems—can often be consumed.

When foraging, it's important to know what you're harvesting. Some plant friends can have look-alike foes and it takes a knowing eye to discern them. (For example, wild carrots can resemble poison hemlock, which can be deadly!)

Each region has its own unique combination of wild plants. I incorporate many of them into the recipes with notes about how to harvest and process them if you happen to live in that region. If you are not already a forager, consult an expert in your region before you harvest and consume anything.

When cooking with any new ingredient for the first time, it's best to start by using small amounts to make sure you're not allergic. If you're pregnant or breastfeeding, take medication, or suffer from a chronic condition, always check with a healthcare provider before ingesting a new ingredient—especially those as powerful as wild plants.

At NATIFS, the nonprofit I founded, ethnobotanist Linda Black Elk is our education director. She is creating some incredible resources to teach people about wild foods. If you're looking to learn more about foraging, I encourage you to follow her work and first seek out any field guides or websites written about the wild plants in your region by Indigenous peoples.

For general research, I also recommend the work, including books and websites, of Alan Bergo (also known as Forager Chef), Pascal Baudar, and Alexis Nikole Nelson (also known as Black Forager).

Here are some of the wild seasonings I use the most:

Alliums: There are many, many species of wild alliums—the plant family that includes onions, garlic, shallots, and leeks—that grow in Turtle Island, some that have been here long before colonization and others that have not. I also use cultivated alliums in my cooking, but I'll seek out wild varieties when I can. Most wild alliums have very small bulbs with long, thin greens. Each has its own nuanced flavor, with some leaning warmer and more garlicky and others greener and sharper. In the recipes, I'll often call for wild alliums by colloquial names, say, prairie onion or field garlic. It's okay if you use them interchangeably with other wild alliums and I'll often offer a substitution with cultivated alliums as well.

Wild bergamot: This native plant in the mint family, also known as bee balm or monarda, has no relation to bergamot, the citrus fruit. The flowers—which can come in bright red, pale blue, and other colors in between—are beloved by bees and hummingbirds, so planting them in your garden supports native pollinators. You can use the peppery-tasting flowers and leaves as a seasoning that resembles oregano.

Conifers: Evergreen trees and shrubs, including species of spruce, pine, fir, juniper, hemlock (not to be confused with poison hemlock!), redwoods, and cedar, have long provided Indigenous peoples with medicine. Their needles or leaves as well as cones and sometimes berries can bring their beautiful fragrance to cooking, too. In the spring, many conifers push out new growth at the tips, which are exceptionally tender and flavorful.

These conifers are generally not sold for food purposes, but you can often purchase some pieces of fresh or dried conifers from individual foragers on Etsy. To harvest from conifers, I simply use clean scissors or garden clippers to prune off a few pieces that look especially green and vibrant. I make sure to harvest from different parts of the tree or shrub so I don't leave any visual impact.

As always, make sure you know from what plant you're harvesting and ask before you harvest from someone's property. Be absolutely sure that you avoid all parts of yew trees and shrubs, as they are highly toxic.

If you're pregnant, be extra careful when ingesting conifers as some of them consumed in higher quantities can act as an abortifacient.

Rose hips: In the late fall and winter in many forests, you can see gleaming red rose hips left behind after the flowers die. Rose hips are rich with vitamin C and have a naturally tart flavor. Depending on the application, I use finely ground rose hip powder as well as dried seedless rose hips that I grind myself. You can find these both sold commercially, or you can gather your own rose hips. When processing your own wild rose hips, it's imperative you make sure there are no seeds left, as they are hard enough to chip a tooth.

Sage: In Native culture, sage is viewed as a sacred plant and is used as medicine and in ceremonies. When Indigenous peoples talk about sage, they're often referring to native varieties of sagebrush in the *Artemesia* genus, which is part of the daisy family. Some varieties of Native sage, however, do share the same genus—*Salvia*—as culinary sage, which is in the mint family. These sage leaves can have a more pungent, sometimes medicinal flavor than culinary sage, so I recommend starting with smaller amounts than you're used to.

Sumac: While sumac is well known for its place in Middle Eastern cooking, Turtle Island is home to many species of this shrub. The dried, ground berries have a tart, almost lemony flavor. I reach for them when I want to perk up a dish with some acidity without adding citrus or vinegar.

Game meats and insects

Livestock, including pigs, cows, and chickens, were all brought by colonizers, and they irrevocably changed so many landscapes. Pre-colonization, Indigenous peoples relied on hunting and trapping for meat. Some game meats, including rabbit, turkey, venison, elk, and bison, are often naturally leaner than domesticated animals. Plus, if they are wild, they eat a wild diet instead of a fattening one filled with grain.

While I'd love for you to hunt for your meat if you can, you can also find farmed versions from specialty purveyors.

To learn even more about cooking game, I highly recommend the work of Hank Shaw, including all of his cookbooks.

In some parts of Turtle Island, it was and is completely normal and encouraged to eat insects. I share recipes that include some of the most beloved type of insects in chapters where appropriate.

Fish and shellfish

Indigenous peoples living near streams, rivers, and the sea often pull fish and shellfish from their local waters. Sometimes, they eat them fresh; other times, they smoke or dry them for longer storage. It's amazing to live in a world of refrigerated trucks that can whisk fish and shellfish far from their indigenous waters. But this kind of access has a cost.

Right now, there are many species of fish that are endangered. Our philosophy: Eat only what's abundant and pulled from nearby waters. If you're not fishing yourself, purchase only from suppliers you trust.

Sweeteners

Traditional Indigenous food was never as sweet as modern food is today. Most of the sweetness came from crops like squash and corn or from wild fruits or honey. Depending on the region, Indigenous peoples also tapped trees to harvest tree sap, like maple and birch, to be boiled down and used sparingly as syrup, a tradition that continues today. In the southern desert lands, people have long extracted juice from the agave plant to make everything from vinegar to syrup to fermented beverages. When I cook food inspired by these regions, I reach for agave syrup, which is sometimes sold as agave nectar. After Europeans brought honeybees, Indigenous peoples embraced honey, and I do use it occasionally in my cooking.

Salt

People living along the coasts had easy access to salt in their diet from the ocean as well as from the sea creatures and plants that lived there. Others who lived inland harvested salt from salt springs or traded salt for other essentials with other Indigenous groups. Some vegetables are naturally high in sodium and people also procured the necessary salt in their diet by using ashes made from these vegetables in their cooking. Today, I use fine and coarse sea salts in our kitchen.

Fats

Fats derived from animals were common in Indigenous cooking but people also created what we'd today call nut or seed butters as well as nut or seed milks. They also isolated plant-based oils by grinding up a nut or a seed, boiling it, and then scooping off the fat that rose to the top. In the book, I call for Indigenous fats, like sunflower and avocado oils or duck fat. I also make use of various nut and seed butters and milks.

Starches

In addition to corn, I regularly use a few other starches in my cooking, especially for gluten-free baking. The first is cassava flour, which has a neutral flavor and incredible binding capability. It often lightens the texture of dough.

Amaranth is a weedy plant that produces nutritious leaves and seeds. It grows widely in Turtle Island but was once a very important part of people's diets in Mesoamerica. Throughout the book, I occasionally use amaranth seeds—which are also thought of as a pseudo grain. I reach for the flour in gluten-free baking and pop the seeds (see Popped Amaranth, page 37) to serve like rice or as a garnish.

Speaking of rice, I use wild rice frequently in places where it grows. I also grind it finely for flour.

THE PANTRY RECIPES

When I first read the legendary book *Buffalo Bird Woman's Garden,* I was ecstatic to find such a detailed description of a traditional Indigenous pantry. An expert Hidatsa gardener, Waheenee (also known as Buffalo Bird Woman) describes what a year was like in her village along the Missouri River in the mid-nineteenth century in what is now North Dakota.

This book is beloved by growers to this day for its detailed account of how she set up her gardens, worked the fields, and saved her seeds.

I love her book because she also recounts the ways she preserved the harvest to last for months or even years and describes many of the dishes she made with her bounty.

For decades, so much of this knowledge was nearly lost because of colonization. I'm grateful for sources like this book that give us glimpses into the past so we can recover and reclaim this wisdom to build our future.

In fact, her book inspired much of my vision for the Indigenous Food Lab—a place where people can learn traditional Indigenous ways of food preservation and preparation. It has also inspired numerous recipes I've created over the years.

With these pantry recipes, I want you to see the real craft and care that goes into the traditional ways of processing some of the ingredients for the foods we eat. Do I expect you to make your own maple sugar or grind your own masa from nixtamalized corn for every meal you cook? Of course not. But I want you to know you can.

I've also included recipes for some of my go-to condiments, such as Duck Egg Aioli (page 36) and Dandelion or Milkweed Capers (page 38), that appear in different places throughout this book.

With these pantry recipes, I want you to see the real craft and care that goes into the traditional ways of processing some of the ingredients for the foods we eat.

HOMEMADE NIXTAMAL AND HOMINY

makes about 4 cups

1 pound dried field corn kernels

1 tablespoon cal or 22.5 g culinary wood ash

Nixtamalizing corn is an ancient practice that makes hard field corn tender so it can be ground into masa (dough) for tortillas, tamales, and the like. The process also unlocks corn's nutrients. (Read more about it in On Nixtamalization, page 26.) You can cook nixtamalized corn further, so it's very tender, to use as hominy (also known as pozole).

When making nixtamalized corn with calcium hydroxide (also called cal), be extremely careful handling the alkaline liquid, as it can burn your skin and eyes. I always wear goggles and keep my arms fully covered when adding the alkalizing agent and draining the corn. Keep it simmering at the back of the stove to prevent any liquid from splashing onto you.

You can nixtamalize any variety of dried corn. Each type of corn will produce a slightly different flavor and texture when you make masa, so play around to find your favorite.

In a large nonreactive pot, combine the corn with water to cover by about 1 inch. Set the pot on a back burner and turn the heat to medium-high. Just before the water starts to bubble, carefully add the cal or culinary ash. (Wear goggles and long sleeve clothing when you do.) You'll see the corn change color almost instantly. (For example, yellow corn turns vibrant orange.)

Partially cover and simmer over medium-low heat for 1 hour. Use a slotted spoon to remove a kernel from the water. Run it under cool water, then take a bite. If it breaks in half easily, you're ready to move to the next step. (It should be tender enough to bite, but still white in the center and not pleasant to chew.) If it hasn't reached that stage, keep simmering and occasionally testing until it's ready, up to 1 hour longer. (As the corn simmers, add more water as needed to keep the corn covered with water by 1 inch.)

Drain the corn, then rinse well. In a bowl, cover with lukewarm water and massage to help remove as many of the outer hulls as possible. They will rise to the surface and you can skim them off and compost them. The more hulls you remove, the smoother your masa will be. Aim to remove at least 50 percent.

At this point, you can either make Fresh Masa (page 28) or continue cooking the corn to make hominy.

To make hominy: Transfer the nixtamalized corn to a clean pot and cover with water. Bring to a simmer over medium-low heat and cook for 1 to 2 hours longer, until the kernels are tender. (Add more water as needed to keep the corn covered.)

Drain the corn (but reserve the liquid if you'll use it in a soup or a stew).

Refrigerate the hominy and liquid separately in airtight containers for up to 2 days or freeze for up to 3 months.

ON NIXTAMALIZATION

Nixtamalization is an ancient practice that originated about 3,500 years ago in ancient Mesoamerica. It spread with corn culture north throughout North America to Canada and south through Central America into the Andes highlands as well as other parts of South America. The process involves simmering dried corn kernels in an alkaline solution, which can be made with water and either wood ash, baking soda, or calcium hydroxide (also known as pickling lime or slaked lime and sometimes just called cal).

Nixtamalization helps dissolve some of the outer hulls, making the corn softer and more gelatinous so you can easily grind it into dough, known as masa (see Fresh Masa, page 28). It also makes the corn's protein, important minerals (like calcium, zinc, iron, magnesium, and sodium), and niacin more bioavailable. Finally, it reduces toxins found in moldy corn.

While you can buy dried nixtamalized corn, which you can simply cook without adding the alkalizing agent, you'll find more varieties of dried corn that will need to be nixtamalized.

The resulting corn is called nixtamal in Mexico. When cooked until soft, it's known as hominy in the United States and Canada. In the Northeast, Indigenous peoples often call nixtamalized corn, lye corn, washed corn, or hulled corn. It also sometimes goes by pozole, which is also the name of the stew made with nixtamal.

Each nixtamalization agent has its pros and cons.

Cal: Calcium hydroxide is perhaps the most common agent used because it's powerful and consistent, but it is very harsh. When working with cal, I recommend wearing gloves and goggles and keeping your skin covered.

Ash: If you build fires, ash is free and easy to come by, but you need to use more of it than you would cal. (Also, you want to only use sifted ash from hardwoods that you know haven't been treated with chemicals. Or you can seek out culinary ash.) The corn cooked in ash also requires extensive rinsing afterward to remove any traces of ash. I call for the amount of ash by weight in the recipe on page 25 because the density of it can vary significantly.

Baking soda: This can work as well, but it does leave behind a flavor I don't enjoy, which is why I don't prefer it.

If you want to understand much of the food in Turtle Island, I encourage you to try nixtamalization (see Homemade Nixtamal and Hominy, page 25) at least once. It's a fun, gratifying process and the basis of so many dishes in this book.

ON MASA HARINA

Masa harina allows you to make masa more easily at home. The flour, made from nixtamalized, dehydrated, and ground corn, lets you just add water. For many years, Maseca was the only widely available brand of masa harina, but you can now find better-quality versions online and at some markets.

Masienda (masienda.com), for example, makes masa harina from four different colors of corn, all sourced from heirloom corn grown in Mexico. Bob's Red Mill makes their masa harina from organic yellow corn and King Arthur Flour uses organic white corn.

You can make any of the recipes in the book that call for fresh masa using masa harina. Below are some rough equivalencies. Know that when you use masa harina, you might often end up with a little extra than what's called for in the recipe, but that's okay.

FRESH MASA (by WEIGHT)	MASA HARINA	FINE SEA SALT	WARM WATER
8 ounces	1 cup	pinch	¾ cup
1 pound	1¾ cups	¼ teaspoon	1⅓ cups
1½ pounds	2½ cups	⅜ teaspoon	2 scant cups
2 pounds	3½ cups	½ teaspoon	2⅔ cups

THE METHOD In a bowl, stir together the masa harina and salt, then add the warm water. Knead to form a soft dough, making sure no dry spots remain. Cover and let stand for 20 minutes to 1 hour to allow the flour to fully hydrate before using the masa.

You might need to add a little more water or masa harina to achieve the proper texture, which will depend on the recipe.

FRESH MASA FROM HOMEMADE NIXTAMAL

makes about 2 pounds

4 cups Homemade Nixtamal (page 25), well drained

½ teaspoon fine sea salt (optional)

Masa is the dough made from nixtamalized corn that's used in many recipes throughout this book, including tortillas, tamales, and so many other applications. Like bread baking, masa making is a lifelong practice and one that's much easier to learn by doing rather than from a recipe.

While you can grind your nixtamal using the meat-grinder attachment on a stand mixer, you get better results with a hand-cranked corn grinder followed by a food processor. If you plan to make homemade masa part of your cooking routine, a corn grinder is a wise investment. Below, I offer both methods.

For a deeper dive on masa making, I highly recommend the book *Masa* by Jorge Gaviria, founder of Masienda, a company dedicated to helping cooks make high-quality masa. I also recommend their masa harina, a flour that lets you just add water for making masa.

Throughout the book, I use masa in many different recipes. If you're not up for making your own homemade fresh masa, you can either purchase premade fresh masa from tortillerias or shortcut the process using high-quality masa harina (see On Masa Harina, page 27).

Spin the nixtamal in a salad spinner or pat it dry with a clean kitchen towel.

To use a meat grinder: To grind the nixtamal with a meat-grinder attachment, set up the grinder with a medium grinding plate and have a bowl ready to catch the ground corn. Sprinkle the nixtamalized kernels into the feeder and allow the grinder to do its work without pushing on the kernels. After the kernels have all been ground once, put them through the grinder again, this time using the pusher and a little water as necessary to help move them through.

To use a corn grinder and food processor: To grind the nixtamal with a corn grinder and food processor, attach the grinder to your countertop and set up the grinding plates for a fine grind for tortillas or a more medium grind for tamales. Grind the corn into a bowl according to the manufacturer's instructions, adding 1 tablespoon of water at a time to keep the grinder and corn lubricated. Transfer the ground corn to a food processor and process until it reaches the texture of mashed potatoes.

When your masa is ready, mix the sea salt into the dough, if desired.

You can refrigerate fresh masa in an airtight container for up to 3 days. You might need to add a little water to rehydrate it a bit before using.

You can tightly wrap masa in plastic wrap and freeze for up to 3 months.

CORN TORTILLAS

makes sixteen 6-inch tortillas

At our Indigenous Food Lab, you'll often see griddles lined with tortillas puffed up like balloons. The puff happens after a third flip, during the last few seconds of cooking, when a pocket of steam presses apart the outer edges of the tortilla. It's a sign that the masa was perfectly ground, hydrated, pressed, and seared on a very hot pan, and the tortilla is thoroughly cooked on the inside.

The puff can take practice to achieve but isn't crucial to a delicious tortilla. Whether they perfectly puff or not, these tortillas will still taste so much better than store-bought tortillas that sit on the shelves for weeks at a time.

If you decide you enjoy making tortillas, I recommend getting a tortilla press to help you create consistent rounds. But you can also press them with a pie plate or roll them out with a rolling pin.

1 pound Fresh Masa (page 28) or use masa harina (see chart, page 27)

Knead the masa in a bowl to assess the texture. For soft tortillas, you want the dough to feel moist but not sticky. If it feels a bit dry, add 1 teaspoon water and knead for about 30 seconds, repeating until you have the right consistency.

To test the dough, roll the masa into a ball, the size of a Ping-Pong ball, then flatten into a ½-inch-thick round. If the edge is smooth, the dough is ready. If it cracks, knead in more water, 1 teaspoon at a time. If the dough sticks to your hands, you'll want to add masa harina or just let the dough stand for 10 minutes to allow it to dry a bit and then test again.

Divide the dough into 16 equal portions and roll into balls the size of Ping-Pong balls. Heat a well-seasoned comal, griddle, or cast-iron skillet over medium-high heat for 2 minutes. (You're aiming for the surface to reach at least 400°F.)

Set a piece of plastic wrap or parchment paper on the bottom of a tortilla press or a work surface. Place a ball of the dough on top. Set a piece of plastic wrap or parchment paper on top of the dough. Press or roll the dough into a ¹⁄₁₆-inch-thick tortilla.

Uncover, peel the tortilla off the wrap, and transfer to the griddle. Sear for 20 to 30 seconds, until dry on the bottom with a little bit of blistering in spots. Flip and cook for another 20 to 30 seconds. Flip one last time, pressing the tortilla in spots with a spatula, and cook for 10 to 20 seconds, looking for that magical tortilla puff. (If it doesn't puff, it's okay.)

Transfer to a clean kitchen towel and cover to keep warm as you press and cook the remaining tortillas.

You can place tortillas between layers of parchment paper and freeze in an airtight container for up to 1 month.

AREPA DOUGH

makes about 2 pounds (enough for 8 to 12 arepas)

Arepas are little cakes made from cooked corn dough that has *not* been nixtamalized. They're traditional in Venezuela and Colombia. Most recipes for arepas call for arepa flour, which is typically a highly processed flour made from the cooked dough that has been dehydrated and ground. At our Indigenous Food Lab, we create arepa dough from heirloom varieties of corn.

I adapted it here for the home cook by using either a stand mixer with a meat-grinder attachment or a corn grinder with a food processor. The arepa dough will be more coarse than masa, but the oil helps hold it together.

(Or, you can, of course, use arepa flour. For the method, see page 318.)

- 1 pound dried whole-kernel corn (see Notes), soaked overnight and drained
- 2 tablespoons sunflower oil
- 1 teaspoon fine sea salt

Notes

- *If you can find cracked corn, you can use that instead of cooking a dried whole-kernel corn and rubbing off the hulls. They will also cook a bit faster than whole corn.*
- *To speed up cooking the corn, you can use a pressure cooker. Start by pressure-cooking the corn for 1 hour 15 minutes on high pressure and then move on to the skin removal.*

In a pot, combine the soaked corn kernels with water to cover by 2 inches and bring to a boil over high heat. Reduce the heat to medium-low and simmer for 2 to 3 hours (or sometimes even longer), until completely tender. When you bite into the kernels, the insides should be translucent.

Drain and transfer the kernels to a large bowl filled with water. Aggressively rub the corn together to remove as many of the outer hull layers as you can. The hulls will float to the top. Just skim them off and discard them.

To use a meat grinder: Set up the grinder with a medium grinding plate and have a bowl ready to catch the ground corn. Sprinkle the kernels into the feeder and allow the grinder to do its work without pushing on the kernels. After the kernels have all been ground once, put them through the grinder again, this time using the pusher and a little water as necessary to help move them through.

Knead in the oil and salt until it holds its shape when you roll it into a ball. Cover the dough and refrigerate for 1 to 2 hours before using it to make arepas.

To use a corn grinder and food processor: Attach the grinder to your countertop and set up the grinding plates for a medium grind. Grind the corn into a bowl according to the manufacturer's instructions, adding 1 tablespoon water at a time to keep the grinder and corn lubricated.

Transfer the ground corn to a food processor. Add the oil and salt and process until you have a coarse dough that is not too sticky, sprinkling in a little more water if needed to hold it together.

The dough should hold its shape when you roll it into a ball.

Cover and refrigerate the dough for 1 to 2 hours before using it to make arepas.

GEF GLOBAL ENVIRONMENT FACILITY
INVESTING IN OUR PLANET
CONABIO
Cultivo: Maíz
Clave de ntificación: Z-M-17
Nombre Local: Mezcla
Productor: Daniela Grijalva Olivera
Comunidad: Ejido Unión Zapata
Año: 2020
inifap

MASON
MASON

SEED, NUT, AND GRAIN MILKS

makes 1 quart

Dairy came with European colonization, and the livestock that people brought changed the landscape of Turtle Island, which is why I typically avoid it in my kitchen. Traditionally, some Indigenous groups would pound nuts and seeds and blend the mixture with water to make rich porridges or creamy liquids. So strained seed, nut, and grain milks like the ones here aren't far from tradition.

Each seed or nut has its own distinctive flavor, and nut milks tend to feel the most creamy because of their rich fat. At Owamni, I use wild rice and pepita milk most often, but I also let the region where I am inspire me. For example, in the South, I'd use pecan milk. In the Northwest, hazelnut.

1 cup sunflower seeds, pepitas, pecans, black walnut pieces, skinned hazelnuts, or uncooked wild rice, soaked overnight in 6 cups of water

Pinch of sea salt

Maple syrup (optional)

Drain the soaked nuts, seeds, or grains, then rinse and transfer to a blender, preferably one that's high-powered. Add 4 cups fresh water and the salt and blend until very smooth.

Line a sieve with two layers of cheesecloth or a clean kitchen towel and pour in the nut milk. Pull up the cloth around the puree and twist to squeeze. (Alternatively, use a nut-milk bag to drain.) Whisk in a little maple syrup, if desired, to sweeten.

If desired, reserve the pulp for another use (see Notes).

Notes

- *To deepen the flavor of the milks, you can toast the seeds first before soaking.*
- *You can use the pulp in place of nut flours or bran in baked goods or add it to smoothies.*

SWEET CORN MILK

makes about 3 cups

I reach for sweet corn milk whenever I want to enhance the flavor of other corn in the dish. For example, it brings more sweetness to the Green Corn Soup (page 167). You could also use it in place of some of the water for the Indigenous-Inspired Shrimp 'n' Grits (page 142).

2 cups sweet corn kernels (from 2 to 3 large ears)

Pinch of sea salt

In a blender, combine the corn, 2 cups water, and the salt. Puree until very smooth.

Line a sieve with two layers of cheesecloth and set over a bowl and pour in the puree. Pull up the cloth around the puree and twist to squeeze the corn milk into the bowl. (Alternatively, use a nut-milk bag to drain.) Discard the solids. Refrigerate for up to 3 days.

MAPLE SUGAR

makes 1½ cups

I frequently use maple syrup as a sweetener in my cooking and baking, but sometimes I don't want the added moisture, so I turn to maple sugar. While you can purchase maple sugar, it's also easy and satisfying to make your own.

- **2 cups pure maple syrup**

Pour the syrup into a large, heavy saucepan and clip a candy/deep-fry thermometer to the side. Bring to a boil over high heat, then reduce the heat to medium-high and cook the syrup vigorously without stirring. Keep an eye on the syrup to make sure it doesn't boil over.

Once the syrup's temperature reaches between 257° and 262°F, remove the pan from the heat. Start to stir the syrup with a wooden spoon; it will start to turn granular within a couple of minutes and form large clumps. (If you're using a cast-iron pot, it can take as long as 10 minutes because the pan holds so much heat.)

When the sugar is cooled, shake it through a fine-mesh sieve to help sift it. If any large clumps remain, pulse them in a food processor or blender until they are finely ground and add to the remaining sugar. Store for several months in an airtight container.

DUCK EGG AIOLI

makes about 1¼ cups

This is a bit of an Indigenous mother sauce. Perhaps not traditional, but it's what I reach for whenever I want to add a bit of richness to the plate. This recipe works best in a mini food processor or the smaller bowl of your food processor (if you have the option), but you can also make it in a blender, immersion blender, or whisking by hand. Whatever you do, just make sure to add the oil very slowly to help the emulsion form.

- **1 duck egg**
- **1 tablespoon cider vinegar**
- **1 to 2 garlic cloves, finely grated**
- **½ teaspoon mustard powder**
- **⅛ teaspoon fine sea salt**
- **1 cup sunflower oil**

In a mini food processor, blend the egg for about 20 seconds, until fully combined and slightly aerated. Add the vinegar, garlic, mustard powder, and salt and blend for another 20 seconds, until well combined. Scrape down the sides of the bowl.

With the machine running, gradually add the oil, starting with a few drops at a time and later a very thin stream to develop a thick, emulsified sauce.

Transfer to an airtight container and refrigerate for up to 2 weeks.

QUICK PICKLES

makes 2 cups

Because I don't use citrus in Indigenous cooking, pickles become a fun way to add acidity to a dish. This is a good general quick pickle. I often update the aromatics for these pickles depending on the region.

- 2 cups sliced carrots, burdock root, sunchokes, or other root vegetables, or whole ramp bulbs or asparagus spears (sliced to an even thickness)
- ½ cup cider vinegar
- ¼ cup agave syrup, maple syrup, or honey
- 1 tablespoon fine sea salt
- 2 garlic cloves, peeled but whole
- 2 teaspoons yellow mustard seeds

Pack your choice of vegetable (or a mix of a few) into a clean 1-quart jar or nonreactive airtight container.

In a small saucepan, combine the vinegar, ½ cup water, the agave syrup, salt, garlic, and mustard seeds. Bring to a boil and whisk to dissolve the salt. Pour over the vegetables in the jar. Let cool to room temperature.

For the best flavor, refrigerate them for at least 1 day and use them within 1 month. (The garlic cloves might turn blue over time. It's a natural reaction between the sulfur in the garlic and the acidity. The pickles and garlic are still safe to eat.)

POPPED AMARANTH

makes 1 cup

Packed with protein and fiber, amaranth seeds are often sold as a grain and can be cooked into a porridge or pilaf or ground into a flour. The tiny seeds are also delicious when they're popped, because they lose their naturally grassy flavor and become starchy and crisp. In Mexico, you often see the seeds sold already popped. At home, I generally pop them myself.

While it works best to pop the seeds 1 teaspoon at a time, don't worry. The process moves fast and the seeds pop to about four times their size.

- ¼ cup amaranth seeds

Heat a small dry saucepan over medium-high heat for 2 minutes. Add 1 teaspoon of the amaranth, cover with a lid, and shake the pot. If the grains start popping almost right away, the pot is hot enough and you can keep going. (Otherwise, the grains will likely burn and you'll want to heat the pot some more before starting again.)

After 10 to 20 seconds, when the popping noise slows down, transfer the popped amaranth to a bowl. Continue popping the amaranth 1 teaspoon at a time and transferring to the bowl. You can use the popped amaranth right away or let it cool and store in an airtight container for up to 3 days.

DANDELION OR MILKWEED CAPERS

makes about 1 cup

When harvested while they're tightly closed and green, dandelion and milkweed buds make excellent capers. (You can also make capers out of nasturtium buds if you have them growing in your garden.)

Dandelion buds first appear in large numbers in early spring. You might also find them during other parts of the season. The best dandelion buds for capers are those that are tightly closed and growing close to the ground. Skip any of the buds attached to stems, or any that, when squeezed, reveal the yellow flower within. To find these buds, you sometimes need to push apart the leaves. If you like, you can also dig out the dandelion plant and find some buds growing just below the surface of the ground, waiting for their time in the sun. You can use the leaves for salads or pestos and roast the roots for tea.

You'll generally see milkweed buds in late spring or early summer growing in clusters. Harvest some of the clusters (but leave some on the plant, too!) and separate the individual buds before pickling.

¾ cup dandelion or milkweed buds

½ cup cider vinegar

2 teaspoons fine sea salt

If your dandelion buds have a visible calyx attached (the leaves that fan out from the bottom of the bud), remove it. Put your buds in a bowl of water and swish them around to dislodge any grit or debris. Lift them out of the water to drain.

Bring a medium pot of water to a boil. Add the buds and blanch for about 30 seconds, until bright green. Drain and shake dry, then transfer to a 1-pint jar.

In another pot, combine the vinegar, salt, and ½ cup water and bring to a simmer over medium heat, stirring to dissolve the salt. Pour this hot brine over the buds and let stand until cooled to room temperature.

Seal and refrigerate. Ideally, you'll want to let the buds pickle for at least 1 week before using the capers. Refrigerate for up to 2 months.

Note: *These capers are designed to be refrigerator pickles that you keep for a couple of months. If you prefer to make pickles for long-term storage, you can process the jars in a water bath.*

ROASTED BIRD STOCK

makes 3 to 4 quarts

Anytime you have a leftover roasted turkey, duck, or goose, save the carcass in the freezer to make stock when you want it.

- 1 roasted turkey, duck, or goose carcass
- 2 large yellow onions, halved
- 2 large carrots, scrubbed and coarsely chopped
- Dark-green tops from 1 to 2 leeks (optional)
- 5 garlic cloves, smashed and peeled
- A small handful of savory herbs (optional), such as dried sage, bergamot, or local edible conifer needles

In a large soup pot, combine the carcass, onions, carrots, leek tops (if using), the garlic, and water to cover. Bring to a simmer over medium-high heat. Reduce the heat to medium-low, partially cover, and cook for at least 4 hours and up to 10 to 12 hours (you can do this overnight) if you want a more concentrated and gelatinous bone broth. Skim off any scum or fat on the surface. Add the herbs, if using, and let the stock simmer for another hour.

Turn off the heat and let the stock cool for 30 minutes, then strain through a fine-mesh sieve into a large bowl. Discard any solids.

Cool to room temperature, then skim off as much of the surface fat as you can. Ladle the stock into airtight containers and refrigerate until well chilled. Remove any remaining fat that hardens on the surface. (You can discard the fat or use it for cooking.)

Refrigerate for 4 to 5 days or freeze for up to 6 months.

RICH BISON OR OTHER GAME STOCK

makes about 3 quarts

This roasted bone stock brings a deep rich flavor to meaty stews. You can add herbs and other aromatics that are appropriate to your region if you like.

- 6 pounds bison bones, such as knuckle bones or soup bones, or other bones from large game animals, such as elk, moose, caribou, or deer
- 2 large yellow onions, quartered
- 2 large carrots, scrubbed and coarsely chopped
- 5 garlic cloves, smashed and peeled
- 2 tablespoons sunflower oil
- 1 tablespoon tomato paste (optional)

Preheat the oven to 400°F.

In a large metal roasting pan, roast the bones for about 40 minutes, turning once or twice, until evenly browned.

Add the onions, carrots, garlic, and the oil to the pan and toss until evenly coated. Roast for about 1 hour, tossing the vegetables a few times, until well browned in spots. Transfer the bones and vegetables to a stockpot.

Pour off all but 1 tablespoon of the fat from the roasting pan. Add the tomato paste (if using) to the roasting pan and cook over medium heat just until the paste darkens and starts to glaze the bottom of the pan. Add 2 cups water to deglaze the pan and scrape up any browned bits.

Pour that deglazing liquid into the stockpot. Add enough water to cover the bones and vegetables. Bring to a simmer over medium heat, then reduce the heat to low, skimming off any scum on the surface. Partially cover and cook gently for 10 to 12 hours (you can let it go overnight), until the flavor is deep and rich.

Turn off the heat and let the stock sit for 30 minutes, then strain the liquid through a fine-mesh sieve into a large bowl. Discard the solids.

Let the stock cool to room temperature, then skim off as much of the fat as you can. Ladle the stock into airtight containers and refrigerate until well chilled. Remove any remaining fat that hardens on the surface. (You can discard the fat or use it for cooking.)

Refrigerate the stock for 4 to 5 days or freeze for up to 6 months.

GREAT PLAINS

THE WILD FOODS OF THE PRAIRIE

THE VAST PRAIRIES AND BIG SKIES OF the Great Plains is where it all began for me. The region extends all the way from the southern parts of Alberta and Saskatchewan in Canada down into the United States to portions of Texas and New Mexico. I grew up on Pine Ridge Reservation in South Dakota, on a twenty-acre ranch outside a tiny town. Imagine the scenery from *Lonesome Dove*—blazing sun, star-filled skies, rustling prairie grasses, and endless dust.

The Lakota once stood tall and strong on the Great Plains, living on a diet of hunted bison and gathered plants, with agriculture playing a secondary role. This was one of the last areas of what's now the United States to be colonized, as we fiercely defended our ancestral lands. To weaken the resolve of the Lakota and other Plains tribes, the US government mounted a campaign in the late nineteenth century to decimate bison, our main food source, then pushed us onto reservations. This effectively forced traditionally nomadic hunters into a more stationary agrarian lifestyle, which has forever impacted our foodways.

The legacy I was born into included government-issued food, involuntary boarding schools for my ancestors, forced assimilation to Christianity, the prohibition of Native languages, and the universal destruction of ancient Indigenous ceremonial practices, culinary traditions, and spiritual wisdom. Fortunately, the tapestry of my childhood was rich because our Oglala Lakota people kept our culture alive through celebrations like powwows and ceremonies like sweat lodge.

By the time I grew up, in the aftermath of colonization, Pine Ridge was one of the poorest places in the country and plagued by chronic diet-related conditions, like diabetes, obesity, and heart disease. But I didn't realize we were dirt poor, because my childhood was so rich with beautiful culture, like listening to my grandparents speak fluent Lakota. For big gatherings on our family ranch, we savored traditional meals, including harvested thíŋpsiŋla (wild prairie turnip, aka timpsila), hearty tȟaníǧa (a soup made with bison or beef intestines), and wóžapi (a berry pudding/sauce). Because I grew up eating these dishes with family and referring to them in our language, you'll see those Lakota names reflected in the recipes that follow.

But those flavorful, nourishing dishes stood in stark contrast to the commodity foods lining our kitchen shelves most of the time, like government canned beef with juices, canned vegetables, and bright orange cheese blocks.

I spent most of my waking moments outside with my sister and our cousins, who lived just down the hill. I distinctly remember the smell of hot white sage scorching in the sun and the sight of bright stars glowing on a cloudless night. When we weren't helping with ranch chores, like moving cattle and mending fences, we were out exploring the grasslands on horseback, harvesting thíŋpsiŋla and chokecherries, and hunting pheasants and grouse.

We left the reservation's sense of community, tradition, and pride behind when I was twelve, after my parents split up and our mom moved us to nearby Spearfish so she could pursue a college degree. This gave us access to opportunities we otherwise wouldn't have had, but it also came with a huge culture shock. As brown kids with thick rez accents, we faced ongoing racism in this white conservative town. I eventually made some friends, and we'd ride our BMX bikes through town with our .22 rifles on our backs to go target shooting up in the hills—no one batted an eye at us. I spent most of my teen years with my head buried in a book at the college library alongside my mom, absorbing every bit of information I could.

During college, I worked as a field surveyor for the US Forest Service, where I learned about the culinary and medicinal values of the plants that flourished in the expanse of the Black Hills, which we call Paha Sapa. I also spent time with my uncle Richard Sherman, who has devoted his life to understanding the flora and fauna of South Dakota's wild, rugged, infinitely beautiful Badlands.

Although my work takes me across the globe these days, I return home to the Black Hills whenever possible to stay connected to my roots. After all, it's where my Lakota ancestors' creation story took place, at the sacred Wind Cave. I often find myself daydreaming about what this area looked like before colonialism. Despite the traumas we have overcome and still face today, there is so much hope, beauty, and resilience across the region.

THE LAND

The Great Plains acts as a living record of this land's formation from the collision of continental plates billions of years ago, with ancient rocks exposed in places like the Black Hills and the Central Texas Uplift. Shallow inland seas once blanketed the area, leaving behind a flat floor of layered shale, sandstone, and limestone sediment. Over time, bordering mountain ranges helped form the gently sloping high plains through erosion.

For millennia, this semi-arid region was sparsely populated, until the climate became warmer and wetter—prime conditions for grass growth. That drew bison, followed by nomadic hunters. Soon, the Sioux (including the Dakota, Lakota, and Nakota/Assiniboine), Blackfeet, Cheyenne, Arapaho, Comanche, Crow, Mandan, Hidatsa, and Arikara made their homes there. Today, more than fifty tribal communities inhabit the Plains across the United States and Canada.

Perhaps because of its name, some people mistakenly assume the region is boringly uniform. In reality, it contains several unique ecosystems that offer important habitat to birds, lizards, snakes, beavers, rabbits, prairie dogs, foxes, coyotes, elk, pronghorns, and, of course, bison. The beautiful tree-covered Black Hills, for example, look strikingly different from the flat, almost featureless Llano Estacado of Texas and New Mexico. Despite the varying environs across its 1,125,000 square miles, most of the region experiences a continental climate, with cold winters, hot summers, little rainfall, and high winds.

The region is served by key waterways like the Saskatchewan River in Canada and the Red, Missouri, Arkansas, and Rio Grande rivers in the United States. It is also home to the Ogallala Aquifer, the largest groundwater reservoir in North America and a vital water source that's being depleted due to agricultural overuse and climate change.

Sandy and thorny in some spots and rich and fertile in others, the soil quality varies depending on precipitation, humidity, and natural grass cover. Sadly, the original drought-hardy, high-protein grasslands have all but been destroyed due to settler farmland development and subsequent livestock overgrazing. Colonialism shaped the land space in more subtle ways, too. The purposeful decimation of bison plays a factor, since their saliva contains special enzymes that stimulate plant growth, as does the restriction of traditional land management practices like controlled fires, which have been utilized for eons to maintain a healthy prairie.

Before the now-ubiquitous cattle ranches covered the Plains, bison numbered in the millions and tribes migrated across the area following the sacred animal. This required easily assembled and transported shelters like tepees, which are constructed by stretching a bison hide cover over a frame of pine poles.

Today, the region is also dotted with national parks like the Badlands, Yellowstone, Grand Teton, Glacier, and many more. My uncle Richard, who for a time managed our tribe's wildlife, points out that the maintenance of those lands—careful or otherwise—is wholly dependent on the government superintendent in charge, rather than an unbroken lineage of generations of Indigenous peoples who cared for this land as a central part of our cultures. In fact, he literally wrote the book on the subject (*Indigenous Peoples and the Collaborative Stewardship of Nature*) and developed a stewardship model that shows how traditional ecological knowledge can be used in these and many more settings.

THE HISTORY

When most people think of the quintessential American Indian, they tend to picture Plains Indians. Because we were among the last tribes to face colonialism, we were often depicted on horseback hunting bison in early American artwork and literature. But European horses weren't widely introduced until the 1600s, when Spanish conquistadors came searching for gold—the first of many expeditions to pillage the natural resources of the land we stewarded.

Horses changed life in the region, helping Indigenous groups expand their territories and become more economically and politically powerful. This greater mobility also caused greater competition among the previously relatively peaceful tribes, who could now easily traverse larger swaths of land—inevitably leading to squabbles over hunting grounds and even raids on one another's villages.

The French expanded into the region in the early 1700s from the Mississippi Valley and wisely established trade and military partnerships with the formidable Native communities. The British followed in the late 1700s and developed numerous trading posts. As was so often the case, Europeans brought with them some initial economic opportunities but also problems like guns, alcohol, and epidemic diseases.

In the mid-1800s, the Great Plains was hit with a major influx of Americans due to the Oregon Trail development, the post–Civil War railway expansion, and the Homestead Act of 1862, which allowed settlers to claim 160 "free" acres of land to cultivate. In the process, they destroyed the grasslands, tilled the earth for farming, overhunted bison almost to extinction, and intensified rivalries among tribal nations.

The irrepressible Indigenous communities fought back, which prompted the first Fort Laramie Treaty of 1851 (also known as the Horse Creek Treaty). In an attempt to quell conflict and ensure safe passage for pioneers, US peace commissioners met with the Sioux, Blackfeet, Crow, Cheyenne, Arapaho, Mandan, Hidatsa, and Arikara tribes in what is thought to be the largest ever gathering of Plains Natives, with more than ten thousand people present. The treaty defined each tribe's territorial borders and stipulated that the United States would safeguard those lands from further intrusion. In exchange for annuities and rations, the Native groups agreed to end intertribal warfare and authorized the government to develop roads and military outposts. Of course, all these territories would be whittled down over time through unjust and reneged agreements.

Even with the treaty, encroachment continued and sparked bloody brawls. The US government set out on another peacekeeping mission and signed the second Treaty of Fort Laramie in 1868 with the Sioux, Blackfeet, and Arapaho. This created the Great Sioux Reservation, which then spanned sixty million acres centered around the sacred Black Hills. In exchange for exclusive use of their territories, the tribes agreed not to attack settlers and ceded thousands of acres that had been promised to them, but retained hunting and fishing rights on those lands.

Not long after, famed "Indian fighter" and Army officer George Custer led the 1874 Black Hills Expedition to explore the area's natural resources. When his crew discovered gold, thousands of miners flocked to the unceded Sioux territory. This led to violent clashes, eventually requiring military intervention.

Tribal leaders and US officials tried to reach an agreement but failed. The government then established even smaller reservations and lured people onto them with the promise of food and supplies. When Indigenous dissidents refused to comply, the Great Sioux War broke out in 1876, with Lakota warriors Crazy Horse and Sitting Bull leading the formidable Native forces. Custer and his troops met their demise during the Battle of the Little Bighorn, yet the government continued its ceaseless pursuit of the Black Hills. That ongoing quest precipitated the Wounded Knee Massacre—the deadliest shooting in American history, where US troops slaughtered nearly three hundred Lakota men, women, and children. Resistance leaders Crazy Horse and Sitting Bull eventually surrendered separately, and then were killed.

As for the Black Hills, the US government in 1877 redrew the lines of the Fort Laramie Treaty and seized this sacred site, which remains a point of major contention. In 1980, the US Supreme Court ruled that the government had illegally taken the land and awarded more than $100 million in reparations. But to this day, my tribe refuses to take the money—now worth north of $1 billion—because the Black Hills were never for sale. After all, in our Indigenous worldview, we never thought of land as something to be owned, bought, or sold.

The Dawes Act of 1887 (also called the General Allotment Act) hugely impacted Great Plains tribes, too, by further imposing white values about property ownership. It broke up commonly held reservation lands into small allotments to be parceled out to individuals. For a variety of reasons, many people have opted to sell or lease their allotments to white farmers and ranchers, creating checkerboarded reservations across the region. On Pine Ridge, for instance, around 60 percent of our 2.1-million-acre reservation gets leased out by the Bureau of Indian Affairs often below market value, perpetuating a vicious cycle that limits our ability to develop wealth because many people depend on that short-term payout and therefore aren't able to utilize the land to its greatest potential.

Other Plains tribes suffered similar fates. The Blackfeet, who were shrewd hunters and warriors, were one of the first Indigenous groups to move from the Great Lakes. Before colonization, their sophisticated society was so successful that it actually served as the archetype for the famous psychological concept of Maslow's Hierarchy of Needs, with its tiers of human needs, from physiological basics all the way up to self-actualization. As Blackfeet/Cherokee food sovereignty advocate Mariah Gladstone explains, Maslow, who was also a known eugenicist, spent time observing the tribe and even modeled the triangle shape on the tepee design. But he got it wrong when he placed focus on the individual rather than the community.

Like so many Plains peoples, the Blackfeet faced starvation after the near extinction of the bison, eventually taking up agriculture and signing away their land in order to survive. Today, they are the most populous Native group in Montana and reside on a 1.5-million-acre reservation, about 40 percent of which is owned by non-Natives due to the private land ownership allotment system. And the tribe has had to fight tirelessly in court to protect its ostensibly guaranteed water, hunting, fishing, trapping, and gathering rights. The Blackfeet have three Canadian reserves in southern Alberta and Saskatchewan, too.

Also migrating from the Great Lakes, the Crow call themselves Apsáalooke, meaning "children of the large-beaked bird." For a time, they were affiliated with the agrarian Hidatsa people but then adopted a nomadic hunting lifestyle and developed some of the region's largest horse herds. Under great duress, the tribe ceded most of its 38-million-acre territory across Montana, Wyoming, and South Dakota in exchange for some meager provisions and perpetual hunting rights on those lands, which the US Supreme Court upheld in a 2019 decision. Today, the Crow reservation is the largest in the state of Montana, at 2.3 million acres.

The Cheyenne and Arapaho are now one united nation, but they began as distinct groups before forging a powerful alliance in the early 1800s. Originally pushed out of the Great Lakes and Eastern Woodlands, the two tribes abandoned their agricultural lifeways and took up hunting and gathering upon moving into the Plains. Over time, they split into geographical subdivisions.

The controversial Sand Creek Massacre of 1864, in which US troops attacked a Cheyenne and Arapaho camp and killed more than 230 people, prompted the Colorado War followed by the Medicine Lodge Treaty of 1867. This set up two confederated reservations for the Comanche, Kiowa, Plains Apache, Southern Cheyenne, and Southern Arapaho in Oklahoma Indian Territory. In addition to the united Cheyenne and Arapaho Nation there, the Northern Cheyenne have a reservation in southeast Montana and the Northern Arapaho share a reservation with the Eastern Shoshone in Wyoming's Wind River Valley.

The Three Affiliated Tribes of the Mandan, Hidatsa, and Arikara were among the Plains' first farmers, despite the area's relatively short growing season compared to more southern parts of Turtle Island. They depended mainly on agriculture for their food supply, growing hardy crops like corn, beans, squash, and sunflowers in the moist, fertile soil in the Missouri River bottomland, where they resided in rounded earth lodges. Thanks to forward thinkers like seed keeper George Will, many of the ancient seeds still exist today.

After all, in our Indigenous worldview, we never thought of land as something to be owned, bought, or sold.

Of course, endless modern-day issues threaten our lifeways, including overgrazing by livestock, growth of monocrops on corporate farms, and exploitation of natural resources through mining and pipelines. The Standing Rock Sioux's 2016 protests against the Dakota Access Pipeline construction stands as a shining example of Indigenous activists fighting for our basic human rights. The tribe was rightly worried that a crude oil spill could contaminate its water supply, since the pipeline would cross the Missouri River just upstream from its reservation. Despite those valiant efforts, the pipeline was ultimately built and has been in operation since 2017, although an environmental review was underway at the time of this writing.

THE FOOD

In so many ways, bison shaped the landscape, history, and foodways of the Great Plains. Tatanka, as we call this important relative in the Lakota language, represents life, abundance, and self-sacrifice. For centuries, they roamed the region and provided sustenance, shelter, clothing, and tools for many Native communities, who hunted other wild game like elk and pronghorn.

A lot of Lakota mythology and religion is centered around bison, and these iconic figures are omnipresent throughout our legends, paintings, and ceremonies. Growing up, I heard stories about how Creator gave us bison so we wouldn't starve; I also learned to use every part of the animal so nothing went to waste. I remember seeing herds of these massive creatures out on the prairie as a kid, when they were being reintroduced to Pine Ridge.

The systematic decimation of bison was the United States' answer to the so-called Indian Problem in the West. They realized that removing this main food source helped them control Indigenous peoples and take over our desirable land spaces. So the federal government started encouraging bison hunting en masse, even allowing people to shoot them from railroad train windows. In my extensive research on the topic, one disturbing account that stands out details how a party of sixteen hunters killed 2,800 bison over the course of a single summer.

Thankfully, conservation and activist groups are leading efforts to restore these sacred creatures to the region, which in turn helps regenerate the prairie and strengthen Native sovereignty. This important revitalization also lets more people enjoy the lean yet rich-tasting meat. The versatile protein can be subbed in for ground beef for a leaner, milder, and slightly sweeter flavor profile. It is also delicious braised and cooked into a nourishing tȟaníǧa-inspired dish (see page 58), or dried to make pápa—a survival food that factors into so many traditional Lakota meals—and combined with chokecherries in wasná (see Pápa and Wasná: A Great Plains Tradition, page 51).

I have so many strong childhood memories of chokecherry wožapi—a delicious, thick, traditional berry soup—cooking on my grandmother's stove all day long. As kids, we would spread a blanket under the shrubs in late summer to fill up buckets of this slightly tart stone fruit. Plump and purple when ripe, it grows in clusters like grapes and falls right off the stem. Unfortunately, climate change has impacted fruit yields, resulting in reduced harvests in recent years.

Thíŋpsiŋla (sometimes spelled timpsila) is another staple, and you'll often see braids of this wild prairie turnip hanging in Lakota homes. In ancient times, our people followed the short midsummer harvest across the area, and many families today still forage and eat this valuable food. When I was a kid, my cousins and I would all pile into the bed of my dad's truck to go harvest the tuber. Following an old Lakota story, thíŋpsiŋla's hand-like leaves would point us toward the next plant, and we'd take care only to dig up those that had already seeded so the plant would sprout up again the following year.

Harvesting this tuberous root is hard work, especially in the smoldering summer sun, but it's well worth the effort. When eaten fresh, it has a crisp, sweet taste reminiscent of unroasted peanuts. We peel back the thick brown bark to reveal the pale white vegetable and then braid the tops of the plants to hang-dry in the sun. Thíŋpsiŋla has so many uses, like being added to waháŋpi (soup), served as a side vegetable, shaved into chips for a garnish, or ground into a flour to act as a thickening agent. Similar to dried meats, the prairie turnip is considered a wartime food—lightweight, virtually nonperishable items that ensured our survival.

Much like misconceptions about the landscape, the region's bounty is often underestimated. Beyond these staples, countless wild ingredients grow all over the Great Plains, such as berries, plums, acorns, tons of allium varieties, mustard plants, elm oyster mushrooms, biscuit root, sego lily, rose hips, greens like stinging nettle, and herbs and seasonings, including mint, bee balm, and more. You just need to know how to spot them and then how to transform them into delicious meals, medicines, and teas to nourish the mind, body, and spirit, as the Lakota people have done for eons.

SEASONED PÁPA

makes about 4 ounces

Traditionally, pápa is made without seasoning, but I like to flavor it with maple sugar and salt.

- 1 pound lean bison or elk meat, from cuts such as tenderloin, rump, or round
- 3 tablespoons Maple Sugar (page 36) or store-bought
- 2 teaspoons fine sea salt

Use a very sharp knife to remove fat, gristle, and anything else that's not lean meat. Freeze the meat for about 1 hour to make it easier to slice, then slice the meat as thinly as you can, no thicker than ⅛ inch.

In a bowl, toss the meat with the sugar and salt. Arrange the seasoned meat on a rack set over a baking sheet and refrigerate for 8 hours or overnight.

To dry, either set up a dehydrator or preheat an oven to 170°F (or your oven's lowest setting). Pat the meat dry. If you have a food dehydrator, follow the instructions for making jerky. If you're using the oven, arrange the meat on a clean rack set over a baking sheet and dry for about 4 hours, until leathery. Let cool.

Refrigerate in an airtight container for up to 1 week.

PÁPA AND WASNÁ: A GREAT PLAINS TRADITION

Much of the original Lakota diet is based on dried ingredients, including meat, squash, corn, thíŋpsiŋla (sometimes called timpsila or prairie turnips), and fruits. Dried food is not only energy-dense and shelf-stable but also lightweight for easier travel.

To make pápa (also known as bapa or dry meat in English), people would very thinly pound lean pieces of meat trimmed of all of its fat, and then hang it to dry in the wind and sun. Today, people continue this tradition but use modern equipment, like dehydrators.

Pápa is then used in a host of traditional dishes. For example, we pound the meat until it's feathery and mix it with dried berries and a bit of fat to make a mixture called wasná. (The Dakota have a similar mixture known as pemmican.) I often think of wasná as the original energy mix, as it's full of protein, healthy fat, and vitamins. At Lakota ceremonies, you sometimes see people pass around a bowl of wasná to share.

Sometimes, wasná is stuffed into intestinal casings and smoked to create a dried sausage.

I've added wasná to the leaf wraps on page 54.

There's also waháŋpi, which means soup or stew and can made with pápa and thíŋpsiŋla (see Pápa Waháŋpi, page 53).

NATIVE
LAND

PÁPA WAHÁŊPI

serves 2

Waháŋpi means soup or stew in Lakota, and there are many types of them. Like more traditional versions, this one is made with the dried meat pápa and thíŋpsiŋla, a root vegetable that grows wild on the prairies and can be dried and stored for years. The pápa here provides a deep meaty flavor for the simple broth while the thíŋpsiŋla brings an earthy sweetness.

This is a wonderful dish to make when you have the ingredients on hand but your cupboards are otherwise bare or when you're out camping and you bring your dried foods along.

- 6 fresh or dried thíŋpsiŋla (prairie turnips), soaked overnight if dried
- 12 dried prairie onions or other wild onions or 1 small onion, chopped
- 2 ounces Seasoned Pápa (page 51) or bison jerky, cut into bite-size pieces
- Sea salt (optional)
- A handful of tender wild greens, such as plantain or lamb's quarters

Drain the thíŋpsiŋla if you soaked them and cut into bite-size pieces.

In a pot, combine the thíŋpsiŋla, onions, and seasoned pápa and add just enough water to cover. Bring to a boil over high heat. Reduce the heat to medium to maintain a bare simmer and cook for about 30 minutes, until the thíŋpsiŋla and pápa are tender.

Taste and season with salt if needed. Add the greens and stir just to wilt, then serve hot.

Note: *While the meat provides plenty of flavor, it does not give a lot of body to the broth. For a richer soup, you can make it with Rich Bison or Other Game Stock (page 41).*

WASNÁ AND ANISE HYSSOP WRAPS

serves 4 as a starter

You can make wasná by pounding any type of lean dried meat or jerky with dried fruit. Growing up, we used bison and chokecherries. The mixture can be pressed into cakes, but it's also often left fairly loose, like a meaty trail mix.

While wasná makes a great snack, it's also an incredible umami-rich garnish. At Owamni, we sprinkle it over tartare, soups, and salads. Here, inspired by the types of wraps you sometimes see in Southeast Asian cuisine, I use wasná to make an herbed salad that I wrap in anise hyssop leaves.

Anise hyssop is a plant in the mint family with large anise-flavored leaves. It grows wild on parts of the prairie as well as in the Great Lakes and Eastern Woodlands. It blooms purple flowers throughout the summer that bees love, so it's a great addition to a garden.

WASNÁ

- 4 ounces Seasoned Pápa (page 51) or bison or venison jerky (see Note), torn into pieces
- ¼ cup dried chokecherries, aronia berries, or currants
- 2 tablespoons melted bison fat or other animal fat

WRAPS

- ¼ cup wild mint or other mint leaves, chopped
- 2 wild onions with greens or scallions, thinly sliced
- 2 tablespoons cider vinegar
- 1 tablespoon maple syrup
- 1 garlic clove, minced
- ¼ teaspoon fine sea salt
- ½ cup corn nuts, coarsely chopped
- 20 large anise hyssop leaves, plus some blossoms

Make the wasná: In a food processor, pulse the meat until it's finely chopped. Add the dried fruit and pulse until the mixture is reduced to a powder. Add the fat and pulse again until incorporated so the mixture barely holds together when pressed. You can refrigerate this mixture in an airtight container for up to 5 days.

Make the wraps: Transfer the wasná to a small bowl. Add the mint and sliced onions and toss until incorporated like a salad, then transfer to a platter.

In another small bowl, stir together the vinegar, 2 tablespoons water, the maple syrup, garlic, and salt. Transfer to the platter.

Put the chopped corn nuts in a bowl on the platter.

Arrange the anise hyssop leaves on the platter. Break apart their blossoms and arrange them in a pile on the platter.

To serve, invite people to put a leaf in their hand and add a bit of the wasná, corn nuts, and blossoms to the center. Add a small spoon of the vinegar dressing, then wrap it up and eat in one or two bites.

Note: *If you choose to use jerky instead of making the pápa, look for one that is seasoned very simply.*

DRIED VENISON AND CORN SALAD

serves 4 to 6

In this late-season salad, I toss hominy with sweet-tart dried crabapples and chewy pápa (dried meat). For something that's so neutral-looking in color, it's wildly flavorful thanks to the dried alliums, maple syrup, and cider vinegar.

In traditional Indigenous cooking, people use ash as an alkalizing agent to nixtamalize corn and as a source of minerals, including sodium, which weren't always readily available. Inspired by these traditions, I like to make ash from vegetables to use as a seasoning, because it retains some of the original flavor of the vegetable while also taking on a pleasantly bitter charred element. For this salad, I make ash with spent sweet corncobs.

- 2 ounces Seasoned Pápa (page 51) made with venison, or venison jerky
- 2 cups Hominy (page 25)
- ½ cup Dried Crabapples (opposite) or other dried apples
- ½ teaspoon onion powder
- ½ teaspoon garlic powder
- 1 tablespoon cider vinegar
- 1½ teaspoons maple syrup
- 2 tablespoons sunflower oil
- Sea salt
- Corncob ash (optional; see Note)

In a food processor, pulse the pápa until finely chopped.

Set some aside as garnish and pour the rest into a bowl. Add the hominy, dried apples, onion powder, garlic powder, vinegar, maple syrup, and oil and toss together. Season with salt. If desired, sprinkle with corn ash. Garnish with the reserved jerky.

Note: *To make the corncob ash, use metal tongs to hold a spent corncob over a gas burner or a grill set to medium-high heat, turning until thoroughly blackened. Transfer to a plate to cool completely. Tap off the ash into a small bowl and use it as a seasoning.*

DRIED CRABAPPLES

makes about 2 cups

½ cup cider vinegar

12 crabapples or 2 Granny Smith apples

A lot of fruits that are indigenous to Turtle Island are challenging for our modern foodways and palates because the fruits have fleeting seasons and are harder to ship, or the flavors are less sweet.

Crabapples, tarter and more astringent than commercial apples, are one of those fruits. In the fall, you often see these poor little orbs languishing all over the ground. But when used thoughtfully, they can add a complex acidity and depth of flavor to dishes.

When I can, I like to dehydrate them for the pantry as I do here, and add them to salads (like Dried Venison and Corn Salad, page 56).

Fill a bowl with 2 cups water and add the vinegar. Using a mandoline or very sharp knife, slice the apples ⅛ inch thick across the core and discard any seeds. Soak the apples in the water for 5 minutes. Drain and pat dry.

To dehydrate: Arrange them in a dehydrator and dry for 6 to 12 hours, until they're pliable but no moisture remains.

To oven-dry: Preheat the oven to 200°F. Line two baking sheets with parchment paper.

Spread the apple slices on the lined pans in a single layer and bake for 1 hour. Flip each apple slice and bake for 1 hour longer. Check the apples: If they are pliable but no moisture remains, turn off the oven and let the apples cool completely there. If you prefer crisper apples, leave them in the oven to bake up to 1 hour longer before cooling.

WHEN DRYING FOOD IS KEY TO SEASONAL EATING

Removing moisture from foods—whether leaves, fruits, meats, or seafoods—can preserve them for months to come. Traditionally, people dried food in the sun and wind or near fires, which simultaneously smoked and dried ingredients. Today, I use dehydrators in our kitchen. If you are committed to seasonal eating, I highly recommend investing in a dehydrator. It will allow you to preserve fleeting ingredients, like onion greens and ramp tops, only available in early spring, which you can pulverize into a powder (see page 110) and use as a seasoning any time of year.

BRAISED BISON OXTAIL AND TRIPE
(INSPIRED BY TȞANÍǦA)

serves 4

This dish is based on one we've served at Owamni. Instead of the traditional intestines of tȟaníǧa, it features bison tripe, which is a bit easier to find, as well as oxtail, which enriches a cedar-infused broth sweetened with some apple. To bulk up the meaty stew, I sauté some carrots and turnips and add them to the broth with toothsome hominy.

Hearty and comforting, it's an admittedly fussier recipe than the classic, more rustic version. But taking the time to cook the pieces separately allows you to build the complex and layered flavors of the final dish.

TȞANÍǦA, THEN AND NOW

In Lakota, tȟaníǧa (sometimes spelled taniga) means the stomach or intestine of an animal, but it also refers to a traditional soup we make from it. (Though, you could argue it should then be called waháŋpi tȟaníǧa.) I remember my family making tȟaníǧa when I lived in Pine Ridge. My grandmother would start cleaning cow intestines early in the morning, inserting a broomstick handle to scrape out the insides. Later, the house would smell a bit funky as they stewed all day. She used to try to mask the smell by using plenty of white pepper—and to this day, when I smell white pepper, I think of tȟaníǧa.

Using the whole animal in this way is not a trend for Indigenous peoples. It's part of a way of life. I appreciate the old way of making tȟaníǧa—simmering the intestine with little more than thíŋpsiŋla (prairie turnip) and nixtamalized corn. (And, in the case of my grandmother, plenty of white pepper!)

Over the years, I've experimented with different versions, sometimes drawing inspiration from menudo, a Mexican soup often made with tripe and a chile broth. See this recipe for an updated version of tȟaníǧa inspired by the Great Plains.

Oven-braise the bison oxtail: Preheat the oven to 275°F.

Season the bison oxtail all over with salt. In a large heavy ovenproof pot, heat the oil over medium-high heat until shimmering. Add the oxtail and sear for 10 to 12 minutes, turning frequently, until browned and crusty all over. Transfer to a plate.

Add the leek and garlic to the pot and cook for about 4 minutes, stirring, until softened. Stir in the apple and bergamot.

Return the oxtail to the pot. Add 4 cups water, increase the heat to medium-high, and bring to a boil. Reduce the heat to medium-low, add the cedar, cover, and transfer to the oven.

Braise for about 4 hours, or until tender.

Meanwhile, prepare the rest of the tȟaníǧa: When the oxtails have been cooking for about 1½ hours, cut the tripe into 1-inch pieces and place in a medium saucepan. Add water to cover by 2 inches and bring to a boil over high heat. Season the water with salt. Reduce the heat to medium-low, so the water simmers without rapid evaporation, and cook the tripe for 1½ hours. Scoop out and reserve ½ cup of the cooking liquid, then drain the tripe.

In the same saucepan, heat the oil over medium heat. Add the garlic and cook for 1 to 2 minutes, just until softened. Stir in the tripe and the reserved cooking liquid. Add the maple syrup and vinegar and bring to a boil over medium-high heat. Reduce the heat to medium-low, cover, and cook the tripe for about 45 minutes, or until softened (but it will still be a bit chewy) and flavorful. Stir in the hominy just to heat through. Taste and season with salt.

When the oxtail is done braising, transfer it to a plate. Strain the cooking liquid into a pitcher or measuring cup and skim off as much of the fat as possible. Discard any solids. Wipe out the pot, then return the cooking liquid to the pot. Bring to a boil over high heat and cook until reduced by one-quarter, just to deepen the flavors, about 10 minutes. Return the oxtail to the cooking liquid and keep warm over low heat.

When ready to serve: In a skillet, heat the oil over medium-high heat until shimmering. Add the carrots and turnips, season with salt, and cook for about 3 minutes, stirring, until they start to develop some color at the edges. Reduce the heat to medium, add ¼ cup water, cover, and steam just until the vegetables are crisp-tender.

Serve the oxtails with the tripe, hominy, and vegetables. Ladle the reduced oxtail cooking liquid over top. Garnish with sliced wild onion greens and dried wild bergamot (if using) and serve.

BISON OXTAIL

- 1 pound bone-in bison oxtail
- Sea salt
- 2 tablespoons sunflower oil
- 1 small leek, white and light-green parts only, thinly sliced
- 2 garlic cloves, thinly sliced
- 1 apple, coarsely chopped
- 1 tablespoon dried wild bergamot (bee balm)
- 1 (5-inch) piece cedar

TȞANÍǦA

- 8 ounces cleaned/trimmed bison tripe
- Sea salt
- 2 tablespoons sunflower oil
- 2 garlic cloves, thinly sliced
- 1 teaspoon maple syrup
- 1 teaspoon cider vinegar
- 1 cup Hominy (page 25)

SERVING

- 2 tablespoons sunflower oil
- 2 large carrots, scrubbed well and cut into 1-inch-long pieces that are ½ inch thick
- 4 baby turnips, each cut into 8 equal wedges
- Sea salt
- Sliced wild onion greens or scallions, for garnish
- Dried wild bergamot (bee balm), for garnish (optional)

RABBIT SOUP WITH CORN DUMPLINGS

serves 4 to 6

Throughout many parts of Turtle Island, from Mexico to southern Canada, people historically ate various forms of dumplings, breads, and cakes made from nixtamalized corn. The dumplings here are inspired by Mexican chochoyotes, which have a divot in the center to help them cook through and capture some of the broth.

- 1 medium yellow onion
- 1 rabbit (about 2¼ pounds), cut into 6 serving pieces (rib cage removed)
- Sea salt
- 1 tablespoon crumbled dried prairie sage or culinary sage
- 1 large carrot, scrubbed well and coarsely chopped
- 3 tablespoons maple syrup, plus more as needed
- 2 tablespoons sunflower oil
- 1 pound Fresh Masa (page 28) or use masa harina (see chart, page 27)
- 2 tablespoons melted duck fat or sunflower oil
- Thinly sliced wild onion greens or scallion greens, for serving

Cut the onion in half. Coarsely chop one half and cut the other half into ½-inch pieces

Place the rabbit pieces in a large pot, cover with water, and season generously with salt. Add the sage, coarsely chopped onion, carrot, and maple syrup and bring to a boil over high heat. Reduce the heat to medium-low, cover, and simmer for about 1½ hours, or until the meat is so tender that it pulls apart.

Using tongs, transfer the rabbit to a plate to cool slightly. Strain the broth into a clean pot (discarding any solids), then taste and season with more salt and maple syrup, as needed. Keep the broth warm over medium-low heat.

When the meat is cool enough to handle, pull it from the bones. Be very careful to remove all of the rabbit bones, as they are small.

In a large skillet, heat the oil over medium heat until shimmering. Add the diced onion, season with salt, and cook, stirring, for about 5 minutes, or until softened. Add the pulled rabbit meat, taste and season with more salt and a little bit of maple syrup.

Set a piece of parchment paper on a baking sheet or a work surface. In a large bowl, combine the masa and fat or oil. Test the dough by rolling it into a small ball and pressing it to about ½ inch thick. If the edges crack, add warm water 1 teaspoon at a time and knead for 1 minute, adding more water as needed until the dough is soft and no longer cracks.

Using a 1-ounce scoop, portion the dough into 20 pieces and roll into balls. Press your thumb into each one to create a divot in the center.

Bring the rabbit broth to a simmer and drop the dumplings gently into the broth. Simmer for about 10 minutes, or until the dumplings are cooked through and tender. Be careful not to overcook them or they will begin to fall apart in the broth.

Add the pulled rabbit meat to the broth just to warm it through.

Ladle the rabbit, broth, and dumplings into bowls and garnish with the onion greens. Serve hot.

NOPALES AND ARIKARA BEAN SALAD

serves 6 to 8

My friend Rowen White worked with the Seed Savers Exchange to identify indigenous seeds in their archives that she could help grow out and give back to families who had lost them, a process known as seed rematriation. One of the seeds she found was for a bean that came from the Arikara tribe in North Dakota. This drought-tolerant bean, now known as the Arikara Yellow Bean, was kept alive and sold for many years by the now-defunct Oscar H. Will Seed & Company. (You can find them today from the Seed Savers Exchange.)

The Arikara Nation is a Great Plains tribe that, after decades of smallpox, land loss, and conflict with settlers and other tribes, joined forces with the Mandan and Hidatsa tribes in the 1860s to form the Three Affiliated Tribes, now called the MHA Nation. Historically, the Arikara people were excellent farmers and developed this bean to grow and mature early in the harsh climate of the Missouri River Valley. Many Arikara people now live with other members of the MHA Nation on the Fort Berthold Reservation in North Dakota.

The small beans have a creamy texture and work well as baked beans and in soups and salads, too. People often think of nopales, the prickly pear cactus paddles, as a Mexican and Southwestern ingredient, but they grow in other warmer, drier parts of Turtle Island, including the southern Great Plains. I add some pepitas for crunch and a handful of wild herbs to perk up the flavor.

- 1½ cups dried Arikara Yellow Beans or other small dried beans, such as flageolet, soaked overnight and drained
- Sea salt
- 2 medium nopales (prickly pear cactus paddles), about 5 ounces each before prepping (see Trimming and Cleaning Nopales)
- 2 tablespoons sunflower oil, plus more for brushing
- 1 tablespoon cider vinegar
- 1 tablespoon maple syrup
- ½ small red onion, thinly sliced
- ¼ cup toasted pepitas, for serving
- Small handful of wild greens and herbs, such as wood sorrel, mint, chickweed, lamb's quarters, or young dandelion or amaranth, torn into bite-size pieces, for serving

In a pot, combine the soaked and drained beans with water to cover by 1½ inches and bring to a boil over high heat. Reduce the heat to medium-low, partially cover, and simmer the beans until tender all the way through, 30 to 45 minutes. Drain and run under cold water to cool. Transfer to a bowl, season with salt, and let stand for 10 minutes.

Preheat a grill to high heat. Or preheat a grill pan or cast-iron skillet over high heat. Brush the nopales with the oil and season with salt. Working in batches if necessary, cook the nopales for 8 to 10 minutes, turning frequently, until charred in spots and tender. Transfer to a work surface and cut crosswise into thin strips.

Add the nopales to the beans in the bowl and toss. Add the vinegar, maple syrup, red onion, and the 2 tablespoons sunflower oil and toss again. Garnish with the pepitas and wild greens just before serving.

Trimming and cleaning nopales: *If your nopales aren't precleaned, start by scraping off their thorns and trimming. To do so, use tongs to hold each cactus paddle firmly on a work surface while using a sharp knife to scrape against the grain of the thorns to remove them. Then use the knife or a vegetable peeler to cut off/discard ¼ inch around the edges of the paddles as well as the tough base. Rinse under cold water and pat dry.*

SUNFLOWER SEED "RISOTTO"
WITH MAPLE-ROASTED SQUASH AND PRAIRIE PESTO

serves 4

In *Buffalo Bird Woman's Garden,* the Hidatsa gardener (see The Pantry Recipes, page 24) describes making a dish out of sunflower seeds that gets cooked slowly with vegetables. "Meat was not boiled with the mess, as the sunflower seed gave sufficient oil to furnish fat," she says. Here, I reimagine this Hidatsa family meal as a sort of risotto topped with roasted and glazed squash.

SQUASH

- 1 (1-pound) piece Hidatsa winter squash or kabocha squash, seeded and cut into 1-inch-thick wedges
- 2 tablespoons sunflower oil
- Sea salt
- 1 tablespoon maple syrup

RISOTTO

- 2 cups sunflower seeds, soaked for 8 hours
- 2 tablespoons sunflower oil
- 1 large onion, finely diced
- Sea salt
- 4 garlic cloves, finely chopped
- ¼ cup fresh apple cider
- 1 tablespoon cider vinegar
- 3 cups Roasted Bird Stock (page 40) or vegetable broth
- ½ cup Prairie Pesto (page 68), for serving

Cook the squash: Preheat the oven to 425°F.

Spread the squash wedges on a baking sheet and brush both sides with the oil. Season all over with salt.

Roast the squash for about 30 minutes, or until browned on the bottom and tender. Brush both sides with the maple syrup and continue roasting for another 5 minutes to glaze.

Make the risotto: Drain and rinse the seeds. Measure out ¾ cup of the soaked seeds and transfer to a blender with ¾ cup water. Puree to form a smooth sunflower cream. Set the remaining whole sunflower seeds aside separately.

In a saucepan, heat the oil over medium heat. Add the onion, season with salt, and cook, stirring, for about 5 minutes, or until translucent. Add the garlic and cook, stirring, for about 2 minutes, until fragrant and softened. Add the apple cider and vinegar and bring to a boil, then cook until the liquid reduces to about 1 tablespoon.

Add the reserved soaked sunflower seeds (that aren't pureed) and the stock and bring to a simmer over medium heat. Cover and reduce the heat to medium-low if needed to prevent the liquid from boiling over. Cook for about 25 minutes, or until the seeds are tender but not quite soft.

Uncover and stir in the sunflower cream. Cook until the "risotto" is heated through and the sunflower seeds look like they're suspended in a creamy sauce. (If it seems very loose, increase the heat to medium and simmer, allowing some of the excess liquid to evaporate.)

Taste and season with salt, as needed. Serve topped with wedges of glazed squash and drizzle with the pesto.

PRAIRIE PESTO

makes about 1 cup

This makes a thick, garlicky pesto using Indigenous ingredients. The flavor will vary widely depending on the greens you use, but the seeds give it richness and the sumac a nice bright note. To thin it out, add more oil if you like.

- 2 garlic cloves, peeled but whole
- ½ cup toasted sunflower seeds or pepitas, or a mix of the two
- 2 cups mixed wild greens, such as lamb's quarters, amaranth greens, common plantain, young chicory greens, dandelion, and onion greens
- 1 teaspoon ground sumac
- ½ cup sunflower oil
- Sea salt
- 1 teaspoon cider vinegar

In a blender or mini food processor, pulse the garlic cloves and toasted seeds until coarsely chopped. Add the greens and sumac, then pulse to chop again. With the machine running, add the oil, then pulse in a pinch of salt.

Add the vinegar and pulse just once or twice to combine. Taste and season with more salt, as needed.

The pesto can be refrigerated in an airtight container for up to 5 days.

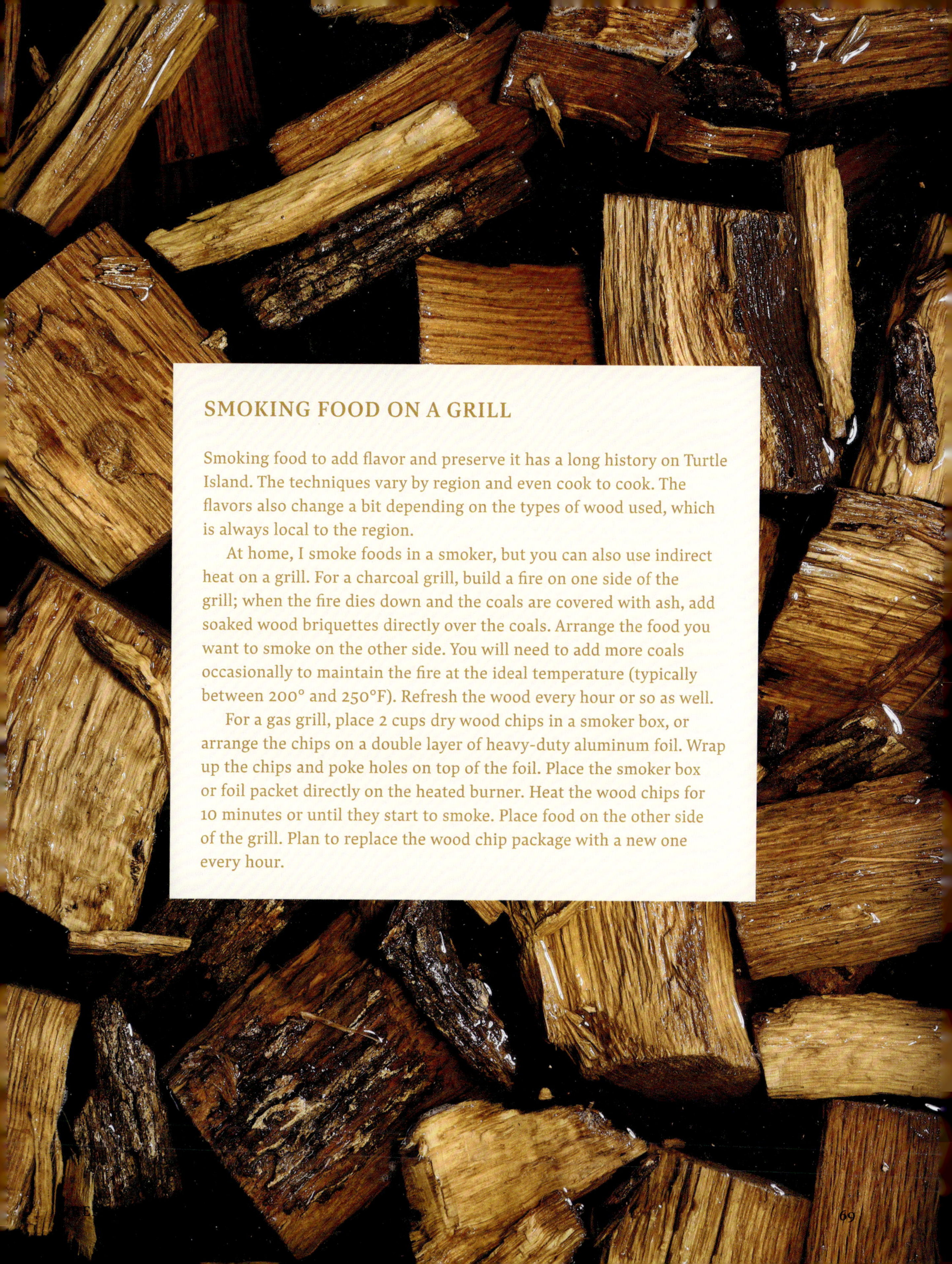

SMOKING FOOD ON A GRILL

Smoking food to add flavor and preserve it has a long history on Turtle Island. The techniques vary by region and even cook to cook. The flavors also change a bit depending on the types of wood used, which is always local to the region.

At home, I smoke foods in a smoker, but you can also use indirect heat on a grill. For a charcoal grill, build a fire on one side of the grill; when the fire dies down and the coals are covered with ash, add soaked wood briquettes directly over the coals. Arrange the food you want to smoke on the other side. You will need to add more coals occasionally to maintain the fire at the ideal temperature (typically between 200° and 250°F). Refresh the wood every hour or so as well.

For a gas grill, place 2 cups dry wood chips in a smoker box, or arrange the chips on a double layer of heavy-duty aluminum foil. Wrap up the chips and poke holes on top of the foil. Place the smoker box or foil packet directly on the heated burner. Heat the wood chips for 10 minutes or until they start to smoke. Place food on the other side of the grill. Plan to replace the wood chip package with a new one every hour.

SMOKED BISON RIB-EYE
WITH PLAINS CHIMICHURRI

serves 2 to 4

Bison steaks tend to be quite lean, so it's best to cook them to medium-rare. At Owamni, we prepare these steaks in a three-step process. First, we dry-brine them in a mixture of salt, maple sugar, and a bit of chile. Then we smoke them to infuse them with more flavor and to slowly bring them up to doneness. Finally, we sear them just before serving.

We tend to prefer oak for smoking the steaks, because it allows the flavor of the meat to shine through. You can also use hickory wood, which will bring a more intense smokiness, or a fruitwood, like apple or cherry, which will bring a delicate sweetness.

If you don't have a smoker, you can set up your grill for indirect cooking (see Smoking Food on a Grill, page 69, starting the steaks at a low temperature and then finishing them off with a sear. Inspired by the traditional Argentinian sauce, I make a chimichurri using wild herbs as well as the usual garlic, vinegar, and oil. It's beautiful with the rich flavor of meats, including bison.

RIB-EYE

- 2 tablespoons Maple Sugar (page 36) or store-bought
- 1½ tablespoons coarse sea salt
- ½ tablespoon smoked salt (or more sea salt)
- 1½ teaspoons ancho chile powder
- 2 bison rib-eye steaks, each about 1½ inches thick
- 1 tablespoon sunflower oil

CHIMICHURRI

- ½ cup wild greens, such as wild parsley, lamb's quarters, amaranth greens, or common plantain
- 2 tablespoons fresh anise hyssop or wild mint leaves
- 4 stalks wild garlic or 4 large garlic cloves, minced
- 3 tablespoons cider vinegar
- 1 teaspoon red pepper flakes
- Sea salt
- ½ cup sunflower oil

GARNISH

- Thinly sliced scallions
- Handful of local berries

Make the rib-eye: In a small bowl, mix together the maple sugar, both salts, and ancho powder. Rub the mixture all over the meat and refrigerate uncovered for at least 4 hours and up to 24 hours.

Preheat a smoker to 250°F (or if you don't have a smoker, see Smoking Food on a Grill, page 69).

Pat the meat dry, insert a probe thermometer into the thickest part of the steaks, and smoke for 10 to 15 minutes, until the internal temperature is 100° to 105°F. Transfer to a plate.

Heat a cast-iron skillet, grill pan, or outdoor grill over high heat. If you're using a skillet or grill pan, add the oil and heat until shimmering. Otherwise, oil the grates. Add the steaks and cook for 2 to 3 minutes, until nicely seared on the bottom. Flip and cook until nicely seared on the other side.

Insert a thermometer into the center part of the steak. If it registers between 120° and 125°F, transfer the meat to a carving board and let rest for 5 minutes. Otherwise, reduce the heat to medium-low and continue cooking, turning the steaks occasionally, until they reach the proper temperature.

Make the chimichurri: In a blender or mini food processor, coarsely chop the wild greens, herbs, and garlic. Add the vinegar and pepper flakes and process until the greens and garlic are finely chopped. Season with salt. Transfer to a bowl, then stir in the oil. Let the chimichurri stand for 10 minutes before serving. You can refrigerate the chimichurri in an airtight container overnight.

After the meat rests, thinly slice it crosswise. Serve with the chimichurri and garnish with the scallions and berries.

SQUASH AND PEPITA TARTLETS

makes 10 to 12 tartlets

When ground with a little oil and sweetener, pepitas form a dough that creates a crisp, crunchy shell for these little tartlets, filled with roasted squash and apple. (As a topping, you can toss some pumpkin seeds and amaranth with maple syrup and bake for a few minutes until crunchy.) Like all Indigenous desserts, this one is free of refined sugar, wheat, and dairy, and it's also nutrient-dense.

FILLING

- 2-pound piece Lakota winter squash, red kuri squash, or kabocha squash, seeded
- 1 cup boiling water
- 1 teaspoon dried pineapple weed or chamomile
- 1 Gala apple, cored and cut into chunks but not peeled
- ½ cup maple syrup
- 1 teaspoon fine sea salt
- ½ teaspoon agar-agar powder

TART SHELLS

- ¼ cup sunflower oil, plus more for muffin tin
- 8 ounces pepitas (about 2 cups)
- ¼ cup amaranth flour
- 1½ teaspoons maple syrup
- 2 teaspoons agave syrup

Make the filling: Preheat the oven to 350°F. Line a baking sheet with parchment paper.

Set the seeded squash on the baking sheet cut-side down and bake until very soft, about 1 hour. (Leave the oven on.) Discard the squash skin and measure out 2 packed cups of roasted squash.

Let the boiling water sit for 1 minute before using. Place the dried pineapple weed or chamomile in a mug and pour the hot water over it to steep for 5 minutes. Strain the tea, discarding the solids.

In a food processor or blender, combine the 2 cups of roasted squash with the apple chunks, maple syrup, and salt. Add ½ cup of the tea and puree for about 1 minute, until smooth, adding more tea if necessary to achieve a smooth consistency. (You'll have about 2½ cups.)

Scrape into a saucepan and set over medium-high heat. Whisk in the agar-agar and simmer for 2 minutes, or until the filling thickens.

Make the tart shells: Lightly oil 12 cups of a standard muffin tin or ten 4-ounce ramekins, then line each with strips of parchment paper (to make pulling out the tartlets easier).

In a food processor, pulse the pepitas and amaranth flour until the seeds are finely chopped. With the machine on, add the oil, ¼ cup water, the maple syrup, and agave and let it run until it holds together like a dough.

Press the dough evenly into the bottoms and up the sides of the prepared muffin cups or ramekins (to create tart shells). (Use about 2 tablespoons per muffin cup.) If the dough gets sticky, wet your hands with a little water as you press.

Pipe or spoon equal amounts of the filling into the tart shells. (Use about 3 tablespoons of filling per muffin cup.) If using ramekins, place them on a baking sheet.

Bake for 15 to 20 minutes, until the crust is browned at the edges and the filling is dry to the touch on top.

Let cool in the pan or ramekins for 10 minutes, then carefully lift out the tarts and transfer to a rack to fully cool. Serve at room temperature or cover and refrigerate and serve chilled.

GREAT LAKES

WHERE FOOD GROWS ON WATER

FOR NATIVE PEOPLES ACROSS TURTLE Island, water symbolizes life, fertility, purity, and sustenance. In the Great Lakes basin—which encompasses the watershed around Lakes Superior, Michigan, Huron, Erie, and Ontario as well as the states and provinces that have come to border these waterways—water also represents a sacred way of life.

So much of my work to revitalize Native foodways has taken place in Minnesota, from the first Indigenous dinner I ever served in Bemidji in 2012 to opening my restaurant, Owamni—named after the Dakota word for the sacred waterfalls it overlooks on the Mississippi River—in Minneapolis in 2021. At the restaurant, we proudly highlight the area's incredible bounty, including staples like wild rice, walleye, and maple syrup, as well as less-known but equally tasty ingredients like ramps, morels, milkweed, anise hyssop, balsam fir, and white cedar.

Although I grew up on the Great Plains, I feel a special connection to this region because my mom's family comes from the Crow Creek Indian Reservation in South Dakota, where the Dakota and the Ho-Chunk peoples were sent after they were expelled from the Great Lakes. My great-grandparents were actually some of the first children raised there.

I look back fondly on that late springtime dinner in the northern lake town of Bemidji. In preparation, I foraged for wild foods—fiddleheads, onions, ginger leaves, wood shelf mushrooms, and an abundance of dandelion leaves—in the woods alongside my friend Simone Senogles (Red Lake Nation), who has such a beautiful awe and admiration for the natural world around us. Together with smoked perch, wild rice, and cattail shoots provided by friends and local farmers, these ingredients became the basis for a multicourse Indigenous dinner for some twenty-five people.

After an Ojibwe elder led a prayer, dinner began with a flatbread made from wild rice—an essential food for Great Lakes tribal peoples—complemented by foraged mushrooms. Next, I served a salad of crisp cattail shoots, wild onion, and dandelion greens topped with local pine nuts and a fragrant, gently sweet birch syrup. Then came the main course, cedar-stewed rabbit with fiddlehead ferns, followed by a sweet corn cake with berry drizzle for dessert. At once makeshift and momentous, that meal laid the groundwork for what was to come.

I later moved from Bemidji to Minneapolis, where I've lived for nearly thirty years. My adopted hometown has played a pivotal role in many Native milestones. In 1968, it was the birthplace of the American Indian Movement, a grassroots effort protesting racist government policies and fighting for self-determination that kicked off the national Indigenous civil rights movement. More recently, the city was ground zero for the global racial reckoning after the police killing of George Floyd in 2020. Today, Minneapolis still has one of the largest urban Native populations in the United States. It's home to the American Indian Cultural Corridor, a hub of Native food, art, and culture in the heart of the city, as well as Little Earth of United Tribes, the country's first and only Indigenous preference project-based Section 8 rental assistance housing complex. I'm so honored to be a part of the Twin Cities' vibrant Native community.

THE LAND

Long before colonists built the city of Minneapolis to help power the agriculture and timber industries, the Anishinaabe (also known as Ojibwe or Chippewa), Dakota (also called Sioux), Ho-Chunk (often referred to as Winnebago), Meskwaki, Odawa, and Potawatomi peoples inhabited the Great Lakes basin for millennia. Some have always been here, like the Dakota and Menominee, who have stories about the glaciers retreating after the last Ice Age. Others, like the Anishinaabe and Meskwaki, migrated from the east. Today, there are more than seventy tribal groups living throughout the region across the United States and Canada.

As the Anishinaabe legend goes, more than a thousand years ago, a prophecy urged them to find "the land where food grows on water." The tribe headed westward and came upon an area glimmering with freshwater lakes in which tall grasses with tassels of milky seeds grew. A passing duck supposedly dropped some kernels into a kettle, introducing them to one of the region's most prized foods: the life-sustaining grain *manoomin* (meaning "the good berry"), more commonly known as wild rice.

Formed more than a million years ago by massive glaciers, the namesake lakes contain the largest supply of fresh water in the world. These immense bodies of water also moderate the humid continental climate caused by air masses flowing in from every direction. Summer is hot and humid, with the lakes releasing stored heat come autumn, making for heavy snowfall and a harsh winter. Then spring, with its thawing and thunderstorms, is a time of beautiful reawakening. The distinct seasons create incredibly fleeting opportunities to harvest wild foods, like ramps in early spring and wild rice in late summer. Here, nature keeps us hyperaware of what's going on around us.

Over the centuries, the Great Lakes tribes developed sophisticated systems to make use of the area's abundance, moving in rhythm with the seasons. They fashioned tools, canoes, and dwellings like wigwams and longhouses from birchbark and tree saplings. Traditionally, men fished the waterways with spears and nets for walleye, trout, perch, bass, muskellunge, northern pike, and whitefish. Using bows and arrows made from copper or stone, they hunted and trapped deer, moose, rabbits, beavers, squirrels, ducks, and other wildlife in the dense forests.

Women, meanwhile, gathered ramps, fiddleheads, and morels in the spring; blueberries, blackberries, and gooseberries in the summer; and beechnuts, hazelnuts, and hickory nuts in autumn. They tapped maple and birch trees to make syrup and grew crops like corn, beans, and squash in the rich soil. The Menominee, for example, developed elaborate raised garden beds on Wisconsin land that they've managed for 160 years, which is today considered one of the most sustainable forest operations in the country. To prepare for the lean winter months, tribal communities preserved much of this bounty by drying, curing, and smoking it. Many of these culinary traditions are alive and well today.

Before settlers clear-cut the landscape for agricultural use, the Great Lakes had plentiful forests, grasslands, and marshy wetlands. When I try to envision what the region might look like had it been properly preserved, I picture the Meskwaki Nation in central Iowa. After losing much of their land through treaties, this longtime Great Lakes tribe purchased their settlement. What began as eighty acres in 1857 has grown to more than eight thousand acres in modern times. Because the land base was purchased, the Meskwaki Nation is not an Indian reservation in the way most tribal territories are. This sovereign nation has stewarded this land for nearly 170 years, carefully cultivating it using traditional ecological knowledge. Today, it's the only place in the state that reflects how Iowa should look—with glistening lakes, rolling hills, dense forests, and a balanced ecosystem—rather than the flat landscape people have come to expect.

THE HISTORY

Not only did the region's waterways supply rich sustenance like fish and wild rice, they also allowed Native peoples to move between villages to trade foods, furs, and other supplies long before initial European contact in the mid-1500s. British and French fishers angling off the coast of northeast Canada were the first to barter guns, cloth, metal tools, and manufactured goods in exchange for beaver, mink, fox, and other coveted furs. Word spread quickly, prompting French explorers to settle in the St. Lawrence Valley.

Recognizing the power of the Great Lakes tribes, the French formed economic alliances with them to help fuel their fur empire. By most accounts, French and Native people lived in harmony for decades and even sometimes intermarried. But the fur trade also caused the spread of European diseases, guns, and alcohol, and it ultimately encouraged voyageurs to move deeper into the Great Lakes region.

As more European settlements encroached on the basin in the mid-1600s, several wars broke out, causing Indigenous communities to migrate both within and out of the region. But it was in the 1800s that life in the Great Lakes was forever changed.

By the time the colonialist machine moved into the region in full force, it had perfected its scheme for pushing tribal groups off their homelands using a lethal combination of treaties, expulsions, and sheer violence. The Anishinaabe, one of the largest Native populations across Turtle Island, signed more than forty treaties with the US government between 1785 and 1867, surrendering land and mineral rights in exchange for the right to hunt, fish, and gather foods like wild rice on the ceded land. These promises have been broken time and again in the ensuing years, but tribal groups have fought hard to protect their rights, including hard-won Supreme Court battles.

Meanwhile, the Ho-Chunk were driven off their ten-million-acre territory across Wisconsin, Minnesota, Iowa, Missouri, and Illinois due to treaties, forced removals, and the Black Hawk War of 1832. But even after their relocation onto reservations in other parts of the country, they returned to their homeland and eventually bought back land tracts when the Homestead Act of 1862—which provided US citizens with 160 acres of federal land as long as they agreed to live on and farm it—was extended in 1875 to Native individuals if they denounced their tribal ways. After years of fighting, in 1974 the tribe won compensation for the land lost through fraudulent treaties. Much like the Meskwaki in Iowa, the Ho-Chunk are the only one of Wisconsin's federally recognized tribes that doesn't live on a reservation but instead on repurchased land.

Like the Anishinaabe, the Odawa in ancient times migrated from the east into Michigan, Ohio, and parts of southern Canada. Widely known as traders, the tribe formed an alliance with the Ojibwe and Potawatomi known as the Council of the Three Fires. During the Seven Years' War (1756–1763) between the British and French in pursuit of North American dominance, they supported their French trading partners. After that defeat, the Odawa organized an uprising against the British known as Pontiac's Rebellion. Although unsuccessful in stopping further encroachment, it caused British powers to issue the Royal Proclamation of 1763, which recognized the legal right of Indigenous communities to lay claim to the lands they occupied—a First Nations protection in Canada to this day. The Odawa surrendered much of their homeland through treaties with both the US and Canadian governments and today live mainly in Michigan, with smaller populations in Oklahoma and Ontario, Canada.

The gruesome fate of the Dakota is perhaps the most infamous atrocity among the Great Lakes tribes. Between 1837 and 1858, they signed multiple treaties exchanging their homeland in Minnesota for money, food, and supplies that never materialized. Facing starvation, hunting parties went on raids, which prompted the Dakota Uprising (also known as the US-Dakota War of 1862). In the ensuing unjust trials, more than three hundred Native men were sentenced to death, followed by the largest single execution in American history, when US forces hanged thirty-eight Dakota men in Mankato. Many of the sixteen hundred Dakota people held at Fort Snelling through the winter died from disease and exposure. The survivors were later expelled to reservations in Nebraska and South Dakota after the government voided its treaties with the tribe. The state of Minnesota apologized for these horrors 150 years later in 2012, but the long-lasting effects still reverberate today.

Although the thirst for controlling spaces and building wealth didn't hit the Great Lakes until a century after other parts of the United States, the basin was similarly ravaged. With its ample timber, minerals, and fertile soil, the region was rich with resources that settlers were hungry to exploit. Land surveyors acquired countless land scrips from the Anishinaabe—who couldn't comprehend the concept of land ownership—then portioned out tracts for sale. This opened up the doors for an influx of Danish, Swedish, Finnish, and German immigrants as well as the extractive lumber, mining, and agricultural industries.

The Homestead Act of 1862 accelerated all of this. It built a class of increasingly wealthy landowners who acquired more and more acreage. Meanwhile, struggling independent farmers with no regard for traditional ecological knowledge started overhunting and overfishing since so few regulations were in place.

What resulted was an absolute environmental catastrophe. Homesteaders and burgeoning industries ripped up the earth to make way for farming and decimated forests to sell as timber. I have even come across little handbooks from the early 1900s explaining how to remove tree stumps after land had been clear-cut. This wiped out wild game and plants; plus, the cows, pigs, and other livestock that were introduced to the area created a totally different ecosystem. All of this eventually led to the industrialization of agriculture and the formation of the corporate farms we see today. A similar story played out in the Great Lakes fishery as large-scale commercial fishing took hold.

Layered onto this long history of deception, displacement, and trauma are modern-day threats like pollution, climate change, habitat mismanagement, and pipeline and mine development. To combat this, tireless land defenders have dedicated their lives to preserving sacred Native traditions and foods in the region. For instance, my friend Simone leads the Indigenous Environmental Network's food sovereignty and climate justice efforts and fights hard against the commodification, commercialization, and genetic modification of wild rice. I've been fortunate enough to learn from these local knowledge keepers, whose invaluable insight has informed my work to revitalize Indigenous foodways.

THE FOOD

Indigenous communities in the Great Lakes have fought hard to protect their way of life, their cultural practices, and their traditional foodways through steadfast determination, peaceful protests, and legal battles. Like so many Native peoples across Turtle Island, they have faced countless broken treaties and ongoing challenges to their rights to hunt, fish, and gather.

To this day, wild rice remains a vital Native food, with an entire economic system built around it. Prized for its nutritional value and earthy taste, it's among the first foods eaten by babies and the last eaten by elders. Wild rice is served during ceremonies, feasts, and potlucks and is also a favorite ingredient in soups, casseroles, and side dishes. Contrary to popular belief, it's super easy to cook.

But the majority of the so-called wild rice sold as a gourmet food in supermarkets isn't wild at all. Instead, it is a farmed counterfeit that's grown mostly in California, in man-made paddies that mimic its natural habitat. Its shiny, jet-black appearance contrasts with natural wild rice's matte finish and varying brown hues. This domesticated paddy rice—which in Minnesota and Wisconsin must be labeled as such—has been tamed over time to make it less delicate, easier to harvest, and therefore more agriculturally profitable.

The traditional harvesting method is a painstaking process that takes years to master, with family techniques being passed down from one generation to the next. In late summer to early fall when the aquatic grass's swollen seeds are ripening, the Anishinaabe return to their secret wild rice beds—similar to favorite fishing holes—to harvest this special plant by hand.

Ricers work in pairs, with one person gently guiding a canoe through the shallow waters using a long push pole and the other person wielding cedar knockers to gently bend the tall grasses and tap the seed heads into the boat. Some kernels fall into the water and sink down into the mud—a critical part of the cycle to plant next year's crop. In Minnesota, which produces much of the world's wild rice, a license is required to harvest the grain, which must be done in this careful manner.

Once back on shore, processing begins. Families dry their harvest in the sun on a blanket, then parch it in a metal kettle over a slow-burning wood fire. Next, they dance on the rice to loosen and remove the outer hull from the seed. Finally, they gently toss it in a shallow birchbark winnowing tray and let the wind carry away the chaff—rendering this important food ready for cooking, selling, or bartering. Those looking for a more efficient approach turn to processor Bruce Savage (Fond du Lac Band of Lake Superior Chippewa), whose Spirit Lake Native Farms

processes thousands of pounds of wild rice every year using his proprietary modern equipment.

But wild rice habitats have been under threat for decades due to unscrupulous harvesters, climate change, and mine and pipeline construction. In 2018, the White Earth Band of Ojibwe passed a groundbreaking Rights of Manoomin law that formally recognizes this sacred plant's right to exist, flourish, regenerate, and be preserved. This set the stage for a 2021 lawsuit against the Minnesota Department of Natural Resources in a valiant but ultimately unsuccessful attempt to halt the destructive Enbridge Line 3 oil pipeline project.

At Owamni and the Indigenous Food Lab, wild rice—both the hand-harvested variety and Indigenous-grown paddy rice—inspires us endlessly. We add it to masa when making tamales, cook it in a dry skillet until puffed and toasty for garnishes and tea, blend it with ground meat for sausages, and also serve it simply, sweetened with a little maple syrup, so people can enjoy its nuanced flavors and fluffy texture. In this chapter, I showcase it multiple ways: as a simple porridge with birch syrup (see page 84), alongside nixtamalized corn in tamales (see page 92), as a crust for walleye fish cakes (see page 88), and as a binder and nutritious mix-in for duck sausage patties (see page 91).

Walleye is another huge economic driver for Great Lakes tribes. Firm enough to grill but mild and subtly sweet enough to fry, this versatile freshwater fish is a mainstay on our menus. Thanks to its elusive nature, walleye is one of the most coveted catches in the region; it typically clocks in at a few pounds but can weigh up to twenty. I admit that I'm actually pretty awful at fishing—after all, I grew up on the Great Plains—but if someone hands me a walleye, I can make it taste delicious in so many ways. For instance, check out the recipe for Wild Rice–Crusted Walleye Cakes (page 88), seasoned with anise hyssop.

For tribal communities here, fishing is a way of life. Unfortunately, they are in constant battle with state and federal management, who try to curtail or altogether quash their treaty rights. This has prompted long legal fights, both triumphant and disappointing. One landmark decision is the 1999 US Supreme Court ruling that upheld the Mille Lacs Band of Ojibwe's treaty rights on ceded public land. This echoed a 1972 Wisconsin Supreme Court ruling that the Bad River and Red Cliff Chippewa bands had the right to fish in Lake Superior without state regulation.

> To this day, wild rice remains a vital Native food, with an entire economic system built around it.

Throughout the years, there has also been ongoing public outcry over when, where, and how Indigenous groups exercise their treaty rights, sometimes leading to violent clashes between Native fishers and non-Native protesters. Resort owners and sport anglers often question off-reservation fishing and oppose the use of spears and nets. A lot of this uproar is ironically focused on the decimation of wildlife populations—the unfortunate consequence of ineffective management policies and extractive practices that ignore traditional ecological knowledge.

A notable example of wildlife decimation is the near extinction of walleye on Red Lake in northern Minnesota. The Red Lake Band of Chippewa's reservation spans 840,000 acres, including 85 percent of the namesake waterway. Walleye has long been an abundant food and income source here, but it was almost lost in the 1990s after decades of overfishing, starting with the establishment of a commercial fishery during World War I. To address the problem, the tribe and the state came to a historic agreement mandating a strict moratorium on fishing across Minnesota's largest inland lake. After extensive restoration efforts, the lake was reopened to limited fishing in the spring of 2006.

Across the region, tribal groups endeavor to protect walleye and other critical fish species from overfishing and disruptions like pollution, warming waters, shoreline erosion, and invasive species. The Great Lakes Indian Fish & Wildlife Commission, which represents eleven Ojibwe nations across Minnesota, Wisconsin, and Michigan, strives to safeguard both the area's natural resources and its members' treaty rights.

Maple syrup is another local dietary staple. Its long shelf life makes it an ideal energy source for the cold winter months. But it's more than just sustenance—it's also a symbol of the symbiotic relationship between Indigenous peoples and the natural world. According to Anishinaabe legend, the trickster figure and cultural hero Nanabozho discovered maple syrup when the thick, sweet substance rained down on him from a tree. Fearing his people would become lazy if given this delicacy so freely, he turned the syrup into sap so that they would have to work hard to enjoy it.

Today, the laborious but worthwhile process of maple sugaring looks much like it did centuries ago, aside from modern tools. In the spring when daytime temperatures rise above freezing but nighttime temperatures remain below, people take to the woods, typically returning to established sugar bush camps.

Quite often, the same family or group has gathered at these special tree groves for generations to not only collect sap but also share stories and pass on time-honored traditions.

To tap for sap, sugar makers drill or gash a small hole in the side of a tree and then pound in a spigot, with a container (historically made of birchbark) placed beneath to catch the diverted sap. They then boil it down for several hours to achieve the desired consistency and sugar content. It's a time-consuming task, since some forty gallons of sap are required to make a single gallon of syrup.

Eaten during feasts, ceremonies, and everyday meals, maple products are also valued for their preservation and medicinal properties. Syrup has been used for millennia to cure and flavor meats so they keep through the long winter. It's also used as an anesthetic and is believed to help naturally cleanse the kidney and liver.

In addition to these staples, there are countless other proteins, plants, and ingredients all around us that make up the Great Lakes Indigenous foodways. But as with wild rice, walleye, and maple syrup, they, too, face modern-day disruptions like climate change and human encroachment. For instance, the vital pollinator plant milkweed—once ubiquitous across the area but now endangered—has been enjoyed by both butterflies and Native peoples for eons. Once-thriving herds of moose, an important protein, have also dwindled over the years.

More than a decade after that first Indigenous dinner in Bemidji, I'm still incredibly honored to showcase the magnificent beauty of the bounty that surrounds us. At Owamni and the Indigenous Food Lab, people are often amazed at how simple yet deliciously nourishing our food is. I truly believe there's no more powerful tool than food to bring people together and educate them about Native cultures. These recipes give us an opportunity to reclaim our cultural identity, restore ancestral wisdom, and reconnect with each other and the world around us. From Wild Rice Porridge with Birch Syrup (page 84) to Beaver Tacos (page 95), these modern-day dishes offer a taste of my adopted home and pay homage to the original peoples of this land—and this water.

HOW TO COOK WILD RICE

Hand-harvested wild rice is more delicate in color, fluffier in texture, and sweeter in flavor than the shiny jet-black grains of cultivated "wild" rice, known as paddy rice. They also cook completely differently, with paddy rice requiring more time and water to become plump.

At my restaurant and for events, I use both hand-harvested rice and paddy rice. I source our paddy rice from Red Lake Nation Foods.

You can cook wild rice on the stovetop using the absorption method as you would other types of rice, or you can boil it like pasta. It's generally fluffier and less swollen with water when you cook it using the absorption method, while boiling it like pasta is often a little bit faster. Note that 1 cup uncooked wild rice (hand-harvested or paddy) will yield 3 cups cooked.

ABSORPTION METHOD

For hand-harvested wild rice

Rinse the rice in a sieve, shaking to remove any excess liquid. In a medium saucepan, combine 1 cup wild rice and 1½ cups water and bring to a boil over high heat. Reduce the heat to medium-low, cover, and cook until the grains are tender and the water is absorbed, about 20 minutes. If the water is absorbed but the rice could be more tender, add ¼ cup more water and continue cooking for 4 minutes longer. Turn off the heat and let it stand 5 minutes, then fluff with a fork.

For paddy rice

Rinse the rice in a sieve, shaking to remove any excess liquid. In a medium saucepan, combine 1 cup paddy rice with 2½ cups water and bring to a boil over high heat. Reduce the heat to medium-low, cover, and cook until the grains split at one edge and the water is absorbed, 45 to 50 minutes. Turn off the heat and let the rice stand for 5 minutes.

PASTA METHOD

In a large pot of boiling salted water, cook the rice uncovered until just tender. For hand-harvested wild rice, 12 to 15 minutes. For paddy rice, 35 minutes if you'd like chewier rice and up to 50 minutes for softer rice; either way, the top of the grains should be split. Drain the rice. To help evaporate and absorb the excess water and give the rice a fluffier texture, return it to the pot, cover with a clean towel followed by a lid, and let stand on the warm burner for 5 minutes.

WILD RICE PORRIDGE
WITH BIRCH SYRUP

serves 2 to 4

When I have leftover wild rice, I like to make a hearty porridge. It's a soothing way to start the day. Cooking the rice with some sunflower milk (or any other milk) makes the porridge richer and more satisfying, and a bit of birch syrup brings out the sweetness of the rice. To make the porridge creamier, you can partially puree it with an immersion blender or a standard blender. Or you can leave it as is for a more toothsome texture.

- 2 cups cooked wild rice (from about ¾ cup uncooked rice; see page 83)
- 1 cup sunflower milk (see Seed, Nut, and Grain Milks, page 35) or other nondairy milk, plus more for serving
- ¼ cup birch or maple syrup, plus more for serving
- ½ teaspoon fine sea salt
- Great Lakes Granola (optional; recipe follows), for sprinkling

In a medium saucepan, combine the cooked wild rice, 2 cups water, the sunflower milk, birch syrup, and salt and bring to a boil over high heat. Reduce the heat to medium-low and simmer the porridge partially uncovered, stirring occasionally, for 30 minutes, or until the rice plumps and fully splits and is suspended in the creamy liquid.

For a creamier consistency, use an immersion blender to partially puree the porridge. (Or transfer about one-third of the rice to a blender and puree, then return it to the pot.)

Spoon the porridge into bowls and serve on its own or with a sprinkle of Great Lakes Granola as well as more sunflower milk and syrup, if desired.

GREAT LAKES GRANOLA

makes about 3 cups

This grain-free, rich, crunchy granola brings together the nuts and seeds from plants that both grow wild and that we cultivate widely in the region. Hickory nuts are probably the trickiest ingredient to find commercially, but they are available online. If you can't find them, you can substitute pecans.

Serve this on its own as a snack, with sunflower milk (see Seed, Nut, and Grain Milks, page 35) for breakfast, and as a topping for porridges and salads.

- 1 cup raw sunflower seeds
- 1 cup raw pepitas
- ½ cup black walnuts
- ½ cup hickory nuts
- ⅓ cup maple syrup
- ⅓ cup sunflower oil
- ¾ teaspoon fine sea salt

Preheat the oven to 250°F. Line a baking sheet with parchment paper.

In a large bowl, toss together the sunflower seeds, pepitas, black walnuts, and hickory nuts. Add the syrup, oil, and salt and toss again.

Spread the mixture on the prepared baking sheet in a single layer and bake for 30 to 40 minutes, or until toasty, stirring about halfway through.

Let the granola cool and dry out on the baking sheet before transferring to an airtight container, where it can be kept for up to 1 week.

CEDAR-MAPLE BAKED BEANS

serves 8

At Owamni, I make a version of these baked beans with many Indigenous varieties. While most lima beans grow best in warm climates, the Potawatomi people in Wisconsin adapted this variety of lima bean, known as the Potawatomi pole bean, to grow well in our region. Over generations, they kept it safe so we can still enjoy it today, and I love these big, flat beans in this dish.

Maple gives these baked beans that characteristic sweetness, but the addition of cedar (or you can substitute with balsam fir) gives them a beautiful, unexpected aroma. Growing up, we traditionally boiled cedar to help purify the air and to drink for tea. It's high in vitamin C, so popular during cold season. While it's safe to ingest in smaller quantities like this, it's a powerful plant and best not to consume every day. Many people also recommend avoiding it when pregnant.

- 2 tablespoons sunflower oil
- 1 large yellow onion, chopped
- Fine sea salt
- 2 cups dried Potawatomi Pole Lima Beans or other multicolored lima beans, soaked overnight, drained, and well rinsed
- ¾ cup maple syrup
- 1 (5-inch) piece fresh or dried northern white cedar, balsam fir, or other edible conifers (see Notes), plus a small piece or a few needles, for garnish

Preheat the oven to 300°F.

In a large Dutch oven, heat the oil over medium heat. Add the onion and 1 teaspoon salt and cook for 6 to 8 minutes, stirring, until the onion is translucent. Add the beans, 4 cups water, the syrup, and ½ teaspoon fine sea salt and bring to a simmer. Arrange the cedar piece on top.

Cover, transfer the beans to the oven, and bake for 30 minutes. Uncover and stir and continue to cook the beans, uncovered, until tender. They should take between 1 hour 30 minutes and 2 hours total to cook. If the water level falls below the beans before they're tender, add just enough water to cover. Ultimately, you want beans that are tender and suspended in a small amount of liquid.

Remove the cedar piece. Taste and season with more salt, as needed. Finely chop a little bit of fresh cedar to sprinkle on top and serve.

The baked beans can be refrigerated in their liquid overnight. Reheat gently over low heat.

Notes

- *I like to soak the beans before I cook them because they cook more evenly this way, so be sure to plan ahead.*
- *Northern white cedar and balsam fir grow prolifically in the Great Lakes, and I can usually harvest from both trees either in my own backyard or with a walk around my neighborhood. See Conifers, page 22, for more about sourcing conifers for cooking.*
- *This recipe is completely plant-based, but if you'd like to enrich the flavor of the bean cooking liquid, you could add shredded smoked turkey during the last 30 minutes of cooking, when the beans are nearly tender.*

WILD RICE–CRUSTED WALLEYE CAKES

makes 8 cakes

Like a good Maryland crab cake, these cakes are made with plenty of fish and very little binder. If you want to bind the mixture together more, making them a bit firmer, you could add a duck egg. Dry mustard gives the cakes a little bit of bite, while hyssop adds an intriguing anise flavor, and the crust of pan-popped wild rice gives them a crunchy, satisfying texture to go with the tender fish inside.

If you use frozen walleye, you can make these cakes year-round. I like to serve them with the luscious duck egg aioli and a simple green salad.

- ½ cup uncooked wild rice
- 1 pound skinless walleye fillets, cut into chunks
- ½ small onion, finely chopped
- 1 medium burdock root, peeled and coarsely grated (about ½ cup)
- 1 tablespoon mustard powder
- 3 tablespoons dried anise hyssop leaves or flowers
- ¼ cup fine cornmeal
- ½ teaspoon fine sea salt
- 3 tablespoons sunflower oil, plus more as needed
- Duck Egg Aioli (page 36), for serving

Put a few grains of the rice in a medium skillet and set the pan over medium-high heat; shake the pan occasionally to prevent them from burning. When the rice starts to pop (it will lighten in color and start to make a crackling sound in the skillet), discard this rice. (Now you know the pan is hot enough to pop rice.)

Return the skillet to the heat. Add ¼ cup of the wild rice to the skillet so it covers the bottom of the pan. Cook the rice for 20 to 40 seconds, shaking the pan gently, until most of the grains are lighter in color and puffed slightly, then immediately transfer the popped rice to a cool plate so it doesn't burn. Repeat with the remaining ¼ cup rice.

When all the rice is cool, transfer it to a spice grinder or mini food processor and pulse until coarsely chopped. Transfer to a plate for coating the fish cakes.

Working in batches as needed, pulse the fish a few times in a food processor until it is coarsely chopped and transfer to a bowl. Add the onion, burdock, mustard powder, anise hyssop, cornmeal, salt, and 1 tablespoon of the oil and mix until well combined.

Using a ¼-cup measure or a 2-ounce scoop, form the mixture into 8 patties of equal size and transfer to a plate.

In a large skillet, heat the remaining 2 tablespoons of oil over medium-high heat until shimmering. Line a plate with paper towels.

Coat half the patties on both sides in the rice, pressing gently so it adheres.

Working in batches to avoid overcrowding, add the coated cakes to the pan and cook for 3 to 4 minutes, until nicely browned on the bottom. (If the cakes seem like they're browning too quickly, reduce the heat to medium.) Flip and cook for 3 to 4 minutes, until browned on the second side. Drain on the paper towels. Repeat with the remaining cakes, adding more oil to the pan as necessary.

Serve with duck egg aioli.

DUCK, WILD RICE, AND CRANBERRY SAUSAGE PATTIES

WITH POACHED DUCK EGGS AND DANDELION CHIMICHURRI

serves 4

Ducks and wild rice share a special relationship. According to an Anishinaabe legend, a passing duck dropped wild rice into a kettle and introduced this life-sustaining grain to people. During the harvest season, people allow some of the rice grains to fall into the water to share with duck relatives, and to help plant next year's crop.

To make these free-form sausage patties, it's easiest to start with ground duck meat. If you can't find it, you can certainly grind your own. Just make sure 10 to 20 percent of the weight includes the fat or skin, so the patties will be juicy.

CHIMICHURRI

- 4 ounces dandelion leaves (tough stems removed), finely chopped
- ½ shallot, finely chopped
- 1 tablespoon dried cranberries, preferably unsweetened, finely chopped
- 2 tablespoons cider vinegar
- ⅓ cup sunflower oil
- Sea salt

PATTIES AND EGGS

- 3 juniper berries
- 1 pound ground duck meat
- 1 cup cooked and chilled wild rice (from ⅓ cup uncooked rice; see page 83)
- ⅓ cup dried cranberries, preferably unsweetened, finely chopped
- 1¼ teaspoons dried wild bergamot (bee balm)
- 1½ teaspoons fine sea salt
- 4 duck eggs
- 1 tablespoon sunflower oil
- Ground sumac, for sprinkling (optional)

Make the chimichurri: In a medium bowl, stir together the chopped dandelion, shallot, and cranberries. Stir in the vinegar and sunflower oil. Taste and season with salt.

Make the patties and eggs: Use a small mortar to pound the juniper berries into a powder.

In a large bowl, mix together the ground duck, chilled wild rice, cranberries, bergamot, crushed juniper, and salt. Using a ½-cup measuring cup or scoop, form the sausage into 8 patties of equal size, about ½ inch thick and place them on a plate.

One at a time, crack each egg into a fine-mesh sieve set over a bowl to allow any of the extra loose egg white to drain. Transfer each cracked egg to its own small bowl.

Bring a medium pot of water to a bare simmer over medium-low heat. Stir the water to create a vortex and add 2 of the eggs, one at a time, and cook for about 3 minutes, or just until the white is opaque and the yolk is still soft. Using a slotted spoon, transfer to a plate and repeat with the remaining 2 eggs. Keep the eggs near the stove so they stay warm.

In a large skillet, heat the oil over medium-high heat until shimmering. Add the sausage patties and cook for 3 to 4 minutes, until browned on the bottom. Flip, reduce the heat to medium, and cook for about 3 minutes, or until browned on the bottom and cooked through or until an instant-read thermometer inserted into the side of a sausage registers 165°F.

Transfer the sausage to plates and serve with the poached duck eggs and dandelion chimichurri. Sprinkle with sumac, if desired.

WILD RICE TAMALES
WITH SMOKED MUSHROOMS AND ROSE HIP

makes about 20 tamales

To showcase two important foods for Indigenous peoples in the region—wild rice and nixtamalized corn—I bring them together in tamales, with the cooked rice blended into the masa. I then stuff the tamales with quickly smoked mushrooms that get a bright citrusy note from rose hips and serve them along a sweet-tart berry sauce known as wóžapi, sometimes spelled wojapi.

Between mixing the dough, cooking the filling, and stuffing the corn husks, tamales can be labor-intensive to pull together on your own. That's why people typically make them in big batches while in community with each other. (If you want to do the same, feel free to double or even triple the recipe.)

You'll need to soak 1 pint of wood chips overnight and soak 24 corn husks for at least 4 hours or up to overnight (plus more for steaming). While you can use any type of wood chips designed for smoking, I like the clean flavor of oak with the mushrooms.

MUSHROOM FILLING

- 2 pounds oyster mushrooms, cleaned and cut into ¼-inch slices
- 1 tablespoon Rose Hip Powder (page 359) or store-bought
- Sea salt

TAMALES

- 2 pounds Fresh Masa (page 28) or use masa harina (see chart, page 27)
- ⅔ cup sunflower oil or melted and slightly cooled duck fat
- 2 teaspoons fine sea salt
- ½ cup Roasted Bird Stock (page 40) or other stock
- 2 cups cooked wild rice (from ¾ cup uncooked rice; see page 83)
- 24 corn husks, soaked for 4 to 24 hours
- Mixed Berry Wóžapi (recipe follows), for serving

Make the mushroom filling: Line a metal roasting pan with aluminum foil. Arrange the soaked wood chips in the pan. Cover the chips with foil and poke holes in the foil.

Arrange an ovenproof perforated pan or fine-mesh rack so it's about 2 inches above the chips. (You can create balls of foil to help elevate the rack.) Spread out the mushrooms on the rack and cover the pan with foil. Set across two burners over high heat for 7 minutes. Turn off the heat and let it stand for 10 minutes. (Alternatively, spread them out on two baking sheets without oil and roast in a 400°F oven until they're wilted, 12 to 15 minutes.)

Uncover the mushrooms, transfer to a cutting board, and finely chop.

Toss the mushrooms with the rose hip powder and season well with salt.

Make the tamales: In a stand mixer fitted with the paddle attachment, combine the masa, oil, and salt and beat on medium speed for about 5 minutes, or until fluffy. Start adding the stock, 1 tablespoon at a time, until you have a soft, slightly tacky dough. Use a spoon or your hands to mix in the wild rice. Arrange 1 soaked corn husk on a work surface with the narrow end pointing away from you and the ribbed side down. Using a ⅓-cup measure, scoop the dough into the center of the husk. Use a large rounded spoon to create a well in the dough, leaving a ½-inch border of husk. Measure out about 3 tablespoons of the mushrooms and arrange in the well.

Fold in the long sides of the husk, overlapping them to enclose the filling. Fold the narrow end toward you, over the tamal; it will remain open at the wide end. Stand the tamal, open-end up, in a very

large steamer insert. Repeat with the remaining corn husks, dough, and filling.

Cover the tamales with more corn husks or parchment paper.

Fill the bottom of the steamer with water so it's below the bottom of the steamer insert. Bring to a boil over high heat, then reduce the heat to low. Cover the steamer with a lid and steam the tamales for 1½ hours, replacing water if needed. To check doneness, remove one of the tamales; if it feels firm, check inside. If it looks shiny and wet or you see a lot of residue sticking to the husk when you pull it away, continue cooking for up to 30 minutes longer. Otherwise, remove all the tamales from the steamer to cool for 15 minutes. The masa inside will continue to firm up during this time.

Serve the tamales with wóžapi.

MIXED BERRY WÓŽAPI

Makes about 2 cups

- 2 cups mixed berries, thawed if frozen
- 1 tablespoon maple syrup

In a medium saucepan, combine the berries and ¼ cup water. Cook over medium heat, stirring, for 3 to 5 minutes, until the berries are softened. Transfer to a blender, add the maple syrup, and puree until smooth.

Transfer to an airtight container and refrigerate for up to 4 days.

BEAVER TACOS
WITH PICKLED ONION AND WATERCRESS

serves 6 to 8

Historically, the beaver was an important animal in the Great Lakes not just for its fur but also for its meat. These days, it's more of a delicacy, but trappers still seek it out. Its tail is leathery on the outside and used to make crafts. The rest of the beaver breaks down like other four-legged animals, with front and hind quarters and loin pieces that have a rich, beefy flavor.

If you're ever breaking down a beaver yourself, the most important thing to know is that you must remove its castor glands, which are used to scent its territory but can unfortunately taint the meat. If you accidentally puncture a gland, you'll discover a scent that haunts your sinuses for days on end.

For this recipe, you can use any cut of beaver you can find because the meat is braised until meltingly tender with garlic, a little chile, maple, tart berries, and aromatic cedar. You can substitute skinned duck legs for the beaver, which have a similarly luscious texture.

PICKLED ONION

- 1 medium red onion, thinly sliced
- 1 (2-inch) piece cedar or balsam fir (see Conifers, page 22)
- ½ cup cider vinegar
- ¼ cup maple syrup
- 1 tablespoon fine sea salt

BEAVER

- 3 tablespoons sunflower oil
- 3 pounds bone-in hunks of beaver meat cut from the front or hind quarters (or substitute skinned duck legs)
- Sea salt
- 1 large yellow onion, coarsely chopped
- 6 garlic cloves, smashed
- 1 ancho chile, stemmed and seeded
- ¼ cup aronia berries or cranberries, fresh or frozen
- 4 cups Rich Bison or Other Game Stock (page 41) or water
- ¼ cup maple syrup
- 1 (5-inch) piece cedar (optional; see Conifers, page 22)
- 2 sage leaves

TACOS

- 24 Corn Tortillas (page 31) or store-bought, warmed
- 2 cups watercress

Make the pickled onion: Pack the onion and cedar into a clean 1-pint jar.

In a small saucepan, combine the vinegar, ½ cup water, the maple syrup, and salt and bring to a simmer over high heat, whisking to dissolve the salt. Pour the hot brine over the onion. Let cool to room temperature, then remove the cedar. Seal and refrigerate for at least 1 hour or up to 1 month.

Cook the beaver: Preheat the oven to 300°F.

In a large heavy pot, heat half of the oil over medium-high heat until shimmering. Season the beaver meat all over with salt. Add half the beaver pieces so they're in a single layer and sear for about 10 minutes, turning occasionally, until browned all over. Transfer to a plate. Repeat with the remaining oil and beaver.

Reduce the heat to medium. Add the onion, garlic, and chile. Season with salt and cook for about 5 minutes, or until the onion is softened. Add the berries and cook for about 4 minutes, stirring, until they soften and start to burst. Add the stock and maple syrup. Bring to a boil and reduce the heat to medium-low. Add the cedar (if using) and sage, then cover, transfer to the oven, and cook for 2½ to 3 hours, until the meat is meltingly tender and falls away from the bones.

Using tongs, transfer the meat to a cutting board. Strain the remaining liquid into a pot and skim off as much of the fat as possible. Bring the liquid to a boil over medium-high heat and cook for about 20 minutes, until reduced by half. Taste and adjust with salt.

Pull the meat off the bones and toss with the liquid.

Serve the tortillas with the braised beaver meat, pickled onion, and the watercress, allowing people to assemble their tacos at the table.

BALSAM FIR BRAISED MOOSE
WITH SUNCHOKE MASH

serves 4

This simple stew brings you a taste of the Great Lakes forests. Gamey moose meat gets braised in a dried mushroom broth with the aroma of fir. Ramps or baby leeks enhance the natural sweetness of the sunchoke mash served alongside. The vegetables in the stew get very soft, so I like to separate them out and serve them as an optional side dish. You can also make this dish with meat from elk or deer.

MOOSE

- 1 ounce mixed dried wild mushrooms
- 1½ cups boiling water
- 2 tablespoons sunflower oil
- 1½ pounds boneless moose stew meat, cut into 2-inch chunks (or substitute elk or deer meat)
- Sea salt
- 1 medium yellow onion, finely chopped
- 1 large carrot, scrubbed well and finely chopped
- 2 tablespoons maple syrup
- 1 ounce fresh or ½ ounce dried balsam fir boughs (see Conifers, page 22)

MASH

- 1¼ pounds sunchokes, each halved lengthwise
- 1 tablespoon sunflower oil
- 4 ramp bulbs, thinly sliced, or 1 baby leek, white and light-green parts only, thinly sliced crosswise
- Sea salt
- Wild onion greens or chives, thinly sliced, for garnish

Cook the moose: Preheat the oven to 300°F.

Place the mushrooms in a heatproof glass measuring cup. Pour the boiling water over them and let them rehydrate while you start the stew.

In a Dutch oven or ovenproof heavy pot, heat the oil over medium-high heat. Season the moose meat with salt. Working in batches, add the meat and cook for about 8 minutes, turning until browned all over. Transfer to a plate.

Reduce the heat to medium, add the onion and carrot, and season with salt. Cook for 3 to 5 minutes, stirring, until softened. Lift the mushrooms out of the water and transfer to the pot, stirring to incorporate. Return the meat to the pot. Pour in the mushroom soaking liquid, stopping before you reach any grit at the bottom of the measuring cup. Add the maple syrup, then add just enough water to come three-quarters of the way up the meat.

Bring the liquid to a boil over high heat. Reduce the heat to medium-low and add the balsam fir boughs. Cover and transfer to the oven. Cook for about 3 hours, or until the moose meat is meltingly tender.

Using a slotted spoon, transfer the meat to a plate. Strain the cooking liquid into a clean pot. Discard the balsam fir and reserve the vegetables, if desired. Bring the liquid to a boil and cook for about 20 minutes, until it is reduced to about 1 cup.

Return the meat to the sauce and keep warm. Reheat the vegetables in a separate saucepan, just until warm.

Meanwhile, make the mash: In a medium saucepan, combine the sunchokes with water to cover by 1 inch and bring to a boil over medium-high heat. Cook for 20 to 25 minutes, until tender.

Using a slotted spoon, transfer the sunchokes to a high-powered blender. Add 2 cups of the cooking liquid and let stand to cool.

Meanwhile, in a skillet, heat the oil over medium heat. Add the ramps and cook for about 3 minutes, or until softened but not browned. Scrape into the blender and puree until smooth. Season with salt.

Spoon the mash onto plates. Top with the braised moose and sauce and serve with the vegetables. Then garnish with green onions or chives.

SWEET CORN PUDDING
WITH WOODLAND BERRY SAUCE

serves 4

While this dessert tastes like summer, you could make it any time of year when you use frozen sweet corn and berries. I don't strain the corn mixture because I like to leave it with a little bit of texture, plus the natural starch from the corn helps to thicken without adding any refined starch. Like many puddings, this one needs to set up in the refrigerator for several hours.

PUDDING

- 3 cups sweet corn kernels, fresh (from 2 to 3 ears) or thawed frozen
- ¾ cup corn or sunflower milk (see Sweet Corn Milk, page 35, or Seed, Nut, and Grain Milks, page 35)
- ½ cup Maple Sugar (page 36) or store-bought
- ¼ teaspoon fine sea salt

BERRY SAUCE

- 2 cups sweet berries, such as blackberries, raspberries, or other summer berries
- ¼ cup dried seedless rose hips
- ¼ cup maple syrup
- Pinch of fine sea salt

Make the pudding: In a high-powered blender, puree the corn, milk, maple sugar, and salt until very smooth. Pour into a medium saucepan. Whisking constantly, bring to a boil over high heat, then reduce the heat to medium and cook for about 10 minutes, or until the mixture is reduced to a thick batter.

Divide among four glasses or ramekins that each hold at least 1 cup. Let cool to room temperature, then refrigerate for at least 6 hours or overnight.

Make the berry sauce: In a blender, puree the berries with the rose hips, maple syrup, and salt. Add a little water if you need to help loosen the puree.

Transfer to an airtight container and refrigerate until well chilled.

Just before serving, pour the berry sauce over each portion of corn pudding.

EASTERN WOODLANDS

THE PEOPLE OF THE FIRST LIGHT

ON A CRISP OCTOBER EVENING BACK IN 2017, New York City diners experienced the first-ever Indigenous meal at the legendary James Beard House. I prepared that dinner with a team of Native chefs, including prodigy Maizie White, the daughter of renowned Mohawk seed keeper and farmer Rowen White. Maizie was just twelve at the time and likely the first Indigenous preteen to make a meal in this prestigious setting.

Whenever I cook in someone else's homeland, I take care to showcase the local culture by using the languages and foods of that region. To honor the area's original Native inhabitants, I spent weeks sourcing ingredients from tribal producers and learning to cook them in a way that respected tradition yet still made them feel new. With help from a friend who's fluent, I wrote that night's menu in Algonquian, a language that most diners had probably never seen or heard before, even though it once was spoken broadly here.

Our multicourse meal showcased the region's delicious, diverse foodways from land and water. Guests savored dishes including Shinnecock oysters on the half shell; hard-shell quahog clams with smoked crawfish and sea lettuce; and rabbit with Buffalo Creek squash, toasted hickory nut, and foraged pawpaw. We closed out the evening with a dessert of nixtamalized maple red corn pudding complemented by hickory, corn shoots, and burnt maple sugar.

From the vantage point of the historic James Beard House, a tiny sliver of a townhouse in the West Village that once belonged to the influential culinary expert and cookbook author, it's hard to imagine what this area previously looked like. Before colonization, the place now known as Manhattan was not a concrete jungle but rather a range of diverse environs, including lush forests, grasslands, freshwater and tidal marshes, hardwood swamps, peatlands, rocky streams, ponds, and eelgrass meadows.

Originally known as Lenapehoking, this land was home to the Lenape people, an Algonquian-speaking group that included relatives across southern New York, New Jersey, Pennsylvania, and Delaware. They ate well from their expansive gardens, hunting expeditions, and the nearby fresh and salt waters.

In addition to providing seemingly endless bounty, the region acts as the backdrop for so many American myths, fueling this country's obsession with Indigenous figures like Squanto and of course with the first Thanksgiving. While based on an actual event between English colonizers and members of the Wampanoag Nation, the November holiday as many people celebrate it today actually took shape in the mid-nineteenth century, to help the United States heal after the Civil War.

Like many teachings perpetuated by our education system, these inaccurate history lessons largely disregard the devastating traumas that colonialism wreaked upon the area's original residents. But against all odds, steadfast cooks, seed keepers, and food sovereignty warriors have strived to maintain connection to their foodways by reviving heirloom varieties and reintroducing important ingredients to their communities.

THE LAND

New York City sits in the middle of the Eastern Woodlands, which spans the Atlantic coast from southern Canada down to Delaware and from the ocean inland to the eastern edge of the Great Lakes. Now one of the most densely populated areas across Turtle Island, the region encompasses coastal plains, river valleys, mountains, and verdant temperate forests. The fluctuating elevation, geography, and climate across the landscape in turn influence the endemic flora and fauna.

Even with its extensive development, the area still has pockets of forests filled with deciduous trees like oak, hickory, poplar, maple, and beech. In the fall, they drop their fire-hued leaves and then spend the winter stretched naked toward the sky to let the sunshine pour through. Come spring, when the longer days and warmth return, the forests reawaken. This region experiences four strongly delineated seasons, which prompted tribes to develop advanced food systems, including savvy preservation methods and impressive reserves to ensure their large communities endured the cold winters.

The lush woodlands have long been prime hunting and trapping grounds thanks to thriving populations of deer, moose, elk, rabbits, beavers, raccoons, and birds, such as turkeys, ducks, and geese. The forests also supply foods and medicines like berries, grapes, wild greens, nuts, seeds, and of course maple sugar. The many waterways, meanwhile, host sturgeon, salmon, shad, and other freshwater fish. In the past, the area's abundant hardwoods also served as a means of housing (taking shape as longhouses and wigwams), transportation (canoes), and countless tools.

To the north and west of New York City sit the fertile fields of the Seneca Nation, the westernmost member of the powerful Haudenosaunee Confederacy (known to the French as the Iroquois). This collective's representative approach served as a model for the formation of the US government and its Constitution.

To the east of the Big Apple are the chilly, salty waters of the gray-green Atlantic, where the Wampanoag, Narragansett, Pequot, Mohegan, and Shinnecock peoples fished, gathered shellfish, and hunted whales with harpoons.

The rich inland soils, meanwhile, let the region's skilled farmers practice the symbiotic three sisters method of growing corn, beans, and squash together, where each plant benefits the other while also feeding the soil. Area tribes developed corn in a rainbow of colors and for a multitude of purposes—flint corn for soups, flour corns for breads, popcorn for toasting over the fire, and more. The many varieties of beans were dried and stored for soups, and firm squashes were put away for the long winters. These sacred crops have nourished Native communities for eons.

The food stockpiles that the largely agrarian, highly entrepreneurial Haudenosaunee (meaning "people of the longhouse") communities accumulated gave them incredible political power. Unfortunately, those caches also became targets for destruction by Colonial forces as a way to weaken Native sovereignty. But these vital reserves are being restored today. The Onondaga Nation, for instance, currently has enough food to feed its tribal members for four years thanks to food sovereignty advocate Angela Ferguson and her farm crew.

The region's diverse terrain has long provided ample food for its residents with a unique combination of ocean access, life-giving waterways, flourishing forests, and fertile soil. The varying landscape and its bounty also influenced the fluctuating population density across the area as well as Native groups' seminomadic nature. Today, more than sixty Indigenous groups inhabit the Eastern Woodlands across both the United States and Canada.

THE HISTORY

Long before Plymouth Rock landed on us in 1620 and the Thirteen Colonies were established, dozens of Native groups inhabited the Eastern Woodlands dating back millennia. Although these communities were and continue to be distinct in many ways, many of them spoke Algonquian or Iroquoian languages. These shared-language families allowed for easier trade and negotiation.

The areas now known as New England, New Brunswick, and Nova Scotia are actually the ancestral homelands of a wide range of tribes, including the Abenaki, Maliseet, Massachusett, Mi'kmaq, Mohegan, Narragansett, Nauset, Nipmuc, Passamaquoddy, Paugussett, Pennacook, Penobscot, Pequot, Pocumtuc, Podunk, Tunxis, Wampanoag, and Woronoco peoples. These probably sound familiar, since they inspired the names given to area states, cities, and sites. Several of these communities banded together to form the Wabanaki Confederacy in the mid-1600s to stand tall against the formidable Haudenosaunee Confederacy as well as encroachment from European settlers.

Farther inland, straddling both sides of the US/Canadian border, are the territories of the powerful Haudenosaunee. Oral traditions suggest that the league was created by a cultural hero known as the Great Peacemaker in 1142. Today, it remains the oldest living participatory democracy on the planet. Now known as Six Nations, the alliance originally included the Iroquoian-speaking Mohawk, Oneida, Onondaga, Cayuga, and Seneca tribes, with the Tuscarora joining later. The coalition often clashed with the Huron and Algonquin peoples who were part of the lesser-known Seven Nations of Canada, an alliance of villages situated along the St. Lawrence River.

Contrary to what US history lessons have taught many people to believe, Eastern Woodlands communities were extremely sophisticated and developed thriving, well-organized villages. But then devastation struck in the early 1600s, when influenza, measles, and smallpox brought on by European fishers and merchants hit these communities hard; Native peoples had no natural immunity. A 1616 epidemic, for instance, killed about 75 percent of the Indigenous peoples living along the Atlantic coast. When the Pilgrims—the first wave of European religious reformers—arrived, they settled in a region ravaged by disease and took over emptied Native villages.

The Wampanoag tribe, who have long resided in Massachusetts and Rhode Island, live on in American culinary lore through the myth of the First Thanksgiving. Prior to the seventeenth century, as many as forty thousand people in some sixty-five villages made up the broader Wampanoag Nation. They took pity on the bedraggled settlers and taught them to farm so they could survive their first challenging year.

The details of the First Thanksgiving are murky, but we know that in 1621 a harvest celebration took place between the barely surviving British colony of fewer than one hundred people and the ninety or so Wampanoag men who arrived for a visit alongside their leader, Ousamequin (also known by the title Massasoit). That same year, Ousamequin and early colony governor John Carver signed a treaty that promised mutual aid and amicable relations. Unfortunately, those efforts didn't lead to lasting peace between the British and the people whose lands they encroached upon.

That shared meal would not look like today's typical Thanksgiving spread. Instead, venison was served, perhaps accompanied by wild turkey, fish, eels, and shellfish. The British also adopted the Wampanoag dish known as nasaump—boiled cornmeal porridge mixed with meats, vegetables, or berries. Many of the contemporary trappings would have been missing from the table, as potatoes had not yet made their way from South America into the global food system and there was no butter, wheat flour, or sugar for pies. And while cranberries grow well on Wampanoag homelands, they would not have been made into a sugary jelly back then.

Long before Plymouth Rock landed on us . . . dozens of Native groups inhabited the Eastern Woodlands.

As was the case across much of Turtle Island, early relationships between tribal communities and European colonists were tentatively harmonious, with some trade and intermarriage taking place. With the British and French vying for North American dominance, alliances were formed and tribal rivalries intensified. The Haudenosaunee originally sided with the British (though that shifted during the American Revolution), and the Huron and some other Algonquian-speaking tribes sided with the French.

Several conflicts followed, including the Beaver Wars (also known as the French and Iroquois Wars), named for their focus on fur hunting and trading territories. King Philip's War (1675–1676) was one of the most brutal brawls, as Native peoples fought to maintain a stronghold in their homelands. Ousamequin's son, Metacom (known to the British as King Philip), was killed and his head mounted on a stake outside Plymouth colony, where it stayed for two decades. His relatives and other tribal members, meanwhile, were shipped to the Caribbean as slaves.

The American Revolution of 1775 to 1783, in which the newly founded colonies sought freedom from Great Britain, shook up prior alliances and divided the Haudenosaunee, who were wary of both British and French promises to support their sovereignty. General John Sullivan's scorched-earth march in 1779 marked a major turning point in the war, when Continental Army troops invaded Haudenosaunee territory with the imperative to carry out "the total destruction and devastation of their settlements," including acres upon acres of corn, beans, squash, pumpkins, cucumbers, watermelons, muskmelons, and stone fruits. Who knows how many important seed varieties were lost to history?

These kinds of campaigns aren't just a thing of the past. As recently as 1990 during the Oka Crisis, the Mohawk community of Kanesatake in southwestern Quebec experienced similar destruction when military tanks plowed through their cornfields during a seventy-eight-day standoff over land disputes, as Mohawk seed keeper Steve McComber remembers.

The Revolutionary War came to an end when the British ceded their US land through the 1783 Treaty of Paris, which created the northern US border without Indigenous consultation. Fearing retribution in this new republic, many Haudenosaunee fled to Canada.

George Washington, who in reality was a glorified land surveyor, pushed for the stealing and commodifying of land spaces using the Northwest Ordinance of 1787 as justification. This one act of legislation was perhaps the most damaging of them all, because it set in motion rapid US expansion by means of violence and laid the foundation for dividing up the land into the perfect grid that we see across much of the country today.

From its very beginning, the US government has undermined Indigenous sovereignty time and again, with policies that erode our rights and increase oversight. It is a maddening irony that this country's origin story—one of supposed uprising against oppression—is laden with oppression of this continent's original peoples. Similarly, although the nascent government modeled itself after Indigenous examples, it had little respect or regard for what the founding fathers called "merciless Indian savages" in the Declaration of Independence.

Furthermore, the "Columbus myth"—the false notion that the infamous explorer "discovered" the already inhabited Americas—as author and historian Roxanne Dunbar-Ortiz calls it in her landmark book *An Indigenous Peoples' History of the United States* is still alive and well, as the very naming of Washington, DC, reminds us. Even today, with historic Indigenous representation in both elected and appointed positions, the federal government remains mercurial. That said, I'm encouraged by well-intentioned individuals, both Native and non-Native, who are working to effect change from within our flawed federal systems. One example is the US Department of Agriculture, which has recently made meaningful strides to support tribal self-determination and restore trust with Native communities by introducing grant-making programs related to Indigenous meat production and food sovereignty while also addressing historic barriers to assistance. Even so, there is still much work to be done.

THE FOOD

While Indigenous peoples of the Eastern Woodlands no longer live in bark-covered longhouses and their communities have adapted to accommodate roads, shops, and non-Native neighbors, they still celebrate seasonal food abundance. For them, Thanksgiving is not a single day but a frequent occurrence.

They celebrate maple sugar thanksgiving when the sap begins to flow in early spring and strawberry thanksgiving when the first sweet red fruits ripen. They have ceremonies for green beans and green corn from the garden in the summer, for cranberries from coastal bogs in the early fall, and autumnal harvest celebrations as the last of the produce is put up for the winter. In between are many small celebrations to express gratitude to the lands and waters for providing such riches.

Many of the foods that have sustained Eastern Woodlands tribal communities for centuries are tied to creation stories that link their arrival on Earth to celestial origins. Perhaps most famous is the Haudenosaunee creation story, in which the Sky Woman plummeted to the Earth, grabbing some seeds from a celestial tree as she fell. Birds caught her and laid her on the back of a large turtle, giving rise to the term Turtle Island. She had a daughter who matured, then became pregnant with twins, one of whom killed her during childbirth.

Afterward, Sky Woman covered her daughter's body with soil, and from it sprouted tobacco and strawberries—the seeds she had grabbed as she fell down to Earth. Her body also produced the important three sisters crops of corn, beans, and squash. The strawberry plant, whose crushed berries resemble blood, sprang from her heart. Corn, whose kernels turn milky as they ripen, sprang from her breasts. Squash, with a curly vine akin to an umbilical cord, grew from her belly button, and long finger-like beans emerged from her hands. From her feet sprang sunchokes, a potato-like tuber native to this region that looks like the pads of human feet that have been walking in fresh dirt.

To delve into Eastern Woodlands foodways, I have been lucky to learn from friends like Mashpee Wampanoag chef Sherry Pocknett. In 2023, she became the first Indigenous woman to win a James Beard Award in celebration of her now-closed Rhode Island restaurant, Sly Fox Den Too. There, she served American comfort foods with Indigenous takes, including her fan-favorite Fish Hash (page 122). Her tribe, the Mashpee Wampanoag, is known as the People of the First Light. They fed European settlers in what is considered the earliest Thanksgiving—which they have long viewed as a national day of mourning.

Sherry grew up on Cape Cod and has been cooking since she got a Suzy Homemaker toy oven as a young girl, which she used to prepare eels, quahogs, and venison for her family. She remembers learning to fish when she was just three years old, foraging for berries and sassafras, digging clams, and eating deer and raccoons that her father hunted.

In the spring when the herring run, Sherry and her relatives would go down to the stream with buckets, separating the male fish from the females—whose eggs would be harvested and sold as caviar or fried in sunflower oil. After tossing the heads, tails, and guts into the garden for fertilizer, they salted the fish and then fried or baked it to be served with cornmeal dumplings, potatoes, green beans, and beets from their garden. This is just one of the many meals Sherry remembers with great nostalgia.

In the summer, families lived closer to the coast in dome-shaped wetus (wigwams) crafted from woven reeds, and in the winter resided farther inland in large, bark-covered longhouses. They tended gardens of corn, beans, squash, and sunchokes; harvested clams, mussels, and scallops from the shoreline; and caught fish and whales in the sea. They dug pits in the sand on the beach, layered in shellfish and seaweed, then built a fire on top to steam them—a practice still enjoyed these days in what's sometimes called a clambake (see How to Have an Appanaug, page 109).

Sherry and I often reunite at Native-focused culinary events, like the Intertribal Food Sovereignty Summit. I remember marveling at her breaking down pounds upon pounds of cooked lobster faster than I ever could, as someone who grew up far from the Atlantic. (See page 118 for a lobster salad recipe inspired by that encounter.) For the 2018 summit, I had the honor of preparing the Feast of the Green Corn Moon, a celebration that occurs when corn kernels first become fully formed and edible.

At that same event, my friend Tawnya Brant, a Mohawk chef who lives in Six Nations territory in southern Ontario, showed me how to make Strawberry Wedding Bread. This pink corn dumpling uses an heirloom variety of red corn grown by her seed keeper mother, Terrylynn.

For this simple yet tasty treat, we combined finely ground corn flour, a little water, and some chopped strawberries; shaped the mixture into palm-size pucks; then dropped them into boiling water to cook.

Tawnya transforms heirloom crops into what she calls Haudenosaunee fusion cuisine. Drawing from her restaurant experience and using ingredients from Native producers, she brings nutritious fare to her community with unique spins on traditional dishes of corn soup and bison stew as well as contemporary favorites including bison shepherd's pie, wild boar lasagna, and elk chimichangas. In doing so, she aims to inspire people to embrace fresh, healthful foods that feel familiar and taste delicious.

A descendant of the strong Mohawk leader Molly Brant, Tawnya talks about how the people of the longhouse have always been open to "extending the rafters" to welcome in anyone who respects the Haudenosaunee way of living. She hopes that those interested in Indigenous cuisine embrace the ethos that guides her work: Everything is a gift. Sherry and Tawnya's approaches to showcasing traditional foods differ slightly from my own decolonized philosophy—they will cook with wheat, pork, and other ingredients that were brought here in addition to their own Indigenous bounty. But, as I always say, there are no rules when it comes to food, and I am so grateful to them for all they've taught me.

In the following pages, you'll find recipes that feature many of the ingredients I've learned to cook from these generous knowledge keepers, including lobster, rabbit, quahogs, creamy potato beans, and heirloom varieties of corn. I hope these dishes let you see this bountiful land with fresh eyes and give you a newfound appreciation for the Indigenous peoples who continue to thrive there.

HOW TO HAVE AN APPANAUG (CLAMBAKE)

Clambakes have been adopted by settlers in what is now New England, but for the Wampanoag and other coastal Indigenous peoples, the tradition is more than a fun cookout. It is also a spiritual ceremony that celebrates the natural resources that surround them, as well as the changing of the seasons. Sometimes, people have a clambake to honor a member of the tribe.

To put on a clambake, you must first choose a spot. It should be close enough to a bay so you can easily bring the rocks and clams from the water there. It can be on a sandy beach or a little farther inland, if you prefer. You should also make sure it's a spot where you are permitted to have a large fire. After you have your spot, you must prepare your fire pit, which you can do a day ahead of time. To do so, dig a large, shallow oval pit that's about 4 feet across at its widest and about 6 inches deep. (The shape represents the Circle of Life to the Wampanoag.) Gather rocks to put into the pit; the ideal rocks are 10 to 12 inches in size and smoothed by the tides.

Arrange the rocks to cover the floor of the large pit, then gather plenty of dry dead wood.

On the day of the clambake, you can forage for the clams, which is easiest to do in the bay during low tide. To find quahogs, wade into the water and dig around with your feet. Each time you feel something hard, pull it out with your hands.

To find sickissuogs, also known as steamer clams, go to the edge of the bay and look for holes in the sand. When you see small bits of water shoot out from the holes, dig down and you will likely find the clam. Wash all of the freshly dug clams in the bay or fresh water to remove any sand.

To create the fire as well as provide the unmistakable flavor of a true clambake, you need to gather rockweed. Rockweed is a greenish-brown seaweed that gets layered over the rocks in the pit to prevent the food from getting scorched. Its pockets full of water also help steam the food.

Gather any other food you might like for the clambake, including live lobsters and sweet corn on the cob. People today often also add potatoes, onions, and sausages. (Sometimes, people put the corn, sausage, and potatoes into cheesecloth packets to keep them tidier.)

About 3 hours before you would like to eat, arrange the wood you gathered over the rocks and light the fire. Maintain a hot fire by adding more wood as needed. As the wood burns and turns to ash, rake the ash over the rocks to help heat them. After about 2 hours, when the rocks are very hot, arrange the rockweed on the hot rocks and allow it to steam and sputter. If you're cooking packets of corn, potatoes, onions, and sausage, arrange them first over the hot rockweed. Next, add the clams followed by the lobsters.

Top the food with more rockweed. To help the food steam more evenly and faster, arrange a heatproof tarp cover on top, weighted down with rocks.

As the food cooks, people often give thanks to the Great Spirit and think about the value of all living things.

After about 1 hour, when the lobster is fully cooked and the clams are open, remove the cover and rockweed. Carefully transfer the food to platters and enjoy.

RAMP POWDER

To make ramp powder, you can dehydrate ramp leaves in a dehydrator or arrange them on racks in a dry room near a fan. When the leaves are completely dry, pulverize them in a food processor. Store at first in a paper bag to make sure there is no residual moisture, then transfer to a jar, seal tightly, and keep in a dark place for up to 1 year.

QUAHOG AND CORN CHOWDER

serves 4 to 6

Quahogs are rounded hard-shell clams that can come in a variety of sizes, and clam chowder is one of those iconic "New England" dishes people love. Instead of relying on flour and cream as thickeners, though, I look to Indigenous ingredients—nixtamalized corn, corn milk, and squash puree—which contribute body and sweetness. Smoked scallops add an appealing richness, replacing the typical bacon; they are available from high-quality seafood shops and some Asian markets.

Ramp powder gives the soup a lovely green hue. If you don't have ramps on hand to make it, you can substitute onion and garlic powders, but your soup will not be green.

- ½ acorn squash, seeds reserved
- ¼ cup plus 1 tablespoon sunflower oil, plus more for rubbing
- Sea salt
- 12 cherrystone or 24 littleneck quahogs (hard-shell clams), scrubbed
- 1 medium yellow onion, diced
- 3 tablespoons Ramp Powder (opposite) or 1½ tablespoons onion powder and 1½ tablespoons garlic powder
- 3 cups Hominy (page 25)
- 4 cups Sweet Corn Milk (page 35)
- 8 ounces smoked scallops, chopped into bite-size pieces if large

Position racks in the upper and lower thirds of the oven and preheat the oven to 350°F.

Remove as much of the stringy flesh as possible from the squash seeds and pat dry. Toss with 1 tablespoon of the oil and season with salt. Spread out on a baking sheet. Rub the cut side of the squash with oil and arrange it cut-side down on a second baking sheet.

Transfer the seeds to the top rack and the squash to the bottom rack of the oven. Toast the seeds for about 20 minutes, tossing once or twice as they cook, until nicely golden. Let cool. At the same time, bake the squash for 45 minutes to 1 hour, until very tender. Let cool.

Scoop the flesh out of the skin and mash the squash or puree it in a food processor. Measure out 1 cup of puree for the soup and reserve the rest for another use.

Bring 2 cups water to a boil in a large pot over medium-high heat. Add the quahogs, cover, reduce the heat to medium, and cook for 8 to 10 minutes, until their shells open. As each one opens, use a slotted spoon to transfer the quahogs to a bowl. If any of the clams refuse to open after most of them have been cooked, discard them. Carefully strain the cooking liquid through a coffee filter or a cheesecloth-lined sieve. Measure out 2 cups of quahog liquid and set aside. Remove the meat from the quahog shells. If the quahogs are large, coarsely chop the meat.

Meanwhile, in another large pot, heat the remaining ¼ cup of oil over medium heat. Add the onion and cook for about 6 minutes, stirring, until the onion is tender.

Add the ramp powder, quahog liquid, hominy, and corn milk. Whisk in the squash puree and bring to a simmer over medium heat. Cook for 20 minutes to meld.

Add the smoked scallops and cooked quahogs and cook for about 2 minutes, just to warm them through. Taste and season with salt as needed.

Ladle the chowder into bowls. Garnish with the toasted squash seeds and serve.

SMOKED RABBIT WITH CRANBERRY BEANS AND DRIED STRAWBERRIES

serves 4

We often think of cranberry beans as tan and speckled with pink, but there is a variety of heirloom cranberry beans that are deep-red before they are cooked. (You can find the seeds from a number of vendors online and can occasionally find the beans from smaller vendors. You can, of course, substitute another bean if you prefer.)

This dish takes several hours over a couple of days to pull together because you must brine, smoke, braise, and sauté the rabbit and soak and cook the beans. The results, however, are worth it, because the rabbit is unbelievably flavorful. Dehydrated strawberries (or store-bought dried strawberries) provide a sweet-and-sour exclamation point to the dish.

You can make all of the components a day in advance and bring them together quickly as you would a pasta dish right before serving.

You will need a smoker for this recipe, or you can rig a charcoal or gas grill to work as a smoker and cook the rabbit low and slow. (See Smoking Food on a Grill, page 69, for the method.)

- 2 cups small strawberries, cut into ⅛-inch-thick slices, or ¾ cup (4 ounces) dried sliced strawberries
- 1 whole rabbit (2½ pounds)
- Fine sea salt
- 1 cup maple syrup, plus more as needed
- 4 (8-inch) pieces white pine (see Conifers, page 22)
- Ground sumac
- 1 cup dried True Cranberry beans or other cranberry beans, soaked overnight and drained
- 3 tablespoons sunflower oil
- 5 whole ramps, wild onions, or scallions, cut crosswise into 1-inch pieces
- 1 cup packed dandelion leaves, coarsely chopped

If starting with fresh strawberries, arrange them on the tray of a dehydrator and dehydrate for 6 to 12 hours, until dry but still chewy. (Alternatively, preheat an oven to 170°F or your oven's lowest setting. Arrange the sliced berries on a rack set over a baking sheet and bake, checking them after 4 hours and once every 30 minutes after that until they are dry but pliable and chewy.)

In a bowl or container large enough to hold the rabbit with brine, stir together 4 cups room temperature water, ¾ cup plus 2 tablespoons salt, and the maple syrup until the salt dissolves. Stir in 12 more cups water. Submerge the rabbit and add half the white pine. Refrigerate overnight.

The next day, rinse the rabbit well and rub it all over with sumac. Discard the brine.

Preheat a smoker to 240°F (or if you don't have a smoker, see Smoking Food on a Grill, page 69).

Smoke the rabbit according to the manufacturer's instructions for 1½ hours. Flip and smoke for another 1½ hours and then remove from the smoker. (The rabbit's internal temperature should register at least 165°F on an instant-read thermometer when inserted into the thickest part of the meat, away from the bone.)

Transfer to a cutting board and cut the smoked rabbit into serving pieces (legs, thighs, and saddle), then arrange in a Dutch oven. Add water to just barely cover and the remaining white pine. Bring the water to a simmer over medium heat, then reduce the heat to medium-low, cover, and gently simmer for about 1½ hours, or until the rabbit is very tender and falling off the bone.

Meanwhile, rinse the beans well and transfer to a pot. Add water to cover by 2 inches and bring to a boil over high heat. Reduce the heat to medium-low, partially cover, and simmer for 40 minutes to 1 hour 15 minutes, until the beans are tender but not overcooked. Drain, then spread out on a baking sheet to cool. Season with salt.

Uncover the rabbit and discard the white pine. Reserving 1 cup of the cooking liquid, drain the rabbit. Pull the rabbit meat off the bones.

In a large cast-iron skillet, heat the oil over medium-high heat until shimmering. Add the smoked and braised rabbit meat and sear for about 5 minutes, stirring occasionally, until the edges of the meat start to brown and crisp a bit. Add the ramps and cook for 2 to 3 minutes, until wilted and nearly tender. Add the cooled cooked beans with ½ cup of the rabbit cooking liquid and stir gently to not break the beans. Taste and season with salt, maple syrup, and sumac.

Reduce the heat to low and cook just until you see steam rising from the skillet, then add most of the dried strawberries and the chopped dandelion leaves and stir gently to incorporate.

Transfer to a serving bowl. Garnish with the remaining dried strawberries and serve.

WILD MUSTARD AND ROOT VEGGIE SALAD WITH SUNFLOWER DRESSING

serves 4

In the spring, garlic mustard (*Alliaria petiolata*) takes over yards and forests in the Eastern Woodlands as well as parts of the Great Lakes and Pacific Northwest. In its first year, the heart-shaped leaves grow low to the ground. The following year, the plant shoots up to knee-high and blooms delicate white flowers so it can spread its seed. While it's a nonnative plant from Europe, it's also invasive, meaning it grows aggressively and can crowd out native plants. The good news is that it's delicious, and you're helping the environment by harvesting it at any stage of its development.

American sea rocket (*Cakile edentula*) is a coastal plant in the mustard family that grows in the sandy, rocky soils along the Atlantic coast. It's tender in spring, but you can harvest it whenever you see it. (And if you can't find it, you can substitute arugula.)

Both greens taste especially nice with earthy burdock roots, which you can forage or find easily at Asian markets. Here, we combine these greens and roots in a simple salad with a creamy sunflower seed vinaigrette that is a true taste of spring in this part of Turtle Island.

- Sea salt
- 3 tablespoons cider vinegar, plus more for the ice-water bath
- 1 large burdock root (7 to 8 ounces)
- ½ cup toasted sunflower seeds
- ½ cup sunflower oil
- 2 tablespoons maple syrup
- 2 medium carrots (7 to 8 ounces total), cut into matchsticks
- 2 wild onions, spring onions, or scallions, cut on the diagonal into thin slices
- 2 cups garlic mustard, American sea rocket, or arugula

Bring a large pot of salted water to a boil over high heat. Set up an ice-water bath and add a few tablespoons of vinegar to it.

Using a vegetable peeler, carefully peel the burdock root trying not to cut too deep. Cut the root into 4-inch lengths. Cut those lengthwise into thin slices, then cut the slices into very thin strips or matchsticks. As you work, transfer to the ice-water bath, because burdock root oxidizes quickly.

When all of the burdock is prepped, scoop it out of the ice water and add to the boiling water. Cook for about 1 minute, until crisp-tender, then drain and return to the ice water to cool. Drain, pat dry, and transfer to a large bowl.

Add 3 tablespoons of the sunflower seeds to a mini food processor or blender, add the 3 tablespoons vinegar, the oil, and maple syrup and puree until smooth and emulsified. Taste and season with salt.

Add the carrots, onions, garlic mustard, and half the sunflower seed dressing to the bowl with the burdock and toss to coat.

Divide the salad among individual bowls and garnish with the remaining toasted sunflower seeds. Pass the remaining dressing at the table.

WHELKS WITH SAMPHIRE AND GARLIC OIL

serves 4 to 6

Whelks are sea snails you'll find frequently off the coasts of North America. They are available mostly shelled and frozen, and they sometimes go by their Italian name, scungilli. They have a sweet, ocean flavor that is reminiscent of clams, but deeper and more mellow. Here, I call for the meat shelled because it's easiest to work with, but if you can only find them in the shell, see Cooking Whelks (below). Paired with another treasure from the coast, salty, crunchy samphire (also known as sea beans), this is a simple dish that highlights two different types of brininess.

- 4 scallions
- 8 ounces young, tender fresh samphire (also known as sea beans, salicornia, and pickleweed)
- ¼ cup sunflower oil
- 4 garlic cloves, thinly sliced
- 8 ounces whelk meat (see Note), rinsed and thinly sliced
- 2 tablespoons cider vinegar

In a medium pot, bring 4 cups of water to a boil over high heat. Set up an ice-water bath.

Cut the scallions into 1-inch lengths, then cut those lengthwise into thin strips. Add them to the ice water.

Add the fresh samphire (but no salt; samphire is naturally salty!) to the boiling water and cook for about 1 minute, until it turns bright green. Drain and transfer to the ice water. When the samphire is cool, drain it and the scallions well—you can use a salad spinner if you like—then transfer to a large bowl.

Line a plate with paper towels and place it near the stove. In a skillet, heat the oil over medium heat until it's warm. Add the garlic and cook for 2 to 3 minutes, stirring and tipping the skillet a bit to help the garlic fry in the oil, until the garlic is golden and crisped. Using a slotted spoon, transfer the garlic chips to the paper towels to drain and cool.

Add the whelk meat to the oil and cook for about 2 minutes, just to warm them through.

Add the whelks, the oil from the skillet, and the vinegar to the bowl and toss to incorporate. Garnish with the garlic chips and serve.

Note: *If you can't find whelks, you can also make this with steamed and shelled mussels.*

COOKING WHELKS

If you can only find live whelks in the shell, start with 1½ pounds. The snails can come in different sizes, from about 12 per pound to each being 6 or 7 ounces. For the Whelks with Samphire salad, you can use either, but you'll want to cut them into bite-size pieces after you cook them.

Before cooking, wash the whelks in several changes of water to remove any sand and grit from within the shell.

Bring a large pot of water to a boil over high heat and salt it heavily. Set up an ice-water bath. Add the whelks and cook for about 4 minutes for smaller whelks and 10 minutes for larger whelks. Drain and transfer the whelks to the ice water to let cool completely.

For small whelks, use a toothpick to remove and discard the tough foot at the entrance of the shell. Then use it to pull out the meat (the entire snail).

For larger whelks, use a fork to remove the tough foot, then use the fork to pry the meat out of the shell. Separate the meat (the part closer to the entrance of the shell) from the digestive tract (the curled part that was deeper in the shell). Thinly slice the meat only, discarding the rest.

LOBSTER SALAD
WITH SWEET CORN IN COOL ELDERBERRY BROTH

serves 2 to 4

One of the first times I met chef Sherry Pocknett, she was covered in lobster juices preparing for a big feast later in the evening. I never saw anyone break down lobsters so fast. This is a dish inspired by the time I met her, which was toward the end of the summer, when sweet corn was juicy and elderberries were ripe. It's served cool, and the sweet lobster and corn are accented with fried garlic, toasted pepitas, and a beautiful, light elderberry broth.

ELDERBERRY BROTH

4 ounces fresh or frozen elderberries (see Note), with or without stems

½ medium shallot

1½ tablespoons pure maple syrup

Sea salt

SALAD

Kernels from 1 ear sweet corn

3 tablespoons sunflower oil

2 garlic cloves, thinly sliced

8 ounces cooked lobster meat (from two 1½-pound lobsters; see Cooking Lobster, opposite), cooled and cut into bite-size pieces

¼ cup sliced scallions, cut on the diagonal

3 tablespoons toasted pepitas

Sea salt

Make the elderberry broth: In a medium saucepan, combine the elderberries (it's okay to include the stems if they're attached), shallot, maple syrup, and 1½ cups water and bring to a boil over high heat. Reduce the heat to medium-low and simmer for 10 minutes, or until the berries are very soft. Press the berries gently to release some of the juice. Strain the liquid through a fine-mesh sieve (do not press on the solids) and let cool to room temperature. Season with salt.

Make the salad: Heat a medium skillet over medium-high heat.

Add the corn kernels, and cook for about 2 minutes, until charred in spots. Transfer to a plate and let cool.

Line a second plate with paper towels and place it near the stove. Add the oil to the skillet and heat over medium heat until it's warm. Add the garlic and cook for 2 to 3 minutes, stirring and tipping the skillet a bit to help the garlic fry in the oil, until the garlic is golden and crisped. Using a slotted spoon, transfer the garlic chips to the paper towels to drain and cool. Reserve the garlicky oil.

In a bowl, toss together the lobster, scallions, pepitas, charred corn, garlic chips, and garlic-infused oil. Taste and season with salt.

Mound the salad into the center of shallow bowls. Pour the cool elderberry broth into the bowls so it pools around and under the salad and serve right away.

***Note:** If you can't find fresh or frozen elderberries, you can make this with 1 ounce dried elderberries and 2 cups water, but the elderberry broth will be less vibrant tasting.*

COOKING LOBSTER

To cook live lobsters, place them in the freezer for no more than 10 minutes.

Meanwhile, fill a pot large enough to hold the lobsters about three-quarters full with water. Bring to a boil over high heat and season generously with salt. To kill the lobsters swiftly and humanely, insert the point of a sharp chef's knife just behind their eyes. Quickly pierce through the shell, and bring the blade down to cut through the head.

From there, you can plunge the lobsters headfirst into the boiling water and cook for 10 minutes (for 1½-pound lobsters), until their shells are bright red and the meat is opaque. Drain and let the lobster cool before separating the claws and tails from the body, cracking the shells, and pulling out the meat.

PINE-BRAISED VENISON WITH BUFFALO CREEK SQUASH AND CRABAPPLE SAUCE

serves 4 to 6

Because deer are often hunted in the fall, I built a dish around it using some of autumn's most abundant ingredients: winter squash and crabapples. Buffalo Creek Squash is a large, vibrant orange Hubbard squash and is a Seneca heirloom from the Buffalo Creek reservation. It has thin skin and sweet, dry flesh. Kabocha or red kuri squash would be a good substitute.

The white pine branches added to the top of the braise infuse the meat with its citrusy, piney flavor, and tart crabapples lighten the deep meat flavor.

- 1½ pounds Buffalo Creek Squash, kabocha, or red kuri squash, seeded and cut into 1-inch pieces
- 6 tablespoons sunflower oil
- Sea salt
- Ground sumac
- 2 pounds venison stew meat, cut into 2-inch pieces
- 4 cups Rich Bison or Other Game Stock (page 41) or other meat stock
- ½ cup maple syrup
- 8 ounces white pine branches (cut to fit inside a Dutch oven), plus an optional 1 teaspoon finely chopped white pine needles (see Conifers, page 22), for garnish
- 1 pound crabapples or Granny Smith apples, cut into chunks and seeded but not peeled
- Dried Crabapples (optional; page 57), for garnish

Preheat the oven to 400°F. Line a baking sheet with parchment paper.

On the baking sheet, toss the diced squash with 3 tablespoons of the sunflower oil and season with salt and sumac.

Spread the squash on the baking sheet and roast for 18 to 25 minutes, stirring once halfway through, or until the squash is tender and lightly caramelized.

Reduce the oven temperature to 300°F.

In a large Dutch oven, heat the remaining 3 tablespoons of oil over medium heat until shimmering.

Season the venison all over with salt and sumac. Working in batches, sear the venison meat for about 8 minutes, turning frequently, until browned all over. Increase the heat to high. Add the stock, 2 cups water, ¼ cup of the maple syrup, and the pine branches and bring to a boil. Cover and transfer the pot to the oven.

Cook for 3 hours, then check the meat. If it's pull-apart tender, remove the pot from the oven. If it's not, continue cooking and checking on the meat every 30 minutes. (Add more liquid if the pot starts to seem dry.) When the meat is ready, discard the pine branches and needles and keep the venison warm over low heat.

Meanwhile, in a large saucepan, combine the apples, 2 cups water, and the remaining ¼ cup of maple syrup. Bring to a simmer and cook for about 25 minutes, until the apples are soft. Drain off and reserve most of the liquid, then use a potato masher to mash the apples until they're the consistency of chunky applesauce.

Return the roasted squash to the oven for 5 minutes, just to warm it through.

Transfer the squash to a large shallow serving bowl or deep platter. Using tongs, gently break up the venison meat and arrange it over the squash. Spoon a little of the reserved cooking liquid over top and serve the applesauce alongside. If desired, garnish with chopped white pine needles and rounds of dried crabapple.

SHERRY POCKNETT'S FISH HASH

serves 4 to 6

Sherry Pocknett is a Mashpee Wampanoag chef who is known for the comforting dishes she cooked at her restaurant Sly Fox Den Too, in Charlestown, Rhode Island, just fifteen minutes from the coast. The inlets nearby are a favorite spot for large striped bass and bluefish—and, thus, the people who fish for them.

Here, she shares a simple hash you can serve with the catch of the day.

4 tablespoons sunflower oil, plus more for the pan

1½ pounds skinless local fish fillets, such as striped bass, haddock, or bluefish

Sea salt

1¼ teaspoons Ramp Powder (page 110) or garlic powder, for seasoning

1½ pounds Yukon Gold potatoes, scrubbed and cut into ¾-inch pieces

1 large yellow onion, diced

4 to 6 duck eggs (optional), pan-fried

Greens from 2 ramps or scallions, thinly sliced

Preheat the oven to 400°F.

Lightly grease a 9 × 13-inch baking dish with some oil. Arrange the fish in the baking dish and season with salt and the ramp powder. Roast for about 10 minutes, or until just opaque throughout. Use a fork to flake the fish.

Meanwhile, in a large pot, combine the potatoes with water to cover and season the water generously with salt. Bring to a boil over medium-high heat and cook for 7 to 12 minutes, until just barely tender. Drain.

In a large well-seasoned cast-iron skillet, heat 2 tablespoons of the oil over medium heat. Add the onion, season with salt, and cook for 6 to 8 minutes, or until tender and starting to brown. Add the remaining 2 tablespoons of oil. Stir in the potatoes, then spread out the mixture into a single layer. Increase the heat to high and cook for about 5 minutes, pressing occasionally with a spatula, until crusty on the bottom. Working in sections, turn the hash over and cook for 3 to 5 minutes, until browned on the other side. Stir in the flaked fish and its juices.

Serve the hash with fried duck eggs, if desired, and garnish with the ramp greens.

DESERONTO POTATO BEANS, ROASTED MUSHROOMS, AND PURSLANE

serves 4 to 6

The Deseronto Potato Bean is a Mohawk heirloom from the Tyendinaga Reservation in Ontario that has a starchy, potato-like texture. You can seek out seeds to grow in your garden or substitute other large white beans in this simple, earthy dish, featuring roasted mushrooms, ramp powder, and the juicy crunch of purslane. You'll need to soak the beans overnight.

- 1 cup dried Deseronto Potato Beans or other large white beans, such as cannellini, soaked overnight and drained
- Sea salt
- 1 pound mixed wild mushrooms, such as chanterelles, sliced ½ inch thick
- 1½ teaspoons Rose Hip Powder (page 359) or store-bought
- 2 tablespoons Ramp Powder (page 110) or 1 tablespoon garlic powder and 1 tablespoon onion powder
- 2 tablespoons cider vinegar
- 1 tablespoon maple syrup
- ¼ cup sunflower oil
- 1 cup fresh purslane, coarsely chopped, for garnish
- 2 tablespoons fresh or dried wild bergamot (bee balm) flowers, for garnish

In a medium pot, combine the soaked beans with water to cover by 2 inches and cook for 45 minutes to 1 hour 15 minutes, until tender. Drain and let cool. Season with salt and let stand so the beans can absorb the seasoning.

Position the rack in the middle of the oven and preheat the oven to 400°F.

Spread the mushrooms over a large baking sheet and roast for about 15 minutes, stirring once halfway through, until wilted and tender. Season well with salt and sprinkle with the rose hip powder.

In a bowl, whisk together the ramp powder, vinegar, syrup, and oil. Fold in the seasoned mushrooms and the cooked beans. Taste and season with salt.

Transfer to a serving bowl, garnish with fresh purslane and wild bergamot flowers, and serve.

BLUEBERRY LEATHER

makes about 4 ounces

Making a fruit leather is a simple way to preserve peak-season fruit. At Owamni, we often use fruit leathers as sweet, chewy garnishes, but I also love them as a snack on their own. I use a dehydrator to make fruit leathers, but you can also use a low-temperature oven.

- 2 cups fresh blueberries, stemmed as needed
- 1 medium to large apple, cored but not peeled
- ⅓ cup Maple Sugar (page 36) or store-bought

In a blender (preferably high-powered), combine the blueberries, apple, and maple sugar and puree until smooth.

Preheat a dehydrator to 130°F. Line dehydrator trays with parchment paper. Spread the mixture on the trays. Place in the dehydrator for 8 to 10 hours, until dried but still pliable. (Alternatively, preheat the oven to 170°F or its lowest setting. Line a baking sheet with parchment paper or a silicone liner. Spread the mixture on the baking sheet and bake for 5 to 7 hours.)

Let cool, then cut into equal strips and roll each one in parchment paper strips. Refrigerate in an airtight container for up to 2 weeks.

SOUTHEASTERN WOODLANDS

AND THE BAYOU

IN WHAT IS NOW THE UNITED STATES, this is where the story of colonization begins. A century before Plymouth Rock landed on us, the Spanish and French were fighting for footholds in the Southeastern Woodlands and the Bayou. But this region was already inhabited by robust Indigenous societies, as European explorers discovered while scouting the Atlantic seaboard in the sixteenth century. The centuries-long battle between the area's original residents and white settlers was hard-fought.

Stretching from the coastal lowlands of Maryland down the coast to the subtropics of Florida and over to southern Appalachia, the Southeast is home to dozens of Indigenous groups. My work to revitalize Native foodways has taken me all over Turtle Island, and I've been fortunate enough to spend time with a number of communities there.

One foggy evening back in fall 2018, I visited the Catawba Nation—the only federally recognized tribe in South Carolina—to give a talk and enjoy a meal together. Over dinner in that woodland setting, we discussed decolonized fare as we savored it, nibbling on sunflower seed–crusted trout, hunter's stew, wild rice, and maple-sage roasted vegetables.

Afterward, Faye George Greiner presented me with a beautiful handmade basket. This revered elder is one of few Catawba basket weavers and is single-handedly responsible for reviving this traditional practice. She adorns her work with a wooden heart tag—a fitting token because she is sharing a piece of her heart. I feel the same way when I'm making nourishing, nutritious food for people.

I've similarly shared meals and stories with the Eastern Band of Cherokee, the Lumbee Tribe of North Carolina, the Seminole Tribe of Florida, and more. Although these communities are certainly distinct from one another, they have a collective history of dispossession and displacement due to the waves of colonialism that pummeled the area time and again.

The most infamous instance of removal in the region is of course the Trail of Tears. This mass eradication of the so-called Five Civilized Tribes—the Cherokee, Chickasaw, Choctaw, Muscogee (Creek), and Seminole—followed Andrew Jackson's Indian Removal Act of 1830. That's why so many food traditions with roots in the Southeastern Woodlands have branches extending out across the country into places like Oklahoma, where the US government forcibly relocated these groups.

The interlacing story of Indigenous and African cultures is also really evident in this region. Both Native and Black peoples faced oppression due to colonialism, because the United States was built upon stolen Indigenous lands and upon the backs of enslaved African people. In fact, what many Americans have come to think of as Southern cuisine is actually an amalgamation of the time-honored culinary traditions of these marginalized and siloed groups, along with European influences. (Consider, for example, rouxless filé gumbo that employs native sassafras and African okra as thickening agents.) It was no mistake that colonialists did their best to divide and conquer us.

Of course, this often-overlooked shared history is super complicated. During the push to assimilate into European society, groups like the aforementioned Five Tribes enslaved Black people.

Native peoples were also forced into chattel slavery, and enslaved African and Indigenous individuals often intermarried. These communities also joined forces in fighting against settler encroachment, such as when the Black Seminoles (a group of freed and runaway slaves) helped defend the namesake tribe's Florida foothold during the Three Seminole Wars.

Further complicating matters are laws like Virginia's 1924 Racial Integrity Act, which was intended to bolster white supremacy by classifying people as either white or Black. For many mixed-race Native Americans, it highlighted the complexities of Indigeneity and perpetuated discriminatory practices in the region. Although racism is still alive and well even in our tribal communities, there are countless Afro-Indigenous individuals across the Southeast and beyond who take great pride in all aspects of their ancestry.

Perhaps no place better exemplifies this blending of Indigenous, Black, and white heritage than New Orleans, or Bulbancha, as it was called before European arrival. Meaning "place of many tongues" in Choctaw, that name refers to the many tribal nations that resided here for centuries—including the Biloxi, Houma, Natchez, Tunica, and others. Researcher and writer Jeffery Darensbourg, who is Louisiana Creole and a member of the Atakapa-Ishak Nation, is of "triplicate ethnicity," with Indigenous, West African, French, and Spanish ancestry. Through his articles and speaking engagements, he is illuminating the real origins of Louisiana's storied soul food—think crawfish boils, maque-choux, and corn bread—which he explains is overwhelmingly Indigenous, secondarily African, and just tertiarily European when it comes to both ingredients and techniques.

This collision of cultures in the Southeastern Woodlands is also probably how the Cherokee princess myth came about. This trope has become a running joke in Indian Country, but it still points to a problematic phenomenon. Even today, during a time of unprecedented authentic Native representation, many people still questionably claim to be Indigenous thanks to a great-great-great-grandmother who just happened to be Cherokee royalty. (Hearing this growing up, I always wondered how so many people were somehow part Cherokee.)

While we tend to laugh it off, this misappropriation is just one of the latest layers of colonialism that the tribal communities of the Southeastern Woodlands and the Bayou face after ongoing encroachment by French, Spanish, British, and eventually American settlers. Despite centuries of oppression and suppression, the more than twenty-five tribal groups that call this region home are actively restoring their important cultural and food traditions.

THE LAND

This vast swath of land space is extremely ecologically diverse, yet is characterized by a few overarching ecoregion provinces that curve along the contours of the coastline and layer inland from there. These include the outer coastal plains mixed province, the southeastern mixed forest, the central Appalachian broadleaf forest, and the Everglades in the far southeast.

Adjacent to the Atlantic, the outer coastal plains follow the eastern seaboard from Maryland all the way down into parts of Georgia, Alabama, Mississippi, and Florida. With plentiful lakes, marshes, and swampland across its gently sloping terrain, this temperate rainforest experiences mild winters, hot summers, and heavy precipitation. The woodlands are dominated by smaller trees with a less dense leaf canopy, letting sunshine peek in on the many ferns, shrubs, palms, and herbaceous plants dotting the forest floor.

Slightly farther inland spanning across many of those same states (save for Florida) sits the southeastern mixed forest. Encompassing the Piedmont, this ecoregion province is very true to its name, with a wide range of trees including pine, oak, hickory, dogwood, red maple, black

gum, and sweetgum as well as beautyberry and highland blueberry shrubs.

Moving even more inland and sticking more northward, we encounter the central Appalachian broadleaf forest, which includes the Appalachian, Allegheny, and Blue Ridge mountain ranges. This area has incredible biodiversity that reflects its varying elevation, ranging from 300 to more than 6,600 feet above sea level.

For millennia, the Cherokee—who are the original Appalachians—relied on this lush temperate rainforest's many foods and medicines, such as ramps, mushrooms, herbs, berries, and wild greens. In addition to providing habitat for endless woodland animals, the region's ample trees are prized for the treasures they yield—that is, their nuts, which have been staples in Cherokee and Choctaw food systems for centuries.

Tucked at the southern tip of Florida, the Everglades sit upon a mostly flat marl and limestone shelf. Part of an immense drainage basin, this subtropical wetland boasts diverse habitats including naturally flooded grasslands, freshwater marshes, mangrove estuaries, and moist hardwood forest. It's home to alligators, snakes, and other reptiles as well as deer, bears, panthers, bobcats, raccoons, and small game. Sadly, this ecologically rich area is now half its original size due to human development—a literal draining of the swamp—that has diverted hundreds of millions of acre-feet of water for agricultural and urban use. This has caused irrevocable damage to the land, and, in turn, its animal inhabitants, including countless bird species (some of which are now endangered).

Early Indigenous peoples, such as the Calusa, Ais, Jega, Mayaimi, and Tequesta, inhabited and traversed South Florida, relying upon the natural bounty for sustenance, shelter, and tools. They lived in elevated, open-air thatched huts known

as chickees, traveled using dugout cypress canoes, built shell formations, and crafted tools from shells, bones, and other natural materials. For food, they fished, harvested shellfish, hunted everything from deer to alligators, and even grew some crops on the hillocks. Later when colonists pushed tribal communities off their ancestral homelands, the Miccosukee and Seminole sought refuge in the Everglades.

The term bayou describes a shallow, slow-moving portion of a body of water, derived from the Choctaw word bayuk (meaning "small stream"). Over the years, it has come to define the parts of the Southeast where bayous are most prevalent, including Louisiana, Mississippi, Alabama, and parts of Arkansas. The Gulf Coast region is full of these freshwater, saltwater, and brackish waterways that host fish, shrimp, frogs, lizards, turtles, tortoises, snakes, alligators, and crocodiles. Hundreds of bird species nest or stop over along their migratory paths, too. Indigenous peoples such as the Choctaw as well as the Cajun and Creole peoples made their homes there and lived off the land's abundance.

Sadly, the innumerable negative effects of human development are readily apparent across this region. Important ecologically diverse ecosystems were forever changed when settlers flattened and plowed up millions of acres for the industrial farming and livestock raising we now see in the area. Waterways, meanwhile, have been overfished and contaminated—but Native communities are taking the lead to restore them.

For instance, in Virginia, the Nansemond Indian Nation is restoring thousands of oysters to its namesake ancestral waterway, while the Pamunkey people are helping bring back the culturally important American shad after a massive decline in the twentieth century. These are just a couple of instances showing how Indigenous and conservation groups are working to mitigate pollution, coastal erosion, and climate change in order to protect and preserve the Southeastern Woodlands.

THE HISTORY

The Indigenous story most of us know of the Southeastern Woodlands is the Trail of Tears, but Native history there begins long before that. The tribal communities of the densely populated region consider themselves "first-contact" people, meaning they were the earliest groups to encounter Europeans within what is now the United States.

Dating back millennia, the dozens of sophisticated societies were well adapted to the area's varying ecosystems. They had powerful chiefdoms—such as the commanding Powhatan Confederacy of more than thirty Algonquian-speaking tribes—as well as major urban trade centers, monumental sites, prosperous agricultural production, and vast hunting and foraging territories. In some places, there's still evidence of complex ancient earthen settlements, such as Cahokia near St. Louis, Missouri; Moundville in Alabama; and Poverty Point in Louisiana. Although there was some intertribal conflict, shared Caddoan, Iroquoian, Muskogean, and Siouan language families allowed for robust trade networks.

Famed conquistador Juan Ponce de León is thought to be the first European to set foot in Florida in 1513, but Spanish explorer Hernando de Soto's expedition beginning in 1539 was when many regional Indigenous groups came in contact with colonizers. With his army, horses, dogs, and a herd of pigs in tow, he set out on a mission to conquer La Florida. They marched inland for thousands of miles in search of gold and silver (which they didn't find), along the way battling with Native peoples and leaving behind a trail of disruption, destruction, and diseases like smallpox and measles that decimated the Indigenous population.

The Spanish hogs, which wreaked havoc on the environment, gave rise to the American pork industry and are the likely ancestors of the wild swine that roam the region today. Native communities eventually incorporated pigs into their foodways and also embraced other imported ingredients like field peas, watermelons, and peaches, as Choctaw Tribal Historic Preservation Officer Ian Thompson explains.

In the decades that followed, the Southeast became a colonial battleground between the Spanish and French, with the former prevailing. Despite Indigenous communities' efforts to stave off encroachment, La Florida grew to encompass much of the region. The Spanish introduced even more infectious disease, converted countless Indigenous individuals to Catholicism, and established some of the country's first plantations, using enslaved African and Indigenous peoples to grow corn, rice, sugar, and the citrus that's now synonymous with the Southeast. The Native slave trade became a lucrative business, as did eventual cash crops of cotton and tobacco.

Determined to corral Spanish Florida, the British developed strategic settlements to the north, including the 1607 establishment of Jamestown, Virginia, and later the Province of Carolina, which overlapped with Spanish claims. The French, meanwhile, took control of a massive ribbon of land farther west stretching from southern Canada to the Gulf of Mexico that they dubbed Louisiana. Life in the Southeastern Woodlands wasn't easy for European colonizers, who faced famine, extreme weather, attacks from local tribal nations, and other hardships that early on caused them to abandon some settlements.

Of course, the land they were fighting over had for centuries been inhabited by Indigenous peoples, who were now being displaced by hundreds of thousands of settlers lured to the coveted area by its lush vegetation, fertile soil, long growing seasons, and promise of prosperity. Some Native groups defended their ancestral homelands, while others developed diplomatic relationships with the intruders and even adopted their practices in an attempt at coexistence.

By the late seventeenth century, area tribes were involved in the many wars between these European powers in hopes that their allegiances might help them maintain their shrinking land base—which obviously didn't pan out. When the British won the French and Indian War (1754–1763), several territories changed hands. The French ceded Louisiana to the Spanish and all its land east of the Mississippi to the British, while the Spanish gave up Florida to the British. But after the Revolutionary War (1775–1783), the burgeoning US government took over much of the region. The seemingly ceaseless American thirst for land continually pushed Southeastern Woodland tribes off their ancestral homelands.

Of course, the land they were fighting over had for centuries been inhabited by Indigenous peoples.

In the early nineteenth century, when Florida was still under Spanish rule, the area served as a safe haven for escaped enslaved Africans, who sought refuge among the Seminole. This sparked the first of Three Seminole Wars between 1817 and 1858, all led by Andrew Jackson. Throughout these conflicts, the Seminoles were never "conquered," and they never signed a treaty with the US government. A small contingent remained in the Everglades even after the Indian Removal Act was signed into law in 1830 and many other Indigenous peoples were forcibly relocated to Indian Territory, the land west of the Mississippi that the United States acquired in the 1803 Louisiana Purchase.

In the aftermath of that law, Jackson and his agents coerced the Cherokee, Chickasaw, Choctaw, and Muscogee (Creek) to sign treaties ceding their territories. Upward of 100,000 people traveled en masse along what became known as the Trail of Tears, with thousands dying along the way. But, like the Seminole, factions from these groups refused to leave, hiding within the environs they'd come to know so well. (For more on the Trail of Tears, see Indian Territory: Oklahoma, page 156.)

Those who survived the treacherous journey to what would become Oklahoma did their best to maintain their cultural traditions and foodways in a foreign place. Those who stayed in the Southeast worked to rebuild. These important reclamation and revitalization efforts are still underway today for these communities, who bore the brunt of colonialism centuries before it hit other parts of Turtle Island.

THE FOOD

Southeastern Woodlands foodways are as rich and diverse as the region itself, thanks to its temperate climate, fertile soils primed for farming, and natural bounty from both forest and sea. Lots of us have some familiarity with these dishes, because so much of what we know as Southern cuisine was heavily influenced by Indigenous and African traditions—after all, we were the ones primarily growing and cooking the food there. A prime example is shrimp and grits, which I reimagine with purely Native ingredients on page 142.

Many area Indigenous groups, including the Five Tribes as well as the Catawba, Lumbee, Shawnee, and others, are considered expert horticulturists. They have long carefully managed the land, generally employing the slash-and-burn method to clear forests in the past while simultaneously fertilizing the soil with nutrient-rich ash. During the long growing season, they cultivate crops like corn, beans, squash, sunflowers, pumpkins, sweet potatoes, tomatoes, grains, and dozens of other vegetables.

Corn plays such a vital role in Southeast foodways. Often nixtamalized with wood ash to increase nutrient bioavailability, the many cultivated varieties show up in endless dishes—grits, breads, stews, soups, succotash, and traditional foods like banaha (cornmeal tamales) and sofkee, a pungent fermented food whose thickness ranges from a drink to a porridge. As in so many other places across Turtle Island, corn was grown alongside beans and squash as part of the symbiotic three sisters. In the recipes that follow, I showcase this cornerstone ingredient in a Summer Succotash (page 153), Corn Mush (page 147), and cakes that combine the Cherokee staples of nixtamalized corn and chestnuts (see page 149).

While some area tribes certainly did have large community fields filled with crops, other agricultural efforts didn't resemble how we've come to picture farming today. Indeed, Native peoples have long cultivated wild foods such as ramps, cattails, mushrooms, and the like in their natural settings, explains food sovereignty researcher Troy Wiipongwii, who is of Chickahominy descent.

Foraging played a significant secondary role in agricultural practices. Packed with protein and fat, acorns, chestnuts, pecans, black walnuts, and especially hickory nuts get transformed into drinks, breads, soups, porridges, and more.

Other important wild ingredients include tender greens like chickweed, dandelion, purslane, sochan, watercress, and lamb's quarters (many of which come together in a salad on page 138); roots like greenbrier, American groundnut, and sunchoke; and fruits like pawpaws, persimmons, berries, and grapes. The Cherokee, Chickasaw, and Choctaw each have their own name for the sweet dumplings made from wild grapes (see page 154). Indigenous communities also dried and ground sassafras leaves into the flavoring and thickening agent known as filé powder, and turned yaupon holly leaves into a naturally caffeinated tea used for ceremonies and purification purposes.

Southeast tribal communities have long hunted deer, wood bison, possums, rabbits, squirrels, groundhogs, turkey, waterfowl, small reptiles, turtles, and even alligators in the far south. From the ocean and the area's many inland waterways, they catch saltwater and freshwater foods including fish, clams, cockles, crabs, oysters, frogs, and crawfish (crayfish). Although crawdads (crawfish) are typically associated with Cajun cuisine, these freshwater crustaceans are of such significance to several Southeast communities that they're featured in multiple tribes' creation stories.

Cooking in pits, using earthen ovens, or over open fire has traditionally been extremely common among the area's Native peoples, which helped inspire the South's famed barbecue culture. Of course, tribal communities also began incorporating European and African ingredients and cooking methods into their food systems post-contact, resulting in the region's unique blended-culture cuisine.

For a true taste of the Bayou, Louisiana Creole researcher and writer Jeffery Darensbourg shares a recipe for a staple he's savored since childhood. His take on gumbo (see page 144) features duck, shrimp, and venison sausage, but this is also a great opportunity to play around with Native proteins: rabbit, turkey, oysters, crabs, or even alligator or turtle. It's also an introduction to important foraged foods of the Bayou, which include bull thistle, chicory, ramps, mushrooms, swamp lotus, arrowhead roots (wapato or duck potatoes), wild lettuces, and much more. Sadly, these plants are being harvested less and less due to pollution and contamination concerns.

With his work, Jeffery reminds us that many beloved Louisiana culinary traditions have Indigenous origins. Inspired by food sovereignty warriors like Jeffery, I shaped these recipes with key regional ingredients such as oysters, shrimp, chestnuts, pawpaws, wild greens, and grapes, and, of course, all-important corn to honor and reflect the foodways of the Southeastern Woodlands.

BLISTERED MILKWEED PODS

serves 2

- 24 young milkweed pods
- Sunflower oil
- Flaky sea salt, for serving

Milkweed is often known as a crucial food source for Monarch butterflies. While monarchs exclusively eat the leaves, I enjoy the buds—I use them to make capers (see page 38)—and the fleshy pods. The pods form in summer after the plant flowers, and they taste best when they're young. They're at the right stage when the pods are 1 to 2 inches long, have soft green spikes, and have a texture similar to okra. Their outer casing becomes smooth and firm as they age.

You can batter and fry the pods, like okra. Or you can treat them like shishito peppers, as I do here, and simply blister them in a hot pan. Enjoyed this way, they have a firm crisp-tender texture and a gentle green bean–like flavor.

When harvesting milkweed pods, be sure to use principles from the honorable harvest: Only gather pods from places where the plants are plentiful, and take no more than one or two pods per plant.

Scrub the milkweed pods under cool running water. Cut them in half lengthwise. You will find the immature seeds, which have a cheese-like texture or are a little bit fluffy. Remove the seeds and reserve for salads.

Heat a large skillet over medium-high heat. Add a very thin layer of oil, and once it shimmers, add the pods in a single layer, cut-sides down, and cook for 2 to 3 minutes, until browned along the edges. Flip and cook the pods for about 1 minute longer, until blistered in spots

Sprinkle with flaky salt and serve.

WILD GREENS SALAD
WITH PERSIMMONS AND HICKORY NUTS

serves 4

North American persimmons have a fleeting season in late fall. They don't last very long fresh, so I always recommend freezing or drying them to extend their shelf life.

You can make this salad, which pairs their sweetness with rich nuts and wild greens, from spring through fall using whatever tender foraged greens you find.

- ½ cup hickory nuts or pecans
- Sea salt
- Ground sumac
- ½ cup diced fresh persimmons or 2 ounces dried persimmons, preferably the North American variety, cut into bite-size pieces
- 1 tablespoon cider vinegar
- 1 teaspoon maple syrup
- 8 cups loosely packed wild greens (see Note)
- ¼ cup mountain mint or other wild mint, leaves torn
- 2 tablespoons thinly sliced green parts of ramps, wild onion, or scallion
- 2 tablespoons sunflower oil

Spread the nuts in a large skillet in a single layer. Toast over medium heat for 3 to 5 minutes, stirring frequently, until they smell fragrant. Transfer to a plate and season the nuts with salt and sumac.

If you're using dried persimmons, bring a small saucepan of water to a boil. Add the persimmons and remove them from the heat. Let them stand for about 10 minutes to rehydrate, then drain.

In a large bowl, whisk together the vinegar and maple syrup. Add the wild greens, mountain mint, and ramps. Taste and season with salt. Drizzle in the oil while tossing to coat the greens evenly, then add the nuts and persimmons and toss again. Serve right away.

Note: *In the spring, look for dandelion, plantain, chickweed, and sochan (see below). In the summer or fall, look for purslane, lamb's quarters, or plantain.*

SOCHAN

Sochan, which comes from the green-headed coneflower plant, *Rudbeckia laciniata*, is an important green for Cherokee people as well as other Indigenous peoples in the region. It's a plant that's been gathered since time immemorial and enjoyed for its robust flavor. The leaves are most tender and best for a salad like this one in spring, and they can be sautéed or added to soups and stews in fall.

OYSTER STEW
WITH PAWPAW AND CORN CREAM

serves 2 to 4

While they taste like a tropical fruit, pawpaws (*Asimina triloba*) are native to the eastern part of Turtle Island. They have a fleeting season, ripening toward the end of the summer into September. Their sweet, custardy flesh is a natural addition to desserts, but I also like their flavor with seafood—particularly oysters and clams. Here, inspired by a Southern oyster stew, I make a cream for poaching the oysters from sweet corn as well as the pawpaw.

- 2 large ears sweet corn, husked
- 1 tablespoon sunflower oil
- 1 large yellow onion, quartered
- 2 pawpaws (6 to 7 ounces each), halved lengthwise, or 1 cup frozen pawpaw puree
- 12 large Southern oysters, scrubbed and shucked, with briny liquid reserved
- Sea salt (optional)
- Ground sumac, for sprinkling
- Wood sorrel, for garnish

Using a serrated knife, cut the corn kernels from their cobs, reserving the cobs.

In a large saucepan, heat the oil over medium-high heat until shimmering. Add the onion and corncobs and cook, turning a few times, until charred in spots.

Carefully add 4 cups water (it will cause a rush of steam) and bring to a boil. Reduce the heat to medium and simmer for 20 to 30 minutes, until the liquid is reduced to 1½ cups. Turn off the heat and let cool to barely warm.

While the broth simmers, remove and compost the seeds from the pawpaw flesh if you have fresh pawpaws. Transfer the flesh or thawed puree to a blender, along with the reserved corn kernels.

Strain the reduced broth directly into the blender, discarding the solids, and puree until very smooth.

Using a flexible spatula, push the puree through a fine-mesh sieve into the saucepan. Compost any excess pulp. Bring the corn and pawpaw cream to a simmer over medium heat and cook for about 3 minutes, until the foam subsides.

Add the shucked oysters and their briny liquid to the cream and cook for about 2 minutes, or just until the oysters are firm.

Taste the cream; the oyster liquid should provide enough salinity, but if not, season with a bit of salt.

Sprinkle with sumac, garnish with wood sorrel, and serve.

INDIGENOUS-INSPIRED SHRIMP 'N' GRITS

serves 4

In much of the Southeast, as well as other parts of Turtle Island, cornmeal-based porridges were a staple for Indigenous peoples and still are today.

This recipe is an homage to the Southern classic that has its roots in Africa and was likely first cooked in the United States by African cooks in the Carolina Lowcountry.

Rich with smoked turkey and fresh corn, these shrimp 'n' grits take some time to put together. To build flavor for the gravy, you need to make a stock using shrimp shells and husked ears of corn. You can then thicken it with filé powder, which is made with sassafras leaves and popular in gumbo (see page 144).

- 1 pound large shell-on wild shrimp (16/20 count)
- 3 large ears sweet corn, husked
- 4 tablespoons sunflower oil
- 8 ramps or scallions, 4 coarsely chopped and 4 thinly sliced crosswise
- 2 red bay leaves or other bay leaves
- 1 cup coarse-ground grits
- Sea salt
- 2 garlic cloves, minced
- Pinch of red pepper flakes
- 4 Roma tomatoes, cored and coarsely chopped
- 1 teaspoon ground sumac
- Meat from 1 smoked turkey drumstick or 2 smoked duck legs, cut into bite-size pieces
- ½ teaspoon filé powder (optional)
- Nasturtium leaves, for garnish (optional)

Peel and devein the shrimp. Reserve the shrimp shells and refrigerate the shrimp until you need them.

Cut the kernels from 1 ear of the corn, reserving the cob and kernels separately.

Use the large holes of a box grater to grate the kernels from the remaining 2 ears of corn. Reserve the cobs and grated corn separately.

In a medium saucepan, heat 2 tablespoons of the oil over medium-high heat until shimmering. Add the shrimp shells and coarsely chopped ramps and cook for about 8 minutes, or until the shells are crisped and pink and the ramps are very tender and browned in spots.

Add the 3 corncobs, 4 cups water, and the red bay leaves and bring to a boil over high heat. Reduce the heat to medium-low, cover, and simmer for about 1 hour, or until the stock is flavorful and reduced to about 1½ cups. Strain into a large measuring cup, discarding the solids.

Meanwhile, in a medium saucepan, bring 4½ cups water to a boil over high heat. Reduce the heat to low and gradually stir in the grits and 1 teaspoon salt. Cook for 45 minutes to 1 hour, until the grits are creamy and tender, stirring occasionally and being sure to scrape the bottom of the pot.

Stir the grated corn into the grits and keep warm.

When ready to serve, in a large skillet, heat the remaining 2 tablespoons of oil over medium heat until shimmering. Add the shrimp in a single layer and cook for about 2 minutes, or until nearly opaque. Stir and cook until the shrimp are opaque throughout, about 1 minute longer. Use a slotted spoon to transfer them to a plate.

Add the thinly sliced ramps to the skillet, season with salt, and cook for about 3 minutes, or just until softened. Add the garlic and pepper flakes and cook for about 1 minute, or until fragrant. Add the tomatoes and

sumac and cook for about 10 minutes, or until the tomato juices release and nearly evaporate.

Add the reserved 1½ cups shrimp/corn stock and bring to a boil over high heat. Cook, stirring a few times, until reduced by half. Reduce the heat to medium, stir in the smoked turkey and whole corn kernels, and cook for about 2 minutes to warm through.

Add the filé powder, if desired, and cook just until the sauce thickens a bit more. Taste and season with salt. Return the shrimp to the skillet and stir to coat and heat through.

Taste the grits and season with more salt as needed. To serve, ladle the grits into bowls. Top with the shrimp and gravy and nasturtium, if using.

JEFFERY'S DUCK AND SHRIMP GUMBO

serves 8 to 12

Gumbo is from the various peoples in Louisiana, including those who are Indigenous, those who have colonized the area, and those who have been brought to Louisiana through the gross injustice of the slave trade.

My friend Jeffery Darensbourg shared this recipe for a gumbo that relies on ingredients that are Indigenous to the Americas and from Africa. He says, *"Indigenous and African Peoples in Louisiana have lived together, been enslaved together, cooked together, and 'did more than shake hands together,' as my friend David Cheramie says."*

It includes duck, shrimp, and smoked venison sausage, but he says you could easily swap in a couple of rabbits, a turkey, and some turtle or alligator meat for the duck. Instead of shrimp, you could add oysters or crabs. And any smoked sausage—preferably Creole-style—will do.

For the vegetables, he uses a mix of wild and cultivated ingredients: *"Some people don't abide tomatoes in gumbo, I know. My rule about it is: If you don't think tomatoes go in gumbo, you probably think you're white. If you don't think okra belongs in gumbo, you definitely think you're white."*

Many gumbos start with a roux—a mix of flour and water that thickens the mix. Because I avoid wheat flour in my recipes, we opted to use a mix of sassafras leaves and okra for their thickening power.

Jeffery adds, *"There is no definitive way to make gumbo. There will never be a definitive way to make gumbo, and I have never made it the same way twice. I have eaten the dish since I was a baby, and I don't use a recipe. I've made countless versions, and this is but one."*

I've left in some of his other colorful notes throughout the recipe.

DUCK AND STOCK

1 whole duck (about 5 pounds)

Sea salt

2 cups coarsely chopped wild onions or 1 large onion, coarsely chopped

GUMBO

Sea salt

8 ounces okra, sliced crosswise (about 3 cups)
This is more okra than I usually use, but as I am forgoing a roux, the extra okra will add to the thickness.

2 cups chopped wild onions, ramps, or spring onion

2 cups chopped pieces bull thistle ribs or stalks (see Notes, page 146) or celery
This plant (Cirsium vulgare), *native to Louisiana, is excellent raw or cooked, and the stalks have a texture similar to celery.*

Cayenne pepper
2 tablespoons is about right for my taste, but you're better off starting with less and adding more.

1 large tomato, coarsely chopped, or 1 (14.5-ounce) can chopped tomatoes

Make the duck and stock: Preheat the oven to 400°F.

Remove and reserve the neck and giblets for making the stock. Using a fork, lightly prick the duck skin all over, being careful not to pierce the meat. Then, using a sharp, thin knife, make shallow cuts in the skin over the breasts and legs making sure you cut through the skin, not the meat.

Transfer the duck to a rack set in a roasting pan. Season the duck all over with salt. Pour in enough water to cover the bottom of the pan without reaching the duck, about 2 cups.

Roast the duck breast-side up for 25 minutes. Use tongs to flip it and roast for another 25 minutes. Then flip the duck so it's breast-side up again and continue roasting for 15 to 25 minutes longer, until the meat in the thickest part of the thigh registers 165°F on an instant-read thermometer.

Gently tip the duck to drain any liquid from the cavity into the pan. Transfer the duck to a work surface and let cool.

Pour the pan juices, including the fat, into a heatproof container, cool,

(recipe and ingredients continue)

cover, and refrigerate. When the duck is cool enough to handle, remove the skin (eat it, or save it for another use), and pull all of the meat off the bones (reserving them), then refrigerate the meat overnight in a separate airtight container.

Transfer the bones to a large stockpot. Add the reserved neck and other giblets (but not the liver) as well as the chopped onions. Add 6 quarts fresh water and bring to a boil over high heat. Reduce the heat to medium-low and simmer gently for 2 to 3 hours, until the stock has reduced to about 4 quarts.

Strain, discarding the solids, and refrigerate in airtight containers overnight. (Please don't skim off any fat, as we will use this in the gumbo.)

Make the gumbo: Whisk 1 tablespoon salt into a large bowl filled with 4 cups water. Add the okra and let it stand for 1 hour, then drain.

Scrape off (and reserve) all of the fat from the surface of the refrigerated drippings and stock. In a large soup pot, melt ¼ cup of the fat over medium heat. Add the onions and bull thistle, season with 1 tablespoon salt and 1 teaspoon cayenne, and cook for 3 to 5 minutes, stirring, until the onions and bull thistle have wilted.

Add the tomato, sausage, duck meat, and okra and cook for 3 to 5 minutes longer, until the okra starts to wilt a bit and the tomato breaks down.

Add the 4 quarts duck stock and bring to a simmer over medium heat. Add the wax myrtle leaves and several shakes of hot sauce (if using). After the stock comes to a simmer, transfer 2 cups of it to a separate bowl and whisk in the filé until well combined, then return it all to the pot. This is for thickening.

Bring the liquid back to a simmer, reduce the heat to low, and cook uncovered for 2½ hours.

Long cooking on low heat gets the goods here. It also helps the liquid reduce a bit and thicken.

Add the shrimp and cook uncovered for 30 minutes.

I know it sounds long, but you want the shrimp to cook long enough that they infuse the gumbo with their deliciousness.

Just before serving, discard the wax myrtle leaves. Taste, and add salt, cayenne, and/or hot sauce, as needed. Ladle the gumbo into bowls and add a scoop of popped amaranth or rice.

As with the wonderful Vietnamese dish pho, eating a bit too much, until one's face is red, is expected.

Notes

- **Bull thistle:** *When foraging bull thistles, wear gloves to harvest them and process them. If you want the stalks, remove the leaves (carefully), then use a vegetable peeler to strip the stalk. Chop the bull thistle stalk crosswise. You can also fold over the leaf (as you would a kale or Swiss chard leaf). Cut off and discard the spiky leaves and keep the ribs. Chop the ribs crosswise.*
- **Wax myrtle** (Myrica cerifera) *is a native plant with waxy, aromatic leaves that are somewhat similar to bay leaves.*

1 pound smoked or cured venison sausage links, cut crosswise into ½-inch slices

4 wax myrtle leaves or fresh bay leaves (see Notes)
Used in a manner similar to bay leaves

Louisiana hot sauce, such as Crystal (optional)

¼ cup filé powder (ground sassafras leaves)
Commercial versions are fine, but I always prefer small-batch artisan varieties when possible.

2 pounds large peeled and deveined wild shrimp (16/20 count)
There is a terroir of shrimp, and for this recipe, I strongly prefer shrimp from the Gulf of Mexico.

6 cups Popped Amaranth (page 37) or cooked wild rice (see page 83)
You can also serve it with cooked rice, if you prefer. It's not native, but grows well in Louisiana.

CORN MUSH

serves 4

Southerners call it grits. Italians, polenta. And in English, we call it corn mush, although it goes by many different names across Turtle Island.

In places where people grew corn, simple corn porridges from dried cornmeal were the base of many meals. Today, they are still a comfort food for Indigenous peoples—sometimes the first food we eat as babies and our last food as elders.

The corn used for mush can be white, yellow, blue, green, red, or even multicolored. Sometimes the cornmeal is roasted first to give it a toasty flavor.

The corn for this dish is not always nixtamalized, but some people add alkalizing agents as they cook their mush to enhance the flavor and soften the texture. For example, in the Southwest, the Diné (Navajo) cook their blue corn mush with juniper ash. (As with nixtamalization, adding an alkalizing agent also boosts the corn's nutritional value.)

In the Southeast, there is also a long Indigenous tradition of sometimes eating (or drinking) thick porridges of soured corn, known as sofkee, which are made with green corn or nixtamalized corn and left to ferment for a little while.

For something drinkable, like an atole (see page 270), fine-grind masa harina is mixed with a higher ratio of liquid.

- 1 teaspoon culinary ash (optional)
- 1 cup medium-grind cornmeal (any color)
- ¼ teaspoon sea salt

In a medium pot, bring 2 cups water to a simmer over medium-high heat. Add the ash if you're using it.

In a bowl, whisk together the cornmeal and salt and then whisk in 2 cups water, making sure to dissolve any lumps. Carefully and gradually add the cornmeal slurry to the simmering water while whisking. Cook for 30 to 45 minutes, stirring occasionally, until the porridge thickens enough that it starts to hold the streaks of the whisk or spoon you use to stir. Taste the mush and if you like the texture (see Note), it's ready to serve. If it seems like the corn needs more softening, continue cooking, adding more water if necessary. Depending on the corn, this might take minutes, or in some cases, an hour or more. It's a matter of your preference and how smooth a texture you want to achieve.

Serve hot.

Note: *When making corn mush, the ratio of liquid to cornmeal can vary immensely based on the texture of the cornmeal grind and the consistency of the mush you prefer. For example, to create a stiff mush, you'll use 1 cup medium-grind cornmeal to 3 cups water. For something looser, you'd increase the water to 5 or 6 cups. The recipe here starts with 4 cups liquid, but feel free to adjust as you like.*

CORN AND CHESTNUT CAKES
WITH GREENS

serves 2 to 4

Much like Haudenosaunee cooking and other Indigenous cooking further north, corn formed the backbone of Cherokee cooking throughout the Southeastern woodlands. People traditionally made different types of corn breads by pounding together nixtamalized corn with cooked beans, chestnuts, hickory nuts, or sweet potatoes and rolling the mixture together with a bit of fat into dumplings. For a treat, they were sometimes sweetened with maple syrup or honey.

The breads were either boiled in water or baked within bark over a fire. They could then be served alongside cooked greens, mushrooms, meats, or fish.

In the spirit of Cherokee-style breads, I created these chestnut-studded corn cakes but turned to several modern conveniences. Instead of nixtamalizing and hand-pounding corn, I use a high-quality masa harina. I also use preroasted chestnuts.

If you like, you could add some smoked turkey or duck to the greens to enrich their flavor even more.

CAKES

- 1 cup high-quality masa harina
- 1 teaspoon baking powder
- ¼ teaspoon fine sea salt
- 4 tablespoons sunflower oil, plus more for the baking sheet
- 3½ ounces shelled roasted chestnuts, finely chopped

SERVING

- 1 tablespoon sunflower oil
- 1 medium yellow onion, chopped
- Sea salt
- 3 ramps or wild garlic bulbs and stalks, chopped, or 3 cloves garlic, thinly sliced
- 5 ounces tender wild greens (about 8 cups), such as sochan (page 138) or lamb's quarters
- 1 teaspoon ground sumac

Make the cakes: In a bowl, stir together the masa harina, baking powder, and salt. Add ½ cup water and 2 tablespoons of the oil and stir together to form a soft dough. Cover and let stand for 20 minutes to allow the masa harina to fully hydrate. Mix in the chestnuts and knead until they are incorporated.

Roll the dough into a ball and divide it into 4 equal portions. Roll each portion into a ball and then flatten into cakes that are about ½ inch thick.

Preheat the oven to 400°F. Lightly oil a baking sheet.

In a large skillet, heat the remaining 2 tablespoons of oil over medium heat. Add the cakes and cook for about 3 minutes, or until they turn golden and crisp on the bottom. Flip and cook for 2 to 3 minutes longer, until golden and crisp on the other side. Transfer the cakes to the prepared baking sheet and bake for about 15 minutes, or until the masa is no longer wet in the middle. Let stand for 3 minutes before serving.

Meanwhile, for serving: In the same skillet, heat the oil over medium heat. Add the onion, season with salt, and cook for about 8 minutes, stirring, until translucent and soft. Add the ramps or garlic and cook for about 3 minutes, or until softened. Stir in the greens with a few tablespoons of water, cover, and cook for about 2 minutes, or until wilted. Stir in the sumac and season with salt.

Serve the cakes topped with the greens.

TURKEY AND MUSHROOM STEW
WITH SASSAFRAS AND PINE BROTH

serves 4 to 6

Sassafras has a long history of medicinal and culinary use in the Southeast. Tribes, including the Cherokee, Choctaw, and Seminole, make tea and other medicines from the roots and bark to resolve respiratory and digestive illnesses or just to enjoy. The flavor of the infusion is reminiscent of a popular drink—root beer—because sassafras roots were one of the components of its original recipe.

The Choctaw people also historically used the leaves, pounding them to thicken and flavor soups. Today, those pounded leaves are known as filé, a popular ingredient in gumbo (see page 144). Here, I use both the roots and leaves in this dusky stew of turkey leg meat and earthy dried and fresh mushrooms, flavored with elements of the forest.

- 2 fresh sassafras roots from saplings (see Note), cleaned, or 1 teaspoon dried sassafras bark
- 1 tablespoon coarsely chopped Virginia pine needles or white pine needles (see Conifers, page 22)
- 1 ounce dried mixed wild mushrooms
- 3 cups boiling water
- 3 tablespoons sunflower oil
- 1 large whole turkey leg (leg and thigh), or 2 turkey thighs or 3 turkey drumsticks
- Sea salt
- 1 large yellow onion, chopped
- 3 large garlic cloves, thinly sliced
- 1 large carrot, scrubbed well and chopped
- 1 cup very thinly sliced fresh wild mushrooms, such as oyster or hen of the woods
- 1 heaping teaspoon filé powder
- ¼ cup tender wild greens (such as chickweed, lamb's quarters, plantain, dandelion, or wood sorrel), coarsely chopped, for garnish
- Corn Mush (optional; page 147), for serving

Combine the sassafras roots and pine needles in a tea bag or in some tied cheesecloth. Place in a large heatproof bowl or liquid measuring cup, add the dried mushrooms and boiling water, and let that steep while you cook the stew.

In a large heavy pot or Dutch oven, heat 2 tablespoons of the oil over medium-high heat until shimmering. Season the turkey with salt and sear it, skin-side down, for 8 to 12 minutes on the first side, until nicely browned and some of its fat has rendered. Flip and cook on the second side for about 8 minutes longer, or until browned. Transfer to a plate.

Reduce the heat to medium and spoon off all but 2 tablespoons of the fat. Add the onion, garlic, and carrot and cook for about 5 minutes, or until the onion is translucent.

Remove the tea bag from the steeping liquid and squeeze out as much liquid as possible. Gradually pour the soaked dried mushrooms and all the soaking liquid into the pot, stopping before you reach the grit that has fallen to the bottom of the bowl or cup.

Return the turkey to the pot. Add more water to the pot as needed so the turkey is about three-quarters submerged. Bring to a boil over high heat. Reduce the heat to medium-low, cover, and simmer for 1½ to 2 hours, until the meat is pulling away from the bone.

Meanwhile, in a skillet, heat the remaining 1 tablespoon of oil over medium-high heat until shimmering. Add the fresh mushrooms and cook for about 8 minutes, stirring, until they release their liquid and start to brown.

Transfer the turkey to a bowl to cool.

Increase the heat under the pot to high and cook until the liquid has thickened and is reduced to about 1½ cups.

Meanwhile, pull the turkey meat from the bones, discarding them, and return the meat to the pot. Add the cooked mushrooms and filé powder and cook, stirring, until the liquid thickens some more.

Serve the stew garnished with wild greens, with the corn mush if desired.

Note: *You can find sassafras trees in certain forests throughout the Eastern woodlands. The trees have three different-shaped leaves and a sweet aroma. They also frequently throw off saplings, which you can dig up for their roots. (Or you can purchase bark and leaves from medicinal herb providers.)*

SUMMER SUCCOTASH

serves 4

Succotash is often described as an early Colonial dish, but when you look at the major ingredients—corn and beans—it's clear that its origin is Indigenous. The name succotash is thought to come from the Wampanoag word misickquatash, meaning corn and beans together. Today, this dish is far more popular in the South.

There are endless recipes for succotash, and the dish can be adapted for the seasons. For example, during certain times of year, you might use cooked dried corn instead of sweet corn and cooked dried beans instead of fresh.

This recipe celebrates peak summer, when you can find sweet corn, green beans, fresh tomatoes, and a gift from Africa that has found another home in the South: okra.

- 2 tablespoons sunflower oil
- 1 small onion, finely chopped
- Sea salt
- 2 garlic cloves, thinly sliced
- ½ red fish pepper or other hot red chile (optional), seeded if desired and minced
- Kernels from 2 ears sweet corn
- 8 ounces fresh Cherokee Trail of Tears beans or other green beans, halved crosswise
- 8 ounces okra, cut crosswise into rings
- 1 large Cherokee Purple tomato or other heirloom variety, cored and cut into ½-inch pieces
- 2 tablespoons finely sliced wild onion greens or chives
- Ground sumac

In a skillet, heat the oil over medium heat. Add the onion, season with salt, and cook for about 5 minutes, or until softened. Add the garlic and chile (if using) and cook for about 2 minutes, or until softened. Add the corn kernels and cook for 4 minutes, or until starting to brown. Add the beans, a pinch of salt, and ½ cup water and cook for 2 to 3 minutes, stirring, until the water has evaporated and the beans are crisp-tender.

Add the okra and cook for 2 to 3 minutes, stirring, just until tender. Turn off the heat and stir in the tomato and onion greens. Taste and season with salt and sumac as needed.

WILD GRAPE DUMPLINGS
WITH PECAN BRITTLE

serves 4 to 6

Many Cherokee and Chickasaw cookbooks feature a version of these grape dumplings, known as panki' alhfola' in Chickasaw. Today, they are often made with all-purpose flour and butter. Traditionally, though, they featured corn. This recipe leans more traditional but takes advantage of a modern convenience: high-quality masa harina. Combined with cassava flour's satisfying chewiness, these dumplings are especially delicious coated in a deep purple sauce made from fresh grapes.

To flavor the sauce, I add a little bit of wild ginger, which you can substitute with fresh ginger. A crunchy maple-pecan brittle finishes off the dessert.

BRITTLE

- ½ cup maple syrup
- ¼ teaspoon sea salt
- 1½ cups pecan halves (5 ounces), coarsely chopped

DUMPLINGS

- ¾ cup masa harina, plus more for rolling
- ¼ cup cassava flour
- 1 teaspoon baking powder
- ⅛ teaspoon sea salt
- 3 tablespoons sunflower oil
- 1½ teaspoons maple syrup

SAUCE

- 2 cups Muscadine grapes or other purple grapes, preferably wild (they don't need to be seedless)
- 2 cups Muscadine or other purple grape juice
- 1 small piece wild ginger, scrubbed and coarsely chopped, or a couple of ¼-inch-thick slices fresh ginger
- 2 tablespoons maple syrup

Make the brittle: Preheat the oven to 325°F. Line a baking sheet with a silicone baking mat or parchment paper.

In a small saucepan, combine the maple syrup and salt and cook over medium-high heat until the syrup reaches 250°F on an instant-read thermometer. Carefully stir in the pecans, then quickly scrape the mixture onto the lined baking sheet. Using a spatula, spread it in a single layer.

Transfer to the oven and bake for about 15 minutes, or until the brittle is dry to the touch. Let cool completely.

Make the dumplings: In a bowl, stir together the masa harina, cassava flour, baking powder, and salt. Add ½ cup water, the oil, and maple syrup and stir together to form a soft, springy dough.

Divide the dough into 24 equal portions and roll into balls. Place them on a baking sheet and lightly flatten each with your palm. Cover with a clean towel to prevent them from drying out.

Make the sauce: In a wide, shallow, heavy-bottomed pan, combine the grapes, 1 cup of the grape juice, and the ginger over medium-high heat. Bring to a boil and cook for about 1 minute, until most of the grapes have burst. Turn off the heat and use a masher or large spoon to help break up any whole grapes.

Strain through a fine-mesh sieve into a bowl, reserving the solids for composting. Return the grape juice mixture to the pan and stir in the remaining 1 cup of grape juice and the maple syrup. Cook over medium heat for about 10 minutes, or until the liquid is slightly thickened.

Carefully add the dumplings to the pan and turn to coat with the sauce. Cover and cook over low to medium heat for 10 minutes, gently flipping halfway using a spoon, until they're no longer raw in the center when you cut one in half.

Coarsely chop or break up the cooled pecan brittle and scatter over the dumplings. Serve warm with the sauce.

INDIAN TERRITORY

OKLAHOMA

THERE'S NO PLACE QUITE LIKE Oklahoma. Across Turtle Island and indeed the planet, it is a situation all its own. Also known as Indian Territory, it's the place where Andrew Jackson forcibly relocated tens of thousands of Native Americans after he signed the Indian Removal Act into law in 1830.

Despite its atrocious origins, Oklahoma has come to represent Indigenous resilience, with dozens of tribal nations now proudly calling the South Central state home. When these groups were banished from their expansive ancestral homelands and packed into less than seventy thousand square miles, they brought with them their important cultural and culinary traditions. So many of my fellow food sovereignty warriors who are revitalizing Indigenous foodways have ties to or roots in Oklahoma that inform the cuisine they're cooking, no matter how far from Indian Territory their life journeys have taken them.

First and foremost, we all owe a debt of gratitude to legendary chef, educator, and advocate Loretta Barrett Oden, whose efforts to uplift Native foods far preceded the modern-day movement. After growing up and raising her family in Oklahoma, she traveled far and wide to learn about Indigenous food traditions. Then in 1993, she opened the Corn Dance Cafe in Santa Fe, New Mexico, as an homage to her Potawatomi heritage. That groundbreaking restaurant quickly became nationally recognized for its authentic Indian food, as it was dubbed at the time.

But as I have long said, you don't need a restaurant to make an impact through food. After working in the industry, Nico Albert Williams started the nonprofit Burning Cedar Sovereign Wellness in her hometown of Tulsa to offer healing and reconnection through Cherokee foodways. Freelance chef and food stylist Bradley Dry, also from the Cherokee Nation, serves up fresh takes on Appalachian favorites like chicken and dumplings for clients including the *Reservation Dogs* cast; he even prepared prop foods of frybread and meat pies for the acclaimed TV series from showrunner Sterlin Harjo highlighting contemporary Native life. And Choctaw Tribal Historic Preservation Officer Ian Thompson, who wrote the book *Choctaw Food: Remembering the Land, Rekindling Ancient Knowledge*, is doing just that at his 160-acre Nan Awaya Farmstead.

The Oklahoma influences reach far beyond the borders of the Sooner State, so named for the white settlers who staked their claims during the Land Rush of 1889. My friend Crystal Wahpepah dishes up Kickapoo fare like peeskipaateeki (coarsely cracked corn porridge) and chipaeesiihooni aapikooni (wild mushroom pumpkin seed mole) at her eponymous Oakland restaurant, the first woman-owned Native spot in Northern California. (See her recipe for Peeskipaateeki on page 164.) Meanwhile, Osage chef Ben Jacobs cofounded Tocabe, the first Native-owned restaurant in the Denver area, which offers build-your-own Indian tacos, a robust online Indigenous marketplace, and a Native meal delivery service.

I jump at any opportunity to partner with these talented individuals in and from Oklahoma, which Loretta fittingly calls the "melting pot of Indian Country." It's home to thirty-nine federally recognized tribes, whose diverse food traditions have organically woven together over time to create the beautiful tapestry of this unique place.

THE LAND

With its memorable rectangular shape and prominent panhandle, this landlocked state is located between the Rocky Mountain foothills to the west and the Ozark Plateau to the east. Yes, there's plenty of prairie throughout Oklahoma, but the land space is so much more diverse than that, with twelve unique ecoregions. That includes mountain ranges, deep basins, thick forests, prized tallgrass prairies, limestone and gypsum caves, cypress swaps, otherworldly salt flats, and more.

The state's diverse terrain and rich natural resources—including oil, gas, coal, granite, limestone, shale, and the like—are the result of a long geological history that involved volcanic activity, the development of shallow seas, and tectonic plate shifting and collision. Those factors yielded varying soil qualities across the state, from rich loam, in which large-scale and family farmers grow hay, wheat, corn, soybeans, sorghum, cotton, peaches, watermelons, peanuts, and pecans, to less fertile sand, where ranchers raise livestock like cattle, pigs, and chickens. Sadly, an overdependence on agriculture has caused irreparable environmental damage in areas.

Long before Oklahoma's famed oil boom, Native peoples sought out natural oil and gas seeps to treat chronic ailments such as rheumatism. Then in the late 1800s, entrepreneurial oilmen convinced local tribes to lease out their land for drilling. By 1901, Tulsa had become the "oil capital of the world." It wasn't long before the value of petroleum, gas, and minerals outweighed the value of human life—at least Native life—as exemplified by the Osage Reign of Terror during the 1920s, when white hustlers brutally murdered families in pursuit of their oil headrights. The land keeps the score and bears the scars, including oil spills, abandoned wells, and other devastating effects from more than a century of excessive natural resource extraction.

Because Oklahoma sits at the intersection of the Great Plains, the Southeastern Woodlands, and the Desert Southwest, the climate ranges from semiarid in the western panhandle to humid subtropical as you head east. The state experiences four distinct seasons, with hot, humid summers and cool but short-lived winters. Precipitation also varies greatly, necessitating extensive irrigation for the agricultural enterprises.

One of Oklahoma's most unique geological features is the salt flats in the north-central part of the state, a vestige of an ancient sea where early Indigenous peoples flocked to hunt wild game and gather salt for preserving food. In the northwest corner of the panhandle sits the Black Mesa, so named for the black lava that coated it thirty million years ago. In the southeast are the notable Ouachita Mountains, which were formed some three hundred million years ago when the North and South American tectonic plates collided.

But the Sooner State is perhaps best known for its prairie grasslands. That includes the Tallgrass Prairie Preserve—the planet's largest protected prairie grass area, comanaged by the Nature Conservancy and National Park Service—where less than 40,000 acres remain of what was once an expanse of more than 140 million acres that fostered endless flora and fauna. Today, the preserve is home to at least 750 plant species and 350 animal species, including bison, deer, coyotes, bobcats, beavers, and even armadillos.

Beyond the preserve, several tribal nations now manage their own bison herds on their respective tribal lands, including the Cherokee, Cheyenne and Arapaho, Modoc, Muscogee (Creek), Osage, and Quapaw. Even though some of these communities don't have an ancient relationship with this sacred animal because their ancestral homelands are in other regions, they all hope to restore so-called Indian Country to what it once was before it was overtaken by settlers. A full return to pre-Colonial times isn't possible, but these initiatives are vital to being in right relation with nature.

Oklahoma is within the drainage basins of the Mississippi, Arkansas, and Red Rivers. In recent years, the state's more than one hundred major reservoirs have hit record lows amid intense droughts that rival the Dust Bowl. That water scarcity is juxtaposed with flash flooding, heat waves, devastating tornadoes, and other extreme weather as a result of climate change. All these factors make efforts to revitalize Indigenous lifeways in the area that much more challenging—and that much more crucial.

THE HISTORY

My Oklahoma friends say it best: This has always been Native land. Thousands of years before the Spanish arrived in the region in the mid-1500s, Indigenous peoples lived in and traveled through what would eventually be dubbed Indian Territory by the US government. Of course, their habitation and hunting areas spanned beyond the arbitrary colonialist borders developed in 1907, when Oklahoma became a state. But as we know, Native American history far predates American history.

Likely between 500 and 1300 CE, the Caddoan Mississippians took up residence near modern-day Spiro, along the banks of the Arkansas River, a natural passage between east and west. These sophisticated traders were as politically powerful as the Aztec and Inca empires, though their legacy is far less known. They developed sophisticated farming communities that included earthen platforms and burial mounds, some of which still stand today. For some time, they experienced great prosperity thanks to long growing seasons for crops like corn, beans, squash, and sunflowers, but a major drought forced them to eventually abandon the site.

The Spiro mound builders are believed to be the ancestors of the modern-day Caddo and Wichita peoples. Along with the Osage, Pawnee, Quapaw, and Plains Apache tribes, they called this place home centuries before it was called Oklahoma. They settled mainly along the area's waterways, and over time faced raids from the Arapaho, Cheyenne, Comanche, and Kiowa, who eventually claimed hunting territories there.

The Caddo have long been excellent horticulturalists, growing corn, beans, squash, pumpkins, watermelons, sunflowers, tobacco, amaranth, and native grasses. For centuries, corn was by far their most important food; they grew multiple varieties and created a robust maize economy with neighboring communities. Although they largely led a more sedentary agrarian lifestyle, they also hunted for deer, bison, and bear using bows and bone-tipped cane arrows. Those who lived near saline marshes and springs boiled down brine to make salt, a valued commodity.

The Wichita, who are known as the People of the Grass House, are now recognized as one tribe

along with the Waco, Tawakoni, and Keechi. They have long led a seasonal lifestyle that allows them to make the most of the area's abundance. In the past, during the warmer months, the women grew corn, beans, squash, and pumpkins that they then dried and stored in bison-hide satchels stocked away in underground cache pits. In the winter, they left behind their grass house villages to go on bison hunts, with men pursuing the prized animal and women preparing the catch by thinly slicing the meat and then hanging it in the winter sun to dry.

But the Indigenous history most people associate with Oklahoma is the Trail of Tears—the mass migration of Native Americans that followed the Indian Removal Act of 1830. That law remains one of the ugliest parts of Andrew Jackson's racist legacy, which closely resembles Donald Trump's extreme xenophobia. While earlier US presidents had taken, in comparison, a more tempered approach to the so-called "Indian problem," Jackson had one goal: to eliminate us.

Answering settlers' fervor for land and the US government's desire for North American domination, that law allowed for the expulsion of tribal groups from their ancestral homelands. In exchange, they were granted land in the unsettled, supposedly uninhabitable area west of the Mississippi River that had been acquired from the French in the 1803 Louisiana Purchase, as well as financial assistance and forever protections in their new home. Sadly, but unsurprisingly, these were just more broken promises from the United States.

The Indian Removal Act was the most egregious step in Jackson's long crusade to drive out Southeastern Woodlands Indigenous communities, who had already ceded much of their land to make way for American expansion. (For more on that region, turn to the Southeastern Woodlands and the Bayou chapter.) Soon after the bill's signing, Jackson sent federal agents to negotiate and enforce removal treaties—nearly seventy of which were put in place during his presidency. Although relocation was in theory supposed to be voluntary and nonviolent, that wasn't what happened. In reality, the government bribed, coerced, and forced some 100,000 Indigenous peoples off their lands. Along the way, countless lives, traditions, and cultural ties were lost.

The law greatly impacted the Five Civilized Tribes—the Cherokee, Chickasaw, Choctaw, Muscogee (Creek), and Seminole—who had earned that nickname for their assimilation of European societal norms like Western education, Christianity, and even slave-holding in an attempt at coexistence. Those efforts ultimately were futile, since these tribal nations were still exiled to Indian Territory.

The term Trail of Tears has come to represent the collective expulsion of Native Americans from the Southeast, but it actually involved several different treks that took multiple routes and happened over the course of more than a decade. The Choctaw were the first people to sign a removal treaty and, between 1831 and 1833, some fifteen thousand people embarked on the treacherous journey along what one leader dubbed the "trail of tears and death." About a third of them perished from disease, starvation, exposure, and attacks.

The Muscogee (Creek), who had already been pushed out of Georgia, attempted to stay in Alabama by signing an 1832 treaty that opened up a large swath of land for white settlement. That tactic proved unsuccessful and, starting in 1836, around fifteen thousand citizens were forced west anyway, with about thirty-five hundred dying along the way.

The Chickasaw negotiated financial compensation of $500,000 for their relocation, which began in 1837. About five thousand people traveled along the same paths taken by the Choctaw and Muscogee (Creek), with lesser loss of life. They settled on leased Choctaw land as a result of the 1837 Treaty of Doaksville, which both tribes signed under duress.

The plight of the Cherokee is perhaps most prominent, though the preceding events are lesser known. In 1832, the landmark US Supreme Court case *Worcester v. Georgia* upheld that the Cherokee had sovereign powers and couldn't be regulated by the state. Despite the promise of that ruling, Jackson refused to enforce it. Facing incursion and expulsion, the tribal nation became divided on what to do next. Part of the Cherokee community signed the 1835 Treaty of New Echota—ceding seven million acres in exchange for $5 million—while others later challenged its validity since the tribal chief hadn't been involved. Nevertheless, it was signed into law and used as justification starting in 1838 to round up and expel an estimated sixteen thousand people, more than a quarter of whom died along the Trail of Tears. (That agreement also reaffirmed a previous commitment to seat a Cherokee delegate in the US House of Representatives—a promise that remains unmet as of this writing.)

Throughout Jackson's long bid to banish the Seminole from the Southeast, they refused to go quietly, resulting in three separate Seminole Wars dating from 1817 to 1858. Despite the tribe's effective resistance, several waves of citizens were forcibly removed. But thousands of people from the Five Tribes refused to leave, eventually becoming citizens of those states. That's why some groups, including the Cherokee, Choctaw, and Seminole, have distinct modern-day tribes in both Oklahoma and the Southeastern Woodlands. Those who relocated to the Sooner State did their best to honor their long-held cultural and food traditions in this new and unknown environment.

In the decades that followed, even more tribal nations were banished to Indian Territory, including the Cheyenne and Arapaho, Comanche, Iowa, Kiowa, Pawnee, Ponca, Potawatomi, Sac and Fox, and several others. This exile came with a promise that Indian Territory would remain undisturbed by the US government and white colonialists, but that was yet another empty promise.

That sense of sovereignty was disrupted by the Dawes Act of 1887 (also known as the General Allotment Act), which parceled out shared land into small allotments for individual ownership; the Indian Appropriations Act of 1889, which opened up unassigned land to settlers under Homestead Act provisions; Oklahoma's statehood in 1907; and countless times when valuable natural resources were discovered on tribal lands. More recently, tribal sovereignty in the Sooner State has been further dismantled, with the 2022 US Supreme Court ruling in *Oklahoma v. Castro-Huerta* that gave states the power to prosecute some crimes on reservations—upending centuries of precedents confirming tribes' right to self-govern.

Today, these Indigenous communities who once resided all across Turtle Island—each with their unique creation stories, lifeways, and food traditions—have well-established relationships with the land space of Oklahoma and a kinship with one another due to their collective displacement there. Their horrific shared history has been flipped on its head to become a united story of resistance and revitalization, with numerous tribal food sovereignty initiatives all across the state, like Ian Thompson's Nan Awaya Farmstead, the Osage Nation's similar Harvest Land farm, and the Cherokee Nation's Heirloom Garden—all aimed at saving traditional foods.

THE FOOD

For the many tribal nations in Oklahoma, the removal from their ancestral homelands caused massive disruption to their food systems. In this new place, they no longer had access to many of the plant medicines, wild animals, and growing conditions to which they'd grown accustomed. In many ways, they were forced to start over, yet they were guided by the traditional ecological knowledge passed down by their ancestors. These adapted foodways reflect Indigenous innovation and ingenuity.

Loretta's "melting pot of Indian Country" metaphor is an apt one, given that Native communities from coast to coast have converged in Oklahoma. From the Southeastern Woodlands, the Five Tribes brought their agricultural traditions centered around the three sisters—corn, beans, and squash. From the Great Lakes, the Illinois, Iowa, Kickapoo, Miami, Potawatomi, and Sac and Fox brought food systems focused on freshwater fish, wild game, and foraged foods like wild rice. From the Great Plains, the Comanche, Cheyenne, Arapaho, and Ponca brought their bison-hunting traditions. The list goes on and on. While there's no such thing as pan-Indigenous cuisine, these distinct foodways have become more intertwined over time due to such close proximity.

Chef Taelor Barton likes to say that the Cherokee are tree people because of the vital role that trees and their fruits—hickory nuts, chestnuts, pecans, walnuts, and more—play in their food traditions. Those show up in important dishes like kanuchi, a rich and creamy soup made from hickory nuts (see On Kanuchi, page 168). I also offer a sweet take in the form of a Black Walnut Cream Tart (page 183) with seasonal berries.

Hickory trees are abundant in Oklahoma, but other important species, such as chestnuts, don't grow there. That requires cooks to use store-bought Asian chestnuts when making staples like chestnut bread (a variation on bean bread). Chef Nico says these ingredient substitutions feel a bit sacrilegious, but she acknowledges how crucial it is that her community have access to these ancient foods.

Likewise, the Choctaw people have created modern versions of traditional foods, unfortunately sometimes employing unhealthful processed ingredients, says scholar Ian Thompson. For instance, walakshi (a fruit dumpling) today is often made with grape juice concentrate, wheat flour, and white sugar (see Wild Grape Dumplings with Pecan Brittle on page 154 for a modern take using only Indigenous ingredients). That dessert is typically served at traditional gatherings alongside tanchi labona (a corn and meat stew, now often made with pork) and banaha bread (a meatless cornmeal tamal).

For the Osage, contemporary feasts involve pit and big-batch, wood-fired cooking of meats like pork, beef, bison, and chicken. Those proteins are paired with dishes like grape dumplings, yonkapin soup (lily pad root), and frybread. Although some of the ingredients have shifted from solely the proteins that were available in ancient times, the time-honored techniques remain the same, explains Ben Jacobs. Reflecting the importance of these culinary practices, the cooks who prepare the feast have proven themselves to earn their spots; it is an honored position in the tradition. For this reason, Ben often says he is an Osage who cooks, not an Osage cook, so as not to detract from those prominent roles.

Because of their displacement to this foreign land space from their vast ancestral homelands, many Indigenous communities in Oklahoma have depended on government commodity foods for decades—white flour, refined sugar, and other hyperprocessed foods—which have perpetuated problems like obesity, heart disease, and type 2 diabetes while also changing Native youth's palates over time. To address this, Indigenous advocates like educator Melissa Lewis are working to preserve culture while also improving health outcomes. Her Little Cherokee Seeds program aims to revitalize both language and traditional ecological knowledge among very young children, including infants.

But the story of Indigenous foodways in Oklahoma is not a tale of loss—rather, it's about adaptation and evolution. In addition to growing culturally important foods like corn, beans, squash, pumpkins, peppers, melons, and all sorts of herbs in gardens and greenhouses, Native cooks also make use of the state's abundant wild foods and game. That includes morels, onions,

Native communities from coast to coast have converged in Oklahoma.

plums, ground cherries, and berries galore as well as plentiful deer, elk, pronghorn, and birds like quail and turkey. Those ingredients come alive in Venison and Tepary Bean Chili (page 176), Hickory-Smoked Quail (page 179), and Slow-Roasted Turkey Breast with Sand Plum Sauce (page 171).

Bradley Dry jokes that you can tell where a Cherokee person is from depending on whether they think springtime is ramp or onion season, because ramps don't grow in Oklahoma but are rampant in the Southeastern Woodlands. His grandmother and aunt taught him how to find, clean, and cook wild onions, and today he still follows their simple yet delicious recipe of briefly boiling the alliums then frying them with eggs. Similarly making use of the land's bounty, Nico stews foraged greens such as kochan, pokeweed, watercress, lamb's quarters, lovage, and peppery creasy greens, which she boils and then fries in fat to be served alongside corn grits.

Nico points out that having so many Indigenous groups in such close proximity yields so many riches. She is honored to cook with ingredients she receives thanks to the Cherokee people's fellowship with other tribal nations, although those ingredients might not be their traditional foods—such as bison from Ponca friends, wild rice from Anishinaabe friends, and chokecherries from Lakota friends. A sense of camaraderie and community is palpable throughout this place, which is why I'm always thrilled at the chance to collaborate with cooks, chefs, and knowledge keepers who have rightly reappropriated the idea of Indian Territory.

PEESKIPAATEEKI

serves 4

My friend, Kickapoo chef Crystal Wahpehpah, runs Wahpepah's Kitchen in Oakland, California, on Ohlone land, where she grew up. She is an enrolled member of the Kickapoo Nation of Oklahoma, and her food at the restaurant brings together her heritage as well as the bounty that surrounds her.

In the Kickapoo language, peeskipaateeki is both the name for corn and for dishes made with corn. Here, Crystal shares a recipe for a breakfast porridge peeskipaateeki using an heirloom white corn. The kernels get cracked in a high-powered blender before cooking into a porridge that's lightly sweetened with maple syrup. By leaving some of the corn pieces fairly large, you get an appealing mixture of textures in the porridge. Crystal likes to top this with blackberries, but you could use any berries.

1 cup dried white whole-kernel corn

1 tablespoon maple syrup, plus more for serving

½ teaspoon fine sea salt

Blackberries, for garnish

In a saucepan, bring 4 cups of water to a boil over high heat.

Place the corn in a blender, preferably high-powered, and pulse to crack the kernels. Stop when most of the corn is finely ground, with a few pieces that are the size of small peas.

Reduce the heat to medium-low and when the water is simmering, stir in the corn. Cook for 40 to 50 minutes, until you have a thick and creamy porridge and the largest pieces are tender if a little chewy. You will want to stir the porridge occasionally for the first 20 minutes and more frequently as it thickens.

Stir in the maple syrup and salt. Divide among bowls. Garnish with the berries and serve warm.

GREEN CORN SOUP

serves 4 to 6

The Green Corn Ceremony is a tradition brought to Oklahoma by many of the Eastern and Southeastern nations who now call Indian Territory home. It happens each summer, around the time the corn crop is first edible and the kernels are milky and sweet. It celebrates not only the new harvest but also the connection people have with each other and all that surrounds them. For some nations, it also represents the beginning of a new year.

Before enjoying green corn and the festival and feast that go along with it, it's traditional for people to resolve conflicts and make amends. Some people fast or partake in purification rituals.

At the celebration, people typically dance and sing, sometimes for a few days on end. Inspired by this important time of year, I created this soup that you can make with green corn—which is named for the fact that it's young, not the color. Historically, most of the corn people cooked was not the sweet corn we see in grocery stores today, but the type dried to store and use in stews or grind into flours. For a brief window each season, this corn is tender and can be eaten with light cooking, much like sweet corn. When it's extra young, you can eat it, cob and all.

To source green corn, you will have to grow it yourself, or ask a farmer to harvest some corn early for you. But you can also make the soup with fresh sweet corn. Dried apples and sumac provide sweetness and an acidic balance to the soup while the corn and sunflower seed milks make it creamy. The sumac gives the soup a bit of a ruddy color.

¼ cup sunflower oil

1 medium yellow onion, diced

1 cup dried apples, chopped into ½-inch pieces

1½ teaspoons onion powder

1½ teaspoons garlic powder

3 tablespoons ground sumac

Sea salt

4 small ears green corn, cut crosswise into ½-inch pieces, or kernels from 2 large ears sweet corn (about 3 cups) or a mix of both

2 cups Sweet Corn Milk (page 35)

2 cups sunflower seed milk (see Seed, Nut, and Grain Milks, page 35)

2 cups coarsely chopped dandelion or amaranth leaves, plus more for garnish

¼ cup toasted sunflower seeds, coarsely chopped, for garnish

In a large saucepan, heat the oil over medium heat. Add the onion, dried apples, onion powder, garlic powder, and sumac. Season with salt and cook for about 6 minutes, or until the onions are translucent and soft.

Add the corn, corn milk, and sunflower seed milk and bring to a simmer. Cook for about 30 minutes, or until the corn is tender and the flavors meld. Taste and season with more salt as needed. Stir in the dandelion greens.

Serve garnished with the toasted sunflower seeds and more greens.

ON KANUCHI

Kanuchi is the Cherokee word for a traditional soup and drink made by cooking mashed hickory nuts, which taste like extraordinarily sweet and buttery pecans. While it can be made conveniently today with store-bought shelled nuts, these nuts can be tricky to find and quite expensive—the meat is just hard to pick out! So Indigenous peoples came up with an ingenious way to process and enjoy the nuts without needing to pick out the nut meat.

To make kanuchi, people start by gathering hickory nuts in the fall, sometimes waiting until after the first frost. They dry them in a warm, dry spot until they crack, which can take a few weeks to a month. Once they're dried, they'll use a hammer or rock to crush each one into large pieces. When smashing the nuts, it's important to discard any that have nut meat that looks dark or smells rancid.

After smashing all the nuts, they'll do a first sift and shake the nuts through a large-holed colander or basket. This removes the bigger pieces of shell.

Then the nuts get ground into a paste. Traditionally, people pound the nuts by hand until they're finely ground and the nuts release enough oils that they hold together when squeezed into balls. Today, some people will pulse the nuts in a food processor, but many people still prefer to pound the nuts by hand, often in community with others.

The balls of nut paste are then stored for long-term keeping. (Historically, they were kept in barrels or pots, and today, they're usually frozen.)

From here, the methods for making kanuchi can vary. If the balls are made from preshelled nuts, they can generally be whisked into water and simmered for about 30 minutes until thick and rich. More often, however, the balls are boiled and incorporated and then strained through a fine-mesh sieve to remove any remnants of shell.

Some people will reduce the liquid to make it very thick while others will keep it more milky. It is then sweetened, if desired, and served on its own as a warm drink or soup or stirred in with nixtamalized corn or wild rice.

For convenience, some people will now make kanuchi with shelled pecans, which grow throughout southern parts of the United States, including Oklahoma, and are easier to find commercially.

BLISTERED DEVIL'S CLAW PODS

serves 4 to 8

Devil's claw is one name for a native plant, *Proboscidea louisianica*, that grows in parts of Oklahoma as well as the desert Southwest. While it's often wild, you can cultivate it in a drought-prone garden.

The plant gets its name from the curvaceous seed pods that look like claws when dried (which is why it's also called ram's horns). People harvest the pods in early summer when they're green, fleshy, and immature; at this stage, they're eaten as a vegetable. They can range in size quite a bit, from 2 to 4 inches long at their thicker ends and skinny curled tails that are about double that length. Like okra, the pods have an appealing mucilaginous quality but a slightly more bitter flavor.

Serve them on their own as a snack, like shishito peppers, or use as a garnish for the Slow-Roasted Turkey Breast with Sand Plum Sauce (page 171).

12 to 24 young devil's claws

Sunflower oil, as needed

Flaky sea salt

Clean the devil's claws under cool water, then pat dry.

Coat a large skillet with a splash of oil, and heat over medium-high heat, until shimmering. Working in batches if needed, add the devil's claws and cook for about 4 minutes, turning a few times with tongs, until tender and blistered in spots. Transfer to a plate, sprinkle with salt, and serve.

SLOW-ROASTED TURKEY BREAST
WITH SAND PLUM SAUCE

serves 8

Sand plums, also known as sandhill plums or Chickasaw plums, grow on a shrubby plant called *Prunus angustifolia* in Oklahoma and other dry prairie areas. While they do grow wild, some people cultivate them in their gardens.

Of course, humans aren't the only ones who love this sweet fruit, which grows throughout the summer. Birds enjoy it, too. To beat the birds to a delicious harvest, pick the fruit while it's still yellow or just starting to blush orange, then allow it to ripen for a few days at room temperature.

Most people turn their sand plums into a sweet jelly set with pectin. When lightly sweetened, as they are here, sand plums create a nice sauce for different kinds of game meats, including wild turkey.

Gently roasting the herbed turkey breast with some stock keeps it moist.

TURKEY

- 2½ tablespoons coarse sea salt
- 2 teaspoons dried wild bergamot (bee balm)
- 2 teaspoons ground sumac
- 1 bone-in turkey breast (7 to 9 pounds)
- 2 leeks, white and light-green parts only, coarsely chopped and rinsed of grit
- 4 cups Roasted Bird Stock (page 40)

SAUCE

- 2 pounds sand plums, other wild plums, or small reddish plums (slightly bigger than a cherry), plus a few pitted plums, for garnish
- ¼ cup honey or agave syrup
- Pinch of sea salt
- Fresh wild bergamot (bee balm) leaves or flowers or other wild herbs, for garnish

Roast the turkey: In a small bowl, mix together the salt, bergamot, and sumac. Use it to season the turkey all over and let stand at room temperature for 1 to 2 hours or refrigerate, uncovered, for up to 2 days.

If the turkey has been refrigerated, let it stand at room temperature for 1 to 2 hours before roasting.

Preheat the oven to 275°F.

Transfer the turkey to a roasting pan breast-side up. Add the leeks to the pan and pour in the stock. Insert a probe thermometer in the thickest part of the breast near where the wings were attached but away from the bone. Cover the turkey with parchment paper followed by aluminum foil, sealing the edges of the pan. (You will need to use a couple of sheets of each.)

Slow-roast for 2½ to 3 hours, until the thermometer registers 165°F. Remove the turkey from the oven to rest for 20 minutes. Reserve some of the pan juices.

Meanwhile, make the sauce: Using a cherry pitter or a paring knife, remove the pits from the plums. Put 1 inch of water in a large saucepan and add most of the pitted plums. Bring the water to a boil over medium-high heat, cover, and cook for about 10 minutes, just to soften them. Let the plums cool slighly and drain.

Working in batches as needed, transfer the softened plums to a blender and puree.

Pour into the empty saucepan and add the honey and a pinch of salt. Cook over medium heat, stirring frequently, for about 5 minutes, or until it's thickened to a spoonable consistency.

Slice the rested turkey breast and brush on a little bit of the reserved pan juices in the bottom of the pan to keep it moist.

Spoon the plum sauce on a platter. Arrange the turkey on top. Garnish with pitted plums and wild bergamot.

GOLDENROD SHOOTS AND MAPLE PECANS

serves 4

Many of us know goldenrod for its swaths of yellow blooms that signal summer is about to transition to fall. While goldenrod has many medicinal uses, the plant is also edible. In spring, when the shoots first appear, they are tender enough to eat raw. As they grow, but before they flower, you can blanch the shoots. Their bitter, ever-so-slightly celery-like flavor is best with rich sauces, like a Duck Egg Aioli (page 36). I add a sprinkle of candied pecans, too, for extra sweetness and crunch.

- ¼ cup pecan halves
- 1 teaspoon sunflower oil
- 1½ teaspoons maple syrup
- ¼ teaspoon fine sea salt, plus more as needed
- 16 tender young goldenrod shoots or 8 midseason shoots
- 2 teaspoons cider vinegar
- ½ cup Duck Egg Aioli (page 36), for serving

Preheat a toaster oven or other oven to 250°F.

Spread the pecans on a small baking sheet and toast for about 10 minutes, or until fragrant. Pull out the pan just long enough to toss the pecans with the oil, 1 teaspoon of the maple syrup, and the salt and toast for about 10 minutes longer, or until dry to the touch. Let cool, then coarsely chop.

If you're using early-season shoots, you can just coarsely chop them.

If you're using midseason shoots, bring a large pot of water to a boil over high heat and salt it well. Remove the lower leaves from the midseason shoots to reveal the stems but keep the top leaves. Add the shoots to the water and boil for about 1 minute, or until bright green and just tender. Drain in a colander, then pat dry with a towel.

In a large bowl, whisk together the vinegar and remaining ½ teaspoon of maple syrup. Add the raw or blanched shoots and toss.

Use the duck egg aioli to create a large smear on a platter. Arrange the shoots on top and sprinkle with the candied pecans.

CHICORY-BRAISED BISON SHANKS

serves 2 to 4

In Oklahoma, large herds of bison roam the Wichita Mountains Wildlife Refuge and the Tallgrass Prairie Preserve.

Inspired by meaty dishes that sometimes include coffee in their braising liquid, here we make a coffee-like infusion with roasted chicory root powder, which is available as a coffee alternative at many health food stores and online. Chokecherries provide acidity and astringency. If you can't find them, substitute with half the amount of blackberries.

The thickness of bison shanks varies tremendously and can affect the cooking time, so be mindful of that as you plan to cook this dish.

- 1 tablespoon roasted chicory root powder
- 1 cup boiling water
- 1 cup chokecherries, fresh or frozen, or ½ cup blackberries
- 4 cups Rich Bison or Other Game Stock (page 41)
- 2 meaty bison shanks (sometimes sold as osso buco), about 1 pound each
- Fine sea salt
- 2 tablespoons rendered bison fat or sunflower oil
- 1 large yellow onion, coarsely chopped
- 1 large carrot, scrubbed well and coarsely chopped
- 1 tablespoon honey
- Corn Mush (page 147), for serving
- Sliced wild onion or scallion greens, for garnish

Preheat the oven to 325°F.

Put the roasted chicory root powder into a heatproof measuring cup. Stir in the boiling water until well incorporated and let steep for 10 minutes.

In a small saucepan, combine the chokecherries and 1 cup of the stock and bring to a simmer over medium heat. Cook for 1 to 2 minutes while mashing the fruit with a spoon, until it bursts and releases its juices. Remove from the heat.

Season the shanks generously with salt. In a large heavy ovenproof pot with a lid or a Dutch oven, heat the fat over medium-high heat until shimmering. Add the shanks and sear for about 10 minutes, turning them frequently, until the shanks are well browned all over. Transfer to a plate.

Stir in the onion and carrot and cook, stirring, for 6 minutes, or until they start to turn brown at the edges.

Gradually pour the steeped chicory liquid into the pot, stopping before you reach any grit at the bottom of the cup. Add the remaining 3 cups of stock and the honey. Using a fine-mesh sieve, strain the fruit mixture into the pot, pressing on the chokecherries to release as much liquid and pulp as possible. Discard the solids. Nestle the seared shanks into the pot and bring to a boil over high heat. Cover and transfer to the oven.

Cook for 2 to 4 hours (depending on the thickness of your shanks), until the meat is so tender it's falling off the bone. Transfer them to a plate.

Skim and discard some of the fat from the surface of the cooking liquid. Bring to a boil over high heat and cook for 15 to 20 minutes, until the sauce is glossy and thickened and reduced to about 1½ cups.

Reduce the heat to medium-low and return the bison shanks to the sauce, turning to coat them evenly. Cook gently for about 2 minutes, just until they are heated through.

Serve the bison shanks and the sauce with corn mush. Garnish with onion greens.

VENISON AND TEPARY BEAN CHILI

serves 8 to 10

Warmly spicy and comforting, this chili gets its robust flavors from both fresh and dried chiles and, of course, ground venison. (You can use any type of lean ground meat here.)

Tepary beans are drought tolerant and have an especially dense, meaty texture. If you substitute other beans for them, you might need to adjust the cooking time a bit, since tepary beans typically take longer to cook, even after you soak them overnight.

To soften the heat of the chili a bit, you can serve it with Corn Mush (page 147). And though avocados are not native to the region, the avocado crema (Crema de Aguacate, page 237) is also delicious with this.

- 1 cup dried tepary beans (any color), soaked overnight and drained
- Sea salt
- 2 guajillo chiles
- 2 morita chiles
- 1 ancho chile
- 4 tablespoons sunflower oil
- 2 pounds ground venison or other ground meat
- 1 medium yellow onion, chopped
- 1 poblano chile, stemmed, seeded, and chopped
- 5 garlic cloves, minced
- 2 pounds fresh tomatoes, cored and chopped
- 3 cups Rich Bison or Other Game Stock (page 41) or other meat stock
- 1 tablespoon cider vinegar
- 1 tablespoon honey
- Corn Mush (page 147), for serving

In a medium saucepan, combine the soaked beans with water to cover by 1 to 2 inches. Bring to a boil over medium-high heat, then reduce the heat to medium-low and simmer for 1½ to 2 hours, until the beans are tender. Add water as needed to keep them well covered. Remove from the heat, season them with salt, and let stand for 20 minutes.

Meanwhile, heat a large cast-iron skillet or a comal over medium-high heat. Toast the guajillo, morita, and ancho chiles for 1 to 2 minutes, turning frequently, until they're pliable and fragrant. Transfer to a work surface to cool, then discard their stems and seeds.

Place the toasted chiles in a medium saucepan, add 3 cups water, and bring to a boil over high heat. Turn off the heat and let stand for 30 minutes, then transfer the chiles and their cooking liquid to a blender and puree. Push the puree through a fine-mesh sieve into a bowl.

In a large heavy saucepan, skillet, or Dutch oven, heat 2 tablespoons of the oil over medium-high heat until shimmering. Add the venison and season with salt. Cook for about 5 minutes, breaking up the meat with a spoon, until evenly browned and cooked through. Using a slotted spoon, transfer to a plate.

Add the remaining 2 tablespoons of oil to the pan and heat over medium heat. Add the onion and poblano and cook for about 8 minutes, or until softened.

Add the garlic and cook for about 1 minute, stirring, until fragrant and soft. Stir in the tomatoes and cook until they start to release their liquid, then add the cooked beans and cooked venison as well as the chile puree and the stock. Bring to a boil over medium-high heat, then reduce the heat to medium-low and simmer for about 40 minutes, or until the chili is thick and flavorful. Stir in the cider vinegar and honey. Taste and season with more salt, as needed.

Serve the chili with corn mush.

HICKORY-SMOKED QUAIL
WITH GROUND CHERRY SALSA

serves 2 to 4

Ground cherries are one of those fruits you can grow in your garden, but you'll also see them growing prolifically in the wild all over Turtle Island, including in Oklahoma. Our native species, *Physalis pruinosa,* has a flavor that's a little bit like a tomato and strawberry combined. They can also have a tropical edge with a pineapple flavor. Each plant can produce hundreds of fruits, each one wrapped in a little husk to protect it from predators. (No surprise, these fruits are related to tomatillos.)

I love to use ground cherries to make salsa, which is especially delicious with the sweet quail meat. You can serve these quail whole with the salsa or pull the meat and make the tostadas on page 180.

QUAIL

- 2 cups cider vinegar
- 3 garlic cloves, smashed and peeled
- 2 tablespoons agave syrup
- 1 tablespoon fine sea salt
- 4 semi-boneless quails (about 4 ounces each)

SALSA

- 2 tablespoons sunflower oil
- ½ small white onion, chopped
- 2 garlic cloves, coarsely chopped
- ½ serrano chile, stemmed, seeded, and chopped
- Sea salt
- 8 ounces ground cherries, husked
- 1½ teaspoons cider vinegar, or more as needed

Prepare the quail: In a bowl large enough to hold all the quail, whisk together the vinegar, 2 cups water, the garlic, agave syrup, and salt until the salt has dissolved. Add the quails, cover, and refrigerate for 4 to 6 hours. Drain the quails (discarding the brine), rinse, and pat dry.

Preheat a smoker to 225°F using hickory wood chips or pellets. (Or if you don't have a smoker, see Smoking Food on a Grill, page 69.)

Smoke the quails for 30 minutes. Transfer them to a baking sheet just long enough to wrap the legs in aluminum foil. Return the quail to the smoker and continue smoking for 15 to 30 minutes longer, until an instant-read or probe thermometer registers 165°F when inserted into the inner thigh. Transfer to a cutting board to cool.

Meanwhile, make the salsa: In a medium saucepan, heat the oil over medium heat. Add the onion, garlic, and serrano and season with salt. Cook for about 6 minutes, stirring frequently, until softened. Add the ground cherries and cook for about 10 minutes, stirring, until they release a lot of their liquid and that liquid begins to thicken. Turn off the heat and stir in the cider vinegar. Let cool slightly.

Using an immersion blender, pulse the mixture to a chunky salsa. (Alternatively, you can transfer the mixture to a blender to puree, but be sure to leave it a little chunky.) Taste and season with more salt and/or vinegar, as needed.

Serve the quails with the salsa.

TOSTADAS WITH SMOKED QUAIL AND GROUND CHERRY SALSA

serves 4

While you can enjoy the smoked quail in the preceding recipe simply with its ground cherry salsa, I like to stretch the meat from these tiny birds a bit further by making these tostadas. As 10-inch rounds, the tortillas are a bit bigger than your usual tostada and resemble a Oaxacan-style tlayuda, without the beans. If you can find them at a Mexican market, buy tortillas made specifically for tlayudas.

- 1 pound Fresh Masa (page 28) or use masa harina (see chart, page 27)
- ¼ cup pepitas
- ¼ cup sunflower seeds
- Sea salt
- Hickory-Smoked Quail with Ground Cherry Salsa (page 179), meat pulled from the quails
- 1 cup lightly packed wild greens and herbs, such as purslane, lamb's quarters, dandelion, plantain, wild onion greens, wild mint, and wood sorrel

Preheat the oven to 450°F. Line two baking sheets with parchment paper.

Divide the masa into 4 equal portions and roll each one into a ball. Using a large tortilla press or a rolling pin, press or roll each ball between 2 sheets of plastic wrap or wax paper into a 10-inch round.

Arrange 2 dough rounds on each baking sheet, leaving a little space between the rounds. Bake one sheet at a time for 10 minutes, then flip, and bake for 10 minutes longer, or until golden with dark edges.

Remove the tortillas from the oven and let cool. Leave the oven on.

In a small, dry skillet, toast the pepitas over medium heat for about 2 minutes, or until lightly puffed and starting to brown. Transfer to a bowl. Repeat with the sunflower seeds in the same skillet and transfer to a bowl. Season with salt.

Spread about half the ground cherry salsa over the tortillas while they're on the baking sheets, leaving a ½-inch border.

Arrange the quail meat on the tortillas and return both baking sheets to the oven for about 2 minutes, just to heat through.

Transfer the tostadas to a cutting board. Sprinkle with the seed mixture and the wild greens. Cut or break into wedges and serve with the remaining salsa.

BLACK WALNUT CREAM TART
WITH SUNFLOWER CRUST AND SEASONAL BERRIES

makes one 9-inch tart

It's remarkable how rich black walnuts become when pureed; their fat makes the puree very creamy, and their funky, sweet scent is floral and unique. This might sound odd, but I really feel like you can taste that black walnuts came from a tree. They make an incredible stand-in for dairy in this tart, nicely set in a crisp sunflower seed crust. To highlight their sweetness and depth of flavor, I toast the walnuts, but if you want a more neutral-tasting cream, you can skip that step.

Agar-agar is a natural, vegetarian gelatin-like agent for setting the cream. I use ½ teaspoon of the powdered form, which makes the filling sliceable but still softly creamy. If you prefer a firmer set, increase the agar to ¾ teaspoon.

CRUST

- ¼ cup sunflower oil, plus more for the pan
- 8 ounces sunflower seeds (about 2 cups)
- ¼ cup amaranth flour (see Note)
- ¼ teaspoon fine sea salt
- 2 teaspoons agave syrup
- 1½ teaspoons maple syrup

FILLING

- 8 ounces black walnut meat (about 1½ cups small pieces)
- ½ teaspoon agar-agar (or ¾ teaspoon for a firmer set)
- ⅔ cup maple syrup
- ¼ teaspoon fine sea salt
- Fresh seasonal berries, such as mulberries, wild blackberries, or other berries, for garnish

Make the crust: Preheat the oven to 350°F. Using a little sunflower oil, lightly grease the sides of a tart pan with a removable bottom (one that holds at least 6 cups of volume) or a 9-inch springform pan.

In a food processor, combine the sunflower seeds, flour, and salt and pulse until the seeds are finely chopped. With the machine running, add the oil, ¼ cup water, the agave syrup, and maple syrup and let it run until it holds together like a dough.

Press the dough into the bottom and at least 1 inch up the sides of the pan. If the dough gets sticky, dampen your hands with a little water as you press.

Bake the tart shell for 20 to 30 minutes, until dry to the touch, deeply golden at the edges, and lightly browned everywhere else. Let cool. Leave the oven on.

Make the filling: Spread the walnuts on a baking sheet and toast in the oven for about 4 minutes, until fragrant.

Transfer the walnuts to a small saucepan. Add 2 cups water and the agar-agar and bring to a boil over medium-high heat. Turn off the heat and let cool so it's warm but no longer steaming. Transfer the walnuts and their cooking liquid to a high-powered blender. Add the maple syrup and salt and puree until smooth.

Pour the filling into the cooled shell and refrigerate uncovered for at least 2 hours, until chilled and set. Garnish the top of the tart with fresh berries and serve.

Note

- *You can purchase amaranth flour, but if you can't find it, you can grind 3 tablespoons amaranth seeds in a spice grinder to yield about ¼ cup. Sift the flour through a fine-mesh sieve, if needed, to remove any larger pieces. (If you need to clear any lingering flavors in your grinder before you make the flour, grind 1 tablespoon amaranth first and discard.)*

DESERT LANDS

SOUTHWESTERN UNITED STATES AND NORTHERN MEXICO

SOME OF MY EARLIEST EXPERIENCES uplifting Native foodways took place in the deserts of the American Southwest, where many Indigenous cultures remain impressively intact despite the evident Spanish influence. Although I traveled to this vast region as a kid to visit some relatives, I hadn't spent much meaningful time there until 2013, when I spoke at the Native American Culinary Association (NACA) symposium. At that point, I was still developing The Sioux Chef in my mind but hadn't yet launched the business, so this was a catalyzing moment for me.

My friend Nephi Craig, who is a White Mountain Apache and Diné (Navajo) chef, founded the Arizona-based organization in 2000, long before the idea of Indigenous foods hit the American cultural zeitgeist. Each year, he brought together chefs, scholars, and other knowledge keepers from across Turtle Island to discuss Native foodways—a meeting of the minds that was a pretty novel idea at the time.

The 2013 conference took place in Tucson, set within the picturesque Sonoran Desert against a backdrop of saguaro cacti juxtaposed with distant mountains. Nephi was such a strong voice and advocate even back then, when there were just a few of us chefs focused on Native cuisine. I was honored to be featured alongside food sovereignty warriors like Xicana culinary anthropologist Claudia Serrato, Muckleshoot nutrition educator Valerie Segrest, Diné (Navajo) chef Walter Whitewater, and Mixtec cook/educator/activist Neftalí Durán. I also remember marveling at the artistry on display, including Hopi culture bearer Ruby Chimerica making piki bread from blue cornmeal, as well as Arapaho, Diné (Navajo), and Tohono O'odham basket weavers selling their intricate creations.

Being in community with these like-minded individuals was so energizing and so affirming. Within a year of that event, I quit my last paying job and started my catering company, The Sioux Chef, with an emphasis on Indigenous foods. I'm forever grateful to Nephi for helping me make those inspiring connections early on in my journey. These days, he focuses on the healing power of Indigenous foods at Café Gozhóó in Whiteriver, Arizona, which doubles as a vocational training center for those recovering from substance abuse. He works alongside student chefs, serving up Western Apache dishes like red chili, acorn stew, and three sisters salad.

Since that 2013 symposium, I've spent more time in the Southwest exploring the arid environs with knowledge keepers like San Carlos Apache forager and educator Twila Cassadore and Tewa/Xicana cook and curandera (traditional healer) Felicia Cocotzin Ruiz. During my adventures there, I've encountered echoes of plants that I grew up with in the desert-like Badlands, including cacti and yucca. Witnessing everyday life in the more rural, more rugged communities reminds me of my feral childhood spent outside on Pine Ridge in South Dakota. Obviously, the cultures of the Southwest and the Great Plains are unique from one another, but I still find these commonalities comforting.

Even from my earliest experiences there, I've had an urge to wipe away the colonial border separating the United States and Mexico and to stop segregating people based on the colonial languages they speak. After all, there are more similarities than there are differences across this imaginary line. That's probably because up until the mid-1800s, the US-Mexico border remained pretty fluid, with Indigenous peoples like the Apache, Comanche, Huichol, and Yaqui moving easily between the two countries. These days, the border is the site of so much dehumanizing strife—including the unimaginable separation of families, unnecessary loss of life, and massive displacement of endemic flora and fauna.

Just as that border was once fairly fluid, so too are the boundaries of this region. For our purposes, it includes Arizona and New Mexico as well as portions of California, Nevada, Utah, Colorado, and Texas along with the Mexican states of Sonora, Chihuahua, Coahuila, Nuevo León, Tamaulipas, Durango, and Sinaloa. While Native lifeways are comparatively intact in the American Southwest due in part to US imperialism hitting them at a later time—with rich cultures and languages still very much alive today—that's not necessarily the case in Northern Mexico. Fewer people who identify as Indigenous live there compared to other parts of the country, and sadly many traditions have been lost.

Whenever I get a chance to visit this enchanting area, I'm endlessly inspired by the artistry and ingenuity of its Indigenous groups, who have lived sustainably in the desert since time immemorial. There's just something so incredible about being surrounded by all these plants—yucca, mesquite, pinyons, smooth sumac, ocotillo blossoms, and other desert blooms—and savoring the region's distinct spices and flavors.

THE LAND

Three major deserts—the Sonoran, Mojave, and Chihuahuan—nearly join together there, creating stunning, warmly lit landscapes. Along with the arid Colorado Plateau, these deserts have long been home to tribal communities including the Apache, Cocopah, Comanche, Cora, Diné (Navajo), Havasupai, Hopi, Hualapai, Huichol, Karankawa, Maricopa, Mayo, Mojave, Opata, Pima, Pueblo, Rarámuri (Tarahumara), Seri, Tepehuan, Tohono O'odham, Ute, Yaqui, Yavapai, Yuma, Zuni, and others. Today, more than fifty-five tribes inhabit the Southwestern United States and Northern Mexico.

But there's more to this area than just desert. The bright sun shines down over its rugged yet picturesque terrain, including mountain ranges, canyons, mesas, buttes, plateaus, high plains, grasslands, and even conifer forests. Within the American Southwest, this diverse topography encompasses four major physiographic zones: the Colorado Plateau, the transitional highlands, the Southern Basin and Range, and the Southwestern plains. The landscape of Northern Mexico is similarly diverse, with several parallel subregions that run north to south, including the Sonora and Sinaloa Plains, Western Sierra Madre, Central Highland Plains, Eastern Sierra Madre, and Gulf Coastal Plains.

This region is unified by its arid and semiarid climate, characterized by little rainfall, pleasantly mild winters, and blazing hot summers. The area typically experiences two wet seasons in summer and winter, when heavy monsoon rains can cause intense flooding. But it'd be a serious oversimplification to lump together all the varying topography of the Southwest—from the snowy Colorado Rockies to the glistening white sands of New Mexico, where fossilized footprints dating back at least 21,000 years challenge previous assumptions about human life in the Americas. It's scientific proof that Indigenous peoples have always been here.

The mountains experience wintertime snowfall, creating critical spring snowmelt that provides life-giving water during the drier months. Sadly, the area has been experiencing a megadrought since 2000, thought to be the driest period since 800 CE. For evidence, just look to the Rio Grande (known as the Río Bravo in Mexico), which forms part of the US-Mexico border and therefore has become a highly politicized place.

The important waterway has been in decline for decades due to climate change, overuse by farms and corporations, and contentious water rights on both sides of the border.

Despite the dry climate, the land provides a wonderfully wide variety of wild foods and medicines. The Sonoran Desert, for instance, is actually one of the most biodiverse places on the planet, plus there are tons of cultivated plants thanks to Indigenous ingenuity. Dating back centuries, Native groups like the Pueblo developed dry farming methods that rely on rainfall catchment, storm runoff, and flood irrigation. The Zuni, in particular, invented the Latdekwi:we technique—also known as waffle gardening based on its appearance—where people dig one-square-foot beds sunken into the ground and surround them by short earthen walls to simultaneously conserve water and protect plants from high winds. The area's tribal communities also adapted crops to the arid soil; for example, corn grows with especially deep roots in the desert.

Long before the Grand Canyon became a popular tourist destination, it was home to tribes like the Havasupai (whose name means "people of the blue-green water," referring to the spectacular waterfalls along Havasu Creek). Today, they're the only full-time residents below the natural wonder's rim and rightly consider themselves its guardians. For centuries, the Havasupai hunted deer, pronghorn, and bighorn sheep as well as gathered amaranth, mescal, blazing star, and pinyon nuts in the area. The Hopi, meanwhile, made annual pilgrimages to the salt mines there to collect the mineral for food preservation and other uses.

This region is also rich with natural resources like copper, uranium, silver, gold, petroleum, and natural gas, all of which have been majorly exploited to devastating effect. Diné (Navajo) uranium miners—who were not warned of the risks of their work—and so-called "downwinders" living near nuclear testing sites experienced major radiation exposure and therefore suffer high incidence of cancer and respiratory illnesses. Today, the landscape is marred by hundreds of abandoned uranium mines that threaten human, animal, and plant life by contaminating the soil and water. Diné (Navajo) advocates are still fighting for recognition and reparations.

Similarly, for more than a decade, Indigenous activists have been protecting Arizona's Oak Flat—a sacred place for the Apache—from the development of a massive copper mine. The 740-acre swath sits within the Tonto National Forest and is rich with Emory oak, whose acorns are crucial for sustenance and ceremony alike. Low in tannins, they don't require leaching in order to be dried and eaten or transformed into flour for foods like stew, dumplings, and baked goods. A group of land defenders called the Apache Stronghold is on the frontlines of that fight, which as of this writing is potentially headed to the US Supreme Court.

These days, water is one of the region's most prized resources since it's in such short supply due to human development and climate change. The Colorado River—which powers electric grids, irrigates farmland, and supplies drinking water for some forty million people—is the poster child for this crisis. In 2023, the Navajo Nation took its battle centered on the vital waterway to the US Supreme Court, which ruled that the federal government isn't required to ensure the tribe's water access—setting a dangerous precedent. Unfortunately, it looks like we're headed toward a future where water is a luxury rather than a right.

Despite these ongoing issues, the Native peoples of the region are resilient as ever. That's because their well-adapted lifeways and foodways are guided by ancestral wisdom and traditional ecological knowledge that's been passed down from generation to generation since the dawn of time.

THE HISTORY

Before those fossilized footprints at New Mexico's White Sands National Park upended previous theories about Indigenous peoples, archeologists and historians thought that Native groups began inhabiting this area around 7000 BCE, likely in pursuit of giant Ice Age animals. Those ancient tribal communities hunted, foraged, and farmed, eventually establishing settlements centered around their agricultural enterprises. Corn arrived from Mesoamerica some four thousand years ago, giving rise to a maize-based economy.

The Ancestral Puebloans (also called the Anasazi), Hohokam, and Mogollon were the three main Indigenous cultures that had emerged by 2000 BCE. The region is marked with clear evidence of their existence in the form of artifacts, ancient civilization ruins, and rock art painted and pecked onto the rugged landscape. They lived in subterranean pit houses and sophisticated villages situated in canyons and cliffsides.

These early Native peoples were innovative horticulturalists and developed complex canal systems to irrigate their desert crops, like the three sisters of corn, beans, and squash. They also had extensive trade networks that connected countless communities. Over time, some of them abandoned their villages, likely due to drought conditions and intertribal conflict. Many of the region's modern-day tribal nations can be traced back to these three groups.

Millennia ago, the Apache and Diné (Navajo) migrated from the Athabascan homelands in what's now Alaska and Canada, quickly developing a prominent presence in the Southwest. Known for their power and prowess, both tribes hunted and foraged for sustenance, raided other Indigenous communities, and eventually adopted some agrarian practices from their Pueblo neighbors. Because they followed the seasonality of the land's abundance, they lived in more temporary dwellings, such as hogans (often east-facing homes made from wood and covered in packed mud) and wickiups (dome-shaped shelters made from saplings, brush, and grass).

The Yaqui—who have been called the "only unconquered Indians in America"—once occupied a vast territory ranging from Northern Mexico into the Southwestern United States. Their dozens of villages dotted the coastline, the mountains, the desert, and the banks of their namesake river. Like many regional tribes, they depended on hunting, gathering, and farming for sustenance.

Life was forever changed for these Indigenous groups when the Spanish invaded the area in the early to mid 1500s. Having colonized parts of the Caribbean, Central America, and South America, they turned their attention to Mexico in pursuit of more resources to exploit—namely gold, silver, and Native workers. After overpowering the Aztec empire in 1521, conquistadors eventually worked their way northward looking for the fabled Seven Cities of Gold. The discovery of silver deposits in Northern Mexico prompted the development of mining towns and the expansion of Indigenous slavery. (For more on the colonization of Mexico, read Mesoamerican Highlands and Pacific Coast: Central Mexico, page 214.)

The Yaqui fiercely defended their territory and even led a rebellion against the Spanish, which in turn prompted extermination attempts. Of the once vast population, many people were either killed or captured and then forced into indentured servitude alongside enslaved Black people in Southern Mexico. Survivors dispersed across their ancestral homelands, which is why there are small Yaqui communities scattered across the region (though most live in the Mexican states of Sonora and Sinaloa). Just as they once fiercely defended their territory, they now fiercely defend their namesake river.

The first Spanish expeditions into what's now the American Southwest in the 1540s yielded few riches, incited deadly brawls, spread infectious diseases, and introduced cattle, sheep, goats, and European horses to the area. Conquistadors were deterred for several decades until the late sixteenth century, when the Roman Catholic church insisted upon expanding its reach into the region. To meet this demand, the Spanish established settlements like Santa Fe, New Mexico (the country's oldest capital city), in the early 1600s.

Despite these ongoing issues, the Native peoples of the region are resilient as ever.

In the ensuing decades, Spaniards built numerous missions, converting thousands of Native individuals to Catholicism and pushing them into the encomienda forced-labor system. Tribal groups resisted, organizing uprisings like the Pueblo Revolt of 1680, which drove Europeans out of northern New Mexico for nearly twelve years. To appease their wards upon their return, the Spanish made more than twenty land grants to Pueblo villages, which are some of the country's oldest continuously inhabited communities. Today, there are nineteen Pueblo tribes in New Mexico.

A former faction of the Shoshone, the Comanche migrated from the Great Plains into the Southwest by the early 1700s and established a territory known as Comancheria that spanned some 250,000 square miles across Texas, New Mexico, Colorado, western Oklahoma, and Kansas. To protect their empire from European encroachment, they destroyed Spanish ranches, farms, and food systems and also led raids into Northern Mexico. The destruction drove many people out of the countryside, which left vast portions of those northern states sparsely populated.

In 1821, Mexico gained independence from Spain, only to be overtaken by the nascent United States in the Mexican-American War (1846–1848). The 1848 Treaty of Guadalupe Hidalgo established

the Rio Grande as the US-Mexico border, adding about 525,000 square miles to the United States (including California, Nevada, Utah, New Mexico, most of Arizona and Colorado, and parts of Oklahoma, Kansas, and Wyoming). For Indigenous groups, this arbitrary boundary cut off access to their traditional territories, including important hunting and gathering grounds.

Particularly puzzling to the US government was how to handle the Pueblo peoples, who had been Mexican citizens and were considered "half-civilized" due to their robust adobe settlements, agrarian lifestyle, and stable political structure. Although Congress confirmed their Spanish land grants in 1854, the federal government didn't protect that land from claims by private settlers and corporations until 1913, when the Pueblo were recognized as Indians and given federal protections. The Pueblo Lands Act of 1924 sought to rectify the situation by restoring their land rights.

American settlers descended upon the Southwest after its annexation, driven in large part by the California Gold Rush. Indigenous groups like the Apache and Navajo fought back, prompting the US Army to attack with full force. One of the vilest acts was the 1863 scorched-earth campaign against the Navajo, including the systematic destruction of villages, farm fields, livestock, and water sources. Upon surrendering, thousands of Navajo were forced to march more than three hundred miles to Bosque Redondo in what's known as the Long Walk—not unlike the Trail of Tears in the Southeastern Woodlands. In total, around ten thousand Navajo and five hundred Mescalero Apache people made the trek, with thousands dying along the way and during their four-year internment due to starvation and disease.

Colonizers not only separated the Indigenous prisoners from their ancestral homelands and their traditional foods but also prohibited them from practicing their ceremonies, speaking their language, or otherwise honoring their culture. For subsistence, detainees received meager rations of foreign foods like white flour, lard, sugar, salt, baking powder, dried milk, coffee beans, and small amounts of often rancid beef and pork. According to Navajo stories, Bosque Redondo captives used those ingredients to invent frybread—which has become a simultaneous symbol of Indigenous oppression, ingenuity, and resilience.

Although some people escaped, the imprisonment officially ended with the signing of the Navajo Treaty of 1868 that recognized the tribal nation's sovereignty while relegating them to a much smaller portion of their ancestral homelands. The legacy of the Long Walk is still palpable on the Navajo Nation, which is the largest reservation in the United States, spanning more than 27,000 square miles across portions of Arizona, New Mexico, and Utah.

The defiance of the Apache is also legendary. They had long safeguarded their ancestral homelands from encroachment, which was heightened after the Mexican-American War. That kicked off the Apache Wars, a two-decade period of guerilla warfare protesting incursion, subjugation, and forced removal to reservations. US forces were outwitted time and again by a much smaller Apache force led by the likes of Cochise, Mangas Coloradas, and Geronimo. Although he eluded capture for twenty-five years, Geronimo eventually surrendered in 1886, signaling the overall surrender of the Apache people.

These examples highlight the determined resistance of the region's Native groups, many of whom would sign treaties that relocated them to reservations but also reaffirmed their water rights as well as hunting and gathering rights on parts of their traditional territories. In the centuries that followed, area tribal nations faced ongoing oppression, including broken promises and forced assimilation. Indeed, the Southwest was once the site of the more than one hundred Indian boarding schools—among the most in the United States—designed to replace Indigenous knowledge with Western teachings.

Despite the American campaign for coast-to-coast dominance, Arizona and New Mexico weren't admitted to the union until 1912 (the newest states save for Alaska and Hawaii), probably because of the area's complex history. Today, the tribal communities of the Southwest account for more than 20 percent of the nation's Native population—which is why their rich and vibrant cultures permeate the region and imbue any experience there.

THE FOOD

I've learned so much from my peers who live in these desert lands and carry on the traditions of their ancestors while also adapting to their ever-evolving environs. It might seem counterintuitive that this arid climate yields so much natural bounty, but the landscape's abundance is apparent once you learn to recognize the foods all around you.

The Native peoples of the region have a millennia-old appreciation for wild foods, including all kinds of cactus—including cholla, saguaro, and prickly pear (also known as nopal), as well as mesquite beans, acorns, pinyon nuts, seeds, agaves, mescals, onions, herbs, greens, and fruits like currants, chokecherries, gooseberries, squawberries, wolfberries, juniper berries, and sumac berries.

Traditionally, area tribes relied on plants for much of their protein, but they have also long hunted wild game such as deer, elk, bighorn sheep, antelope, rabbit, prairie dog, and javelina (wild boar), as well as birds like turkey, quail, and dove. Some Indigenous groups, like the

Zuni, relished cicadas and other insects. In Northern Mexico, food systems also feature toads, snakes, iguanas, and armadillos (thought to have medicinal properties, like treating respiratory ailments). Those who live along the sea and inland waterways harvest many types of fish and shellfish to this day. Depending on their toughness, these meats are often grilled, roasted, slow-cooked, stewed, or dried.

Of course, agriculture plays a huge role for these communities, especially the Pueblo. They historically cultivated foods such as corn, tepary beans, squash, pumpkins, chiles, tomatoes, and more. The Spanish ushered in crops like wheat, melons, and stone fruit as well as livestock like cattle, chickens, goats, and sheep (from which the notable Navajo-Churro breed descended). Europeans presented wheat as a superior grain to corn, so it soon started appearing in traditional foods like tortillas.

Along the US-Mexico border, there began to emerge what Xicana culinary anthropologist Claudia Serrato calls culinary mestizaje: fusion foods with Indigenous, European, and African influences. The most prominent example is Tex-Mex, which was once thought of as bastardized Northern Mexico food but really is a cuisine all its own, characterized by mild heat, smoky flavors, and copious amounts of cheese. Although Tejano people (Texans of mixed-race descent) take great pride in Tex-Mex, it's also a prime case of Indigenous erasure, since its Native origins aren't really acknowledged. The cuisine's foundation of corn, beans, and chiles clearly points to its roots in Mesoamerican foodways.

As for so many Native communities across Turtle Island, corn remains an absolute cornerstone of regional diets. The many varieties grown in the desert lands get made into endless foods, including tortillas, tamales, pozole, soups, piki bread, and atole (a hot masa-based beverage with Mexican origins), to name a few. In this chapter's recipes, blue corn gets made into Blue Corn Pozole Verde with Crisped Rabbit (page 208), while masa is made into tamales with aromatic mesquite flour and a savory bean filling (see page 200).

Coming in all shapes, sizes, and colors, cultivated chiles also factor heavily into these foodways—and even double as decor. People mistakenly associate peppers solely with heat due to their capsaicin content, but in reality these fruits can lend sweet, smoky, earthy, and tangy elements to sauces, salsas, and other dishes. In the recipes that follow, you'll find them flavoring foods like Elk Sausage with Chiles (page 207) and even a glaze that tops a Sweet Tepary Bean Cake (page 212).

During my visits to the region, I've noticed people routinely using wood ash in their cooking—a tradition dating back millennia. Juniper ash, for instance, imparts foods like Hopi piki bread and Navajo blue corn mush with important minerals like calcium, magnesium, sodium, potassium, and phosphorus while also unlocking the niacin in corn through the nixtamalization process.

Felicia Cocotzin Ruiz points out that while the traditional cooking methods—in baskets, in clay pots, underground—vary across peoples and places, they all carry the energy of the land. She thinks that's one of the most crucial components in any dish, which is why as a curandera (traditional healer) she helps people find their way home via food—something she herself has done, too. After her own family's displacement and disconnection, she learned in her early forties that she belongs to the tobacco and corn clans. Now, she carries those medicines with her whenever she travels as an amulet of sorts.

Even though they certainly honor tradition, these foodways aren't stuck in the past. That's thanks to people like chef Justin Pioche, who along with his sister, Tia, and mother, Janice, is honoring his Diné (Navajo) heritage with modern interpretations of Indigenous staples. The James Beard finalist presents his creations—think juniper venison cheeks with potato puree and microgreens—at sell-out pop-up dinners across the Southwest. I was honored to cook alongside

Justin and Tia during my 2023 residency at the James Beard Foundation's dining space in New York City.

The Southwest is also home to lots of Native-owned farms that provide ingredients for Owamni and the Indigenous Food Lab. Ramona Farms in Arizona, for example, is our go-to purveyor for heirloom corn and tepary beans (see page 205 for my Tepary Bean and Squash Chili). Meanwhile, Indigenous-led advocacy groups like Hopi Tutskwa Permaculture, Navajo Ethno-Agriculture, and the Zuni Youth Enrichment Project are passing down traditional ancestral knowledge to the next generation in order to safeguard their connection to both their heritage and their health. That's also a major focus for my friends Thosh Collins (Onk-Akimel O'odham/Wa-zha-zhi/Haudenosaunee) and Chelsey Luger (Anishinaabe/Lakota), who live in the region and founded the grassroots initiative Well for Culture. They're working to restore community health through a return to the ancestral wisdom that once guided our lifeways—important lessons for all of us.

PIKI BREAD: A HOPI STAPLE

In Hopi Lands in northeastern Arizona, women learn to make a melt-in-your-mouth, gossamer bread known as piki. It's a staple dish at ceremonies and celebrations that's been made the same way for centuries, if not millennia, using hand-polished slabs of soapstone handed down through generations.

First the stone slab is set over a hot fire to heat up. Then to make piki, the women combine juniper ash with boiling water and strain the mixture over finely ground blue cornmeal to create a dough. They knead the dough to help make sure all of the cornmeal is well hydrated, then blend it with cool water to form a thin batter. When the batter is ready, they dip their fingers in the batter to quickly and expertly spread it in horizontal bands on the hot stone, starting from the edge of the slab that's farthest away from where they're working. They continue dipping and spreading until they've formed a very thin rectangle that's about the size of the stone.

Within seconds, the edges of the rectangle start to peel up. As the rest of the bread sets, they use their hands to carefully peel the thin layer from the stone. Sometimes, they roll a single layer into a scroll. Other times, they layer a few piki together to fold. The type of celebration often dictates the folding pattern. Before they start working and in between cooking a few piki, they grease the stone with melon seeds, which release their oils, or with bone marrow or sheep brain fat. The resulting bread is pleasingly crisp with a little smokiness from the ash and a distinctive corn flavor.

As they make the piki, the cooks constantly adjust the fire or fill in areas of each piki where the batter looks too thin. While Hopi women make the process look easy, it takes years of practice to properly make piki. It's not a food you can learn to make well from a recipe. Instead, it's best to sit with an expert and practice over and over again.

SUMACADE

makes about 1 quart

Many edible varieties of sumac grow all over Turtle Island and are related to the variety often found in Eastern Mediterranean and Middle Eastern food. When infused, the berries produce a tart lemonade-like drink that can look like tea or have a blush pink color.

- 2 clusters fresh sumac berries or ¼ cup ground dried sumac
- 3 to 4 tablespoons agave syrup or honey
- Ice, for serving

If using fresh sumac berries: Pull apart the berry clusters and discard any large stem pieces. Place in a bowl, cover with fresh water, and agitate them so that any debris falls away. Lift the berries into a colander and rinse some more, then let drain.

Transfer the berries to a large measuring cup or pitcher and use a large spoon to mash them up for 1 minute. Add 4 cups water and let stand for 4 to 8 hours. (The longer it steeps, the stronger it will be.)

Strain the infusion through a fine-mesh sieve or cheesecloth into another pitcher, then stir in 3 tablespoons agave syrup. Taste and add the remaining tablespoon, as needed. Serve over ice.

If using ground dried sumac: In a saucepan, bring 4 cups water to a boil over high heat. Remove from the heat, stir in the ground sumac, and let it steep for about 20 minutes.

Proceed with the same straining, sweetening, and serving instructions here.

Cover and refrigerate the sumacade for up to 2 days.

ATOLE DE PINOLE AND PINYON DESERT GRANOLA

serves 4

Pinole is a toasted cornmeal that's often made into a drink or porridge known as atole. You sometimes see it in the Southwest and Mexico seasoned with cacao or cinnamon. Here, I make it into a comforting porridge with sunflower milk, letting its toasted corn flavor shine, and serve it with a seedy granola flavored with sweet toasty mesquite flour.

GRANOLA

- 1/3 cup pepitas
- 1/3 cup sunflower seeds
- 1/3 cup pinyon pine nuts (see page 324)
- 2 tablespoons mesquite flour
- 2 tablespoons Popped Amaranth (page 37; from 1½ teaspoons dried)
- 1/4 cup agave syrup
- 1/2 teaspoon fine sea salt

PINOLE

- 1/2 cup pinole
- 4 cups sunflower milk or other seed or nut milk of choice (see page 35)
- 1/4 cup agave syrup
- 1/2 teaspoon sea salt

Make the granola: Preheat the oven to 250°F. Line a baking sheet with parchment paper.

In a bowl, toss together the pepitas, sunflower seeds, pinyon, mesquite flour, popped amaranth, agave syrup, and salt until evenly coated. Spread the mixture on the baking sheet in a single layer.

Bake for 30 to 40 minutes, stirring every 10 to 15 minutes (with a greased spatula), until the mixture is lightly browned and toasted. (It's okay if it's still a little wet. It will dry as it cools.) Let cool and break into clumps. (You'll have a heaping cup.)

Make the pinole: In a liquid measuring cup, whisk together the pinole and 1 cup water.

In a medium saucepan, whisk together the sunflower milk, agave syrup, and salt and bring to a boil over medium-high heat. Whisk in the pinole mixture, reduce the heat to medium-low, and cook for 5 to 10 minutes, stirring frequently, being sure to scrape the bottom of the pot, until you have a porridge.

Serve with the granola.

DESERT GREENS

WITH QUICK-PICKLED WOLFBERRIES, DESERT FLOWERS, AND POPPED AMARANTH

serves 4

People often think very few plants grow in the desert, but that couldn't be further from the truth. You just have to know where and when to look, a kind of knowledge that Indigenous communities have developed and passed on for millennia. This salad showcases some of the abundance available in a desert spring, such as lamb's quarters, purslane, and amaranth greens, but you can use this recipe to feature wild greens from your area. It includes chewy, sweet-tart dried wolfberries, which I pickle lightly with chile to make them plump and juicy. They are closely related to goji berries so you could use them as a substitute. Popped amaranth seeds add a bit of crunch.

If there are any available, I also like to add some desert blooms to the salad, such as the pleasingly bitter white yucca blossoms or the juicy young petals from a prickly pear cactus flower bud.

- ⅓ cup dried wolfberries or goji berries
- 2 tablespoons agave syrup
- 2 tablespoons cider vinegar
- 1 dried chile de árbol
- Fine sea salt
- 1 large prickly pear flower bud or 8 yucca blossoms (optional)
- 6 cups wild baby greens, such as lamb's quarters, purslane, or amaranth
- 3 tablespoons sunflower oil
- ½ cup Popped Amaranth (page 37; from 2 tablespoons dried)

In a small saucepan, combine the wolfberries, agave syrup, vinegar, ½ cup water, the chile, and ¼ teaspoon salt. Bring to a boil over medium-high heat, then reduce the heat to low and simmer gently for about 4 minutes, or until this pickling liquid has reduced by half. Let cool completely. Reserving the pickling liquid, drain the berries.

Pull apart the prickly pear flower bud or yucca flowers, if using, then discard the center stamens and pistils, reserving the petals for the salad.

In a large bowl, combine the greens, flower petals, pickled berries, and 1 tablespoon of the pickling liquid and season with salt. Drizzle with the oil and toss to coat evenly. Sprinkle with popped amaranth and serve.

Note: *Save the remaining pickling liquid for use in future salad dressings, if you like.*

MESQUITE TAMALES
WITH TEPARY BEANS AND GREEN CHILE

makes 12 tamales

Mesquite flour brings an intriguing roasty sweetness to these plant-based tamales, filled with savory mashed tepary beans, which are native to the desert and grow well in dry climates. They come in several colors, from black to brown to white, and tend to take longer to cook than other beans, finishing with a meaty flavor. (You may use black or pinto beans as a substitute.) You can serve these for breakfast alongside scrambled eggs and your favorite salsa. (The Salsa Macha, page 226, or the Nopales Salsa, page 204, are especially good with these.)

FILLING

- ½ cup dried tepary beans (any color), soaked overnight and drained
- 2 garlic cloves, smashed
- 2 tablespoons sunflower oil or melted animal fat
- 1 teaspoon ancho chile powder
- ½ teaspoon dried epazote or oregano
- Sea salt
- 1 large poblano chile

TAMALES

- 2 pounds Fresh Masa (page 28) or use masa harina (see chart, page 27)
- ¾ cup mesquite flour
- 2 cups warm vegetable broth or water
- ¼ cup sunflower oil or melted animal fat
- 1 teaspoon fine sea salt
- 12 dried corn husks, soaked for at least 4 hours, plus more for steaming
- Salsa of your choice, for serving

Make the filling: In a large saucepan, combine the soaked beans, garlic, and water to cover by 2 inches. Bring to a boil over medium-high heat. Reduce the heat to medium or medium-low and cook for 1½ to 2 hours, until the beans are tender. Add water as needed to keep the beans well covered. Reserving ½ cup of the bean cooking liquid, drain the beans.

In the same saucepan, heat the oil over medium heat until shimmering. Add the chile powder and epazote and toast for 10 seconds, until fragrant. Stir in the drained beans and reserved cooking liquid. Using an immersion blender, pulse the mixture into a coarse mash, then taste and season with salt.

Light a gas flame or a grill to medium-high heat or preheat your oven's broiler. Char the poblano directly over the flame or grill or under the broiler for about 10 to 15 minutes, turning frequently, until blackened all over.

Transfer to a bowl, cover with another bowl or plate, and let stand for 10 minutes to steam. Uncover the poblano and rub off the skin. Remove the stem and seed cluster from the chile and cut the chile into 12 strips, scraping away any stray seeds.

Make the tamales: In a stand mixer fitted with the paddle, combine the masa, mesquite flour, 1½ cups of the broth, the oil, and salt. Beat on medium speed for about 5 minutes, until fluffy. Start adding the remaining ½ cup of broth, 1 tablespoon at a time, until you have a soft, slightly tacky dough. Add a little more liquid if the dough feels too thick or dry.

Arrange 1 soaked corn husk on a work surface with the narrow end pointing away from you and the ribbed side down. Using a ⅓-cup measure, scoop the dough into the center of a corn husk. Use a large rounded spoon to create a well in the dough. Spoon 2 tablespoons of the bean mash into the well. Top the filling with a strip of poblano.

Fold in the long sides of the husk, overlapping them to enclose the filling. Fold the narrow end toward you, over the tamal; it will remain open at the wide end. Stand the tamal, open-end up, in a very large steamer insert. Repeat with the remaining corn husks, masa, bean filling, and poblano strips.

Arrange the 12 tamales so they're standing open-side up in a steamer basket. Place any other corn husks or parchment paper over the tamales to keep the steam close.

Fill the steamer pot with a couple inches of water (just below the steamer basket) and bring to a boil over medium-high heat. Reduce the heat to low. Cover the steamer with a lid and steam the tamales for 1½ hours, checking to maintain the water level as needed. Remove one of the tamales from the steamer. If it feels firm, check inside it. If it looks shiny and wet or you see a lot of residue sticking to the husk when you pull it away, continue cooking for up to 30 minutes longer. Otherwise, remove all the tamales from the steamer and let cool for 15 minutes. The masa will continue to firm up during this time.

Serve warm, with salsa.

CASSAVA FLOUR TOSTADAS
WITH NOPALES SALSA, CRICKETS, AND OCOTILLO BLOSSOMS

makes 8 tostadas

Cassava flour, made from the yuca root, creates beautiful tortillas. When soft, cassava tortillas are flexible like flour tortillas but are a little more chewy. When fried for tostadas, as they are here, they become gorgeously crisp, almost shattering when you bite into them.

Nopales are a hydrating superfood—perfect for eating in the desert. For an extra hit of protein, I top these with fried crickets, but you could use sunflower seeds instead.

I like to add the tangy ocotillo blooms when I can find them. They're in season in the spring, and you can sometimes source them from Mexican markets.

TORTILLAS

- 1½ cups cassava flour
- ½ teaspoon fine sea salt
- ¼ cup sunflower oil
- ¾ cup warm water, plus more as needed

TOSTADAS

- Sunflower oil, for frying
- Fine sea salt
- Nopales Salsa (page 204)
- 1 cup roasted crickets or toasted sunflower seeds (or a mixture of both)
- ½ cup ocotillo blossoms or other edible dessert blooms (optional)

Make the tortilla dough: In a bowl, stir together the cassava flour and salt. Stir in the oil and warm water, mixing until no dry spots remain. Knead to form a dough.

Divide the dough into 8 equal portions and roll each piece into a ball. Place a ball between two sheets of parchment paper. Using a tortilla press or a rolling pin, press or roll out a round that's ⅛ inch thick and about 5 inches in diameter.

Heat a dry cast-iron skillet over medium-high heat. Cook each tortilla for about 1 minute on each side, until both sides are dry to the touch. Wrap the tortillas in a towel and when they're cool, place them in an airtight bag or container and refrigerate for at least 1 hour, and up to overnight.

Assemble the tostadas: When ready to assemble, set a wire rack over a baking sheet or a sheet of parchment paper and place near the stove.

Pour a ½ inch of oil into a cast-iron skillet and heat over medium heat to about 350°F.

One by one, carefully add the tortillas and fry for about 1 minute, turning once, until golden and blistered on both sides, adding more oil as needed. Transfer them to the rack as you work and season with salt.

When all of the tostadas have cooled, top each one with some of the salsa. Sprinkle with the crickets and the ocotillo blossoms (if using) and serve.

(recipe continues)

NOPALES SALSA

makes about 3 cups

- 3 medium nopales (prickly pear cactus paddles), trimmed
- Sunflower oil, for brushing
- Sea salt
- 1 small white onion, cut into quarters
- 4 medium tomatillos, husked
- ¼ cup culantro or cilantro leaves

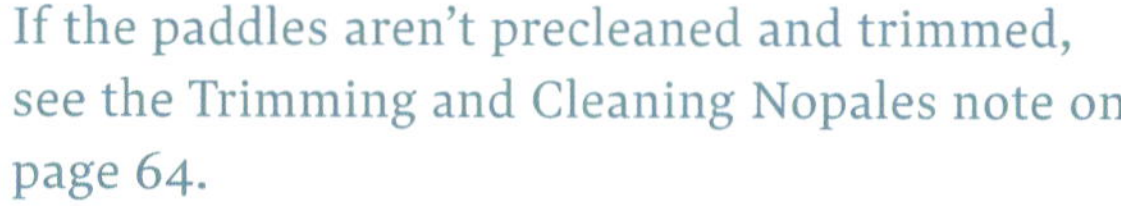

If the paddles aren't precleaned and trimmed, see the Trimming and Cleaning Nopales note on page 64.

Rinse the paddles under cold water and pat dry.

Preheat a grill, grill pan, or cast-iron skillet over high heat. For easier cleanup, you can line your pan with foil first.

Brush the nopales with oil and season with salt. Working in batches, cook the nopales for 8 to 10 minutes, turning frequently, until tender. Transfer to a work surface, cut into strips, and transfer to a bowl.

Using the same grill or pan, cook the onion quarters over high heat, turning frequently, until charred. Remove any of the root ends, as needed, then transfer to a food processor.

Grill or cook the whole tomatillos on all sides until partially blackened, then transfer to a bowl. Cover with another bowl to steam for a few minutes, then discard the skins and place the tomatillos in the food processor.

Add the culantro to the food processor and pulse until the mixture is finely chopped. Add a bit of water if this salsa base seems dry. Transfer to the bowl with the nopales and stir to blend well. Taste and season with salt.

TEPARY BEAN AND SQUASH CHILI

serves 4

Native to the desert lands, tepary beans are drought-tolerant and have a dense, almost meaty texture. Even when soaked, they can take a bit longer to cook than common beans.

Here, I cook them into a chili made with roasted poblanos and dried New Mexico chiles. Squash brings some welcome sweetness and the mesquite flour helps thicken it further. You can serve the chili as is, or top it with Elk Sausage (page 207).

- 1 cup dried tepary beans, soaked overnight and drained
- 1 large onion, halved, and one of the halves chopped
- 4 large garlic cloves, 2 smashed and 2 thinly sliced
- Sea salt
- 1 large poblano chile
- 2 dried New Mexico chiles
- 2 cups vegetable broth
- 3 tablespoons sunflower oil
- 2 cups diced peeled winter squash
- 1 tablespoon mesquite flour
- 1 teaspoon dried Mexican oregano
- ½ teaspoon smoked paprika
- 2 tablespoons cider vinegar
- Elk Sausage with Chiles (optional; page 207), crumbled, for serving
- Finely chopped greens, such as culantro leaves or wild onion or scallion greens

In a large pot, combine the soaked beans, onion half, the 2 smashed garlic cloves, and water to cover by 2 inches. Bring to a boil over high heat. Reduce the heat to medium-low and cook the beans for 1½ to 2 hours, until tender. Add more water as needed to keep them well covered. Remove from the heat, season with salt, and let stand for at least 20 minutes to absorb the seasoning. Reserving 2 cups of the cooking liquid, drain the beans.

Light a gas flame or a grill to medium-high heat or preheat your oven's broiler. Char the poblano directly over the flame or grill under the broiler for 10 to 15 minutes, turning frequently, until blackened all over. Transfer to a bowl, cover with another bowl or plate, and let stand for 10 minutes to steam.

Meanwhile, over the burner or grill, use tongs to hold the dried chiles above the flame and toast them for about 2 minutes turning, until warm and fragrant. (Alternatively, you can toast them in a dry skillet.) Let cool slightly.

Using scissors, snip off the stems of the dried chiles. If you want to reduce the chiles' heat and bitterness, shake out the seeds. Transfer the dried chiles to a small pot and add the broth. Bring to a boil over high heat. Remove from the heat and let stand for about 30 minutes, until the chiles are very soft. Transfer the dried chiles and broth to a blender.

Meanwhile, uncover the poblano and use your hands to pull off and discard the skin. It should slip right off. Remove the stem, open up the poblano, and scrape out the seeds.

Cut the poblano into strips and transfer half of them to the blender. Puree with the dried chiles and liquid until smooth. Set the chile liquid and poblano strips aside.

Wipe out the large pot (used to cook the beans) and warm the sunflower oil over medium heat. Add the chopped onion and the sliced garlic, season with salt, and cook for about 8 minutes, stirring occasionally, until the onion is translucent. Add the diced squash and mesquite flour and stir to coat evenly.

(recipe continues)

Add the drained beans, their reserved cooking liquid, the chile liquid, poblano strips, oregano, and smoked paprika. Bring to a boil over medium-high heat. Reduce the heat to medium-low and simmer for 20 to 30 minutes, until the squash is tender and the chili is thick and flavorful.

Stir in the vinegar and cook for 3 minutes longer, to let the flavors meld. Taste, and season with more salt as needed.

Serve, topped with the elk sausage, if desired, and the greens.

ELK SAUSAGE WITH CHILES

makes 1½ pounds

Inspired by Mexican-style chorizo, I created this loose sausage blend you can serve over the Tepary Bean and Squash Chili (page 205), in tacos, or really anywhere you want a burst of savory flavor. If you can't find ground elk, you can use ground venison or bison.

- 2 tablespoons sweet paprika
- 1 tablespoon ancho chile powder
- 1 tablespoon guajillo chile powder
- 1 tablespoon garlic powder
- 1 tablespoon onion powder
- ½ to 1 teaspoon cayenne pepper
- 1 teaspoon dried Mexican oregano
- 1 teaspoon fine sea salt
- ½ teaspoon ground allspice
- 1½ pounds ground elk meat
- 2 tablespoons cider vinegar
- 2 tablespoons sunflower oil

In a large bowl, stir together the sweet paprika, ancho powder, guajillo powder, garlic powder, onion powder, cayenne, oregano, salt, and allspice. Add the elk meat and vinegar and mix until well combined.

In a large skillet, heat the oil over medium-high heat until shimmering. Cook a small spoonful of the sausage mixture and taste; season the mixture with more salt, if desired. Add the sausage mixture to the pan and cook for about 5 minutes, using a wooden spoon to break it up into crumbles, until cooked through.

Note: *Alternatively, you can form the sausage meat into patties and cook them for a few minutes on each side.*

BLUE CORN POZOLE VERDE
WITH CRISPED RABBIT

serves 4

Pozole is a word for both nixtamalized corn kernels as well as a chunky soup made with them. This version includes a rabbit and tomatillo-based broth that gets a spicy kick from roasted green chiles. While you can use canned hominy, it will be infinitely better if you start with dried pozole that you soak and boil . . . or even better, if you start with dried blue corn and nixtamalize it yourself; blue corn tends to have a deeper, more complex flavor than other types of corn.

The method, however, takes several hours, so you'll need to plan ahead.

RABBIT

- 1 whole rabbit (2½ pounds)
- 1 medium yellow onion, halved
- 2 jalapeños, stemmed, halved, and seeded
- Sea salt
- 1 teaspoon dried sagebrush
- 1 tablespoon agave syrup

POZOLE

- 1 large yellow onion, cut into 8 wedges
- 1 head garlic, halved through the equator
- 1 pound tomatillos, husked and halved
- 2 large poblano chiles, stemmed, seeded, and cut lengthwise into quarters
- 2 jalapeños or serrano chiles, stemmed, seeded, and halved lengthwise
- 4 tablespoons sunflower oil
- Sea salt
- ¼ cup pepitas
- 1 teaspoon dried epazote
- 1 teaspoon dried Mexican oregano
- 1 cup dried blue corn, nixtamalized and cooked (see page 26) or 3 cups cooked hominy
- Ground sumac (optional)
- Diced avocado, for serving

Prepare the rabbit: In a large pot, combine the rabbit, onion, jalapeños, and water to cover by 1 inch. Season generously with salt and add the dried sagebrush and agave syrup. Bring to a boil over high heat. Reduce the heat to medium-low and cook for about 1½ hours, or until the meat easily separates from the bone. Transfer the rabbit to a bowl and let cool.

Strain and reserve the rabbit broth. Ideally, you have at least 6 cups. If you have less, you can supplement it with vegetable broth or water.

When the meat is cool enough to handle, pull the meat from the bones, removing all of the tiny bones. Cover and reserve the meat until you're ready to serve or refrigerate for up to 2 days.

Make the pozole: Preheat the oven to 400°F. Line a baking sheet with parchment paper, if desired.

On the baking sheet, toss the onion, garlic halves, tomatillos, poblanos, and jalapeños with 2 tablespoons of the oil, season with salt, and toss to coat evenly. Arrange the tomatillos and chiles skin-sides up. Roast for about 25 minutes, or until the skins of the poblanos and tomatillos are wrinkly and blistered in spots and the garlic and onion are softened. Keep the oven on at 400°F.

Transfer the roasted vegetables to a blender, squeezing the garlic cloves out of the papery skins. Add the pepitas, epazote, Mexican oregano, and 2 cups of the rabbit broth and puree until smooth.

Transfer the puree to a large pot and add 4 more cups of the broth. Add the corn and cook for about 20 minutes, stirring, until the corn is tender and the flavors meld. Season with more salt as needed.

Meanwhile, as the pozole cooks, toss the pulled rabbit meat with the remaining 2 tablespoons of oil and spread it out on a baking sheet. Roast the meat for 15 to 20 minutes, until it starts to dry out and crisp up. Taste and season with more salt and a bit of sumac, if desired.

Serve the pozole topped with crisped rabbit meat and diced avocado.

JAVELINA Y NOPALES TACOS

serves 4 to 6

Javelina is a peccary—a type of wild pig native to the desert Southwest and Mexico. When I'm focusing on foods native to Turtle Island, I like to use it in place of pork.

People in the region hunt the animals, and there are now also invasive species of wild boar that people hunt throughout the region, too.

For these tacos, we marinate javelina shoulder (you can also substitute wild boar) in vinegar, agave syrup, and pungent epazote, an herb popular in Mexico with an appealing earthy scent. Then we braise it with aromatics and shred the tender meat. A "slaw" of tangy grilled nopales completes the taco with its bright flavor, so there's no need for lime.

While this recipe calls for shoulder meat, if you happen to be handling a whole javelina, it's important to remove its scent gland in the center of its lower back. The animals use this gland to mark their territory and they can stink, like a skunk. When accidentally pierced, the gland can taint the meat.

JAVELINA

- 2 tablespoons cider vinegar
- 2 tablespoons agave syrup
- 1½ teaspoons dried epazote
- 2 pounds javelina or wild boar shoulder meat, cut into 4 chunks
- Sea salt
- 1 yellow onion, halved
- 1 head garlic, halved through the equator
- 2 jalapeños, stemmed, seeded if desired, and halved lengthwise

SLAW

- 2 nopales (prickly pear cactus paddles), about 5 ounces each (before cleaning)
- 2 tablespoons sunflower oil, plus more for brushing
- Sea salt
- 1 to 2 jalapeños, stemmed, seeded if desired, and finely chopped
- 1 tablespoon cider vinegar
- 2 teaspoons ground sumac

TACOS

- 12 to 16 Corn Tortillas (page 31) or store-bought
- Handful of wild greens, for serving

Prepare the javelina: In an ovenproof pot, combine the cider vinegar, agave syrup, and epazote. Add the javelina and turn to coat, then season the meat with salt. Cover and refrigerate overnight.

The next day, preheat the oven to 250°F.

Cover the meat and marinade with water and add the onion, garlic, and jalapeños to the pot. Bring to a boil over medium-high heat. Cover with a lid, transfer to the oven, and braise for about 6 hours, or until the meat is pull-apart tender.

Transfer the meat to a bowl and reserve some of the cooking liquid. Use two forks to shred the meat. Add a little liquid to help moisten the meat, then taste and season with salt. Keep the meat warm.

Make the slaw: If your paddles aren't precleaned, see the trimming and cleaning note on page 64. Rinse the paddles and pat dry.

Preheat a grill, grill pan, or cast-iron skillet over high heat.

Brush the nopales with a little oil and season with salt. Working in batches as needed, cook the nopales for 8 to 10 minutes, turning frequently, until tender. Transfer to a work surface, cut into strips, then transfer to a bowl.

Add the 2 tablespoons oil, the chopped chiles, vinegar, and sumac to the nopales and toss.

Assemble the tacos: When ready to assemble, if your tortillas aren't fresh, warm them on a comal, griddle, or over a gas flame set at medium heat for about 20 seconds per side. Transfer to a towel and cover to keep warm.

Spoon the shredded meat onto the tortillas and top each with the nopales slaw and wild greens.

SWEET TEPARY BEAN CAKE
WITH GUAJILLO GLAZE

makes one 8-inch cake or 2 small layer cakes

YouTube sensation Dianxi Xiaoge shares dreamy videos about cooking in the Yunnan province of China, often starting with her foraging for ingredients and then processing them in a traditional way. Watching these videos often reminds me of the slow and careful ways our ancestors made our foods. In one video, she shows how she makes a sweet cake out of little more than beans and a sweetener, and I was so inspired.

I've played around with many versions of this over the years, and now I often serve this cake at events. This version makes a fudgy textured cake with a not-too-sweet cocoa glaze that gets a whisper of fruity heat from guajillo chile. You can spread the glaze over the whole cake, or for a prettier presentation, you can bake this cake in a 9-inch pan and use a ring mold to stamp out 2-inch rounds of the cake and glaze between the layers.

CAKE

- Oil, for greasing the pan
- 1¼ cups dried black or brown tepary beans (about 8 ounces)
- 2 cups agave syrup
- ½ teaspoon fine sea salt

GLAZE

- 1 guajillo chile
- ¾ cup agave syrup
- ¼ cup unsweetened cocoa powder
- 2 tablespoons cassava flour
- 1½ teaspoons agar-agar powder
- Cacao nibs, for sprinkling

Make the cake: Preheat the oven to 350°F. Oil an 8-inch round cake pan and line the pan with parchment paper so it overhangs the pan.

In a food processor or high-powered blender, pulse the beans to coarsely chop, then grind them until they resemble a flour. Sift through a fine-mesh sieve to remove any larger gritty chunks. Return any chunks to grind again. (You want 1¼ cups bean flour.)

In a medium saucepan, combine 2 cups water and the agave syrup and bring to a simmer over medium heat. Slowly whisk in the salt and bean flour to form an almost immediately thickened batter.

Scrape the batter into the prepared pan, spreading into an even layer.

Bake for 35 to 45 minutes, until the cake is pulling away from the sides and a toothpick inserted into the center comes out clean. Transfer to a rack to cool completely, then use the parchment to lift the cake out the pan.

Make the glaze: Toast the guajillo in a dry skillet over medium heat for about 30 seconds, turning a few times, until fragrant and pliable. Remove the stem from the chile and shake out and discard the seeds.

In a small saucepan, combine the toasted guajillo, the agave syrup, and ½ cup water. Bring to a boil over medium-high heat. Remove from the heat and let stand for about 15 minutes, or until the chile is very soft and the liquid has cooled a bit.

Transfer the chile with the syrup to a blender and puree until smooth. Add the cocoa powder, cassava flour, and agar-agar and blend to form a thick glaze.

Spread the glaze over the cooled cake and let it run down the sides. Sprinkle with cacoa nibs.

Serve immediately or refrigerate for up to 2 days.

Note: *Alternatively, bake the cake for 25 to 35 minutes in a 9-inch pan and use a ring mold or biscuit cutter to cut out rounds of cake. Make the mini layer cakes with the rounds. Spread the bottom layers with some of the glaze before finishing the top layers with more glaze.*

MESOAMERICAN HIGHLANDS AND PACIFIC COAST

CENTRAL MEXICO

A LIFE-CHANGING SOJOURN TO THIS region was really the impetus for my work to revitalize Native foodways. It was the mid-aughts, and I was feeling totally burned out on chef life, as anyone working in the restaurant industry can probably relate to. I knew I needed to get away, so I set my sights on Mexico's Central Pacific Coast, having vacationed there in the past. I bought a one-way ticket and by happenstance landed in San Pancho. That was a serendipitous twist of fate, because the then-sleepy beach town served as a great gateway to the robust Indigenous cultures of the area—though that's not what originally brought me there.

I hadn't set out on an *Eat Pray Love*-esque excursion in hopes of having some major epiphany; I was really just in need of a break from the nonstop grind of the restaurant world. But as anyone who knows me knows, I don't sit still for very long. Even though I was supposed to be relaxing and decompressing, I soon found myself curious to learn more about the history and the people of this place. (I've always been a bit of a history nerd, so this is what I consider fun.)

As I started reading up and exploring around, I immersed myself in Mesoamerican knowledge and tradition, which allowed me to see Mexico in a completely different light. I shifted my focus beyond what most Americans associate with the country south of the border—tacos and tequila—to learn about the lifeways of peoples like the Cora and Huichol, who would migrate great distances in order to survive off these lands.

A friend of mine loaned me a VW van, and I tooled around to places like Puerto Vallarta, San Blas, Guadalajara, Morelia, Pátzcuaro, and Zihuatanejo. I was still very young at that point and didn't have a set purpose, but I felt such a sense of freedom and really started to see Turtle Island as a whole, and not through a colonial lens. I ended up working on a biodynamic farm run by this American expat, Joaquin, who would take me hiking and identify all these wild plants along the way. He also taught me how to plant seeds and tend to the soil, which really inspired my interest in seed saving.

As I was learning about the area's rich biodiversity, I was also voraciously studying Mexico's history. After all, this is where Spanish colonialism began back in the early 1500s, then spiraled out to devastating effect for Indigenous peoples. Before that, my knowledge was pretty much limited to what I learned in high school, mostly focused on the ancient Aztec and Maya empires.

This fixation on these supposedly "conquered" societies perpetuates the myth that Mesoamerican cultures no longer exist and that instead there's some single pan-Mexican identity. Quite the contrary—today, more than thirty Indigenous communities reside in this part of Mexico alone, including the Amuzgo, Chatino, Chinantec, Chocho, Chontal, Huave, Mazahua, Mazatec, Mexica (Aztec), Mixe, Mixtec, Nahua, Otomí, P'urhépecha, Tepehua, Zapotec, and more.

All told, I spent about a year down there, just living and learning. Over time, this newfound knowledge began to fit together like puzzle pieces in my mind. I can't totally explain it, but at one point while I was exploring the region, I saw the future all in one flash. This big door opened up in my mind; I realized that the Indigenous cultures around me weren't all that different from the Indigenous culture I grew up in, and what I really needed to be doing was focusing on my own heritage. When I returned to the United States, I was a man on a mission, all thanks to that time spent in Central Mexico.

THE LAND

There's much more to Mexico than just beaches. In reality, the country's most dominant geographical feature is the great highland central plateau flanked by the Sierra Madre Occidental and Sierra Madre Oriental. With volcanic origins and an arid to semiarid climate, the Mexican Altiplano is an extension of the tableland north of the US-Mexico border near El Paso, Texas, that stretches all the way south to the Isthmus of Tehuantepec. Like the continent's First Peoples, the topography of Turtle Island knows no borders.

Central Mexico includes all three of the country's altitude-driven climatic zones: the low-lying tierras calientes (hot lands) of the coastlines, the tierras frías (cold lands) of the mountainous areas, and the tierras templadas (temperate lands) of the inlands and valleys in between. As expected, the tierras calientes have a tropical clime with high temperatures and humidity, fostering lush greenery. The aptly titled tierras templadas boast relatively moderate weather and more arid environs; this is where the major cities of Mexico City, Monterrey, and Guadalajara are located. The less densely populated tierras frías, meanwhile, experience real winters and markedly cooler year-round temperatures.

The country has distinct rainy and dry seasons, with total precipitation varying greatly across the central area's diverse landscape of rugged mountains, high desert, rolling hills, deep valleys, vast plains, thick forests, and xeric scrublands. These ecosystems nurture so much plant and animal life that factor heavily in Mesoamerican foodways. The ocean, of course, supplies seafood, while the inlands are replete with deer, rabbit, iguanas, snakes, armadillos, and turkeys, as well as insects from ants to cicadas to maguey worms.

However, animal proteins actually didn't play a huge role in pre-colonial food systems, as my friend Claudia Serrato, a Xicana culinary anthropologist, explains, pointing to the research of historian Rebecca Earle. Rather, many Indigenous communities largely relied on cultivated and foraged flora to meet their nutritional needs. The land has long provided keystone plants including cacti, mushrooms, beans, agave, yucca, squash, chia, amaranth, and tons of wild greens and herbs like chaya, romeritos, hoja santa, chipilín, epazote, and more (collectively known as quelites, which takes its name from the Nahuatl word for "edible plants").

The soil across much of Central Mexico is extremely fertile thanks to the region's volcanic history, but more waterlogged spots have required Indigenous ingenuity to foster agriculture. The Great Valley (also known as Anahuac) was once the catchment for a group of five interlocking lakes upon which many Mesoamerican communities built their settlements. These savvy early horticulturists adapted their lifeways to the landscape, creating canals and developing highly productive "floating" gardens known as chinampas. This innovative method involves building islands in those canals with staked wattle fences and then piling in layers of vegetation, sediment, and dredged nutrient-rich bottom soil. Still in use today, they yield multiple annual harvests of crops like maíz, beans, squash, tomatoes, chile peppers, herbs, and a range of ornamental and edible flowers. In the highlands, meanwhile, Indigenous farmers employ terraces to manage water and avoid soil erosion.

Of course, these earth-friendly approaches stand in stark contrast to the industrial agriculture that now pervades the region. Mexico actually has one of the highest deforestation rates on the planet, with forests and jungles regularly being cleared for livestock ranching and monocrop farming of wheat, sugarcane, corn,

coffee, sorghum, and more. That's particularly troubling since Mexico is considered one of the world's most megadiverse countries, holding 12 percent of global biodiversity in just 1.5 percent of the planet's land surface.

Large-scale farming represents economic opportunity but also environmental disaster amid the current climate crisis, when we should be protecting natural resources rather than exploiting them. Just like parts of the United States, the region is experiencing extreme weather events like droughts, wildfires, and heat waves that are devastating rural communities. Thankfully, the modern-day slow food movement is nurturing a network between the more isolated Indigenous pueblos and championing traditional ecological knowledge at festivals, through workshops, and even on social media.

Mesoamericans are also fighting to protect one of Mexico's most important cultural and culinary assets: maíz. Indigenous farmers have long preserved the country's sixty-some recognized strains (known as landraces) by saving seeds and planting native varieties, but so many issues threaten that diversity, including US/Mexico trade. The Mexican government is safeguarding heirloom maíz by prohibiting GMO corn production and use, but American Big Ag is of course pushing back with an eye on profit. Meanwhile, land defenders have spent decades protecting this national treasure, including the powerful Sin Maíz No Hay País (Without Corn, There Is No Country) campaign that kicked off in the early 2000s and continues on today.

THE HISTORY

There's long been debate about how and when humans began inhabiting Turtle Island, with Western thinking cutting short the timeline outlined in Native oral histories—since time immemorial—based on a lack of "scientific evidence." (Western and Indigenous sciences have often been at odds for this reason, though we're starting to see these two schools of thought converge more and more these days.) Well, some of the latest archeological findings—nearly 2,000 stone tools discovered at Chiquihuite Cave in Central Mexico—show that people inhabited this region up to 33,000 years ago. Of course this sparked even more controversy, but it proves what we already know: Thriving societies have existed on this continent for eons.

Those First Peoples lived off the fruitful land, developing their food systems around hunting, fishing, gathering, and most of all farming. They domesticated maíz from the wild plant teosinte at least 8,500 years ago, likely in the Balsas River Valley of south-central Mexico. From there, this keystone crop made its way along trade routes south to Panama, Colombia, Ecuador, and Uruguay and then eventually north to the United States. Other early Mesoamerican cultivated foods include squash, beans, chile peppers, tomatoes, avocados, and cacao.

This agriculture became the bedrock for Central Mexican Indigenous communities such as the Olmec, Totonac, and Zapotec as well as the Maya, who have long inhabited Southern Mexico and the Yucatán Peninsula. (For more on Maya cultures, turn to Mesoamerican Rainforest and Gulf Coast: Southern Mexico, page 244.) Far from primitive, these sophisticated societies built millennia ago boasted complex settlements with spectacular architecture, organized governments, thriving economies, and extensive networks for trading goods such as salt, ceramics, animal pelts, precious stones—like obsidian, jade, and turquoise—and jewelry made from precious metals, such as gold, silver, and copper.

Other groups eventually made their way there, including the Toltec, who for a time commanded the Central Valley. But the arrival of the Mexica (also known as the Aztec or Tenochca) hugely shaped the area. Migrating from their legendary homeland of Aztlán, likely in what is today the southern United States and/or Northern Mexico, they quickly established their settlement on Lake Texcoco. In a bid for regional domination, the Mexica aligned their capital of Tenochtitlán with the city-states of Texcoco and Tlacopan to form the formidable Aztec Triple Alliance.

Mexico very much became a country all its own, with blended Indigenous and Spanish influences.

That empire was in power for nearly a century before the Spanish arrived. In 1519, conquistador Hernán Cortés and his crew set sail from Cuba and made landfall along the Yucatán coastline. He led a march inland, along the way plundering some communities and forming alliances with others, such as the Tlaxcalan.

When they reached Tenochtitlán, the Spaniards marveled at the exquisite island city's riches, which reaffirmed their mission to pillage this place. Emperor Moctezuma II initially welcomed them but soon became rightly wary. The invaders and their Indigenous allies took him into captivity (where he later died) and began their slaughter of the Mexica, who fought back ferociously but eventually were overcome due to disease, starvation, and violence. All told, an estimated 240,000 Aztec people died during the war that brought down the empire.

Upon the ruins of the razed Tenochtitlán, Cortés began building Mexico City as the capital of New Spain. Hungry for more land, power, and wealth, the Spanish soon pressed south, expanding their rule as far as Guatemala and Honduras. They struggled to overtake the Maya of the Yucatán Peninsula and were slow to expand into Northern Mexico, deterred by its arid environs and assumed lack of resources to exploit (namely labor and precious metals). Indigenous groups in more isolated areas weren't as hard hit by the subjugation and therefore didn't experience the same degree of cultural destruction due to epidemic diseases, widespread displacement, and forced assimilation.

As if on cue after the overthrow of the Aztec Empire, missionaries began arriving, eager to convert Mesoamericans to Catholicism. More and more Spaniards emigrated to Mexico, pushing out its original inhabitants. Settlers tore up the land to grow foreign crops like wheat, barley, sugarcane, oats, alfalfa, and fruits and vegetables. The introduction of domesticated livestock like cattle, sheep, goats, pigs, and chickens spelled environmental disaster. As they continued to spread across the region, explorers discovered silver, gold, and other precious metals, leading to even more land exploitation in addition to the rampant timber industry.

The Spanish pushed as many Indigenous peoples as possible into indentured servitude at mines and haciendas (essentially plantations), but there was still a need for labor, so they imported enslaved peoples from Africa and the Caribbean to help power the new colony's encomienda economy. As these groups began intermingling and intermarrying, the abhorrent casta system emerged with specific categories for mixed-race people. Popularized by paintings of the same name, those rankings determined individuals' social status and rights, and the effects of this horrific hierarchy are still apparent today.

Despite Spain's ongoing attempts to eradicate Mesoamerican cultures during its 300-year rule of this place, Mexico very much became a country all its own, with blended Indigenous and Spanish influences. Over time, its residents grew tired of the rigorous rule of their European overlords, and after more than a decade of attempted revolts, Mexico gained its independence in 1821. Unsurprisingly, early rallying cries for racial equality and the redistribution of land went unfulfilled in the aftermath of that emancipation.

The nascent Mexican government remained relatively unstable leading up to the Mexican-American War (1846–1848), which resulted in the United States annexing a huge chunk of land stretching from the Rio Grande River in Texas all the way to the Pacific Ocean. For more than three decades starting in 1876, Porfirio Díaz presided over the country as a dictator. Despite his humble upbringing in Oaxaca as a mestizo of mixed Mixtec and Spanish ancestry, he limited freedoms and oppressed lower class and Indigenous communities to benefit the wealthy elite. Rising political tensions preceded the Mexican Revolution (1910–1920), a bloody civil war in which 900,000 people died. It also ultimately led to the creation of a constitution, which recognized Indigenous groups' rights to communal lands known as ejidos.

During the revolt, thousands of Mexicans made their way to US border states like California and Texas to pursue economic opportunity and escape ongoing violence and volatility. Although Mexico eventually found greater political stability in the ensuing decades thanks to a focus on (oft-destructive) industrial development, crime and corruption have continued to run rampant.

A second migration surge into the United States happened during the Mexico oil bust and economic crisis of the 1980s. That prompted the Immigration Reform and Control Act of 1986, which granted an estimated 2.3 million Mexicans legal permanent residence. The Indigenous peoples who made the treacherous trek brought with them their rich cultures and created large expat communities in places like Los Angeles and Houston. Although the US border has become increasingly militarized in recent years, people from Mesoamerica are still migrating into the United States due to worsening poverty, violence, and environmental issues in their home country.

As to be expected, shifting US/Mexico relations have had ongoing negative impacts on Mesoamericans. The 1994 North American

Free Trade Agreement (NAFTA), in particular, disproportionately devastated rural Indigenous agricultural communities by challenging their communal land rights and undercutting prices for key crops like maíz, beans, and coffee due to an influx of subsidized US products. To expose Mexico's egregious social inequities on an international stage, the Zapatista Army of National Liberation (EZLN) seized several towns for nearly two weeks in the southern state of Chiapas on the same day NAFTA went into effect. Although it took place more than thirty years ago, the uprising has since been credited with advancing democratization and the rights of Indigenous peoples, codified by the San Andrés Accords—and the movement marches on today amid ongoing assaults to Indigenous self-determination.

THE FOOD

Just as it's impossible to encompass all of Mesoamerican history in a single chapter, I can't fully describe the richly diverse foodways of Central Mexico in such a small section. The recipes that follow are inspired by pre-contact techniques and ingredients from the region, eschewing Eurocentric foods like beef, pork, chicken, and dairy—though those foods are very much part of modern Mesoamerican cuisine, as I experienced on a recent trip to Oaxaca. One constant throughout the centuries is maíz, a cornerstone food that works its way into several dishes here (just like it does in Mexico). The Corn Four Ways Tacos (page 229), in particular, really highlight the versatility of this staple, which takes shape as tortillas, dumplings, salsa, and a palate-pleasing popcorn garnish—all on one plate.

To savor Central Mexico flavors in the context of their place, in 2024 I made my way to Oaxaca, where Mixtec and Zapotec cultures are incredibly intact. The central-southern state is considered a stronghold for native corn, with thirty-five different strains actively being grown and conserved by area Indigenous farmers. Home cooks, meanwhile, are upholding traditional masa-making techniques—nixtamalizing and grinding dried heirloom corn to create a dough for tortillas, tamales, and other staples—and wouldn't hear of using the more contemporary masa harina (packaged nixtamalized corn flour).

There's just so much to see, taste, and try in Oaxaca that arouses all the senses. The storied Tlacolula Sunday market, for instance, has an entire section dedicated to barbacoa—tender stewed chiva (goat) or borrego (lamb) that's been pit-roasted underground. Many regions in Mexico have their own distinctive style of barbacoa, a technique that originated with the Taíno people in the Caribbean and moved to Mexico before colonization. The earthen ovens crafted for barbacoa are reminiscent of the pibs the Maya build to cook some of their most iconic dishes (see Mesoamerican Rainforest and Gulf Coast: Southern Mexico, page 244). While absorbing all the vibrancy of the busy market, I devoured a bowlful of the delicacy served with *consomé* (broth) and fresh vegetable garnishes.

I also sipped on a mug of atole, dipping concha sweet bread into this warm, creamy traditional corn beverage, as is customary. It comes in countless variations employing local ingredients, like cacao (see page 270). Another popular Central Mexican drink is pulque, an ancestral alcoholic beverage made from the fermented sap of the maguey plant (agave) and fruits like pineapple.

Back in Oaxaca City, the Mercado 20 de Noviembre's popular Pasillo de Carne Asada is a meat lover's paradise. There, I noshed on DIY tacos made with cecina and tasajo (paper-thin cured beef from different cuts), chorizo, nopales, chopped vegetables, guacamole, and fresh salsa.

At night, Oaxaca City comes alive with artisans, makers, and street food vendors slinging must-try tacos, tortas, and especially tlayudas. Long lines form for these fan-favorite grilled oversize artisan maíz tortillas typically topped with *asiento* (pork lard), refried beans, beef or pork, and strings of the region's famed quesillo. After trying my take made with beans, huitlacoche (corn smut), and optional escamoles (ant larvae) on page 235, I encourage you to tailor this endlessly versatile dish to your liking.

At every opportunity, I tried as many of Oaxaca's storied moles as possible; there are far more than just the seven varieties the Mexican state is known for. Prized family recipes for this famed food—which gets its name from the Nahuatl word for "sauce"—are passed down from generation to generation. Most of us are familiar with mole negro, made with chocolate, but Mesoamerican cooks use all sorts of foraged and cultivated ingredients from their respective homelands—including quelites, onions, tomatoes, peanuts, pepitas, sesame seeds, garlic, herbs, and spices—that imbue each variation with a distinct taste and hue. Making this Central Mexico staple is a labor of love, as ingredients can number in the dozens and cook time in the hours thanks to a long, low simmering period. The vibrant mole pipián (see page 241) comes together more quickly than that and is delicious served with your protein of choice, including iguana, a traditional meat in the area.

One of the most memorable meals of that trip was the tasting menu at La Cocina de Humo. In an enchanting al fresco smoke kitchen featuring adobe walls, woodstoves, and earthen comal griddles, talented rising chef Thalia Barrios García and her team presented course after course of traditional foods prepared using traditional methods right before our eyes—making for a multisensorial dining experience.

Most travelers tend to stick to Oaxaca City, but there's much more to be experienced in the nearby pueblos, where Indigenous cultures really shine. As we traveled out of town, I marveled at the endless agave fields, with giant blue-green plants lined up in tidy rows. The Mexican state has become world famous for its mezcal, which has been a boon to the local economy but has also caused massive deforestation and habitat loss. Small-scale distilleries still do exist and adhere to ethical, artisan practices, but they're quickly being overshadowed by profit-driven US companies infiltrating the area. It's a prime example of the omnipresent tug-of-war between honoring tradition and pursuing progress that's so prevalent across Mexico.

My favorite part of the trip, though, was spending time with José Bautista Maldonado, president of the Community Seed Bank in Unión Zapata. Local farmers founded this pilot program in 2021 in response to the climate crisis, which has hampered their livelihoods. While the bank might seem minuscule in size at about three hundred square feet, it's mighty in mission: to ensure the survival of ancient and heirloom plant varieties, especially maíz.

As I sat in the petite Unión Zapata seed bank with José and his wife, Reina, surrounded by dozens of jars of seed varieties—maíz, beans, pumpkins, quelites, and even teosinte (the mother of corn)—I felt such a sense of kinship and appreciation. That enlightening encounter provided a reassuring reminder that Indigenous peoples across time, space, and generations are stewarding ancestral wisdom into the future.

PUESTO
MOLE NEGRO, ROJO Y COLORADITO,
ESTOFADO Y CHILE PARA BARBACOA...

ADOLFA
PUESTO DE BARBACOA
BLANCA Y ENCHILADA
BENEVA

CHAPULINES AL AJO CON CHILE Y SAL

Garlicky Chapulines with Chile and Salt

makes 1 cup

In the United States, you'll generally find chapulines that are already dehydrated and sometimes seasoned. I recommend choosing unseasoned chapulines so you can season them yourself. For a smokier flavor, use chipotle chile powder. For some heat with no smoke, go for ground chile de árbol.

- 3 tablespoons sunflower oil
- 2 garlic cloves, smashed
- 1 cup dried chapulines, preferably unseasoned
- ½ teaspoon fine sea salt
- 1 teaspoon ground chipotle or chile de árbol

Line a plate with paper towels and place near the stove. In a medium skillet, heat the oil over medium heat. Add the garlic, tilting the skillet if necessary to allow it to fry a bit in the oil, and cook for about 2 minutes, or until fragrant. Using a slotted spoon, remove the garlic from the oil and discard or add to a salsa.

Add the chapulines to the skillet and stir to coat evenly. Toast for 3 to 4 minutes, stirring frequently, until crisped. Using a slotted spoon, transfer the chapulines to the paper towels to drain. Season them with the salt and chile powder and serve.

CHAPULINES: A BELOVED SNACK

In Oaxaca and Puebla, families—typically the men and the boys—head out before sunrise to hunt grasshoppers, locally known as chapulines. These are just one type of the many insects people in central and southern Mexico have been eating since before Spanish colonization.

Gathering and eating them is a way to manage their population without pesticides, and prevent the grasshoppers from decimating crops. They're also a sustainable source of protein, and cooked crisp, they have a delightful texture and great flavor, not too dissimilar from shrimp cooked in the shell. (Crustaceans are basically the insects of the sea, after all.)

After they're captured, they're brought back to their homes where other members of the family are ready to help cook and process them. First, they're cleaned and then boiled in a lemony-salted water before being laid out to dry in the sun.

In Oaxaca, people often toast or fry chapulines to eat as a bar snack, use as a crispy topping, or incorporate into salsa. They have a lightly briny flavor and can serve as a vehicle for other seasonings.

SOPA DE CAMOTE CON VENISON SECO Y CHILE

Sweet Potato Soup with Dried Venison and Chile Oil

serves 4

Sweet potatoes are native to South America and have been cultivated in Mexico for countless generations. At Owamni, we serve roasted and grilled sweet potatoes with what we call Indigenous Chile Crisp, a crispy, crunchy condiment inspired by Chinese chili crisp. Our version includes fried chiles and garlic, of course, but it's sweetened with maple sugar.

Chinese chili crisp is quite similar to Mexican salsa macha from Central Mexico.

Inspired by the pairing at Owamni, I top this simple but satisfying soup of pureed sweet potatoes with some salsa macha, which gets warmed with a little bit of dried venison for savoriness. Marigold petals and leaves have a citrusy note that's delicious with the soup. You can use them as an optional garnish.

SOUP

- 2 tablespoons sunflower or avocado oil
- 1 medium yellow onion, thinly sliced
- Sea salt
- 3 medium sweet potatoes (1½ pounds total), peeled and diced
- 3 cups vegetable broth
- 2 cups pepita milk (see Seed, Nut, and Grain Milks, page 35)
- 1 tablespoon cider vinegar

SERVING

- ½ cup Salsa Macha (page 226)
- 1 ounce venison jerky, finely chopped, for garnish
- Marigold petals or leaves (optional), for garnish

Make the soup: In a large pot, heat the oil over medium heat. Add the onion, season with salt, and cook for about 8 minutes, stirring, until it is starting to brown a bit. Add 2 tablespoons water and scrape up any browned bits. Allow the water to evaporate and continue cooking for about 10 minutes longer, adding a tablespoon of water each time more browned bits form on the bottom of the pan, until the onion is richly browned.

Add the sweet potatoes, broth, and pepita milk. Bring to a boil over high heat. Reduce the heat to medium so the liquid simmers, cover, and cook for 15 to 20 minutes, until the sweet potatoes are tender.

Remove from the heat, stir in the vinegar, and let cool to warm. Working in batches, ladle the soup into a blender and puree until very smooth.

When ready to serve: Strain the soup, if desired, into a clean saucepan and warm it over medium heat. If the soup is thicker than you like, add a little more broth, pepita milk, or water to thin it to your preferred consistency. Taste and season with salt, if needed.

While the soup warms, spoon off 2 tablespoons of the oil from the salsa macha. In a small skillet, gently heat the oil over medium heat. Tilt the skillet so the oil pools. Add the venison jerky and cook in the pool of oil, stirring, just until it's warmed through and starts to crisp up at the edges. Add the remaining salsa macha to warm it through.

Drizzle each portion of soup with the warm salsa macha and crisped venison jerky. Garnish with marigold petals or leaves, if using, and serve.

SALSA MACHA

makes about 2½ cups

Salsa macha is a warmly spicy fried chile salsa you'll find on the tables in home kitchens or out at restaurants all over Mexico. Besides heat, it brings a delightful crispy texture to a dish. You can drizzle it over almost anything, from eggs to sandwiches to tacos to soups.

It's often made with peanuts, which are native to the Andes in South America. There's conflicting evidence about when they came to Mesoamerica—whether before colonization or after. I'm including them here, but you could substitute pine nuts.

- 4 dried chipotle or morita chiles (about ½ ounce)
- 3 guajillo chiles (about ½ ounce)
- 1 small ancho chile (about ½ ounce)
- 2 cups sunflower oil
- ⅓ cup raw peanuts or pine nuts
- 4 garlic cloves, minced
- 2 tablespoons agave syrup
- 2 tablespoons cider vinegar
- Fine sea salt

Using scissors, cut off the stem ends of the chipotle, guajillo, and ancho chiles. Shake out and remove the seeds. Cut the dried chiles into 1-inch pieces.

In a large saucepan, combine the oil and nuts and gently fry over medium-low heat for about 1 minute, until just barely starting to brown. Add the garlic and cook for about 1 minute, being careful not to let it brown.

Carefully add the dried chile pieces and stir to coat. Remove from the heat, cover, and let stand for about 10 minutes, stirring once or twice, until the chiles are slightly softened.

Pour the oil with the chiles and garlic into a blender and blend at medium speed. With the machine on, add the agave syrup, vinegar, and 1 teaspoon salt and puree until it resembles a thick pesto.

Scrape it into a bowl. Let the salsa stand at room temperature for at least 6 hours before serving to allow the flavors to meld. Taste and season with more salt as needed. The salsa can be refrigerated in an airtight container for up to 2 weeks.

TACO DE MAÍZ DE CUATRO MANERAS

Corn Four Ways Tacos

makes 12 tacos

Owamni Executive Chef Lee Garman created this popular dish, which nicely showcases the reverence for maíz in Oaxaca. The main filling is a bouncy corn dumpling made with arepa dough and topped with a mellow sweet corn salsa and popcorn for crunch. The fourth form of corn comes in with the tortilla, of course.

CORN SALSA

- 2 tablespoons sunflower oil
- ¼ cup chopped white onion
- 1 teaspoon ground sumac
- Sea salt
- 2 ears corn, husked
- 1 tablespoon cider vinegar
- ¼ teaspoon chile de árbol powder or other ground chile, plus more as needed

POPCORN

- ½ teaspoon ground sumac
- ½ teaspoon fine sea salt, plus more as needed
- 1 tablespoon sunflower oil
- ¼ cup unpopped popcorn kernels

CORN DUMPLINGS

- 8 ounces Arepa Dough (page 32) or Easy Arepa Dough (page 318)
- Sunflower oil, for the pan

TACOS

- 12 (6-inch) Corn Tortillas (page 31)
- Wild greens, such as purslane, wood sorrel, and papalo, for serving
- Pickled Habanero Chiles (optional; page 234), for serving

Make the corn salsa: In a large skillet, heat 1 tablespoon of the oil over medium heat. Add the onion and sumac, season with salt, and cook for about 4 minutes, stirring, until translucent. Scrape into a blender.

Increase the heat to medium-high. Add the ears of corn and cook, turning occasionally, until the kernels are blistered in spots.

Let the corn cool, then cut off the kernels (so you have about 2 cups) and add to the blender. Puree the corn and onion, then add the remaining 1 tablespoon of oil and the vinegar and puree again until smooth. Season with more salt and the chile powder.

Make the popcorn: In a small bowl, stir together the sumac and salt.

In a pot with a tightly fitting lid, heat the oil over medium-high heat for about 1 minute, until shimmering. Add the popcorn kernels, cover, and cook, shaking the pan frequently, until there are 3 seconds between pops, meaning most of the kernels have popped.

Transfer to a large bowl, discarding any unpopped kernels. Season the popcorn with the sumac salt and toss to coat evenly. Taste and season with more salt, as needed.

Make the corn dumplings: Using a 1-inch scoop or tablespoon, scoop the dough into 24 equal pieces (about 2 teaspoons each). Roll each piece into a ball and press to flatten into rounds so they're about ½ inch thick.

Preheat the oven to 350°F. Line a baking sheet with parchment paper.

Brush a comal, griddle, or large skillet with oil and heat over medium-high heat. Working in batches, add as many dumplings as will fit in a single layer. Cook for about 2 minutes, or until blistered in spots. Flip and cook until the other side is blistered. Transfer to the baking sheet.

Bake the dumplings for about 10 minutes, or until they sound hollow when tapped and no raw dough remains in the center.

Make the tacos: Warm the tortillas, either by quickly heating one by one in a hot pan or microwaving them. Build the tacos by drizzling the warm tortillas first with the corn salsa, setting 2 dumplings on top, and finishing with the popcorn, wild greens and herbs, and pickled chiles (if using).

SOPES CON AGUATE Y CHAPULINES

Sopes with Avocado and Grasshoppers

makes 12 sopes

In Mexico, you'll often find sopes, palm-size cakes of masa with ridged edges, filled with toppings, sold in the street as a snack. Beans are a popular addition, and you could certainly make the Pasta de Frijol Negro Oaxaqueña (page 237) and include them here. But they're also tasty this way, with a very simple avocado mash and a crisp sprinkle of chapulines. (Yep, that's grasshoppers.) For a bit of heat and acidity, add some Pickled Habanero Chiles (page 234).

- 1 pound Fresh Masa (page 28) or use masa harina (see chart, page 27)
- 2 tablespoons avocado oil or sunflower oil
- 2 Hass avocados, halved and pitted
- Sea salt
- 1 cup Garlicky Chapulines with Chile and Salt (page 224), or use store-bought preseasoned chapulines, for serving

In a large bowl, mix the fresh masa with the oil. Divide the dough into 12 equal portions and roll each one into a ball. (Cover the balls with a clean towel.)

Using your hands or a tortilla press, press the balls into rounds that are about ¼ inch thick and 4 inches wide.

Heat a well-seasoned comal, griddle, or cast-iron skillet over medium-high heat. Working in batches, add the rounds and cook for 1 to 2 minutes until lightly charred on the bottom and they release easily from the pan. Flip and cook for about 1 minute longer, until the second side is lightly charred and they release easily again.

Working with one cooked round at a time, while it's still hot—you can use a towel to hold the hot edges—lightly pinch up the edges of the sope to create a ridge that will help contain the toppings.

Working with a few at a time, return the shaped sopes to the griddle with the ridged sides up and cook for about 1 minute, to heat through. Transfer to a tortilla warmer or cover with a clean towel to keep warm.

Scoop the avocado flesh into a molcajete or a bowl and use the tejolote (pestle) or a fork to lightly mash the avocado with some salt, just enough so it's easy to spread and scoop, but you can still see some of the distinction between the darker green and lighter green coloring.

Dollop the avocado mash on top of each sope. Sprinkle with the chapulines and serve.

TLACOYOS CON CALABAZA Y XOCONOSTLE PICO DE GALLO

Tlacoyos with Squash and Green Cactus Fruit Pico de Gallo

makes 10 tlacoyos

A tlacoyo is a pre-Hispanic dish in which a pocket of masa is stuffed with filling, typically beans. They're then served with a bright, fresh salsa and other toppings.

Here, I make tlacoyos but stuff them with some sweet, mashed squash, seasoned with a bit of roasted onion, garlic, and chipotle. I serve it with a pico de gallo made with xoconostle, a tart green cactus fruit. While there is no substitute for xoconostle, you could serve these with a pico made from underripe tuna, which is the name for the more typical variety of prickly pear cactus fruit you see in markets. Or substitute another fruit of your choice.

FILLING

- 1 small acorn squash (about 1 pound) or other similar size winter squash, halved
- ½ small yellow onion, cut lengthwise into 2 wedges
- 2 large garlic cloves, unpeeled
- Avocado or sunflower oil
- Sea salt
- ½ teaspoon chipotle chile powder, plus more as needed

PICO DE GALLO

- 4 xoconostle (green cactus fruit)
- 4 Roma tomatoes, diced
- ¼ small white onion, chopped
- 1 jalapeño, halved lengthwise, seeded if desired, and finely chopped
- 3 culantro leaves, finely chopped
- Sea salt
- 1 Hass avocado, diced

Make the filling: Preheat the oven to 350°F.

Remove and reserve the seeds from the squash halves. Rub the cut sides of the squash as well as the onion wedges and garlic cloves with oil and sprinkle with salt. Set the squash cut-sides down on a baking sheet along with the onion and garlic.

Bake for about 45 minutes to 1 hour, until the squash is tender.

Meanwhile, clean the seeds, discarding as much of the stringy flesh as possible, and pat them dry. Toss with 1 tablespoon oil and season with salt. Spread in a single layer on a small baking sheet. Bake for about 20 minutes (at the same time as the squash), tossing once or twice as they cook, until blistered in spots. Reserve them for garnish.

Remove the vegetables from the oven and let cool to warm. Scoop the squash flesh into a food processor, discarding the skins. Add the onion wedges and squeeze the garlic cloves from their skins into the processor. Add the chipotle powder and puree until smooth. You'll only need 1½ cups of the puree; reserve the rest for another use.

Make the pico de gallo: Using a sharp knife, cut the ends off the cactus fruit and stand it up on one of the cut sides. Use the knife to carefully remove the skin. Cut the fruit in half lengthwise and use a spoon to remove the seeds. (If you're using the more common green prickly pear fruit, you will not need to remove the seeds.) Cut the fruit into bite-size pieces and transfer to a bowl.

Add the tomatoes, chopped onion, jalapeño, and culantro to the bowl and season with salt. Just before serving, gently stir in the avocado.

Make the tlacoyos: If you're using the fresh masa, mix in the oil. If using masa harina, follow the chart to make the dough, but add the oil when you add the water.

(recipe and ingredients continue)

Divide the masa into 10 equal portions and roll each one into a ball. Cover them with a clean kitchen towel or plastic wrap while you work. One by one, use your hands or a tortilla press to flatten each ball into a disc about ¼ inch thick and about 3½ inches wide.

Scoop about 1½ tablespoons of the squash filling into the center of each disc. Fold the dough over the filling, pressing the edges to seal. Set the tlacoyo seam-side up and gently press to flatten into a football shape or use a rolling pin. (There will be some squash filling left over; hold on to it.) Cover the tlacoyos with a clean towel as you fill and shape each one.

Heat a comal or griddle over medium heat and brush with a thin layer of oil. Working in batches, cook the tlacoyos for 3 to 4 minutes, until dark brown spots form on the bottom. Flip and cook until golden with browned spots on the second sides.

Spread a little more of the squash filling on top of the tlacoyos and serve hot, topped with the pico de gallo and pickled habaneros (if using). Garnish with the toasted squash seeds and serve.

TLACOYOS

- 1 pound Fresh Masa (page 28) or use masa harina (see chart, page 27)
- 1 tablespoon avocado or sunflower oil, plus more for the pan
- Pickled Habanero Chiles (optional; recipe below), for serving

CHILES HABANEROS EN VINAGRE

Pickled Habanero Chiles

makes 1 pint

Habanero chiles are especially popular in Southern Mexico. I love their sweet, fruity, fiery heat with so many dishes. I recommend wearing gloves when handling habaneros.

- 5 habanero chiles
- 2 tablespoons sunflower oil
- ¼ cup thinly sliced red onion
- ¼ cup thinly sliced carrot rounds
- 2 garlic cloves, thinly sliced
- 2 allspice berries
- 1 bay leaf
- ½ teaspoon fine sea salt
- ¾ cup cider vinegar
- ¼ cup plus 2 tablespoons agave syrup

While wearing gloves, cut off the stems from the habaneros. Remove the seeds and interior ribs for a milder pickle. (It will still be very spicy.) Cut the chiles crosswise into rings ¼ inch thick.

In a nonreactive medium saucepan, heat the oil over medium heat. Add the chiles, onion, carrot, garlic, allspice, and bay leaf. Stir to coat and cook for about 3 minutes, or until everything is fragrant and the vegetables start to soften.

Turn off the heat and stir in the salt, ¾ cup water, the vinegar, and agave syrup. Let cool to room temperature. Ladle everything into a jar, close the jar, and refrigerate for at least 24 hours before using. The pickled chiles can be refrigerated for up to 2 weeks.

TLAYUDA CON FRIJOLES, HUITLACOCHE Y ESCAMOLES

Tlayudas with Black Beans, Huitlacoche, and Insect Caviar

serves 4

The Oaxacan genius with masa continues with these tlayudas, large, crisped tortillas covered in toppings. (A tlayuda is sometimes called Mexican pizza.) As they do in Oaxaca, I top these with the beloved frijoles. But instead of adding the usual cheese, I reach for two pre-Hispanic ingredients still enjoyed in Mexico today: huitlacoche, the sweet and earthy mushroom-like fungus that grows on corn, and escamoles, which are ant larvae.

Escamoles are a delicacy in spring and beloved for their buttery, nutty flavor. If they're not in season, you can leave them off. For a little bit of creaminess and acidity, I finish the dish with an avocado crema.

To make these easier to prepare at home, I roll out the tortillas so they're about 10 inches across and bake them. For larger tlayudas more akin to the type you'd find in Oaxaca, you can divide the dough in half and roll each piece out so it's about 14 inches across. Then bake each tortilla one by one on a pizza stone in the oven.

- 1 pound Fresh Masa (page 28) or use masa harina (see chart, page 27)
- 2 tablespoons sunflower oil
- 1 small yellow onion, chopped
- Sea salt
- 2 garlic cloves, minced
- 1 dried chile de árbol, stemmed and crumbled
- 1 cup cleaned fresh huitlacoche or 1 (7-ounce) can, drained and rinsed
- ½ cup escamoles (optional)
- 2 cups Oaxacan Black Bean Paste (page 237)
- Avocado Crema (page 237)
- Chopped fresh culantro, for serving

Preheat the oven to 400°F. Line two baking sheets with parchment paper.

Divide the dough into 4 equal portions and roll each one into a ball. Use a large tortilla press or a rolling pin to press or roll each ball between two sheets of plastic wrap or wax paper into a 10-inch round. It's okay if the edges crack a little bit. Transfer the rounds to the baking sheets, leaving a little space between the rounds.

Bake for 12 minutes. Flip and bake for 10 to 12 minutes longer, until golden and a bit crisp.

Meanwhile, in a medium skillet, heat the oil over medium heat. Add the onion, season with salt, and cook for 5 minutes, or until tender. Add the garlic and crumbled chile and cook for about 1 minute, or until the garlic is softened. Add the huitlacoche and cook for about 10 minutes, stirring, until it releases all of its moisture and very little liquid remains in the pan. Add the escamoles (if using) and cook for 1 to 2 minutes, stirring occasionally, until white and tender. Keep the mixture warm over low heat.

When the tortillas are golden, spread about ½ cup of the black bean paste on each tortilla. Bake for 6 to 7 minutes, until the edges are curled up and browned.

Top the tlayudas with the huitlacoche and escamoles mixture. Drizzle the tlayudas with some of the avocado crema, top with culantro, and serve.

PASTA DE FRIJOL NEGRO OAXAQUEÑA

Oaxacan Black Bean Paste

makes 4 to 5 cups

This is about as classic as it gets in Oaxaca. These beans form the base of so many dishes. The herbal licorice notes of the dried avocado leaves and pungent oregano-like scent of epazote are essential to get the right flavor, so I encourage you to seek them out here.

- 1 pound dried black beans, soaked overnight and drained
- 1 small white onion, cut into quarters
- ½ head garlic, halved horizontally to expose the cloves
- 2 dried avocado leaves
- Sea salt
- 1 sprig of epazote
- 2 tablespoons sunflower oil
- 1 small yellow onion, finely chopped

In a large pot, combine the beans with water to cover by 2 inches. Add the quartered white onion, garlic, and avocado leaves and bring to a boil over high heat. Reduce the heat to medium-low, partially cover, and simmer for 1 to 2 hours, until tender, depending on the freshness of the beans. Add more water if necessary to keep the beans covered.

Season the beans with salt and turn off the heat. Add the epazote and let steep for 15 minutes. Remove and discard the onion, garlic, avocado leaves, and epazote.

Using a slotted spoon, transfer the cooked beans to a blender. Add about the same volume of cooking liquid as the beans and puree for 30 seconds or so, until smooth.

In a deep skillet or large saucepan, heat the oil over medium heat. Add the diced yellow onion and cook for about 5 minutes, stirring, until tender. Add the bean puree and cook for 4 to 5 minutes, stirring, until any liquid evaporates and the puree thickens to a paste. Taste and season with more salt if needed.

Refrigerate the black bean paste in an airtight container for up to 4 days.

CREMA DE AGUACATE

Avocado Crema

makes about 2 cups

So many dishes in Mexico are finished with crema, so I wanted to see if I could create a version that didn't rely on dairy. With avocado for creaminess and tomatillos for acidity, this one comes close. Drizzle it anywhere you want some crema.

- 1 Hass avocado, halved and pitted
- 4 small tomatillos (about 7 ounces total), husked and coarsely chopped
- ¼ teaspoon fine sea salt

Scoop the avocado flesh into a blender. Add the tomatillos, ½ cup plus 2 tablespoons water, and the salt and puree until smooth. Pour into a bowl or airtight container and give it a stir to help it release the air that built up when it was blended.

Serve immediately or cover and refrigerate for up to 2 days.

TLAPIQUES CON PESCADO, NOPALES Y VERDURAS

Tlapiques with Freshwater Fish, Nopales, and Vegetables

makes 6 tlapiques

The word tlapique comes from the Nahuatl word tlapictli, which means "things wrapped in corn leaf." While it looks like a tamal, it doesn't contain any masa. Instead, it's a mixture that can include meat, fish, and vegetables with seasonings and typically cooked over an open flame or comal.

It's a pre-Hispanic dish of the Xochimilca people, who moved to what is now the Xochimilco in Mexico City about one thousand years ago. Traditionally, people made tlapique with aquatic creatures that were plentiful in the wetland area, including frog legs and tadpoles. Today, people often make this dish with freshwater fish or chicken giblets, nopales, vegetables, and seasonings.

Here, I stuff the corn husks with fish and fresh vegetables, including tomatoes, chiles, and cactus. A little bit of ground chipotle chile brings a smoky depth that permeates everything and brings all of the flavors together.

- 1 pound freshwater fish fillets, such as trout, skinned if desired and cut into 1-inch pieces
- 1 medium white onion, chopped
- 1 large nopal (prickly pear cactus paddle), trimmed (see Trimming and Cleaning Nopales, page 64) and diced
- 2 medium tomatoes, cored and chopped
- 2 to 3 fresh green chiles, such as serrano or jalapeño, stemmed, halved, seeded if desired, and thinly sliced
- 4 garlic cloves, minced
- 3 sprigs of epazote, leaves removed and finely chopped
- 1 teaspoon dried Mexican oregano
- ½ to 1 teaspoon chipotle chile powder, to taste
- Fine sea salt
- 1 tablespoon avocado or sunflower oil
- 12 dried corn husks, soaked for at least 4 hours or overnight
- Warm tortillas (optional), for serving

In a large bowl, toss together the fish, onion, nopal, tomatoes, green chiles, garlic, epazote, oregano, and chipotle powder. Add 1¼ teaspoons salt and drizzle with the oil, then toss again until everything is evenly coated.

Double up the corn husks to create 6 two-layered portions. Add about one-sixth of the mixture to the center of each doubled husk.

Fold the sides and top and bottom of each corn husk over the filling to create a packet. Pull a strip of corn husk from one of the husks and use it to tie each packet closed. (Or tie it with kitchen string.)

Heat a comal or large cast-iron skillet or griddle over medium heat.

Add the 6 packets to the comal and cook for about 10 minutes, turning frequently, until the husks are blistered all over and the fish is cooked. (You will likely need to take a peek at the fish to make sure it's done.)

Let the packets rest for 3 minutes before opening. Serve with tortillas, if desired.

IGUANA EN MOLE PIPIÁN VERDE

Iguana with Green Mole

serves 4

Some people who hunt and cook iguanas serve the meat with the skin and all. If that's your preference, you can absolutely do that. But for those of us who aren't regularly capturing iguanas, the boneless or bone-in meat is sometimes available at markets in Mexico and the United States and through exoticmeatmarkets.com. The online store sources iguanas from Puerto Rico, where the animals are invasive and damaging to the ecosystem.

Sometimes known as chicken of the trees, iguana meat is mild-tasting and should be handled much like chicken because it can carry salmonella.

- 1 pound boneless iguana meat, cut into 1-inch pieces, or 2 pounds bone-in meat cut into serving pieces
- 1 small yellow onion, cut into quarters
- ½ head garlic, halved horizontally to expose the cloves
- 4 culantro leaves
- Sea salt
- Mole Pipián Verde (opposite)
- Popped Amaranth (optional; page 37), for serving

Place the iguana meat in a large saucepan and add water to cover. Add the onion, garlic, culantro, and season generously with salt. Bring to a boil over high heat, then reduce the heat to medium-low and cook for about 1 hour (boneless meat) or 1½ hours (bone-in), until tender. When the iguana is done, strain and reserve the cooking liquid for the mole.

Meanwhile, make the mole, using 1 cup of the iguana broth in place of the broth called for in the mole recipe.

Add the cooked iguana and another ½ cup of the iguana cooking liquid to the pot of mole. Cook for about 15 minutes to allow the flavors to meld.

Serve over popped amaranth, if desired.

Note: *If you don't want to go through the trouble of seeking out iguana, the mole is also quite delicious made with turkey or vegetable broth and served over roasted turkey.*

MOLE PIPIÁN VERDE

Green Mole

makes about 4 cups

When you think of Oaxaca, you likely think of moles—the complex sauces made with toasted nuts, seeds, chiles, fruit, and sometimes cacao. Mole pipián verde is one of my favorites. It's creamy from the pepitas and sunflower seeds, with brightness from the tomatillos and herbal notes because of all the greens.

To create this recipe, I use ingredients that were available before Spanish colonization, including wild greens, chiles, tomatillos, pepitas, and sunflower seeds. It's a sauce you could serve with almost anything, including many kinds of meat or fish, roasted vegetables, or grains. I suggest pairing it with iguana because it's a food that Indigenous peoples have eaten in parts of Mexico—including around Oaxaca—for thousands of years.

- 1 cup pepitas
- ½ cup sunflower seeds
- 1 cup vegetable broth or turkey broth (see Note)
- 1 small yellow onion, coarsely chopped
- 2 garlic cloves, smashed and peeled
- 1 pound tomatillos, husked and halved
- 3 cups quelites, such as chaya (tree spinach), quintoniles (wild amaranth greens), or quelites de cenizo (lamb's quarters)
- 2 serrano chiles, stemmed, halved lengthwise, and seeded, if desired, coarsely chopped
- 1½ cups loosely packed culantro leaves, coarsely chopped
- 2 tablespoons sunflower oil
- 2 teaspoons dried Mexican oregano
- 1 teaspoon ground allspice
- Sea salt

In a large skillet, toast the pepitas and sunflower seeds over medium heat for 2 to 3 minutes, stirring occasionally, until fragrant and slightly darker in color. Transfer to a plate and spread out to cool, then transfer to a blender.

Add the broth to the blender along with the onion, garlic, tomatillos, quelites, chiles, and culantro leaves. Puree until smooth.

In a pot, heat the oil over medium heat. Add the puree and cook for about 15 minutes, stirring occasionally, until it starts to lose its raw flavor. Add the oregano and allspice and continue to cook for 10 minutes longer, or until the mole thickens enough to easily coat the back of a spoon. Taste and season with salt.

Note: *If you are poaching meat to go with the mole, use some of the poaching liquid in place of the broth called for.*

ALEGRÍA DE CACAO

Chocolate-Amaranth Candy

makes one 8 × 8 pan

Alegría, a candy made with popped amaranth seeds blended and set with honey, lives on in Mexico today and it's one you can imagine has been made in similar ways for centuries. This chocolate alegría is inspired by a version photographer David Alvarado brought me from Mexico City. I think it nicely honors the ancient Indigenous tradition of eating both amaranth and cacao.

- 2 cups Popped Amaranth (page 37) or store-bought
- ¼ cup pepitas
- 3 ounces unsweetened chocolate, coarsely chopped
- ½ Mexican vanilla bean, split lengthwise
- 3 tablespoons honey
- ⅛ teaspoon fine sea salt

Line an 8-inch square baking pan with parchment paper or wax paper that overhangs on two sides.

In a bowl, toss together the popped amaranth and pepitas.

Set a medium saucepan over medium-low heat. Add the chocolate and cook, stirring constantly, just until it starts to melt. Scrape in the vanilla seeds, stir in the honey and salt, and continue cooking until the chocolate is fully melted.

Pour the mixture over the amaranth and seeds and quickly stir until evenly coated. Scrape the coated amaranth into the prepared pan, use a spoon to press into an even layer, and let cool completely.

Use the paper overhang to lift and transfer the slab of the alegría to a cutting board. Cut it into 16 equal pieces (or cut how you like). Store in an airtight container for up to 5 days.

AMARANTH: AN ANCIENT SUPERFOOD

Amaranth is one of those ingredients that shows the resilience of Indigenous peoples on Turtle Island. The tiny seeds—also thought of as a pseudo-cereal grain—are rich with protein and were an important food for people in Mesoamerica precolonization. In the Aztec empire, people built statues using amaranth and honey that were eaten during ceremonies. When Spanish conquistadors took over, they burned amaranth fields and forbade people from growing it—perhaps because of its use during non-Christian ceremonies.

As a major food crop, amaranth fell out of favor for centuries, although some people continued to grow it at a smaller scale and people continued to harvest the wild leaves. With its nutritional profile, amaranth seeds have been hailed as a superfood. The Mexican government has been actively promoting amaranth as a healthful addition to people's diets. Because it is a hardy plant and drought-resistant, it's also valuable as water becomes more scarce.

Amaranth can be cooked like a pilaf or risotto or ground into a flour for baking. It also is satisfying to eat popped. In fact, popped amaranth is used in many different sweets in Mexico, like this Alegría de Cacao.

MESOAMERICAN RAINFOREST AND GULF COAST

SOUTHERN MEXICO

I'LL ADMIT THAT MY FIRST TIME experiencing Southern Mexico was as a typical tourist visiting Cozumel for my thirtieth birthday, long before I started down my current path. I didn't know any better, so I mainly just basked in the sun and partied on the *playa* (beach). Fast-forward about fifteen years, and I revisited the Yucatán Peninsula with eyes wide open.

On that 2019 trip, I was eager to learn more about Maya corn culture, so I started by touring the Tulum ruins, then made my way inland to the pre-colonial city-state of Chichén Itzá, one of the world's best-preserved archaeological sites. I was really trying to peel back the layers of tourism and go beyond that surface-level script that locals serve up for travelers. Everywhere I went, I noticed maíz motifs quite literally carved into the walls of these ancient, sacred sites.

Even though my mission on this trip was to dig deeper, I also realized that if this is as deep as most visitors will ever dig, many people will continue to mistakenly place the Maya in the past. But despite the ongoing onslaught on their cultures, these peoples and their dynamic lifeways are still very much alive. Just look at their language: An estimated six million people across Southern Mexico, Belize, Guatemala, Honduras, and El Salvador speak some thirty dialects. That statistic alone is a testament to the resilience and resistance of these Indigenous communities, given that many others have lost their native tongue due to colonialism and forced assimilation. Just as Indigenous cultures and communities continue to thrive here in the United States, they do in Mexico, too.

During that trip, I also enjoyed a beautiful meal at Ka'an, situated in the Sian Ka'an Biosphere Reserve south of Tulum. Indigenous chef Hugo Durán helmed the kitchen of the now-shuttered al fresco restaurant, which was getting a lot of acclaim at the time. It was situated in this beachside bamboo hut, with a super-simple central kitchen where everything was cooked over fire. That meal was so memorable, not only for the delectable cuisine—spear-caught snapper wrapped in hoja santa, pib-cooked guajolote (turkey roasted in an earthen oven), and handmade bean tamales—but also for the juxtaposition of all these well-to-do tourists dining in this rustic, no-frills space.

Hugo is quick to point out that he's not originally from that area; rather, he was born and raised in Mexico City. He has no formal culinary training but started traveling to better connect to his Mesoamerican roots, along the way learning from knowledge keepers like agricultural engineer Amado Ramírez Leyva and Paula Pedro, who worked with him at Ka'an and came to be known as maestra de maíz—the master of corn. His culinary journey has been life-changing, transforming the childhood shame he felt about his Indigeneity into celebration. That ingrained sense of self-doubt and self-loathing is such a common phenomenon among Native peoples; after all, that's what colonialism was designed to do.

I totally understand Hugo's desire to pay homage to Maya culture through modern Yucatecan cuisine. Another person who's done that in recent decades is renowned Danish chef René Redzepi, of Noma fame. But when he and his team popped up in Tulum in 2017 for a seven-week stint, it hit differently. Although the prices at Ka'an were by no means cheap, they didn't come close to Noma Mexico's $750 fifteen-course tasting menu. Sure, tickets sold out in a matter of hours and rave reviews poured in, but so, too, did a distaste for such an expensive meal in a place where much of the local population lives in poverty, as noted by former *New York Times* restaurant critic Pete Wells (who refused to review the experience).

Don't get me wrong; I have huge respect for René as a culinary thought leader who really jumpstarted the contemporary local, sustainable fine-dining movement. But there was something all too ironic about a European restaurant swooping in to cook Mesoamerican food—essentially bringing their prestige to "elevate" the food to the point where wealthy white people would fly in and pay thousands of dollars to try it. I think we've probably had enough "discoveries" of Indigenous cultures for one millennium.

Like so many Native peoples the world over, the Maya communities of Southern Mexico and Central America have fought hard to preserve their rich cultures, which go so far beyond the ruins of their once-flourishing civilizations. If you push beyond the colonialist mindset, you can see that these lifeways are as strong and sophisticated as ever, despite a Spanish conquest aimed at snuffing them out. In fact, there are an estimated eight million Maya people currently living in that part of the world—around the same size of the population at the time of European contact—protecting not only their traditional practices but also this beautiful, bountiful place.

THE LAND

So much more than just a tourist attraction, the tropical Yucatán Peninsula is an incredibly ecologically rich region. The Isthmus of Tehuantepec, where the land narrows as it curves eastward, acts as the rough western boundary for the area. It includes the Mexican states of Chiapas, Tabasco, Campeche, Yucatán, and Quintana Roo, hugged by Guatemala and Belize to the southeast. Just like in other parts of Turtle Island, the arbitrary border separating Mexico from these countries is nothing more than a colonialist construct. This area has fittingly been dubbed El Mundo Maya (the Maya World), which is divided into three zones demarcated by subtle environmental shifts: the northern lowlands, the southern lowlands, and the southern highlands.

Despite the blanket term used to describe the region, the Maya comprise nearly thirty unique groups delineated by their distinct languages and locales, including the Akateko, Ch'ol, Chontal, Chuj, Huastec, Jakaltek, Kaqchikel, K'iche', Mam, Mopan, Q'anjob'al, Q'eqchi', Tojolab'al, Tzeltal, Tzotzil, Yucatec, and more. (As these Indigenous communities move toward greater sovereignty and self-determination, their preferred names may continue to shift, including shedding the overarching "Maya" term.)

From the very start, these groups tailored their lifeways to the diverse landscape, which encompasses both wet and dry tropical forests, temperate sierras, coastal plains, mountain ranges, mangrove swamps, wetlands, and more. The region is considered a neotropical biogeographic realm based on the flora and fauna it fosters, as compared to the Nearctic realm of the rest of the continent. In this way, Southern Mexico has much more in common with Central and South America than it does with North America. Weather there tends to be hot and humid, with fluctuating rain during the wet season of May to October (though that's changing amid the climate crisis).

The northern part of the peninsula features karst terrain, with few surface rivers or lakes, and in their place water-filled sinkholes known as cenotes that have formed over time due to collapses in the porous limestone bedrock. The region's vast subterranean karst aquifer system—one of the most extensive on the planet—forms

a neat half-circle atop the edge of the deeply buried Chicxulub asteroid impact crater. This massive space object hit the Gulf of Mexico some 66 million years ago, causing extensive climate and environmental change thought to have killed off 75 percent of the Earth's species, including the dinosaurs.

For Maya people, the area's thousands of cenotes are not only sacred sites but also vital water sources. As such, they built some of their estimated forty city-states like Chichén Itzá in close proximity. To accommodate these vast settlements, the Maya also developed sophisticated rainwater collection infrastructure. Echoing the natural phenomenon that creates cenotes, they built subterranean chultúnes for storage and also constructed dams atop hills to let the natural grade distribute it throughout their extensive canal systems. Given the influx of human development in the area today, the cenotes face major threat from pollution and land mismanagement.

The region's thin, poor soil sitting atop a limestone slab poses another challenge to agricultural efforts, leading to even more Indigenous ingenuity in the form of the intercropping milpa system. Centered around maíz, these "forest gardens" take many years to cycle through multiple stages: first clearing a plot using the slash-and-burn method; next cultivating symbiotic crops like corn, beans, and squash, as well as chile peppers, avocados, tomatoes, sweet potatoes, cacao, greens, and herbs; then finally allowing for an extended fallow period to reestablish the forest. This method not only enhances soil fertility for better yields, it also maintains land cover, reduces soil erosion, and promotes biodiversity.

As the landscape shifts across the region, so, too, do the innovative approaches. In the low-lying swampy areas, for example, Maya communities employ raised-bed farming, not unlike the Aztec chinampas (see Mesoamerican Highlands and Pacific Coast: Central Mexico, page 214). In the southern highlands, where the soil quality improves thanks to a long history of volcanic activity, Indigenous agriculturists utilize terrace farming. Unsurprisingly, Spanish-introduced crops such as melons, mangoes, bananas, and citrus fruits have made their way into these Maya farms. Still in use today, the milpa system is rightly heralded for its environmental soundness, but is also being negatively impacted by climate change effects, including droughts and heat waves.

Water becomes much more readily available moving westward toward the Isthmus of Tehuantepec. In fact, the state of Tabasco contains about one-third of Mexico's surface fresh water. The area is subject to major flooding that regularly causes extensive damage and requires evacuation of coastal villages. Chiapas, meanwhile, constitutes the most mountainous part of the region. It's home to the southernmost extension of the Sierra Madre range as well as plentiful lakes, lagoons, rivers, and waterfalls throughout its varying elevation.

Mexico is considered one of the world's most megadiverse countries, in large part thanks to the biodiversity of this region. A prime example is the lush Maya Forest, the second largest remaining tropical rainforest in the Americas after the Amazon. Hundreds of plant and animal species—some of them endangered—inhabit its twenty-plus micro ecosystems. Upward of 600,000 people, including Maya and other Indigenous groups, have also made this bountiful place their home and continue to steward the land through agroforestry and other traditional practices. Although many parts of this jungle are protected, there are still major deforestation and degradation problems due to the extractive agriculture, timber, and mining industries. So much stands to be lost with the ongoing destruction of biodiversity havens like this.

While sustainable agriculture lays the foundation for Maya foodways, fishing and hunting play a secondary role, which is where that biodiversity factors in. The varying landscape fosters an unbelievable amount of flora and fauna. Coastal communities harvest tuna, jack, grouper, lobster, shrimp, and similar bounty from the sea. Typically preserved with salt in ancient times, these foods made their way across the region along trade routes. Farther inland, Maya groups have long hunted deer, javelina, armadillo, rabbit, turkey, duck, turtle, iguana, and other game.

Of course, colonization hugely impacted not only Maya ways of life but also the landscape of Southern Mexico. Although the infertile soil and inhospitable clime of the Yucatán wouldn't support cash crops like wheat, barley, and other cereal grains, the Spanish did manage to grow corn, citrus, sugarcane, cotton, and henequen there. What really ravaged the region, though, was the introduction of livestock like cattle, pigs, goats, and sheep. Today, Indigenous communities across the peninsula are fighting back against the widespread industrial ranching that's causing massive habitat loss and threatening the crucial underground cenote water system. These profit-driven practices stand in total opposition to the ecologically sound methods that Maya communities have employed since time immemorial.

THE HISTORY

Known for developing some of the most complex cultures in the ancient Americas, the Maya began inhabiting the Yucatán millennia ago after migrating from what's now Central America. They oriented their more than forty city-states around their innovative agriculture that fed a huge population—upward of ten million at its peak. Maíz, in particular, not only served as a staple but also propelled Maya communities to prosperity.

In addition to building their impressive stone settlements and ceremonial centers—whose ruins famously dot the area—the early Maya developed elaborate calendars, writing and mathematics systems, and bark-paper books known as codices detailing their religions, rituals, and more. They also produced incredible artwork, ceramics, textiles, baskets, and jewelry featuring precious metals and gemstones, which were widely traded through well-established networks. Even with the Spanish destroying and hoarding many of these important artifacts, it's still so apparent how advanced these cultures have been since the very beginning.

The Maya's stronghold on the peninsula prevented much incursion from other Mesoamerican groups, but they still faced challenges. Around 800 CE, they began abandoning their robust cities, especially in the southern lowlands, for reasons largely unknown. Anthropologists and historians have proposed possible causes like drought, overpopulation, and battles between competing Maya city-states. In reality, it was probably a combination of these factors that caused them to move to smaller agricultural villages and leave behind their splendid settlements, which over time became cloaked in the vines and vegetation of the rainforest.

The Maya briefly encountered the Spanish a few times when explorers made landfall along the coastline before their official pursuit of Mexico. After conquistador Hernán Cortés and his crew overtook the Aztec Empire in 1521, they quickly expanded New Spain's reach as far as the Isthmus of Tehuantepec. (For more on the colonization of Central Mexico, see Mesoamerican Highlands and Pacific Coast: Central Mexico, page 214.) Numerous attempts to claim the Yucatán in the following decades proved unsuccessful, but European diseases did decimate the Maya population. While some Indigenous communities initially tried to civilly coexist with the intruders, most fiercely defended their homelands. All told, it would take more than a century and a half of relentless conflict and much bloodshed for the Spanish to colonize the region.

> Maíz, in particular, not only served as a staple but also propelled Maya communities to prosperity.

The dispersed, politically fragmented nature of the Maya settlements—as opposed to one central stronghold, like the Aztec capital city of Tenochtitlan—impeded conquest. The varying topography of the landscape also posed problems. By 1528, the Spanish were successful in establishing a settlement in the Chiapas Highlands. Farther north, the western part of the peninsula wasn't subdued until 1542. But these occupations didn't automatically spell defeat for the eastern part of the region; rather, they prompted several Maya communities to band together for a united front against the invasion.

After a coordinated uprising ended poorly for those Indigenous groups, many people sought refuge in the densely forested southern lowlands. One of the last holdout communities was the Itzá of northern Guatemala, who remained independent until 1697. The Lacandon, meanwhile, evaded Spanish oppression by escaping into what's now known as the Lacandon Jungle, where they lived relatively unbothered until loggers, archeologists, and missionaries showed up there around the turn of the twentieth century.

As they settled parts of the region, the Spanish immediately gave out land grants and implemented the encomienda system, forcing Indigenous individuals into indentured servitude on haciendas. (Later laws prohibiting this slavery had little real-world impact.) Franciscan friars also descended upon the area to evangelize the Maya peoples and aided in rounding them up into centralized cities. Refusing to be subjugated, these Indigenous groups rebelled against the violent,

exploitative conditions and led several revolts over the next few decades.

This resistance continued through the declaration of Mexico's independence in 1821. Inspired by this act of liberation and fed up with oversight by a central government so far away in Mexico City, the Yucatán proclaimed its sovereignty the following year. That lasted a few years until it willingly rejoined Mexico in 1824, shortly after the country became a republic. History repeated itself with the Yucatán again declaring independence in 1841, but this time it was met with harmful trade restrictions and an army invasion. The state finally rejoined the republic in 1848, around the same time of the Mexican-American War.

Amid this political chaos, the Caste War of Yucatán began in 1847 as a protest to the oppressive exploitation, ongoing land loss, and social and economic inequalities that Maya peoples had been experiencing for decades. Led by Jacinto Pat and Cecilio Chi, the insurrection intended to drive out the wealthy land-owning Europeans and mestizos (people of mixed Indigenous and Spanish ancestry). Although Mexican forces eventually defeated the Indigenous insurgents in 1901, the Caste War brought about meaningful change, including improved social conditions, political reform, and the eventual dissolution of the hacienda system in the area. The effects of the Mexican Revolution (1910–1920), including the establishment of a constitution recognizing Indigenous land rights, wouldn't truly impact parts of Southern Mexico until much later.

This long history of Indigenous resistance and resilience in the region continues on. In 1994, for instance, the poverty-stricken state of Chiapas was the site of the Zapatista uprising, orchestrated to bring attention to the country's social inequities as the North American Free Trade

Agreement (NAFTA) went into effect. But even with all these uprisings, the agricultural, timber, and tourism industries—all major offenders on the environmental and social justice fronts—are booming in Southern Mexico.

One of the most recent examples of the Mexican government prioritizing so-called progress over people is the development of the Maya Train carrying tourists across the Yucatán. Building the 1,525-kilometer track required clearing out a large swath of the Maya Forest and also displacing nearly 3,000 households. Alongside other activists, advocates from the affected Maya communities fought hard against the megaproject, ultimately to no avail. Although they've taken new forms, these modern-day assaults to hard-won Indigenous sovereignty echo the egregious acts of the region's complex history.

THE FOOD

For the Maya peoples, food offers more than just nourishment; it's also a crucial part of ceremony. Their sophisticated belief systems are interwoven, and food is no exception. Of the many deities associated with specific plants and animals, one of the most revered is Hun Hunahpu, who is closely associated with maíz.

Just as there's no single Maya identity, there's no single Maya cuisine. Each community's unique culinary practices are tied to their specific land space and history. Of course, that history includes colonization, and current Maya food systems have the indelible imprint of Spanish influences. Modern dishes often marry introduced foods like pork and chicken with traditional preparation techniques.

The Yucatán fan-favorite cochinita pibil (which literally translates to "cooked underground"), for instance, calls for cooking citrus-marinated pork in an earthen oven known as a *pib*. This ingenious method of slow-cooking in a pit lined with hot stones and firewood imparts the banana leaf–wrapped meat with that signature smoky flavor. Renowned Maya chef Rosalía Chay still prepares it this way and offers a rare opportunity to witness the process—and savor the dish—through her culinary experiences.

As I always say, there are no rules in food, and I find cochinita pibil quite tasty. But in my work to revitalize Indigenous foodways, I challenge myself to prepare meals without relying upon the Eurocentric ingredients that are now ubiquitous across Turtle Island. For the purposes of this book, I'm inviting home cooks to do the same.

My version of this staple subs in native turkey and skips the sour orange (see page 262). But believe me, you won't find it lacking in any way, since achiote (ground annatto seeds) gives this beloved dish its unique taste, color, and depth. Indeed, in Maya cuisine, it's the recados—blends of roasted chiles, dried herbs, garlic, and other spices—that really make the meal. They're traditionally ground on a stone metate, but a food processor will also do the trick.

My take on poc chuc (see page 264), a popular grilled pork dish that translates to "toast" over "fire," swaps in javelina for domesticated pork, because these wild pigs were roaming the region prior to European contact. This lean meat gets marinated with tomatillos for extra tenderness and served alongside handmade corn tortillas.

But let's be real about the real star of the show here: maíz, which acts as the cornerstone of Maya cuisine. In the recipes that follow, it shows up in delicious and nutritious corn fritters (see page 255) paired with the superfood huauzontle, also known as Aztec broccoli. It's also the main attraction in chochoyotes (see page 261), masa dumplings served in a vegetable soup.

Dzotobilchay (page 257) is another traditional meal whose translated meaning tells you everything you need to know: corn dough cooked with chaya, a wild green sometimes called tree spinach. The dough gets filled with hard-cooked duck eggs and toasted pepitas—making for a tamal unlike any you've ever tried. Similarly, these dishes show off a side of the Yucatán most people never get a chance to savor.

ENSALADA DE JÍCAMA Y PIÑA CON SAL DE CHILE Y ACHIOTE

Jicama and Pineapple Salad with Chile and Achiote Salt

serves 4 to 6

This juicy salad is exactly what I want to eat on a sweltering day. The combination of salt, achiote, and chile is one you'll see used throughout Southern Mexico and one you could sprinkle over almost any combination of raw vegetables and fruit. For this salad, you ideally want a ripe, sweet pineapple. Look for fruit with some yellowing on the skin and sweet smell at the base. Avoid pineapples that have no aroma or smell sour or fermented.

1 dried chile de árbol

2 teaspoons coarse sea salt

1 teaspoon achiote seeds

1 medium ripe pineapple

½ medium jicama

1 tablespoon agave syrup

Tear the chile(s) into small pieces and place in a mortar, discarding the stem. Include the seeds for a spicier salt or discard them, if you prefer. Add the salt and achiote and use the pestle to pound until you have a cohesive salt mixture.

Use a sharp knife to remove the leafy top and outer skin from the pineapple. Cut the pineapple vertically into quarters and then remove the wedges of central core from each one. Cut the cored pineapple quarters into ½-inch pieces and place in a serving bowl.

Peel the jicama and cut it into the same size of ½-inch pieces, adding them to the bowl.

Drizzle the fruit with the agave syrup, sprinkle with the chile salt, and serve.

THE FRAUGHT HISTORY OF PINEAPPLE ON TURTLE ISLAND

Native to South America, pineapples have been cultivated in Mesoamerica for thousands of years. The Maya people in particular often planted the regal fruit among other crops, including tomatoes, avocados, chiles, sweet potatoes, and jicama.

Colonizers in the Caribbean and later Mexico were immediately enamored of pineapples' curious shape and delicious, sweet flavor. They brought them back to Europe, where they became a fashionable status symbol. Eventually, European land thieves built monoculture plantations in the tropical "New World" to grow pineapples at scale with enslaved labor. In the nineteenth century, the appetite for pineapples led to even more land theft in Hawaii.

I hesitated to include an ingredient with such a dark history for Indigenous peoples, especially considering pineapple is still often grown on a large scale using extractive agricultural methods. But it's also important to share these histories so we can appreciate an ingredient's origins and work toward growing them in better ways in the future.

TORTITAS DE HUAUZONTLES CON SALSA DE CACAHUATE, TOMATE Y CHILE DE ÁRBOL

Fried Huauzontle Fritters with Peanut, Tomato, and Chile Salsa

serves 4 to 6 as a starter

Huauzontles (*Chenopodium nuttalliae*) are one of the many quelites—or wild greens—beloved in Mexico. The plant is closely related to lamb's quarters, amaranth, and quinoa but highly prized for its cluster of buds that form, which resemble broccoli in texture but spinach in flavor. (Some people call this vegetable Aztec broccoli, in fact.)

There are several typical dishes made with this vegetable, often involving cheese and a roasted tomato sauce. For these huauzontles, I blanch them and then toss them in a batter to make crispy, lacy-edged fritters that I then serve with a version of salsa de cacahuate, a peanut salsa popular in central and southern Mexico.

- 1 long bunch huauzontles (12 to 16 ounces)
- Fine sea salt
- 1 duck egg
- Pinch of baking soda
- 1 cup chilled sparkling water
- ½ cup fine cornmeal
- ½ cup cassava flour
- Sunflower or avocado oil, for frying
- 1 cup Salsa de Cacahuate (recipe follows), for serving

Pull the bud clusters off the stems from the huauzontles. Rinse the huauzontle buds in several changes of water to remove any grit.

Bring a large saucepan of salted water to a boil over medium-high heat. Add the huauzontle buds to the boiling water and cook (blanch) for about 2 minutes, just until bright green and tender. Drain and run them under cool water. When they're cool enough to handle, squeeze out any excess water, then roll into towels to dry.

In a medium bowl, lightly beat together the egg, baking soda, and ¼ teaspoon fine sea salt. Gently stir in the sparkling water.

In a separate bowl, whisk together the cornmeal and cassava flour. Gradually add the flours to the egg mixture and mix it in gently to form a slightly lumpy batter. Fold in the blanched huauzontle buds, making sure they get evenly coated.

Line a plate with paper towels and set it next to the stovetop. In a cast-iron skillet, heat ¼ inch of oil over medium heat to about 350°F.

Working in batches to avoid overcrowding, scoop 2 to 3 tablespoons of the batter for each tortita into the oil and fry for about 2 minutes, or until golden brown on the bottom. Use a spatula to carefully flip and fry for 1 to 2 minutes longer, until golden and crisped on the second side.

Transfer to the paper towels to drain and season with salt. Serve with the salsa.

(recipe continues)

SALSA DE CACAHUATE

Makes about 2 cups

- 3 dried chiles de árbol
- 1 large tomato, cored
- ¼ medium white onion
- 4 garlic cloves, unpeeled
- ¼ cup avocado or sunflower oil
- ½ cup unsalted roasted peanuts
- ¼ teaspoon dried Mexican oregano
- 4 allspice berries
- Sea salt
- 1 tablespoon cider vinegar

Heat a cast-iron skillet over medium heat. Add the chiles in a single layer and toast for about 2 minutes, turning frequently, until they're pliable, fragrant, and blistered in spots. Transfer to a bowl to cool. Snip off the stem end of the chiles. If you prefer a less spicy salsa, shake out the seeds.

Add the tomato, onion, and garlic to the skillet. Cook the garlic for about 3 minutes, turning frequently, until blackened in spots all over, and 4 minutes for the onion and tomato, turning and blackening them in spots as well. Transfer to a plate to cool.

Peel the garlic and add it to a blender along with the onion and tomato.

Heat the oil in the same skillet. Add the peanuts, charred chiles, oregano, allspice, and a pinch of salt. Cook for about 1 minute, stirring, until everything is fragrant and the peanuts darken slightly.

Scrape everything from the skillet into the blender. Add ¼ cup water and pulse until nearly smooth but with some texture. Add the vinegar and pulse just to incorporate. Ultimately, you want a pourable salsa. If it's too thick to pour, add more water, 1 tablespoon at a time, as needed. Taste and season with more salt as needed. You'll have about 2 cups of salsa.

If not using right away, store in an airtight container in the refrigerator for up to 1 week.

DZOTOBILCHAY

Maya Tamales with Chaya and Eggs in a Roasted Tomato Sauce

makes 8 tamales

Dzotobilchay is a tamal from the Yucatán Peninsula made using masa mixed with chaya leaves. Chaya is a perennial tropical shrub that produces nutrient-dense leaves that taste like spinach. (In fact, chaya is sometimes called tree spinach or Maya spinach.)

Today, you'll often see dzotobilchay wrapped in banana leaves, but I use corn husks here. Otherwise, with its pepitas and hard-boiled egg filling and pan-roasted tomato sauce, this dish is fairly traditional.

TAMALES

- ¾ cup pepitas
- 4 duck eggs
- Sea salt
- 8 ounces chaya leaves, lamb's quarters, or spinach
- ½ cup duck fat
- 1 pound Fresh Masa (page 28) or use masa harina (see chart, page 27)
- 8 dried corn husks for tamales, soaked overnight, plus more for the pot

SAUCE

- 2 tablespoons avocado or sunflower oil, plus more for brushing
- ½ small white onion, cut into 6 wedges
- 1 garlic clove, unpeeled
- 1 jalapeño, halved lengthwise and seeded
- 5 plum tomatoes, halved lengthwise
- 1 teaspoon cider vinegar
- Sea salt

Make the tamales: In a large dry skillet, toast the pepitas over medium heat for about 2 minutes, or until they start to darken. Transfer to a food processor.

When the seeds are cool, pulse them until they are coarsely ground. Scrape into a bowl.

Set up a bowl of ice and water and place it near the stove. In a medium saucepan, bring several inches of water to a boil over high heat. Reduce the heat to medium-low so the water simmers and carefully lower the eggs into the pot, making sure they are submerged. Cook for 10 minutes. Using a slotted spoon, transfer the eggs to the ice bath. Let cool, then peel the eggs. Leave the water at a simmer.

Chop the hard-boiled eggs and add them to the bowl with the pepitas. Season with salt and toss to combine.

Add the chaya leaves to the simmering water and cook for about 1 minute, until bright green. Drain the leaves in a colander and run them under cool water. Squeeze out as much of the liquid as possible and coarsely chop the leaves.

In a bowl, using an electric mixer, beat the duck fat on high speed until fluffy. Add the masa, a little at a time, until incorporated. Scrape the chopped greens into the masa and stir until evenly distributed.

Arrange 1 husk on a work surface, ribbed-side down, with the narrow end pointing away from you. Using a ¼-cup measure, scoop dough into the center of the husk. Use a large rounded spoon to create a well in the dough, leaving a ½-inch border of husk. Measure out about 3 tablespoons of the pepita/egg filling and arrange it in the well.

Fold in the long sides of the husk, overlapping them to enclose the filling. Fold the narrow end toward you, over the tamal; it will be open at the wide end. Stand the tamal, open-end up, in a steamer insert. Repeat with the remaining husks, dough, and filling.

Cover the tamales with more corn husks or parchment paper.

(recipe continues)

Fill the bottom of the steamer with water to come no higher than where the bottom of the steamer insert will be. Bring to a boil over medium-high heat. Reduce the heat to low. Add the steamer insert, cover the pot, and steam the tamales for 1½ hours. Remove one of the tamales from the steamer. If it feels firm, check inside. If it looks shiny and wet or you see a lot of residue sticking to the husk when you pull it away, continue cooking for up to 30 minutes longer. Otherwise, remove from the steamer and let cool for 15 minutes. The masa will continue to firm up during this time.

While the tamales cook, make the sauce: Heat a comal or heavy skillet over medium-high heat. Lightly brush it with some oil. Add the onion wedges, garlic, and jalapeño and cook, turning frequently, for 5 to 8 minutes, or until charred in spots. Let the garlic clove cool, then peel and transfer to a blender. Remove the stem from the jalapeño and transfer to the blender along with the onion.

Add the tomatoes skin-sides down to the pan and cook for about 2 minutes, or until blistered on the bottom. Flip and cook them for about 30 seconds, just until the flesh side is blistered in spots.

Transfer the tomatoes to the blender and pulse until nearly smooth but with some texture.

In a skillet, heat the 2 tablespoons oil over medium heat, until just warmed through. Carefully stir in the pureed sauce (it may steam and bubble up) and cook for 3 to 5 minutes, until slightly thickened and darker. Stir in the vinegar. Taste and season with salt.

Serve the tamales with the roasted tomato sauce.

SOPA DE MILPA CON CHOCHOYOTES Y CHIPILÍN

Garden Vegetable Soup with Dumplings

serves 4 to 6

Just as they have in other parts of Turtle Island, the Maya people in the Yucatán and other Indigenous peoples in central and southern Mexico, interplant corn, beans, squash, chiles, tomatoes, and other crops in a system known as the milpa. Sopa de milpa is a soup that reflects what might be growing in people's gardens at any time, changing from season to season and cook to cook.

When they're available, I like to add chipilín leaves to this soup, which taste like a milder version of spinach with a green bean edge. This shrub grows wild in South and Central America and southern Mexico. You can occasionally find people cultivating the leaves in the United States, too, but you can substitute baby spinach.

To make the soup more filling, I slip chochoyotes—simple dumplings made of masa—into the broth, but you could skip them if you prefer.

- 8 ounces Fresh Masa (page 28) or use masa harina (see chart, page 27)
- 3 tablespoons avocado or sunflower oil
- 1 bunch chipilín leaves (picked from the stems) or 3 cups baby spinach
- ½ medium white onion, chopped
- Sea salt
- 6 garlic cloves, minced
- 1 jalapeño or serrano chile, stemmed, seeded if desired, and thinly sliced
- 1 pound summer squash, such as zucchini, cut lengthwise into quarters and crosswise into ½-inch pieces
- 2 medium tomatoes, cored and chopped
- 6 cups Roasted Bird Stock (page 40) or vegetable broth
- 1 sprig of epazote
- 2 ears corn, husked and cut crosswise into 1-inch-thick rounds
- 1 tablespoon cider vinegar
- 12 squash flowers, stemmed, halved lengthwise, stamen or pistil removed

Mix the masa with 1 tablespoon of the oil.

Finely chop half of the chipilín leaves. Add those to the masa and use your hands to mix them in. Cover the masa while you form the dumplings and keep the dumplings covered once they are made.

Set a piece of parchment paper on a baking sheet or cutting board. Using a teaspoon, scoop the masa into ½-inch balls and place them on the parchment. Press your thumb into each ball to create a divot in the center.

In a large pot or Dutch oven, heat the remaining 2 tablespoons of oil over medium heat. Add the onion, season with salt, and cook for about 5 minutes, or until translucent. Add the garlic and chile and cook for about 1 minute, or until fragrant.

Add the squash and tomatoes, season with salt, and cook for about 5 minutes, or until the tomatoes start to break down and release their juices.

Add the stock, the remaining chipilín leaves, and the epazote. Bring to a boil over medium-high heat. Reduce the heat to medium so the soup simmers. Add the corn cob rounds and cook for about 4 minutes, or until softened.

Gently drop the masa dumplings into the soup and simmer for 7 to 10 minutes, until they are cooked through and tender. Be careful not to overcook, or they will begin to fall apart in the broth.

Discard the epazote sprig and add the vinegar to the soup. Taste and season with more salt as needed.

Stir in the halved squash blossoms, let them wilt, then serve.

GUAJOLOTE PIBIL

Turkey Pibil

serves 4 to 6

Cochinita pibil is often hailed as a pre-Hispanic dish, but that's not entirely true for the modern version. *Cochinita* means "little pig," and domesticated pigs came with the Spanish. The dish was likely made with some form of wild hog, like javelina or peccary, as well as other native animals, including turkey and deer.

Today's recipe also typically relies on citrus—specifically, a sour orange—and citrus, too, came to Mexico with the conquistadors.

It is true, however, that the Maya cooked and continue to cook in an earthen oven known as a pib, which is heated by embers as well as hot rocks. Before food is put in the pib, it is typically wrapped in leaves. The cooking method infuses everything with an incredible smoky flavor while also keeping everything moist. The Maya have also long used marinades made with achiote, the seed of a shrub that imparts a vibrant red-orange color to food and has a slightly peppery flavor.

As I did for many of the recipes in this book, I imagined how a dish might have been before Europeans arrived, but then I adapted it for modern cooks.

Here, turkey gets rubbed with a garlicky achiote marinade warmly spiced with allspice, wrapped in banana leaves to keep in moisture, and then smoked in a smoker. (You can also set up your grill for smoking; see page 69.)

If you have neither a smoker nor a grill, you can slow-roast the wrapped turkey in a 250°F oven and create some smoky flavor by adding ½ teaspoon smoked paprika to the marinade.

- 12 garlic cloves, unpeeled
- 3 tablespoons sunflower or avocado oil
- ¼ cup achiote paste
- 2 tablespoons dried Mexican oregano
- 1 tablespoon allspice berries
- ¼ cup coarse sea salt
- 1 cup cider vinegar
- 3 tablespoons agave syrup
- 2 bone-in turkey thighs plus 2 bone-in turkey drumsticks (about 4 pounds total)
- 4 to 8 banana leaves
- 1 white onion, cut in thin half-moon slices
- 8 Mexican bay leaves
- Warmed tortillas, for serving
- Pickled Onion (page 264), for serving
- Pickled Habanero Chiles (page 234), for serving

Heat a comal or dry skillet over medium-high heat. Add the garlic cloves and cook for 8 to 10 minutes, turning, until the skins are blackened all over. Transfer to a plate to cool.

In a skillet, heat the oil over medium heat. Stir in the achiote paste, oregano, and allspice and cook for 1 to 2 minutes, until fragrant.

Scrape everything from the skillet into a blender. Peel the garlic cloves and add them to the blender. Add the salt, vinegar, and agave syrup and puree until smooth. The marinade will seem strong, but the flavors will mellow.

Pat the turkey pieces dry and transfer to a large bowl. Pour on the marinade and rub it all over the meat, until evenly coated. Cover and refrigerate for at least 8 hours and up to 24 hours.

Remove the turkey from the refrigerator and let it stand at room temperature for 30 minutes.

Preheat a smoker to 250°F (or if you don't have a smoker, see Smoking Food on a Grill, page 69).

For each piece of turkey, you're going to want to wrap it in a banana leaf so it is fully covered. You might be able to use 1 piece of banana leaf for each piece of turkey, but you also might need to overlap 2 leaves to wrap the turkey. Arrange the banana leaves on a work surface, overlapping them as

needed. Lift a piece of turkey out of the bowl and set on the leaves. Top the turkey with some sliced onion and bay leaves and wrap up so it's enclosed in the leaves. Tie the wrap with kitchen string. Repeat to make 4 packages of turkey. Discard any excess marinade in the bowl.

Smoke the turkey for 1½ to 2 hours, until the meat is easily pierced with a skewer and feels like it will pull apart easily. Remove the parcels from the heat and transfer them to a deep platter. Let stand for 5 minutes before opening them, discarding the bay leaves. Use two forks or tongs to shred the meat, discarding the bones.

Serve the shredded turkey with warm tortillas, pickled onion, and pickled chiles.

POC CHUC DE JAVELINA

serves 4 to 6

In the Maya language, *poc chuc* or *pok chuc* means "to toast food over charcoal." Today, this method is often used to cook pork, but it can work for many different kinds of food. Like many dishes in the region, it typically includes a punchy marinade that gets its tartness from sour orange. Here, I make poc chuc with javelina, a type of wild pig, but you can substitute wild boar, and in place of sour orange, which came with European colonizers, vinegar. The garlicky, vinegar marinade cuts through any gaminess.

I suggest you turn the poc chuc into tacos topped with slices of creamy avocado and zippy pickled onion, but you can also serve it with any side dish that inspires you.

To make the meat extra flavorful, it gets brined first and then marinated, so you'll need to plan ahead.

JAVELINA

- ¼ cup fine sea salt
- ¼ cup agave syrup
- 2 pounds javelina or wild boar loin
- ½ cup cider vinegar
- 1 teaspoon ground allspice
- 10 garlic cloves, smashed
- 1 cup avocado oil, plus more for the grill

SERVING

- Warm tortillas
- Sliced avocado
- Salsa of your choice
- Pickled Onion (recipe below)

Marinate the javelina: In a large bowl, combine 4 cups water, the salt, and agave syrup, stirring until the salt dissolves. Add the javelina, making sure it is submerged, cover, and refrigerate overnight.

The next day, cut the meat crosswise into ¼-inch-thick cutlets. (Lightly pound them to thin them out if your slices are uneven or too thick.)

Pour the vinegar into a glass baking dish. Stir in the allspice. Add the garlic cloves and oil. Add the cutlets and turn to coat. Cover and refrigerate for at least 4 hours and up to 8 hours.

When you're ready to cook, preheat a grill, preferably charcoal, to medium-high heat (about 400°F). Oil the grates.

Transfer the cutlets to a plate and pat dry. Discard the marinade. Grill the cutlets for 2 to 3 minutes, until grill marks form on the bottom. Flip and cook for 2 to 3 minutes longer, until just slightly pink within. Transfer to a work surface to rest for 3 minutes, then cut into strips.

To serve: Place the grilled javelina strips on a platter. Serve with the tortillas, avocado, salsa, and pickled onion.

CEBOLLAS EN VINAGRE

Pickled Onion

Makes 1 pint

These zingy, allspice-infused onions are a must-have with Guajolote Pibil (page 262) and the Poc Chuc but are delicious over any taco or masa-based dish.

- ½ large red onion, thinly sliced
- 3 allspice berries
- 1 Mexican bay leaf
- ½ cup cider vinegar
- ¼ cup agave syrup
- 1 tablespoon fine sea salt

Pack the onion, allspice berries, and bay leaf into a 1-pint jar or nonreactive airtight container.

In a small saucepan, combine the vinegar, ½ cup water, the agave syrup, and salt and bring to a boil over high heat, whisking to dissolve the salt. Turn off the heat and pour over the onion. Let cool to room temperature.

Seal and refrigerate for at least 1 hour before serving. The pickled onion can be refrigerated for up to 1 month.

TOSTADAS DE CHARALES FRITOS CON SALSA VERDE CRUDA

Tostadas with Little Fried Fish and Salsa Verde

serves 4 to 8

Charales are the little white fish that inhabit Mexico's lakes and other freshwater sources. They're especially popular in central-western Mexico as well as in Chiapas and often used dried, but you can also cook them when fresh, as they are here. And you eat them heads and all.

I like to marinate them in a vinegary achiote blend so they're super flavorful and have no sense of fishiness. A cornmeal coating helps them become extra crisp once fried. (You can use whitebait or other similar little fish in place of charales.)

When paired with the lush avocado and tangy salsa verde, this dish offers a beautiful mix of flavors and textures.

SALSA

- 1 pound tomatillos, husked and chopped
- 1 jalapeño or serrano chile, stemmed, seeded if desired, and coarsely chopped
- ¼ cup chopped white onion
- 5 culantro leaves or ¼ cup cilantro leaves, coarsely chopped
- 1 garlic clove, peeled
- ¼ teaspoon fine sea salt, plus more as needed

CHARALES

- 1 tablespoon achiote paste
- 1 tablespoon cider vinegar
- 1 garlic clove, minced
- ¼ teaspoon dried Mexican oregano
- ¼ teaspoon chile de árbol powder
- ¼ teaspoon fine sea salt
- 8 ounces cleaned fresh charales or whitebait

ASSEMBLY

- Avocado or sunflower oil, for frying
- 8 (6-inch) Corn Tortillas (page 31) or store-bought
- 1 cup fine cornmeal
- Sea salt
- 2 Hass avocados, halved and pitted

Make the salsa: In a blender, combine the tomatillos, chile, onion, culantro, garlic, and salt and pulse to coarsely chop, then let the blender run at medium speed until the salsa is pureed but with a little texture. Add water as needed to loosen the texture so the salsa is pourable. Taste and season with salt.

Marinate the charales: In a large bowl, combine the achiote paste, vinegar, garlic, oregano, árbol powder, and salt, stirring until well incorporated. Add the charales and toss to coat evenly. Let stand for 15 minutes.

To assemble the tostadas: Pour about ½ inch oil into a skillet over medium heat. Set up two wire racks near the stovetop.

Working with one tortilla at a time, fry for about 1 minute, turning once, until deeply golden and puffed in spots. Transfer to a wire rack. Turn off the heat.

Line a plate with paper towels and place near the stove. Place the cornmeal in a shallow bowl and toss with a pinch of salt. Lift the charales out of the marinade, allowing any excess to drip back into the bowl. Add the marinated charales to the cornmeal and toss.

In the same skillet used for the tortillas, add more oil to reach a ½-inch depth again if needed and heat over medium heat.

Working in batches to avoid overcrowding, shake off any excess cornmeal from the charales and add them to the hot oil in a single layer. Fry for about 2 minutes, turning them as needed, until crisped and golden brown. (Reduce the heat if the cornmeal threatens to burn.) Transfer the charales to the paper towels to drain and quickly season with salt.

Scoop the avocado flesh into a medium bowl and use a fork to mash it. Season it well with salt.

Spread some of the avocado mash over each tortilla. Top with the charales and serve with the salsa.

PESCADO EN HOJA SANTA CON SALSA VERACRUZANA PREHISPÁNICA

Fish Wrapped in Hoja Santa Leaves with a Pre-Hispanic Veracruz Salsa

serves 4

Pescado a la veracruzana is a popular dish often made with white wine, capers, and olives that shows the undeniable influence of Spanish cooking in the region. But the basis for the sauce—tomatoes and chiles—are purely indigenous.

To help keep the lean fish fillets moist, I steam them in hoja santa leaves, which have a fascinating flavor that's reminiscent of root beer. Don't worry. It doesn't make the fish sweet like soda. It just gives it an intriguing herbal flavor that's lovely with the gentle sauce.

- 2 tablespoons avocado or sunflower oil, plus more for drizzling
- 1 medium yellow onion, chopped
- Sea salt
- 2 garlic cloves, minced
- 2 large tomatoes, cored and diced
- 1 jalapeño or serrano chile, stemmed, seeded if desired, and thinly sliced
- 1 teaspoon dried Mexican oregano
- 1 Mexican bay leaf
- ½ cup fish stock or clam juice
- 8 large hoja santa leaves
- 4 skin-on or skinned white fish fillets (6 ounces each), such as snapper or grouper

In a large skillet, heat the oil over medium heat. Add the onion, season with salt, and cook for about 5 minutes, or until translucent. Add the garlic and cook for about 1 minute, or until fragrant.

Stir in the tomatoes, chile, oregano, bay leaf, and a pinch of salt. Cook for about 5 minutes, allowing the flavors to meld and the tomatoes to break down slightly and release their juices. Pour in the fish stock. Bring the mixture to a simmer and cook for 5 minutes longer. Taste and season with salt as needed. Discard the bay leaf and keep the salsa warm over low heat.

Meanwhile, arrange 2 hoja santa leaves on a work surface so they're overlapping slightly. Arrange one of the fish fillets in the center and drizzle lightly with oil. Season both sides of the fish with salt. Wrap the leaves to enclose the fish and transfer to a plate. Repeat with the remaining leaves and fish.

Set a steamer insert in a pot and add about 1 inch water to the pot. Bring the water to a simmer over medium heat. Using tongs, set the wrapped fish, seam-sides down, in the insert, cover tightly, and steam the fish for 8 minutes, checking occasionally to replenish the water as needed. Insert a table knife into the center of one of the fillets. If it's very warm to the touch, turn off the heat. If it's cool or just barely warm, continue steaming for 1 to 2 minutes longer and check the fish again.

Transfer the wrapped fish to plates and serve with the salsa.

ATOLE DE CACAO

serves 4

½ cup unsweetened cacao nibs or ⅓ cup cacao powder

½ cup masa harina

2 cups pepita milk (see Seed, Nut, and Grain Milks, page 35)

Pinch of ancho chile powder

½ vanilla bean, split lengthwise

Agave syrup (optional)

It's believed the Olmec people were the first to cultivate and process cacao and use it to make drinks. For the Maya people, cacao was a sacred food but also consumed daily, much like corn. (In fact, it was often blended with ground corn to make a warm drink like this one.) For people in the Aztec empire, cacao was seen as more special and generally drunk by the elites.

Before colonization, cacao-based drinks were rarely sweetened.

Today, you'll find many warm, often spiced and sweetened cacao-based drinks throughout Mexico. This is a fairly traditional version, unsweetened (unless you'd like to add some agave syrup) and flavored with ancho chile powder and vanilla. It uses the ancient Maya method for aerating by pouring the atole back and forth, although you could use a molinillo or whisk to do so.

Using a metate or spice grinder, grind the cacao nibs into a powder.

In a medium bowl, stir together the masa harina and 2 cups water and let stand for 5 minutes.

Strain the masa and water through a fine-mesh sieve directly into a saucepan, pressing all the solids through. Bring to a simmer over medium heat. Add the ground cacao and stir constantly to try to dissolve.

Stir in the pepita milk and allow it to heat through. Add the chile powder. Scrape in the vanilla seeds and simmer very gently for 5 minutes, allowing the flavors to meld and the masa to thicken the drink slightly.

Pour the drink back into a jicara (a bowl made out of a gourd) or another saucepan and continue pouring it back and forth to aerate it, mix it further, and help it become frothy. (Alternatively, you could use a molinillo or whisk.)

If you'd like to enjoy the atole the way the Maya and Aztec people would, pour it into cups without sweetening. Otherwise, sweeten with agave syrup to taste before serving.

GUANABANA SORBET

Soursop Sorbet

serves 4

Guanabana (also known as soursop) is a large spiky tropical fruit with green skin and white flesh that's both sweet and tart (think pineapple meets apple), with a banana-like creamy texture. It's the kind of fruit that you eat with a spoon or use to make a puree for the base of desserts, like this refreshing sorbet.

The size of the fruit can range from being just larger than a mango to nearly the size of a basketball. You can find them sometimes at Latin or Asian markets or you might also find store-bought frozen pulp.

- 2 cups guanabana pulp (see Note), thawed if frozen
- ½ cup agave syrup
- 1 tablespoon cider vinegar

In a blender or food processor, combine the guanabana pulp, ½ cup water, the agave syrup, and vinegar and puree until smooth. Scrape into a bowl, cover, and refrigerate for 1 hour, or until well chilled.

Churn the mixture in an ice cream maker according to the manufacturer's instructions. Serve immediately or freeze in an airtight container for up to 2 weeks. (Let it sit at room temperature for a few minutes before serving to soften up if it's coming out of the freezer.)

Note: *To make guanabana pulp, choose 1 large ripe guanabana that is fragrant, with a slightly yellow tinge to the skin and just barely soft to the touch. Cut the fruit in half lengthwise. Scoop out the creamy flesh, discarding the large seeds. Measure out 2 cups or use as much flesh as you get out of the fruit, adjusting the ratio of the water, agave syrup, and vinegar as needed to make the sorbet.*

PACIFIC COAST

CALIFORNIA AND BAJA CALIFORNIA

AMERICANS HAVE COME TO KNOW California as many things: the epicenter of entertainment, a bastion of liberalism, a hotbed of golf courses, a leading wine region, and the country's most agriculturally productive state. But the tribal communities that have lived along the southern Pacific Coast since time immemorial know it simply as home. Like Oklahoma, this state has such a singular history that we decided to dedicate an entire chapter to it.

My childhood memories of California include requisite Disneyland visits and time spent with cousins near Los Angeles. As an adult, I've deepened my knowledge of this place thanks to friends and family living there, like my uncle Marlon and his wife, Dale Ann, both of whom taught Indigenous-focused curricula at Cal Poly Humboldt until their recent retirement. I remember visiting them in the early days in 2013, even before I had founded The Sioux Chef, and giving one of my first talks about Native foodways with them in the audience.

A cultural and repatriation consultant who oversees the return of important ancestral belongings to her community, Dale Ann is from Northern California's Yurok tribe, who are the original Redwood people. They recently became the first tribal nation to enter into a comanagement agreement with the National Park Service. Although the 125 acres of Redwood parkland scheduled to be returned to them in 2026 is just a sliver of their original territory, it's a meaningful step toward shared stewardship of this land and its all-important biodiversity.

I've had the opportunity to collaborate with many of California's Indigenous food advocates, like renowned Mohawk seed keeper Rowen White, who lives on the Sierra Seeds sanctuary farm in the foothills of the Sierra Nevada. Back in 2015, she and I hosted the organization's first ever fundraising dinner, a five-course extravaganza of pre-contact cuisine.

To prepare for the meal, we foraged with author and ethnobotanist Alicia Funk, who created the Living Wild Project to help educate Californians about the natural foods all around them. Rowen's then ten-year-old daughter, Maizie, helped us out in the kitchen, plus Xicana culinary anthropologist Claudia Serrato was there to support us, too.

As I do whenever I cook on other people's homelands, I endeavored to honor the foodways of that place. The dinner kicked off with Yurok smoked salmon with yarrow, nettle puree, and a chilled manzanita broth made from the orange-red berries of the area's omnipresent shrubs (which few Californians realize are edible). Our second course was a wild mixed salad topped with an elderberry and ginger dressing, paired with amaranth crackers.

For the entrées, we served smoked elk with yucca flowers, pea shoots, grilled star tulip, and rose hip puree as well as dried duck alongside grilled trumpet mushrooms, miner's lettuce, pine pollen, and balsam fir syrup. I remember when we were plating that dish, we ran out of miner's lettuce (a colonialist-driven name, in case you didn't catch that), so Maizie bolted out of the kitchen and picked some from a nearby patch. That's the beauty of using the natural ingredients that surround us. For a final sweet note, we made a grilled acorn and honey cake with elderflower syrup, mountain mint sauce, and a glazed seed mix.

Even back then, California was experiencing a major drought. I recall it so distinctly—as dinner was wrapping up, the sky cracked open and it started to pour rain, as if on cue. Everyone was thrilled, because they'd been waiting such a long time for a good rain. In so many ways, that event embodied both the beauties and the struggles of Pacific Coast life.

Rowen is just one of many influential expats living in California. Other Native food sovereignty warriors include vibrant Afro-Indigenous chef Crystal Wahpepah, who opened her namesake Oakland restaurant in 2021 after serving traditional Kickapoo cuisine at Silicon Valley giants like Google, Facebook, and Twitter. She grew up in the Bay Area and learned to cook from her aunties at the Intertribal Friendship House, while spending childhood summers back on the family farm in Oklahoma. Her delectable dishes are an amalgamation of those influences.

Meanwhile in nearby Berkeley, chefs Vincent Medina (Chochenyo Ohlone) and Louis Trevino (Rumsen Ohlone) are on a mission to sustain their traditional cultures through their Cafe Ohlone. In addition to offering Bay Area first foods like acorn soup, soft-boiled quail eggs, and chia desserts, the al fresco restaurant creates an interesting juxtaposition for diners to consider, since the nearby Hearst Museum of Anthropology has been notably slow to repatriate the thousands of sacred Indigenous artifacts it holds. As at Owamni, situated along the Mississippi River, a meal at Cafe Ohlone sparks a crucial conversation about tribal sovereignty.

When Potawatomi/Mexican chef Pyet DeSpain moved from Kansas to Los Angeles in 2017 to pursue her dreams of becoming a personal chef, she at first felt like she needed to downplay her Native roots and just make whatever her clients requested. After feeling misaligned with her true identity, she decided to focus on Indigenous fusion cuisine reflecting her multicultural heritage. Her business is booming thanks to a sense of authenticity that shines through in her cooking.

California is also home to a huge community of Mixtecos—Indigenous Mesoamerican peoples from what's now Mexico, particularly Oaxaca. There's even a term to describe this binational culture due to the mass migration in recent decades: Oaxacalifornia. Indeed, Los Angeles has one of the largest Indigenous populations of any US city, including the First Peoples of this place as well as the Pacific Islander and Latin American diasporas.

One of the area's most tenacious Indigenous advocates is Zapotec activist and interpreter Odilia Romero, who moved there from the Oaxaca Highlands when she was ten. Like me, she's fighting for social justice through a cultural lens, but her medium is language while mine is food. Of course, within Native communities, we recognize that these things are inextricably intertwined.

As proud as I am of my peers' accomplishments, I'm not just bragging about the Native food scene in California. Rather, I aim to highlight how the state's vast natural abundance allows many Indigenous lifeways to prosper there, as it has for eons. Whether their ancestors lived there or they more recently made their way from other parts of Turtle Island, these chefs are doing more than just cooking. They're inviting all of us to the table to simultaneously savor the bounty of the Pacific Coast and recognize the environmental and social justice issues at play.

THE LAND

California is a rare place where five climates converge in close proximity, including Mediterranean, continental, highland, desert, and steppe. Along its edges, the state echoes the characteristics of nearby regions, including the Northwest Coast, the Great Basin, and the Southwest desert lands. In combination with the complex topography—mountains, valleys, prairies,

wetlands, rivers, lakes, and more—those climes create a wide variety in weather.

The area tucked between the Pacific Ocean and the Coastal Ranges experiences warm winters and cool summers thanks to the maritime influence. As you'd expect, the Klamath, Cascade, and Sierra Nevada mountain ranges are colder and wetter than the deep valleys, like the extreme Death Valley (the lowest point in the continental United States, which reaches intense temperatures).

Winter brings some rain while summer tends to be drier, making the declining Sierra Nevada winter snowpack of utmost importance. It feeds into the rivers and streams in the spring and early summer, supplying about 30 percent of the state's water needs. Sadly, many of these waterways have been dammed for agricultural, industrial, and domestic use, which alongside overfishing has devastated wildlife populations. There's a movement afoot to remove many of those dams—including the largest US river restoration project to date, as of this writing, along the Klamath—but so much damage has already been done.

The California Current flushes cooler water along the coastline from British Columbia all the way to Baja. Sea breezes not only moderate land temperatures but also push away surface waters, allowing colder, nutrient-dense water to rise up. This process of upwelling creates an extremely fertile ecosystem, supporting vital marine species from kelp to phytoplankton and creating excellent fishing conditions.

Prevailing westerly winds bring that cool, moist air inland, causing greater precipitation in the northern part of the state and along the mountains' western slopes. Much of that air mass gets blocked by the ranges, causing a rain shadow effect on the eastern slopes that yields the more arid environs of the Great Basin and the Mojave and Sonoran Deserts.

The Sonoran Desert continues into the Mexican states of Baja California and Baja California Sur. This narrow strip of land between the Pacific and the Sea of Cortez is dominated by an arid subtropical climate, making for hot summers, mild winters, and little precipitation. Given the dry conditions, flora there is extremely drought-resistant, having evolved over time to regenerate and revitalize itself in that wonderful way that only nature can. These days, there's increasing habitat destruction in Baja due to flooding, collapsing, and land development for hotels and private homes.

It's no coincidence that the Pacific Coast is experiencing outsized climate change effects, including droughts, wildfires, and other extreme weather that's totally reshaping the environs. After all, it's a place whose plentitude has been pillaged by white settlers for centuries and whose original stewards were separated from the land and forbidden from managing it in the holistic manner they'd done for millennia.

THE HISTORY

The area's year-round natural riches that sustained more than five hundred tribes prior to European contact is also what attracted colonists, who have long ravaged the land and sea. Often overlooked in the annals of American history is the all-out genocide that made California what it is today, which is still a place with a very colonialist mindset. We all learned about the Gold Rush and the prosperity it promised prospectors in school, but not of the devastating impacts it had on Indigenous groups.

Of course, the history of California begins long before hundreds of thousands of miners infiltrated this place in the 1840s. Upward of one-third of Turtle Island's First Peoples resided there, speaking more than one hundred different languages and trading extensively with one another. Since time immemorial, they have tailored their lifeways to their respective landscapes and moved across those spaces in harmony with the seasons. Today, California and Baja California are home to more than 150 tribal communities (both federally recognized and unrecognized), including the Achumawi, Chemehuevi, Chumash, Cucapá, Esselen, Gabrielino Tongva, Huchnom, Hoopa, Kiliwa, Kumeyaay, lviatim, Maarenga'yam, Miwok, Modoc, Mojave, Ohlone, Paipai, Paiute, Patwin, Payómkawichum (Luiseño), Pomo, T'epotaha'l, Wintu, Yana, Yokut, and Yurok, to name a few.

The history of California begins long before hundreds of thousands of miners infiltrated this place.

Explorer Juan Rodríguez Cabrillo claimed California on behalf of Spain in 1542, but it wouldn't be until the late 1700s that Spaniards really invaded the area, driven up from Mexico (then known as New Spain) by a desire to stave off Russian incursion from the north and convert the Indigenous communities to Christianity. The twenty-one missions established under Father Junípero Serra along the Pacific Coast from San Diego up to San Francisco were little more than fronts to force Native peoples into indentured servitude after attempting to wipe them clean of their ancestral teachings.

Dubbed Mission Indians, neophytes worked as cooks, craftsmen, farmers, and ranchers, tending to the crops and livestock that pushed out the endemic flora and fauna. The Spanish introduced many of the foreign foods that are now ubiquitous in California, including water-thirsty almonds, oranges, grapes, figs, pomegranates, olives, wheat, cattle, sheep, goats, pigs, and more. Religious leaders known as padres separated Native children from their parents at the age of eight

to get a jumpstart on the cultural assimilation process. The magnitude of this atrocious situation is hard to quantify. An estimated 100,000 Indigenous individuals died as a direct consequence of the mission system, largely due to the oppressive living conditions in dirty, disease-ridden camps.

After gaining independence from Spain in 1821, the Mexican government turned its attention to the California missions and in 1833 ordered them to be secularized—broken up and their property sold or given away. In theory, this was intended to emancipate Indigenous converts and allow them to self-govern on granted land plots—somewhat akin to the seventeenth-century land grants Mexico made to New Mexico's pueblos, which were later upheld by the US government (for more details, read Desert Lands: Southwestern United States and Northern Mexico, page 184). In practice, however, it simply paved the way for the rancho system, in which Native workers toiled under private rancheros instead of Franciscan padres.

But the worst was yet to come for Pacific Coast tribal groups. In 1846, the United States kicked off its Conquest of California as part of the Mexican-American War (1846–1848). In the aftermath of that face-off, the United States annexed California along with Nevada, Utah, New Mexico, most of Arizona and Colorado, and parts of Oklahoma, Kansas, and Wyoming as outlined in the Treaty of Guadalupe Hidalgo.

Just days before that document was signed in 1848, an American carpenter building a water-powered sawmill found gold in a river at the base of the Sierra Nevada. Overblown news reports of the discovery at Sutter's Mill seduced frenzied fortune seekers, who started showing up in the hundreds. When President James Polk wrote about it in his inaugural address that December, it prompted the largest mass migration in US history.

During the nearly ten-year Gold Rush, an estimated 300,000 miners made their way to California, totally displacing its First Peoples. But this incursion was the least offensive act; prospectors then quickly formed citizen militias intended to exterminate the resistant "red devils" who were keeping them from their riches.

When California became a state in 1850, the state legislature passed the Act for the Government and Protection of Indians, which allowed settlers to arrest and enslave Native individuals and take custody of Indigenous children. That set off a state-sanctioned slaughter, during which at least sixteen thousand people were killed. One account from a Sinkyone girl who hid during a brutal attack tells of settlers targeting her family, killing them in front of her, and cutting out her baby sister's heart—which she clutched during that moment of sheer terror. It wasn't until 2019 that Governor Gavin Newsom acknowledged this for what it really was—a genocide—and issued an apology. The California Indigenous population plummeted from an estimated 300,000 people before European contact to as low as 15,000 by the end of the nineteenth century due to disease, starvation, and outright brutality that went on for years.

Also in the 1850s, the federal government began negotiating treaties with dozens of Indigenous groups. The eighteen treaties signed by nearly 140 tribal nations set aside some 7.5 million acres as well as financial support and other provisions, but amid public uproar, Congress never ratified the documents and instead imposed an injunction of secrecy that hid them away for five decades. Subsequent executive orders created small reservations for some Native groups, but many were left landless and on the run, trying to survive, notes California Indian Museum and Cultural Center Executive Director Nicole Myers-Lim (Pomo).

When these "secret treaties" were rediscovered in the early 1900s, Indigenous communities and advocacy groups campaigned for land, unfulfilled treaty rights, and citizenship (which was granted in 1917 by the California Supreme Court). Though the government eventually awarded paltry payouts, the stolen lands were not returned. In the ensuing decades, the Bureau of Indian Affairs developed more minuscule reservations and rancherias in undesirable areas, effectively removing Native peoples from the ancestral homelands they had stewarded for eons. As a result, today California has more tribal nations that are not federally recognized than any other state.

Egregious policies have continued to chip away at tribal sovereignty well into the twentieth century, including the establishment of Indian boarding and day schools; the Indian Relocation Act of 1956 that encouraged Indigenous individuals to leave the reservations for cities; the California Rancheria Termination Act of 1958 that sought to dismantle and distribute communal lands; and similarly discriminatory acts through the decades. This is why landback wins are so monumental for these once landless groups that are fighting not only for the health of their tribal communities but also for the health of the Pacific Coast landscape and seascape.

THE FOOD

The state's dynamic climates foster an incredible amount of biodiversity, even in the desert lands. There's no way to encapsulate all of the area's Indigenous foodways in a single chapter, which is why I offer up other resources. For a closer look at Native California foodways, I suggest reading *Chími Nu'am* by Karuk home cook Sara Calvosa Olson, whose contemporary cookbook features insightful advice for how to respectfully and correctly procure and prepare many cornerstone ingredients.

Like Northwest Coast communities, Northern California Native groups such as the Karuk, Yurok, and Winnemem Wintu built their food systems around salmon (see the traditional method for smoking on page 69 and my home-cooking method on page 281) and other fish, such as steelhead, trout, and lamprey. After all, many tribal nations freely traversed the region before the state lines were drawn, which split the Klamath River Watershed into Oregon and California.

The Pomo and Miwok peoples inhabited Sonoma County long before it became Wine Country. Nicole Myers-Lim explains that her ancestors divided their food regions into three categories: the coast, the valley, and the lake. They have long hunted deer, rabbits, and quail; fished for salmon and abalone; and gathered seaweed, acorns, buckeyes, bay laurel nuts, and manzanita. (Learn how to turn these ubiquitous berries into a cider or sugar on page 280.)

For many California Indigenous communities, acorns hold extreme importance for both ceremony and sustenance. For centuries, they have cultivated oak trees in groves and orchards using traditional ecological methods including controlled burns. Thanks to this sustainable agriculture, the fruit remains a modern-day staple, but there's hard work involved in preparing it, including gathering, drying, shelling, leaching, then storing or making it into flour. I offer a step-by-step guide to this process (see How to Make Acorn Flour, page 288) as well as a recipe for versatile Acorn Cakes (page 290) that can be served sweet or savory.

As you head farther south along the coastline, you enter Chumash Country, home to many groups with shared cultures, foodways, and language roots. Spanning the diverse climes of central and southern California, this vast tribal territory affords natural treasures from both land and water. Unfortunately, procuring first foods such as fish, abalone, mussels, and chia has become ever challenging these days due to human development, pollution, and access restrictions, explains Shmuwich Chumash cultural educator Tima Lotah Link.

Even seemingly barren areas, like the Cuyama Badlands that remind me of my South Dakota homelands, nurture plants like pinyon pine, juniper, and all-important chia sage—a "fire-following" plant whose yield improves after a controlled burn has cleared away old growth. Chia is so vital in Pacific Coast foodways it even inspired a grassroots organization. Aiming to honor the original food systems of Southern California, the Chia Café Collective developed a 2010 cookbook, *Cooking the Native Way*, that offers both recipes and lessons learned from plant medicines such as chia. This staple can be prepared so many ways, like as convenient superfood-fueled energy bars (see page 293).

Crossing south of the US/Mexico border, Baja California offers rich abundance in the form of amaranth, chia, pitaya (dragon fruit), mesquite, coastal sage, and cactus. Animals from both land and sea factor into area food systems, including small game, lizards, snakes, insects, abalone, clams, lobster, and fish galore. Indigenous cooks prepare these animal proteins by smoking, sun-drying, and cooking in earthen ovens or over open flames.

Echoing these tribal foodways, the recipes on the following pages take you from land to sea. From the bountiful ocean come simply prepared West Coast Oysters with Dried Salmon, Manzanita Powder, and Wood Sorrel (page 284). The woodlands and the mountains, meanwhile, inspired a hearty bear stew (see page 297) made with sage, sumac, and fennel, and garnished with blackberries and minty yerba buena leaves.

Of course, we couldn't overlook the importance of the area's immense old-growth forests. Redwood needles flavor simply sautéed mushrooms (see page 292), while California incense cedar seasons succulent Braised Rabbit with Greens (page 294). Taken altogether, these dishes start to paint a picture of the plentiful Pacific Coast, with all its beautiful natural bounty and complex, complicated history.

MANZANITA CIDER AND SUGAR

Different species of manzanita (which means "little apple" in Spanish) grow prolifically in California, and you'll also see the shrubs in the western parts of Turtle Island, from British Columbia down throughout the center of Mexico. They are all part of the Arctostaphylos genus. One species, *Arctostaphylos uva-ursi,* also known as bearberries, grows more widely into the East and as far north as the Arctic.

The plants produce berries, flowers, and leaves that have been important food and medicine for Indigenous peoples for centuries.

People harvest the green or slightly underripe orangey-red berries in early summer or fully ripe red berries in later summer or fall to make a sweet-tart cider-style drink that tastes like apple but with a tea-like tannic edge.

The ripe red berries can also be dried and ground to make a fruity "sugar."

The berries have hard seeds that are best not to eat, but it's OK if they're steeped in the cider.

In spring, you can gather the flowers to add to salads or use as a garnish.

TO MAKE THE CIDER

While you can use the green berries to make a tart cider, I prefer cider made with the slightly sweeter ripe, red berries, and I find it easiest to start with them dried (see Note). Measure out how many cups of berries you have. In a mortar, lightly crush the dried berries with a pestle. Transfer to a bowl or glass jar and add 4 cups of water for every 1 cup of whole berries. Let steep for 2 hours, or refrigerated for up to 8 hours, then strain through cheesecloth, discarding the solids. Return the cider to the rinsed-out jar. Seal and refrigerate overnight, allowing any sediment to settle. Store for up to 5 days and enjoy chilled, avoiding the sediment.

TO MAKE THE SUGAR

In a mortar, crush the berries until the softer outer flesh is ground but the hard seeds are still whole. Transfer to a fine-mesh sieve. Shake the berries through the sieve to capture the sugar. Discard the solids.

Note: You can dehydrate your own berries after you gather them, or you can find dried uva-ursi berries online and from some medicinal herb shops. Occasionally, foragers will sell their harvest of dried manzanita berries online as well.

HOT-SMOKED SALMON

makes about 1¾ cups

During salmon season in Yurok country, it's all hands on deck. The salmon run fast and furious, and an important food source for the whole year must be harvested and processed in a few short weeks.

The Yurok people smoke salmon much like people do farther north, either by staking it alongside an open fire or using a smoke box. To preserve salmon for longer keeping, they'll take some of that smoked salmon and can it.

This recipe is for salmon strips that are rich in smoke flavor, well seasoned, and flaky. I make sure to smoke it to at least 145°F, because wild fish can contain parasites that are killed off by cooking (or freezing).

To preserve the salmon in jars, it's crucial to follow safe canning practices and make sure the jars are fully sealed before storing.

The cure for this smoked salmon is simply salt, but if you'd like to make it sweeter, you can add equal parts maple sugar.

1 (2-pound) skin-on salmon fillet

½ cup coarse sea salt

Sunflower oil, for the grates

Cut the salmon lengthwise into 1-inch-wide strips. Then cut the strips so they're about 4 inches long.

Arrange the strips on a baking sheet and season all over with the salt. Refrigerate uncovered for 1 hour.

Rinse the fish then pat dry. Arrange on a rack, skin-side down, and let it stand at a cool room temperature near an open window for 2 hours, or refrigerate uncovered for up to 12 hours. Drying the fish will help the smoke penetrate more.

To use an outdoor smoker: Preheat a smoker to 175°F, according to the manufacturer's instructions.

Oil the grates and set the salmon on top. Smoke to 145°F for about 2 hours if you want some moisture in the fish or continue smoking for 30 minutes to 1 hour longer until it's dry throughout but still pliable. If you want to jar the salmon, you'll want to smoke it just until the fish reaches 145°F. It will cook further in the pressure canner.

To smoke on a gas grill: Lay 2 sheets of heavy-duty aluminum foil on a work surface. Arrange 2 cups dry (not soaked) wood chips on top. Fold up the chips in the foil to form a packet, then use a pencil or pen to poke holes in the top.

Remove one grate from your grill and arrange the packet directly on the burner. Heat over low heat, aiming to get the grill to about 200°F.

Oil the grates, then arrange the salmon on the opposite side of the grill from the smoking packet (indirect heat). Close the lid and cook for about 1 hour, until the fish reaches 145°F. If you'd like your smoked salmon to be drier, add a new packet of wood chips and continue cooking for about 30 minutes longer, until quite dry throughout but still pliable.

Let cool before enjoying or storing. Refrigerate the salmon in an airtight container for up to 5 days.

SMOKED SALMON–BLACK WALNUT SPREAD

makes about 3 cups

In this riff on a creamy fish spread, smoky salmon is bound together with a rich black walnut cream and made aromatic with herbs and capers. Northern California has its own species of black walnut, *Juglans hindsii*. You can also find eastern black walnut trees growing sporadically throughout the region as well.

If you don't have home-smoked salmon on hand, you can also make this with store-bought hot-smoked salmon.

- 8 ounces shelled black walnuts
- 2 tablespoons agave syrup
- 8 ounces Hot-Smoked Salmon (page 281), flaked
- ¼ cup finely chopped wild onion greens or chives
- ¼ cup Dandelion or Milkweed Capers (page 38), finely chopped
- 2 tablespoons finely chopped fennel fronds, plus a few sprigs for garnish
- Sea salt
- Cassava chips, for serving

In a saucepan, combine 2 cups water, the black walnuts, and agave syrup and bring to a boil over high heat. Reduce the heat to medium-low and simmer for 5 minutes to soften the nuts. Turn off the heat and let cool to warm.

Transfer to a high-powered blender and puree to form a thick cream. Scrape it into a bowl and cool to room temperature.

Fold in the salmon, wild onion greens, dandelion capers, and fennel fronds. Taste and season with salt as needed.

Cover and refrigerate until well chilled, then serve with cassava chips and a few extra fennel fronds on top for garnish.

WEST COAST OYSTERS WITH DRIED SALMON, MANZANITA POWDER, AND WOOD SORREL

makes 2 dozen oysters

To me, this is the taste of Northern California in one bite: a local oyster, topped with feathery bits of dried salmon, sweet-tangy manzanita berry powder, and lemony wood sorrel. I made five hundred of these oysters once at the Worlds of Flavor conference at the Culinary Institute of America in Napa, with one culinary student helping me. Hopefully, shucking two dozen oysters won't feel too taxing.

24 dried manzanita berries or bearberries

½ ounce salmon jerky, torn into small pieces

2 dozen Pacific oysters

24 wood sorrel leaves, for garnish

Using a mortar and pestle or a mini food processor, pound or pulse the manzanita berries to a fine powder. Sift the powder into a bowl to remove the seeds.

Clean out the mortar or mini food processor and dry it well, then use it to pound or process the salmon jerky until it's fluffy. Transfer to a bowl.

Shuck the oysters and arrange them (on the half shell) on a platter or two of ice.

To serve, sprinkle each oyster with equal amounts of the salmon jerky, manzanita powder, and a wood sorrel leaf.

FENNEL AND NETTLE SOUP
WITH CALIFORNIA BUCKWHEAT CRUNCH

serves 2 to 4

Four prolific spring "weeds" in California inspired this smooth, fresh-tasting soup. Fennel is not native, but you can see stalks growing through sidewalk cracks, in empty lots, and along the coast. (Here, I use the bulb variety of fennel, which is typically cultivated in gardens.) Nettles also love growing in disturbed areas, including on the edges of woodlands and agricultural fields. California buckwheat (*Eriogonum fasciculatum*) is a shrubby drought-tolerant plant related to commercial buckwheat. I finish the soup with claytonia, which colonizers called miner's lettuce, and Indigenous peoples have reclaimed as NDN lettuce. It comes into season in early spring—just when we all need to eat a little more green.

Use gloves when handling nettles before they are cooked, as they sting.

- 1 medium fennel bulb, with stalks
- 1 medium leek
- 1 teaspoon fennel seeds
- 4 tablespoons sunflower oil
- Sea salt
- 8 ounces young nettles
- ¼ cup California buckwheat or other buckwheat groats
- 2 field garlic bulbs or small garlic cloves, finely chopped
- ½ teaspoon ground sumac
- Claytonia (aka NDN lettuce), when in season, for garnish

Separate the stalks from the fennel. Remove about 2 tablespoons of the fronds and save for garnish. Core and chop the fennel bulb and set aside. Cut up the stalks with the remaining fronds, and place them in a medium saucepan.

Remove the dark-green parts of the leek, wash them, and add to the saucepan with the fennel. Cut the white and light-green parts of the leek crosswise into thin slices. Submerge the rings in a bowl of cool water and gently swish to loosen any grit, then lift them out of the water and drain.

Add the fennel seeds and 4 cups water to the saucepan with the fennel stalks and leek tops. Bring to a boil over high heat. Reduce the heat to low and cook for 30 minutes to make a simple vegetable broth.

In another medium saucepan, heat 2 tablespoons of the oil over medium-high heat. Add the sliced leek and chopped fennel bulb, season with salt, and cook for about 5 minutes, stirring, until softened. Strain the fennel broth over the vegetables, discarding the solids. Reduce the heat to medium and cook for about 5 minutes longer, or until soft enough that they will puree easily. Using tongs, add the nettles to the pot and stir until wilted. Turn off the heat and let the soup cool to warm.

Working in batches as needed, ladle the soup into a blender and puree until very smooth, then push through a fine-mesh sieve into a clean saucepan. Reheat the soup over medium-low heat, taste, and season with salt. Keep warm.

In a small skillet, heat the remaining 2 tablespoons of oil over medium heat. Add the buckwheat and garlic and cook for 2 to 3 minutes, stirring, until they're both looking and smelling toasted. Remove from the heat and sprinkle in the sumac and reserved fennel fronds.

Serve the soup with some of the buckwheat mixture on top. Garnish with the Claytonia if it's in season and serve.

HOW TO MAKE ACORN FLOUR

For many people along the Pacific Coast, acorns provided a similar type of base for meals that corn does in other parts of Turtle Island. Acorns can produce a nutty, protein-rich flour, and people relied on it for daily sustenance, turning it into porridge, soups, and breads.

While acorns are abundant in many parts of Turtle Island, we don't see a steady supply of commercial acorn flour because producing it is labor-intensive. Before it's edible, you must remove the natural tannins. You can leach them from acorns with boiling water over the course of a few hours, or by soaking them in cold water for a few days. The hot method produces dark-colored, flavorful flour but destroys the starch that gives acorns a binding quality when baking, almost the way gluten does. The cold method maintains this starch and produces a lighter-colored, milder flavored flour.

The most labor-intensive part of making acorn flour is shelling the acorns. If you plan to harvest and shell acorns for years to come, it's worth investing in a hand-cranked nutcracker. Otherwise, in smaller batches, you can do it by hand.

As with many kinds of traditional Native cooking, it's best to process acorns while in community with others, so I suggest you make a day (or two) of it. Get your friends together in the fall, go out into the woods, and harvest as many acorns as you can. Wait for a bit to let the acorns dry out, then sit around as you crack and shell them, telling stories and singing songs to make the time go faster.

For even more about using acorn flour in your cooking, I recommend the cookbook *Chími Nu'am* by Sara Calvosa Olson (Karuk), who also provided this photo.

GATHERING ACORNS

Look for acorns that are smooth and shiny and feel heavy in your hand with no holes or discoloration. As you gather, you might encounter different varieties of acorns from different oak trees. All acorns are edible, but you might want to keep the different acorns separated because their flavor and natural levels of moisture can vary widely.

SHELLING ACORNS

If you're shelling by hand, you can cover a few acorns with a towel and hit each one with a hammer to crack them. Otherwise, crack a few at a time in a hand-cranked nutcracker. If you can remove the nut meat easily from the shells, keep going. If you're struggling, you'll want to dry your acorns a bit more. Arrange them in a single layer on baking sheets or tarps and lay them in the sun for a few hours, then try cracking again. (Try to keep them away from squirrels!)

As you shell the acorns, compost any nut meat that looks eaten or moldy.

At this point, you can dry the shelled acorns until very hard (leave them in the sun for a few more hours) and store them in a cool, dry place or airtight container.

Or you can start leaching right away.

LEACHING ACORNS

To hot leach: Place the acorn meat in a saucepan, cover fully with water, bring to a boil over high heat, then drain. Repeat this process several more times. After you drain them the third time, start tasting. When you're done, the meat should taste nutty with little to no bitterness. If it's still quite bitter, keep boiling it and then draining it.

To cold leach: Cover the acorns fully with water in a high-powered blender and blend until smooth. Transfer to a large glass jar, cover, and refrigerate or keep in a cool place (below 75°F). The next day, line a fine-mesh sieve with cheesecloth and drain off as much of the water as possible before getting to the flour that has settled at the bottom. Return any sediment from the cheesecloth to the jar and cover with clean water. Seal the jar and shake to incorporate. Repeat draining and refilling with clean water each day.

After 3 days, start tasting the ground acorns. Stop the soaking process after they lose their bitter flavor. (This can take a few more days.)

MAKING THE FLOUR

For the hot-leached acorns: Drain them well and pat dry and then grind into a fine meal that's about the consistency of almond flour in a flour grinder or a food processor.

For the cold-leached acorns: Drain well through a fine-mesh sieve lined with cheesecloth.

Spread the acorn meal in a dehydrator or in an oven heated to 170°F and allow to dry completely. (This can take about 10 hours.) You want to make sure the ground acorns are completely dried to a flour-like consistency before storing, to prohibit the growth of mold.

You can sift the flour before storing by shaking it through a fine-mesh sieve and then grinding any of the coarse bits left behind. Or you can do this step later, before you start to bake with the flour.

(Before storing in an airtight container, you could store in a paper bag for a few days, shaking it every so often, to make sure the flour is truly dry.)

ACORN CAKES WITH QUICK BLACKBERRY JAM OR MUSHROOMS AND WILD MUSTARD PESTO

makes 12 cakes

These acorn cakes have a satisfyingly nutty, earthy flavor and can go sweet or savory, depending on what you pair with them. I've suggested a few ideas for toppings below. They're also delicious with the Smoked Salmon–Black Walnut Spread (page 283).

If you use darker hot-leached flour, they'll be more richly flavored, while the cold-leached flour will have a milder taste and slightly springier texture.

If you're not up for making your own acorn flour—an admittedly laborious task—you can purchase acorn flour from foragers and artisans online or the more refined acorn starch from Korean markets. The cassava flour in these cakes helps to bind them, so the recipe will work with both cold-leached and hot-leached acorn flour. The amount of water you need, however, will vary.

- 1 to 1½ cups warm water
- 2 tablespoons honey
- 1 tablespoon sunflower oil, plus more for the pan
- 1 cup fine acorn flour, homemade (see page 288) or store-bought
- ¾ cup cassava flour
- 2 teaspoons baking soda
- ½ teaspoon fine sea salt

TOPPINGS

- Quick Blackberry Jam with Mint (recipe below)
- Wild Mustard Pesto (page 292)
- Sautéed Mushrooms with Redwood Needles (page 292)

In a large liquid measuring cup, whisk together 1 cup of the warm water, the honey, and oil until well blended.

In a bowl, stir together the acorn flour, cassava flour, baking soda, and salt. Add the liquid to the bowl, stirring to form a moist but not sticky dough. (The dough should roll into a ball and hold its shape but not stick to your hands.) Add some of the remaining ½ cup water as needed to moisten the dough if it seems dry.

Divide the dough into 12 equal portions and roll them into balls. Place them on a baking sheet and cover with a damp towel to rest and hydrate for 10 minutes. Using slightly dampened hands, pat the balls down into ¼-inch-thick rounds.

Heat a cast-iron skillet or griddle over medium heat. Lightly oil the bottom of the pan. Working in batches as needed, cook the cakes for about 2 minutes, until dry on the bottom and browned at the edges. Flip and cook for 2 minutes on the second side until dry and darker.

Serve the cakes with your topping of choice.

QUICK BLACKBERRY JAM WITH MINT

Makes 1 cup

Both native and nonnative varieties of blackberries grow wild throughout California. You can serve this quick jam with the Acorn Cakes (here), spread over the Black Walnut Cream Tart (page 183), or alongside meats, like duck or venison.

- 1 pint blackberries
- ½ cup agave syrup
- 2 tablespoons chopped wild mint

Place the berries in a medium saucepan and use a potato masher to partially break them down. Add ¼ cup water and the agave syrup. Set over medium heat and cook for 12 to 15 minutes, until the berries break down further and the liquid thickens into a syrupy jam. Stir in the mint and let cool.

SAUTÉED MUSHROOMS
WITH REDWOOD NEEDLES

serves 4

Mushrooms cooked with conifer needles is one of my favorite combinations. It's always a great way to get a taste of the local forest. Serve these mushrooms as a side dish alongside any meat dish or to continue the California forest vibe, serve with the Acorn Cakes (page 290).

- 2 tablespoons sunflower oil or melted animal fat
- 1½ pounds mixed wild mushrooms, cut into ¼-inch-thick slices
- 2 wild garlic bulbs with stalks or 2 garlic cloves, finely chopped
- 2 teaspoons very finely chopped redwood needles or needles from other edible conifers
- Sea salt

In a large skillet, heat the oil over medium heat. Add the mushrooms, garlic, and redwood needles and season with salt. Cook for about 8 minutes, stirring and tossing, until the mushrooms have released their liquid and the pan is nearly dry. Add 1 to 2 tablespoons water to deglaze the pan and cook just long enough for it to evaporate, scraping any browned bits from the bottom of the pan. Serve hot.

WILD MUSTARD PESTO

makes about 1 cup

Wild mustard is not indigenous to the land and is considered invasive because it overwhelms native plants, especially during a superbloom. However, eating wild mustard is actually helpful to the ecosystem, and it's a delicious and nutritious plant, too. All parts of the plant, including the leaves and blooms, are edible and have a pungent mustardy flavor that becomes mellower when blended with the pine nuts, agave syrup, and sunflower oil.

You can make this to serve with Acorn Cakes (page 290) or alongside any meat.

- ½ cup pinyon pine nuts (see page 324) or other pine nuts, toasted if desired
- 1 wild garlic bulb and stalk, coarsely chopped, or 1 garlic clove, smashed
- 2 cups packed wild mustard greens
- 2 teaspoons agave syrup
- ½ cup sunflower oil
- Sea salt

In a food processor, pulse the pinyon pine nuts until coarsely chopped. Add the garlic and pulse until chopped. Add the greens and pulse until chopped. With the machine running, gradually add the agave syrup and the oil. Taste and season with salt. Refrigerate for up to 3 days.

CHIA ENERGY BARS

makes 12 bars

Desert chia (*Salvia columbariae*) is a plant in the mint family that grows in the Sonoran desert. The seeds are almost identical in flavor to commercial chia seeds, which come from a closely related plant.

Chia seeds are an incredible energy food rich with vital nutrients including calcium and omega-3 fatty acids, not to mention plenty of fiber. These granola bars are inspired by one from Craig Torres of the Chia Cafe Collective, which works to preserve Native foods in Southern California and wrote a book in 2010 called *Cooking the Native Way*. The sweet, softly chewy bars get bound together with reduced honey or agave and have a rich, toasty flavor from pine nuts.

These taste best chilled overnight and last for up to 2 weeks in the refrigerator.

- Sunflower oil, for the pan
- 1½ cups pinyon pine nuts (see page 324) or other pine nuts (6 ounces)
- 1½ cups chia seeds (8 ounces)
- 1 cup soft dried local berries, such as wild strawberries or wolfberries, coarsely chopped
- 1 teaspoon sea salt
- 1 cup agave syrup or lightly warmed honey

Preheat the oven to 325°F.

Line a 9 × 9-inch square baking pan with parchment paper and lightly grease it with sunflower oil.

In a bowl, toss together the pine nuts, chia seeds, dried fruit, and salt. Stir in the agave syrup and scrape the mixture into the prepared pan, pressing it into an even layer. (It will be about ½ inch thick.)

Bake for 20 to 25 minutes, until the pine nuts smell toasty, the liquid is bubbling, and a thermometer inserted into the center of the bar (without touching the pan) registers 235°F. Do not let it heat past 240°F. (It's easiest to use a probe thermometer so you can monitor the temperature while it's in the oven. If you don't have one, start checking the temperature using an instant-read thermometer after 20 minutes.)

Let the bars cool to room temperature, then refrigerate until firmly chilled, at least 4 hours or overnight.

Lift the slab from the parchment paper onto a cutting board. Cut into 12 bars of equal size or slice however you prefer. (Bite-size pieces are also nice.) Refrigerate in an airtight container or bag for up to 2 weeks. Since the bars are a little bit sticky, you can wrap each bar in parchment paper for easy grab-and-go eating.

INCENSE CEDAR–BRAISED RABBIT
WITH GREENS

serves 4 to 6

Incense cedar is native to California and is especially fragrant, with bright citrusy and woodsy notes. To infuse its flavor into this simple rabbit dish, I make a quick stock with it and then also add it to the braise. The combination of agave syrup and vinegar in the sauce gives it a lovely sheen.

2 whole rabbits (2½ pounds each)

STOCK

- ½ large onion
- 1 medium carrot, scrubbed well and coarsely chopped
- 2 wild garlic bulbs and stalks or smashed garlic cloves
- 2 small sprigs of fresh incense cedar or 2 tablespoons dried

BRAISE

- 2 tablespoons avocado oil or sunflower oil
- Sea salt
- 2 teaspoons ground sumac
- 1 large yellow onion, chopped
- 3 wild garlic bulbs and stalks or garlic cloves, chopped
- 1 tablespoon agave syrup
- 2 small sprigs of fresh incense cedar or 1 sprig of dried
- 1 tablespoon cider vinegar
- 3 cups tender wild greens, such as lamb's quarters, amaranth greens, dandelion, or wild mustard
- Finely chopped cedar (optional), for serving

Break down each rabbit into 6 serving pieces: 2 front legs, 2 hind quarters, and 2 saddle pieces. (The saddle includes both loins on either side of the spine. It can be left bone-in; cut it crosswise into two pieces. You can use a cleaver or a knife and kitchen scissors to cut the saddle in half through the spine.) Save the backbones and rib cages for the stock. Refrigerate the rabbit pieces while you make the stock.

Make the stock: In a large saucepan, combine the rabbit backbones and rib cages with 8 cups water. Bring to a boil over high heat, then reduce the heat to medium-low so the liquid barely bubbles. Skim off any scum that rises to the surface during the first 10 minutes of simmering.

Add the onion half, carrot, garlic, and incense cedar and simmer gently for about 1 hour, until the liquid is infused with the flavors.

Strain through a fine-mesh sieve into a large bowl, discarding the solids.

Make the braise: In a large, heavy pot, heat the oil over medium-high heat until shimmering. Season the reserved rabbit pieces with salt and the sumac. Working in batches to avoid overcrowding, cook the rabbit for 10 minutes, turning frequently, until well browned all over (but not cooked through). Transfer to a plate.

Reduce the heat under the pot to medium. Add the chopped onion and garlic and cook for about 5 minutes, or until the onion is softened.

Add the strained stock and agave syrup and bring to a boil over high heat. Reduce the heat to medium-low, return all the browned rabbit pieces to the pot, and add the sprigs of cedar. Cover the pot and cook for about 1 hour, or until the rabbit is tender but not falling off the bone. Discard the cedar. Using tongs, transfer the rabbit pieces to a large bowl.

Bring the liquid left in the pot to a boil and cook for 15 to 20 minutes, until it is reduced to about 1½ cups. Stir in the vinegar. Add the greens and cook until just wilted, about 1 minute.

Return the rabbit to the pot just to warm through. If desired, sprinkle with some finely chopped cedar before serving.

CALIFORNIA BEAR STEW

serves 4 to 6

Before 1849, about ten thousand California grizzly bears roamed the Pacific Coast. It was an important animal relative for Indigenous peoples in the region, not to mention a source of food and tool materials.

The California state flag is emblazoned with the bear, chosen because of its supposed ferocity. As more colonists moved to California, stories spread about the dangers of the bear, and settlers hunted, poisoned, and trapped them into extinction in the wild. The last reported California grizzly was seen in 1924, over a century ago.

It was a brutal demise, based on hysteria, and one that reminds me in some ways of the fate of Indigenous people after the Gold Rush.

More recent research has indicated that California grizzlies were primarily herbivores, but the livestock the colonists had brought turned them more carnivorous. The research also shows that the bears were not as large and violent as settlers often described.

The California Grizzly Alliance is working with tribal leaders and scientists to investigate the possibility of reintroducing these bears into the wild, both to right a historic injustice and restore the local ecosystem.

I look forward to keeping an eye on this work to see how it unfolds.

You might now be asking: Why then are you sharing a recipe for an animal that's nearly extinct? I'm not.

Black bears continue to live along the Pacific Coast and much of Turtle Island. Hunting bear is legal in many states, including California, but highly managed. Some Indigenous peoples avoid eating bear, viewing the animals as sacred, while others enjoy the meat (or have historically). It's nearly impossible to find bear meat commercially, so to try it, you will need to hunt it yourself or know a hunter willing to share. You can also make the stew with a different game meat, if you prefer, but know that bear meat will be quite fatty.

Bear breaks down like many other four-legged animals, with loin sections that are more tender and best for steaks and tougher parts rich with collagen, like the shoulder, legs, and head. You can use any of the tougher cuts here.

For this stew, I cook the meat with some wild aromatics, including sage, sumac, fennel, bay leaves, and a little blackberry for flavor and a balance of tartness. I serve it garnished with more fresh blackberries and minty yerba buena leaves.

- 2 pounds bear stew meat, cut into 2-inch pieces
- 1 tablespoon fine sea salt
- 2 tablespoons fresh native sage leaves, such as black sage or California sagebrush, finely chopped, or 1 tablespoon dried and crumbled
- 1 tablespoon ground sumac
- 1 cup blackberries, plus more for garnish
- 2 tablespoons rendered bear fat or sunflower oil
- 1 large yellow onion, chopped
- 2 to 4 young stalks wild fennel, chopped
- 3 wild garlic bulbs and stalks or garlic cloves, finely chopped
- 1 quart Rich Bison or Other Game Stock (page 41) or water
- 2 tablespoons agave syrup
- 2 California bay leaves
- ¼ cup yerba buena leaves, chopped

In a bowl, combine the bear meat, salt, sage, and sumac and toss to coat evenly. Cover and refrigerate overnight.

Preheat the oven to 300°F.

Set a fine-mesh sieve over a liquid measuring cup and lightly mash the blackberries through the sieve to catch the juice. (You're aiming for about ⅓ cup. More is fine.) Discard the skins and seeds.

(recipe continues)

In a large, heavy pot or Dutch oven, heat the fat over medium-high heat until shimmering. Working in batches to avoid overcrowding, add the meat and sear for about 7 minutes, turning as needed, until browned and crusted all over. Transfer the meat to a plate.

Add the onion and fennel stalks to the pot and cook for about 5 minutes, stirring to help scrape up bits from the bottom of the pot, until they are softened. Add the garlic and cook for about 1 minute, stirring, until fragrant.

Add the blackberry juice and cook for 1 minute. Add the game stock, agave syrup, and bay leaves and bring to a boil. Cover the pot with a tight-fitting lid and transfer to the oven.

Cook for about 3 hours, or until the bear meat is nearly fall-apart tender.

Using tongs, transfer the bear meat to a bowl and spoon off and discard as much fat from the top of the stew as possible. Strain the cooking liquid into a clean saucepan. Bring to a boil over high heat and cook until it's reduced to about 2 cups.

Add the bear meat to the reduced sauce and cook just long enough to warm through. To serve, garnish with more blackberries and the yerba buena.

BERRY AND BAY LAUREL SORBET

makes about 1 quart

Most advice about California bay leaves is to use them carefully, because their flavor is stronger than that of the Mediterranean variety. When adding them to stews, people recommend starting with a single leaf. But here, I encourage you to lean into its sweet, herbal flavor and use a whopping 12 leaves to create a concentrated syrup that then flavors a berry sorbet. If you prefer a less intense bay flavor, you can, of course, reduce the number of leaves.

- **½ cup agave syrup**
- **12 fresh California bay leaves**
- **3 cups frozen local berries, such as blackberries, huckleberries, thimbleberries, or strawberries**

In a medium saucepan, combine the agave syrup and 2 tablespoons water and heat over medium heat until barely bubbling at the edges. Add the bay leaves, being sure they're submerged, and simmer gently for 2 minutes, then turn off the heat. Let the syrup cool to room temperature, then discard the bay leaves.

In a high-powered blender, combine the berries and bay-infused syrup and puree until smooth, using the machine's plunger as needed.

Serve the sorbet immediately. (Alternatively, scoop the sorbet into a loaf pan lined with wax paper and freeze until firm, at least 2 hours. Let stand at room temperature for 10 minutes before scooping.)

THE COLD DESERT

THE GREAT BASIN AND THE COLUMBIA PLATEAU

THE COLD DESERT OF THE COLUMBIA Plateau sits just west of my homelands in the Great Plains and stretches from eastern Washington to Idaho, yet in spots it feels like a world away from where I grew up. When I visited Idaho's Craters of the Moon National Monument and Preserve in 2019 and gazed upon the dozens of lava flows there, I got the surreal sensation I had arrived on a different planet—or the set of a Tim Burton movie. This area has a long history of volcanic activity, but in geologic time, these flows might as well have happened yesterday, leaving otherworldly marks on the land. Some of those solidified molten rock streams date back fifteen thousand years, while others are only a couple thousand years old.

This fantastical place is situated on the ancestral homelands of the Shoshone and Bannock peoples, who knew the basalt lava fields as Tennambo'i (meaning "antelope's trail") and witnessed the transformation of the terrain millennia ago. That moniker is a reminder that these tribes journeyed hundreds of miles each year across the rugged region in pursuit of seasonal sustenance like the namesake animal. Those migratory paths forged centuries ago lead not only to bison hunting territories, salmon fishing spots, and camas (a vital root vegetable) digging grounds, but also to the past. For these communities, the fiery landscape of Craters of the Moon symbolizes their adaptability and indomitable spirit.

In recent years, the Shoshone-Bannock Tribes have collaborated with the National Park Service to ensure their voices and stories are amplified throughout the park. That partnership also involves protecting important ancestral places such as the Camas Prairie Centennial Marsh that's still home to its culturally significant namesake food, using a combination of traditional ecological knowledge and modern Western approaches.

For decades, the tribal nation has also strived to restore the culturally significant Snake River and its salmon and steelhead runs, which were hugely impacted by the damming of the 1,080-mile waterway. Scientists, anglers, and of course Native leaders all warned of the damaging effects before the Army Corps of Engineers built the river's four large dams in the 1960s and 1970s. Fast-forward to 2024, and the Biden administration released a report admitting the harm that the damming of the Columbia River Basin—more than 470 dams across its 260,000 miles—has caused to area tribes.

Not far away in southeastern Idaho is the site of the brutal 1863 Bear River Massacre. I visited the landmark and learned about its horrific history from Darren Parry, the former chairman of the Northwestern Band of the Shoshone Nation. The military killed about 350 of his ancestors there in what's considered the deadliest attack on Native peoples in US history—and yet, many Americans have never heard of it.

To ensure the world knows about this atrocious act, Darren penned a book on the subject, called *The Bear River Massacre: A Shoshone History*. In doing so, he's carrying on the work of his grandmother, noted historian, storyteller, and matriarch Mae Timbimboo Parry. In fact, it's her notes on Shoshone botany that guided the Bear River Massacre site restoration; she was also instrumental in shifting the narrative about that slaughter.

In 2018, the tribal nation reclaimed that massacre site, which was once an important gathering place, as part of roughly 350 acres of its ancestral homelands. Since then, community members and conservationists have been revitalizing the environs, including restoring culturally significant plants, such as serviceberries, chokecherries, cattails, and currants, and removing invasive species like water-intensive Russian olive trees.

When he was young, Darren would go out foraging with Mae, gathering camas bulbs, bitter root, serviceberries, and his favorite wild food: chokecherries. Together, they'd make jam, syrup, and gotsap, a traditional berry gravy (somewhat similar to the wóžapi I grew up savoring). Mae also imparted important ancestral wisdom, like not overharvesting the ripe fruits in order to leave some for others and for future crops. These days, Darren is the elder, and he's teaching others about traditional ecological knowledge to help address our world's climate crises. Efforts like his—and those of so many other thought leaders from the region's more than thirty tribal communities—are absolutely vital in securing our sovereignty as Indigenous peoples and safeguarding the future for the next seven generations.

THE LAND

The Columbia Plateau encompasses eastern Washington and Oregon as well as parts of Idaho and British Columbia, between the coastal and Rocky Mountains. Just to the south is the Great Basin, which includes much of Nevada and portions of Utah, Oregon, and eastern California. Its name refers to the fact that all precipitation in the region sinks underground or flows into basins—some of them massive, like Lake Tahoe and the Great Salt Lake—rather than out to the ocean. Both areas are considered cold desert ecosystems due to their arid to semiarid climate, with cold, snowy winters and hot, dry summers.

The Columbia Plateau sits at a lower elevation and experiences less precipitation than its bordering mountain ranges, including the Cascades to the west, the Rockies to the east, and the Blue Mountains to the south. To the north in British Columbia is the Okanogan Highlands, an elevated hilly plateau that's technically part of the Rockies. The snowfall that accumulates in the mountains melts into the many waterways come spring.

The same volcanic activity that created Craters of the Moon also made the broad Columbia Plateau, which formed from a series of basalt flows that totally covered the existing topography some fifteen million years ago. Indeed, the area has one of the largest outpourings of lava across the planet. The relatively flat region features rolling hills, winding rivers, coniferous forests, sagebrush seas, channeled scablands, and glacial deposits of sand, gravel, and stone. Elevation ranges from sea level up to about four thousand feet along the fringes.

Over time, high winds deposited sand and silt across the terrain, yielding fertile soil ideal for farming. Much of the landscape has been transformed for agricultural use, which relies heavily on irrigation given the semiarid climate. The once extensive wetland prairies have been drained to grow crops like winter wheat, barley, alfalfa, potatoes, lentils, and peas. Livestock like cattle and sheep have grazed upon rangeland for decades, disturbing the soil, decimating endemic plants, and allowing invasive species to spread.

Before European arrival, wild foods abounded across the Columbia Plateau. For instance, when Lewis and Clark explored what's now Idaho in the early nineteenth century and came upon a sea of blooming blue camas, they mistook it for an actual lake. Area tribes carefully managed the land using traditional ecological knowledge to ensure the proliferation of this and other plants like bitterroot, biscuit root, onions, and yampa (wild carrots). Today, there are still some segmented camas prairies, including on the Nez Perce Reservation in Idaho as well as on privately owned lands.

Creatures large and small have long roamed these parts, including elk, deer, moose, bighorn sheep, rock chucks (marmots), and prairie dogs as well as birds, such as doves, quail, and sage grouse. Of course, bison also play a major role in Indigenous food systems. In fact, the area includes one of the country's oldest bison jumps—a cliff formation used to hunt the namesake animals by driving them en masse over the landform—Wiggins Fork, located in the Absaroka Mountains of Wyoming. Fish, like all-important salmon, steelhead, and eel-like lamprey, that once filled the many rivers are now lower in number.

The Columbia Plateau connects the Columbia Basin of Washington and Oregon to the Great Basin of Nevada, Utah, and California. Along its other edges, the bowl-like Great Basin is bordered by the Sierra Nevada to the west, the Wasatch Mountains to the east, and the Sonoran and Mojave Deserts to the south. It's the largest area of closed watersheds across Turtle Island, meaning these waters never flow into the sea and instead make their way into the many valleys. This internal drainage system not only shapes the area's ecosystems but also serves as their main water supply in this largely arid environ.

Despite its name, this region actually comprises dozens of individual basins (rather than one large one), separated by more than 150 mountain ranges that have been compared to northward-crawling caterpillars in appearance. That topography resulted from the Earth's crust expanding, uplifting, sinking, and tilting over millions of years. This stretching is also why the area experiences so many earthquakes.

Though it doesn't necessarily resemble a typical desert, this harsh high desert is actually the largest desert in the country. The landscape is punctuated by those lush mountains, salt flats, saline lakes, sagebrush sea, wetlands, riparian zones along the many waterways, and woodlands filled with juniper and pinyon pine. The region has some of the world's oldest living organisms, including Great Basin bristlecone pines that have withstood extreme conditions for five thousand years.

The so-called rain shadow effect of the Sierra Nevada and Cascades heavily impacts the climate. Winds coming in from the Pacific Ocean lose their moisture over the mountains in the form of rain, then absorb moisture from the surrounding area as they sweep downward—resulting in minimal precipitation (hence the importance of that internal drainage system). Of course, elevation and topography also play a role.

What may seem like an inhospitable environment in actuality has sustained tribal communities for millennia, thanks to its plentiful wild plants and animals. That includes about 70 percent of all North American mammal species, from coyotes and mountain lions to bobcats and bats. The environs are also home to several varieties of snakes and lizards.

Though soil quality varies across the Great Basin, most of it is rocky with high salinity, meaning plants need to be hardy to survive there. Wind erosion is a major issue, causing dust storms, vegetation loss, and prorogation of invasive species like cheat grass—problems that have only escalated amid the climate crisis. Scientists have observed other measurable changes over the past century, including regionwide warming, increasing precipitation, decreasing snowpack, and early spring arrival. All of these issues affect the endemic flora and fauna, of course.

The Great Basin's many riches—gold, silver, copper, iron ore, mercury, lithium, silver, diatomite, and gemstones, to name a few—have been heavily exploited since European contact. But as in the American Southwest, water is becoming a highly valuable resource. Exacerbating the West's historic drought, more people are flocking to urban outposts, plus attractions like ski resorts and golf courses are sucking up the supply. The devastating impacts are readily apparent at Utah's shrinking Great Salt Lake, where low water levels are increasing the salinity—and therefore threatening the delicately balanced food web, especially brine shrimp that feed on phytoplankton while also feeding migrating birds (and helping power the commercial fishing industry). It's a salient reminder just how intertwined our world is and how integral we all are to planetary health.

Like in the Columbia Plateau, Indigenous groups are leading efforts to restore the region's ecosystems. For example, the Pyramid Lake Paiute are restoring sixty-five miles of fish habitat for the Lahontan cutthroat trout and cui-ui (an endangered sucker fish only found there) by modifying the Numana Dam on their northern Nevada reservation. In 2023, the tribe received an unprecedented $8.3 million as part of President Biden's infrastructure law for the fish passage project that will help revitalize the fish population by allowing them to reach their spawning grounds. That's just one instance of Indigenous resistance and resilience at work in the Great Basin.

THE HISTORY

Tribal communities have resided in the Great Basin and Columbia Plateau regions for eons, dating back to at least 10,000 BCE. Semi-nomadic Paleo Native peoples likely followed now-extinct megafauna, such as mammoths, mastodons, and giant ground sloths into the area via ice sheets engulfing the landscape. Those melted and formed the large pluvial lakes that once covered the Great Basin, leading to its namesake features.

These Paleo-Indians, as archeologists have dubbed them, were followed by the Great Basin Desert Archaic (referring to the time period, not their lifeways) and then the Fremont people (a general term describing the area's diverse inhabitants). The landscape served as an ideal canvas for their intricate rock art that's still on display today, while the region's arid climate preserved important artifacts of these early civilizations, like basketry, pottery, and other handcrafted creations. Many of these ancient groups spoke Numic, the northernmost extension of the widespread Uto-Aztecan languages.

Hunting and foraging accounted for the majority of their sustenance, but some ancient Indigenous peoples also cultivated limited crops, like the symbiotic three sisters of corn, beans, and squash, where the landscape allowed. They lived in rhythm with nature, residing in more permanent pit house and tule mat lodge villages along waterways in the winter, then moving to temporary hunting and gathering camps in the warmer seasons. To see them through the colder months, they often preserved that harvested bounty by drying or freezing (simply burying it underground).

These longstanding traditions still influence the modern foodways of the Great Basin and Columbia Plateau's dozens of tribes, including the Bannock, Cayuse, Coeur d'Alene, Goshute, Kootenai, Mono, Nimiipuu (Nez Perce), Paiute, Palouse, Okanagan, Shoshone, Spokane, Tenino, Umatilla, Ute, Walla Walla (Warm Springs), Wanapum, Wasco, Yakama, and more. Throughout history, these groups intermingled, shared natural resources, and traded extensively. In fact, the area served as a trading crossroads, where Indigenous groups from the Pacific Northwest, Pacific Coast, Great Plains, and Southwest all met.

European contact disrupted those balanced lifeways that were so harmonious with and respectful of the natural world. As was often the case, early explorers who encountered area Indigenous peoples described them as primitive and destitute—which couldn't be further from the truth, especially in this harsher environment.

Tribal groups in the southern part of the Great Basin, such as the Ute, interacted with the Spanish venturing north from Mexico as early as the 1600s. Imports like horses, guns, and infectious diseases spread across these regions at that time, but most Indigenous communities didn't come into direct contact with white colonialists until the early 1800s. As in the Great Plains, the introduction of European horses changed life, making hunting easier, expanding trade networks, and also increasing intertribal conflict. Epidemics, meanwhile, wiped out huge portions of the Native populations.

It wasn't until 1805 that Columbia Plateau tribal nations had their first sustained Euro-American contact with Lewis and Clark. Early interactions were friendly, with the Nimiipuu (Nez Perce) serving as their guides and saving the expedition crew from starvation. In what's now central Idaho, they savored salmon for the first time with the Lemhi Shoshone. When they came upon the confluence of the Columbia and Snake rivers—an important gathering spot—they documented thousands of salmon not only in the water but also on drying racks.

The duo's report about the abundance of beavers and other prized fur animals lured trappers to the rugged area, many of whom were on good terms with local Indigenous groups, even sometimes marrying into tribal communities. But the burgeoning Western fur trade brought with it ongoing intrusion, the establishment of local trading posts, and competition for wildlife. Religious crusaders also arrived, with Mormons migrating into the Great Basin and Christian missionaries moving into the Columbia Plateau.

It was the promise of prosperity in Oregon and the siren call of California gold that really wreaked havoc on these regions. For several decades beginning in the 1840s, hundreds of thousands of Americans flocked to and passed through the area on their way west. The local discovery of gold and other natural resources drew prospectors, and the wide-open spaces drew farmers and ranchers. Battles broke out as the intruders encroached upon important hunting and gathering territories, as did additional deadly epidemics.

Per usual, the federal government stepped in to intervene. The Nimiipuu (Nez Perce), with their dozens of bands, were among the first tribes to sign a treaty, thinking early negotiation might save them from a worse fate. Of their original 17-million-acre territory, they retained 7.5 million acres as well as indefinite hunting, fishing, and gathering rights across their ancestral homelands. But before the treaty was even ratified, settlers began trespassing onto the reservation. The Nimiipuu (Nez Perce) petitioned the government to prevent ongoing incursion, but instead their lands got further reduced in size by 90 percent through the so-called Thief Treaty of 1863. A contingent of resisters evaded removal, outrunning and then fending off military forces in the Nez Perce War of 1877. Chief Joseph and his forces were just shy of the Canadian border when they were eventually captured. Today, the Nez Perce reservation spans about 770,000 acres in Idaho, though tribal members still practice their treaty rights across their original homelands. Those rights have been challenged and upheld time and again in state court cases.

In the 1860s, several other Indigenous groups were coerced into signing treaties, including the Ute, Paiute, Shoshone, and Bannock. Just like with the Nimiipuu (Nez Perce), their initial reservation lands were further cut down in subsequent treaties. In the case of the Ute, who fought hard over several decades to retain their vast territory spanning much of the Great Basin, the government only provided promised annuities of food and supplies if they sent their children to Indian boarding schools, among other maddening mandates.

A common experience for these communities after their removal to reservations was the forced adoption of sedentary agrarian lifestyles—a stark contrast to their long histories of hunting and gathering. That often created a dependency on cheap government-issued commodities and, in turn, prompted the diet-related health problems that plague our peoples, including obesity, heart disease, type 2 diabetes, and even early death.

Despite these devastating developments, there's hope on the horizon thanks to Indigenous activists and advocates who, like myself, are reclaiming traditional foodways and wisdom. One outstanding example is the Wind River Food Sovereignty Project on the namesake reservation in Wyoming (home to the Eastern Shoshone and Northern Arapaho). Led by codirector Kelly Pingree of the Shoshone-Bannock Tribes, the organization recently acquired a thirty-acre property, dubbed Trout Creek Farm,

where community members can reconnect to their ancestry and the land through place-based learning.

THE FOOD

The seemingly inhospitable environs of the Columbia Plateau and Great Basin are actually anything but. These regions might not be as lush as others across Turtle Island, but the land has long hosted hundreds of wild plant and animal species that have sustained Native peoples for millennia. That includes a huge variety of roots, berries, nuts (like all-important pine nuts), seeds, herbs, and greens harvested in harmony with the seasons. Just as these areas served as a trading crossroads, the terrains of the surrounding regions converge here, along with the foods they yield in abundance.

Camas, in particular, is a staple for so many Indigenous communities there. While this wildflower is known for its beautiful bluish-purple blooms (like the ones Lewis and Clark mistook for water), it's the underground bulb that's most prized. Traditionally, women gathered the root, which resembles a small white onion, using a fire-hardened digging stick made from hardwood, bone, and/or antler. To ensure the plant flourished for the future, Native groups carefully cultivated the wild meadows, employing traditional ecological knowledge practices like periodic burns, and also planted the slow-growing crop in large gardens. These traditions carry on today, and there are many modern-day ceremonies and events dedicated to this sacred food.

Traditionally, this carbohydrate was baked in an earthen oven for several days or dried and stored for the winter. Like so many other vegetables, I like to simply prepare camas to let its sweetness shine through (see page 313). Given the somewhat unforgiving climate, roots like this are crucial components of these foodways, valued not only for their nutritional content and medicinal properties but also their long shelf life.

Equally important are animal proteins, from fish to fowl to big game. In the Columbia Plateau, freshwater fish abound in the many waterways. Like in the neighboring Pacific Northwest, salmon is a sacred first food for the Wy-Kan-Ush-Pum (the Salmon People), including the Nimiipuu (Nez Perce), Umatilla, Warm Springs, and Yakama peoples. Together, these tribal nations have formed the Columbia River Inter-Tribal Fish Commission to protect the salmon, sturgeon, and lamprey populations as well as their own treaty rights to harvest them. Although the Great Basin is more arid, it still fosters fish, including trout, suckers, and some salmon. To honor these traditions, I created a campfire-ready grilled whole trout dish (see page 315).

Many of the animals that fed my ancestors in the Great Plains—bison, elk, deer, and more—factor into these foodways, too. In the past, they were often cooked in those same earthen ovens or over open fires to bring out their rich flavors. In the recipes that follow, I showcase several ways to prepare these game meats with regional flair. Elk is presented two ways: as melt-in-your-mouth bone marrow (see page 309) served with cassava crackers and dandelion salad, as well as dry-brined with sumac and prairie sage (see Prairie Sage–Seared Elk, page 321), then paired with pinyon pine nuts, greens, and seasonal wild berries. Pronghorn antelope makes its way into tacos (see page 322) with a pinyon chimichurri and prickly pear salsa. And my friend Mariah Gladstone, the Blackfeet/Cherokee founder of Indigikitchen, shares a recipe for shredded bison arepas (see page 317) dressed in a delectable elderberry BBQ sauce. An Indigenous take on an American classic, this fan favorite is sure to find its way onto your dinner table. Taken altogether, these dishes reflect the delicious diversity of the Great Basin and Columbia Plateau regions, where Native communities have thrived for eons thanks to their steadfast determination and resourcefulness.

ELK MARROW BONES
WITH DANDELION SALAD

serves 4 as a starter

Using the whole animal has long been part of Indigenous culture. Bone marrow was and is especially prized for its abundance of vitamins and healthy fats. Because of its nutrition, people historically treated it like a dietary supplement for children.

Here, the bones are simply roasted to add a delicious browned flavor. I like to serve these bones with a bitter, briny salad of dandelion greens and capers that cuts through the richness of the marrow.

- 2 pounds cross-cut elk marrow bones (see Note), ideally 2 to 3 inches long
- Sea salt
- 3 ounces young dandelion greens (about 4 packed cups)
- 1 small shallot, coarsely chopped
- 3 tablespoons Dandelion or Milkweed Capers (page 38)
- 2 tablespoons brine from the capers
- 5 tablespoons sunflower oil
- Cassava crackers or other crackers, for serving

Preheat the oven to 450°F.

Season the open parts of the bones generously with salt. Set them in a cast-iron skillet with one of the cut sides up.

Transfer to the oven and roast the bones for 15 to 20 minutes, flipping halfway through, until the marrow is very hot and soft when tested with a toothpick, but not completely melted.

Meanwhile, finely chop the dandelion greens, shallot, and capers together and transfer them to a bowl. Just before serving, add caper brine and oil and season with salt.

Serve the warm marrow with small forks to scrape the marrow from the bones onto crackers and top with the dandelion salad.

Note: *Unless you have a bandsaw at home, I recommend purchasing them precut, or bringing the bones to a butcher and asking them to cut them for you.*

MAPLE-GLAZED SALMON

serves 4

Salmon is a sacred food for Indigenous peoples in the Columbia Plateau, just as it is for people near the coast. While maple trees are not native in the region, big-leaf maple trees grow not too much farther west. Syrup from this Western maple is deep in flavor with molasses-like notes. If you can find it, use it in this glaze, which is enlivened with vinegar and sumac, but any maple syrup will work well.

- 1 skin-on wild salmon fillet (1½ pounds)
- ¼ cup maple syrup
- 2 teaspoons cider vinegar
- 2 teaspoons sunflower oil
- 1 teaspoon ground sumac
- ½ teaspoon onion powder
- Sea salt
- Simply Cooked Camas (optional; page 313), for serving

Preheat the oven to 375°F. Line a sheet pan with parchment paper or aluminum foil (see Note).

Place the salmon on the pan skin-side down. Feel for any remaining pin bones and use tweezers to extract them, as needed.

In a small bowl, whisk together the maple syrup, vinegar, oil, sumac, and onion powder. Use this glaze to brush the fish, then season well with salt.

Bake for 5 minutes, then brush again with the glaze. Continue baking for about 5 minutes longer, or until a thermometer inserted into the thickest part registers 145°F, depending on the thickness of the fillet. (If the fish was frozen previously, you can cook it slightly less if you prefer salmon cooked to medium.)

If you'd like a bit more caramelization, broil the fish on high heat for 1 to 3 minutes.

Let the fish rest for a few minutes, then cut into portions and serve, accompanied with cooked camas, if desired.

Note: *To line the pan, you can use parchment paper, but if you'd like a more richly browned salmon, line the pan with foil so that you can finish it under the broiler.*

CAMAS: A STARCHY STAPLE

Each spring, blue flowers blanket fields around the Pacific Northwest and into the Columbia Plateau, sometimes creating quite the scene in front of snow-capped mountains. You might assume the fields are wild, but many of them have been carefully, if informally, cultivated by Indigenous people throughout the region for centuries.

In the Northwest, bulbs from the blue camas (*Camassia quamash*) are a hugely important traditional food because they're rich with carbohydrates and can be stored for the whole year. People head out to dig up some of the bulbs as the flowers wither and die back, being careful to leave plenty for the future.

While the bulbs could technically be harvested at almost any time, it's much easier to identify the plants in the spring by their blue flowers. A toxic lookalike, known colloquially as "death camas" and scientifically as *Toxicoscordion venenosum*, can often be hiding nearby. You can tell the difference between the plants because death camas blooms white flowers often a few weeks after the blue camas.

Much like sunchokes, camas is rich with inulin, a fiber that, when your gut isn't used to the food, is hard to digest.

Gently cooked, the bulbs have the texture of an onion but a lightly sweet, very neutral flavor. Traditionally, people cooked camas in earthen ovens for a full day or longer. This method ingeniously breaks down the inulin into a simpler sugar, making the camas easier to digest and also irresistibly sweet, with a caramelly, fig-like sweetness. Today, people get a similar effect by cooking them in their slow cookers for at least 12 hours.

People also dry camas to grind it into a flour.

Valerie Segrest (Muckleshoot) uses freshly harvested camas in spring soup with nettles and smoked salmon. She also freezes the bulbs to keep on hand throughout the year, roasting them and adding them to soups and stews.

As is the case with many wild bulbs, the ecosystem in which camas bulbs thrive is threatened by modern agriculture and urban sprawl. If you harvest camas, please be sure to do so with care. I also suggest you share some of your bounty with tribal elders.

If you don't know places where camas bulbs grow, you can order bulbs from garden suppliers and cultivate them in your own garden if you have wet winters and warm, sunny summers. Before you eat them, be sure they bloom blue flowers just to be sure they're the right variety!

SIMPLY COOKED CAMAS

serves 2 to 4

12 to 24 camas bulbs
Sea salt
Oil (optional)

Remove the papery outer layer of the camas bulbs.

Fill a slow cooker with about ½ inch water and set a steamer basket inside. Add the camas, cover tightly, and steam on LOW for at least 12 hours, and up to 36 hours. Check the cooker every so often and add more water as needed.

At 12 hours, they should be light golden and a bit sweet. At this point, you could remove them from the slow cooker and cut them into slices, seasoning them with salt. You can also fry them lightly in a bit of oil so they become crisp on the exterior.

If you continue steaming the camas in the slow cooker, they'll become more deeply browned and soft and develop a rich, molasses-like sweetness. You can freeze the cooked camas for up to 1 year.

GRILLED WHOLE TROUT
WITH WILD BERRY RELISH

serves 2

This is the kind of dish you can make when you're camping with gathered ingredients. You can cook over a campfire, either directly on grill grates or in a cast-iron skillet. If you're not up for building a campfire, you can cook the whole fish on an outdoor grill on medium heat (at about 350°F).

- 1 cup wild berries, such as serviceberries (saskatoon), huckleberries, strawberries, or thimbleberries (or raspberries)
- 10 or so wild onion greens or chives
- 10 edible conifer needles plus 2 small conifer pieces
- Fine sea salt
- 1 whole trout, scaled and gutted (about 1½ pounds)
- 1 tablespoon sunflower oil, plus more for cooking

Build a campfire and let the wood burn down so it's smoldering and still hot but no longer a flaming fire.

While the fire is burning down, place the berries in a bowl and gently crush them with your hands. Finely chop or tear 2 of the onion greens and 1 of the conifer needles into small pieces, add them to the bowl, folding them with the berries. Season with salt.

When the fire is ready, set a cast-iron skillet directly in the coals or set a grill grate over the fire.

Rub the fish all over with the oil and season with salt. Stuff the trout cavity with the remaining onion greens and conifer pieces. Oil the skillet or grill.

Transfer the fish to the skillet or the grill and cook for 4 to 10 minutes, depending on the size of your fish and the heat of your fire, until the flesh is opaque throughout and flaky. Carefully flip the fish (use sticks or tongs if you brought them) and continue cooking until the bottom flesh is opaque and flaky.

Transfer the fish to a wooden board. Remove the skin, if desired, then gently pull the fish flesh in the top fillet from the bones and transfer to a plate. Remove the backbone and transfer the remaining fish fillet to a plate.

Serve the berry relish with the fish.

PULLED BISON AREPAS
WITH ELDERBERRY BBQ SAUCE

serves 8

The Columbia Plateau falls to the west of Yellowstone and the Rocky Mountain region where bison have roamed since prehistoric times. While they were not common in the region, the meat was sometimes acquired through trade.

Mariah Gladstone (Blackfeet, Cherokee) grew up in Northwest Montana and is the founder of Indigikitchen (Indigikitchen.com), a platform where she teaches people about Indigenous foods both online and off. This sweet-tangy elderberry barbecue sauce is one of her most popular recipes. Here, she makes pulled bison sandwiches with arepas, corn-based flatbreads that use a precooked (but not nixtamalized) corn flour. She likes to braise her meat in a slow cooker for ease. If you'd like the sandwiches to come together faster, you can also use an electric pressure cooker (see Note).

BISON

- 2 to 3 tablespoons Maple Sugar (page 36) or store-bought
- 2½ teaspoons paprika
- 2 teaspoons garlic powder
- 2 teaspoons onion powder
- 1½ teaspoons fine sea salt
- 1 (4-pound) boneless bison roast, such as a chuck roast
- 3 tablespoons tallow, cut into tablespoons, or sunflower oil

BARBECUE SAUCE

- 1 cup dried elderberries
- 1 (15-ounce) can tomato sauce
- ¾ cup maple vinegar or cider vinegar
- ½ cup maple syrup
- 2 teaspoons chili powder
- 1½ teaspoons onion powder
- 1 teaspoon sweet paprika
- ½ teaspoon fine sea salt, plus more as needed
- 2 tablespoons masa harina, or more as needed

Prepare the bison: In a small bowl, stir together the maple sugar (to taste), paprika, garlic powder, onion powder, and salt.

Place the meat a slow cooker. Season with half of the spice mixture, rubbing it into the roast, then flip it over and use the remaining spice mixture to rub into the second side and the ends. Pour ⅔ cup water around the roast, not over it. Top with the tallow pieces. Cover and cook on low for 10 to 12 hours, or until the roast is fork-tender.

Meanwhile, make the barbecue sauce: In a medium saucepan, combine the dried berries and 2 cups water and cook over low heat for 30 minutes, stirring a few times, until the berries are soft and plump and have released much of their flavor into the liquid.

Transfer to a blender and let cool to warm. Puree the berries, then strain through two layers of cheesecloth back into the saucepan, discarding the solids.

Stir in the tomato sauce, vinegar, maple syrup, chili powder, onion powder, paprika, salt, and masa harina. Reduce the heat to low and simmer for 10 minutes, or until the sauce is thickened and there's a nice balance between the sweetness and tanginess from the vinegar. Add more masa harina, 1 teaspoon at a time, for a thicker sauce. Taste and season with more salt as needed.

When the roast is done, transfer to a large cutting board and use two forks to pull apart the meat. Drain and discard the liquid from the slow cooker and return the pulled meat to the slow cooker. Add 1½ cups of the barbecue sauce to the pulled meat. Cover and cook on high for 30 minutes to allow the flavors to meld. (Refrigerate any remaining sauce in an airtight container for up to 2 weeks.)

(recipe and ingredients continue)

Make the arepas: Preheat the oven to 350°F. Line a baking sheet with parchment paper.

Divide the arepa dough into 8 equal portions. Lightly grease your palms with oil. Flatten each dough ball into a disc about 4 inches across and ⅓ inch thick.

Heat a large cast-iron skillet over medium-high heat. Add a little oil and swirl to coat. Working in batches, add the arepas in a single layer so there's a bit of space between them. Cook for about 5 minutes, or until deep golden brown on the bottom (a few blackened spots are okay). You're looking to form a crust.

Flip and cook for about 5 minutes longer, or until the second sides are also browned.

Place on the lined baking sheet and transfer to the oven.

Bake for 15 to 18 minutes, until slightly puffed and a little more golden brown in color. Let cool for 5 to 10 minutes before cutting or splitting the arepas open.

When ready to assemble, divide the pulled bison meat evenly among the arepas, either spooning it on top or stuffing it inside the split ones. Serve with more sauce.

AREPAS

- 1¾ pounds Arepa Dough (page 32) or Easy Arepa Dough (recipe follows)
- Avocado oil, for forming and cooking the arepas

Note: *To cook the meat in a pressure cooker, combine the seasoned roast with ⅔ cup water and cook on high for 2 hours. Let the pressure release naturally, then pull the meat. Add the 1½ cups barbecue sauce to the meat and keep the pot on warm for at least 30 minutes, or until you're ready to serve with the arepas.*

EASY AREPA DOUGH

makes 8 arepas

You can make a simpler arepa dough using arepa flour, which is a precooked cornmeal (not nixtamalized corn) that is sold specifically for arepas.

- 2½ cups warm water
- 1¼ teaspoons fine sea salt
- 2 cups arepa flour

To make 1¾ pounds of dough, in a large bowl, whisk together the warm water and salt until the salt dissolves. Gradually add the arepa flour, vigorously mixing by hand. The mixture will start out thin and quickly become a soft, thick dough when all the flour is added.

Knead in the bowl for about 2 minutes, until there are only a few very small lumps. The dough should be moist and tacky but not sticky. (If the dough feels sticky, add more of the arepa flour a tablespoon at a time, mixing well after each addition. If the edges crack, the dough is too dry. Add more water a tablespoon at a time to adjust texture.)

Cover the bowl tightly with a lid or plastic wrap to rest and hydrate for at least 10 minutes and up to 2 hours.

WILD STRAWBERRIES WITH ROSE HIP SYRUP AND BALSAMROOT FLOWERS

serves 4

¼ cup agave syrup
2 tablespoons dried seedless rose hips
2 cups small strawberries, preferably wild, hulled and thinly sliced
2 balsamroot flowers or other edible flowers, for garnish

When the sunny yellow balsamroot flowers bloom in the Columbia Plateau, wild strawberries are in season. I toss the strawberries with a fragrant rose hip syrup and garnish with the flowers. You can serve them on their own as a fresh dessert or on top of a tart or sorbet.

Arrowleaf balsamroot (*Balsamorhiza sagittata*) is an important plant for people in the region. It has long, almost tropical-looking leaves that can be cooked or used for wrapping food. The roots are bitter with a little bit of a piney edge and can be roasted or steamed. The seeds are rich with good-quality fat, like sunflower seeds, and can be pounded into a flour. The yellow petals of the flowers, which I use as an accent in this salad, have a mouth-tingling quality, a bit like Sichuan peppercorns.

Be sure not to confuse balsamroot flowers—which resemble wild sunflowers—with balsam flowers (*Impatiens balsamina*), which are native to India and are not edible.

In a small saucepan, combine the agave syrup and ¼ cup water and bring to a boil over medium-high heat, forming a light syrup. Crumble the rose hips and add them to the pan. Turn off the heat and let the rose hips steep until it cools to room temperature.

Place the sliced the strawberries on plates. Strain the rose hip syrup through a fine-mesh sieve directly over the berries. Discard the rose hips left in the sieve.

Tear the petals from the flowers to garnish the strawberries and serve.

PRAIRIE SAGE–SEARED ELK

serves 4

Elk is a naturally lean meat, so unless you're braising or smoking it, it's generally best to cook the tender cuts, such as the backstrap (tenderloin) or eye of round, to rare or medium-rare. Here, I dry-brine it with salt, sumac, and prairie sage (*Artemisia ludoviciana*), which is actually part of the sunflower family. (It's also known as sagewort and white sagebrush and tastes somewhat similar to culinary sage, if a bit more bitter and astringent.) If it doesn't grow near you, you can order it from foragers on Etsy or Foraged.com.

I like to serve the seared elk with sweet pinyon pine nuts and berries such as red currants, to add richness and tartness to go with the minerally meat. The garnishes are flexible. Use what's growing around you.

- 4 teaspoons coarse sea salt
- 1 tablespoon chopped prairie sage or 1½ teaspoons dried and crumbled
- 1½ teaspoons ground sumac
- 3 small garlic cloves, finely chopped
- 1 (1½-pound) piece elk backstrap or eye of round, trimmed of fat and silver skin
- 1 tablespoon sunflower oil
- 2 tablespoons pinyon pine nuts (see page 324), for serving
- Flaky sea salt
- Fresh red currants, for serving
- Handful of fresh greens or herbs, for garnish (optional)

In a small bowl, stir together the coarse salt, sage, sumac, and garlic. Rub the meat all over with the mixture. Cover and refrigerate for 24 hours.

Rub off any excess of the salt mixture and pat the meat dry.

In a large skillet, heat the oil over high heat until it just starts to smoke. Add the elk and sear for about 2 minutes, or until well browned. Continue to turn and sear the meat for about 3 minutes longer, until well browned all over and the meat registers 115° to 120°F for rare to medium-rare meat. Transfer to a carving board and let rest for 5 minutes.

Meanwhile, in a small dry skillet, toast the pinyon pine nuts over medium heat for about 2 minutes, until just starting to turn golden and fragrant. Transfer to a plate to cool.

Cut the rested elk crosswise into ½-inch-thick medallions. Season with flaky salt.

Serve with the toasted pinyon pine nuts and currants. Garnish with greens, if desired.

HERB-RUBBED PRONGHORN (OR VENISON) TACOS
WITH PRICKLY PEAR SALSA

serves 6

Pronghorn are a native species sometimes called pronghorn antelope or goat-antelope, though they're related to neither goats nor antelope. They are at home in the grassland and brush prairies as well as desert areas in the Great Basin, Great Plains, and Southwest.

They were historically an important animal for Indigenous peoples in these regions. There's evidence people have hunted them for thousands of years and their images appear on Indigenous pottery and other pieces of art.

As with other large animals, people used their hides for clothing and homes and cooked the meat over open fire, either staking it to spit roast and dry or stewing it in pots.

Pronghorn antelope meat can be especially tender and sweet as long as it's handled properly. (Game-loving chef and author Hank Shaw says it must be gutted and cooled quickly in the field for the best flavor.)

For these tacos, I was inspired by all of the plants that grow around where pronghorn graze, so I rub the meat with a combination of prairie sage, aromatic juniper, and tart sumac and then grill it and serve it in tacos with a sweet-tart prickly pear salsa and a sprinkle of pinyon pine nuts.

If you can't access pronghorn meat (you will need to hunt them yourself or know a hunter who does so), you can substitute this meat with other forms of venison, including deer and elk.

MEAT

- 1 tablespoon coarse sea salt
- 1 tablespoon dried prairie sage
- 4 juniper berries
- 1½ teaspoons ground sumac
- 2 pounds pronghorn leg steak or backstrap, trimmed

PRICKLY PEAR SALSA

- 3 medium tomatillos, husked
- ¼ medium yellow onion
- 1 garlic clove, unpeeled
- 1 small jalapeño or serrano chile
- 3 ripe prickly pear fruits
- 1 teaspoon cider vinegar
- Fine sea salt

TACOS

- Sunflower oil
- ½ cup pinyon pine nuts (see page 324) or other pine nuts
- 12 to 18 Corn Tortillas (page 31) or store-bought, preferably blue corn tortillas
- Crumbled dried prairie sage, for garnish

Prepare the meat: Combine the salt, sage, juniper berries, and sumac in a mortar and pound it with the pestle until finely ground. Rub the meat all over with the seasoning. Cover and refrigerate overnight.

Make the prickly pear salsa: Heat a griddle or large skillet over medium-high heat. Add the tomatillos, onion, garlic, and chile to the skillet. Cook for 3 minutes, turning frequently, until the garlic and chile are blackened in spots all over. Remove them from the pan. Continue to cook the onion and tomatillos for another minute or so, turning and blackening them in spots as well. Transfer the tomatillos and onion to a blender to cool.

Peel the garlic clove and transfer to the blender. Remove the stem from the chile and cut in half to remove the seeds, if you prefer a less spicy salsa. Transfer to the blender.

While wearing gloves, cut off the ends of the prickly pears. Using a knife, cut off as much skin as necessary to remove the prickly parts of the skin. Make a vertical cut that's about a ¼ inch deep on the pears. Slip your finger into the cut and peel back the skin, exposing the flesh of

(recipe continues)

the fruit. Add the peeled fruits to the blender.

Add the vinegar and puree the fruits and vegetables until smooth. Taste and season with salt. You'll have about 2 cups and can refrigerate the salsa for up to 5 days.

Make the tacos: Preheat an outdoor grill or a large cast-iron skillet over medium-high to high heat. Rub the grill grates with oil or add 1 tablespoon oil to the skillet. Add the meat and sear for about 4 minutes, or until well browned. Flip and cook until well seared and an instant-read thermometer inserted into the thickest part registers 115°F to 120°F (rare) or 125° to 130°F (medium-rare). Transfer to a cutting board to rest for 5 to 10 minutes.

In a dry skillet, toast the pinyon pine nuts over medium heat for 2 to 3 minutes, until fragrant and browned in spots. Transfer to the cutting board to cool, then coarsely chop.

If your tortillas aren't fresh, warm them over a comal, griddle, or gas flame set at medium heat for 10 to 20 seconds per side. Transfer to a towel and cover to keep warm.

Cut the meat against the grain into very thin slices and place on a platter. Serve with the tortillas, salsa, pine nuts, and crumbled sage.

PINYON PINE NUTS

Nuts from the eleven species of pinyon pine historically provided a vital source of protein and calories to Indigenous peoples throughout dry western mountainous regions of Turtle Island, especially in the Great Basin. Like camas in the Columbia Plateau and saguaro in the Sonora desert, the plant links the people of the region to their identity.

In addition to gathering the nuts for food, people use the leaves for making tea and the wood for ceremonial smudging.

In the fall, when the nuts are ready to harvest, Indigenous families head up into the mountains and set up camp to gather the nuts from the cones.

Harvesting pinyon pine nuts is a tradition that has gone on for centuries, if not millennia, but it's one that is constantly in peril. Since the late nineteenth century, the pinyon forests have been threatened, first by settlers who chopped down the trees for wood and now by overdevelopment of the land and drought due to climate change.

Plus, harvesting and processing pinyon nuts is time-consuming and labor-intensive. The tradition doesn't currently fit the rhythms of modern life.

The reward for all of the effort, however, is an abundance of exceptionally buttery-tasting nuts that can be roasted or ground into a flour. When kept cool, the nuts can be stored for the year until the next harvest.

While the tradition of gathering pinyon nuts has waned, Indigenous activists are working with land managers to find ways to preserve pinyon forests and help the tradition thrive.

HONEY-VINEGAR ROASTED ROOTS
WITH PINE NUTS

serves 4 to 6

You can make these sweet roasted root vegetables with any local or wild roots. A little toss with vinegar after they come out of the oven brightens them up beautifully and makes them hard to stop eating.

- 1½ pounds burdock root or sunchokes or a mix of both, scrubbed and cut into 2-inch pieces
- 3 tablespoons sunflower oil
- ¼ cup honey or agave syrup
- Sea salt
- 1 tablespoon cider or berry vinegar
- ½ cup pinyon pine nuts (see opposite) or other pine nuts

Preheat the oven to 425°F.

Arrange the burdock root and/or sunchokes on a sheet pan. Drizzle with the oil and honey and toss until evenly coated. Season with salt.

Roast for 35 to 45 minutes, until the vegetables are golden brown and easily pierced with a fork. Pull the sheet pan out and while the vegetables are still hot, toss them with the vinegar.

Reduce the oven temperature to 300°F.

Spread out the pine nuts on another baking sheet and toast in the oven for 2 to 3 minutes, just until fragrant. Let cool.

Transfer the vegetables to a platter, garnish with the pine nuts, and serve.

ROASTED SMASHED BABY POTATOES
WITH WILD GREENS PESTO

serves 4

In the Southwest and some areas of the Great Basin, there is a variety of wild potato (*Solanum jamesii*) known as the Four Corners potatoes. Some Indigenous peoples in the region have long gathered or cultivated the tiny tuber, while others are reintroducing this traditional food to their gardens and diets today.

Unlike the common potato (*Solanum tuberosum*), the Four Corners potato is frost and drought tolerant—perfect for the cold desert climate of the region. They are harvested when they are small (from about the size of marbles up to 1 inch large). While packed with nutrients, they can also have a significant amount of glycoalkaloids. These naturally occurring plant compounds help protect a plant from pests and are found in most nightshades, including tomatoes, peppers, and potatoes. While generally harmless to humans at low levels, too much of them can cause gastrointestinal upset or other adverse symptoms.

At this moment, it's challenging to find Four Corners potatoes commercially or even to grow. If you're lucky enough to gather some, treat them like any other wild food and eat a small amount first before consuming more. If a tuber is especially sour or bitter, it's best not to eat it.

Perhaps, over time, this variety will become more domesticated, with more consistently lower glycoalkaloid levels, and a popular regional food plant. Inspired by this Indigenous potato, though, I created this recipe, which features crisp-edged potatoes flavored with a pesto of garlic, pinyon pine nuts, and wild greens. Use the smallest potatoes you can find.

1½ pounds Four Corners potatoes or baby potatoes, scrubbed well

Sea salt

Sunflower oil, for the pan and drizzling

WILD GREENS PESTO

2 tablespoons pinyon pine nuts (see page 324) or other pine nuts

2 cups packed wild greens, such as lamb's quarters, common plantain, watercress, or wild mustard

1 bulb and greens from wild garlic or 1 small garlic clove

½ cup sunflower oil

Sea salt

1 tablespoon cider vinegar

Preheat the oven to 450°F.

In a large saucepan, combine the potatoes with water to cover by 1 inch and season with salt. Bring to a boil over high heat, then reduce the heat to medium-low and cook for 10 to 20 minutes, just until fork-tender.

Drain the potatoes and return them to the pot. Set them over low heat for a minute or two, just to dry them.

Grease a sheet pan with oil and set it in the oven for 1 minute. Pull it out just long enough to add the cooked potatoes and use the bottom of a mug to lightly crush each one. Drizzle them with oil and season with salt.

Roast for 15 to 30 minutes, until the potatoes are golden brown and crisp at the edges.

Meanwhile, make the pesto: In a small dry skillet, toast the pinyon pine nuts over medium heat for about 2 minutes, or until golden with a few browned spots. Transfer to a food processor to cool.

Add the greens and garlic and pulse to chop. With the machine running, add the oil until incorporated and the pesto is finely chopped. Season with salt. Transfer to a bowl. Just before serving, stir the vinegar into the pesto. Serve the potatoes with the pesto.

SWEET PINYON GRIDDLE CAKES
WITH CHIA BERRY JAM

serves 4

During pinyon season, you sometimes see sweet or savory pancakes using these pine nuts. At times, the nuts are folded into a batter whole. Other times, they're ground into a flour, as they are here, to create almost buttery-rich cakes. Instead of supplementing the cakes with wheat flour the way people commonly do now, these honey-sweetened cakes are made almost exclusively with the pine nuts and just a little bit of cassava flour, which gives them a lightly springy texture, and helps them hold their shape.

To quickly thicken a berry jam to serve alongside, I reach for another regional staple: desert chia seeds. It's okay to use store-bought pine nuts and chia seeds here.

JAM

- 2 cups local berries, such as serviceberries, currants, or thimbleberries (or raspberries), fresh or frozen
- 2 tablespoons desert chia seeds or other chia seeds
- 1 teaspoon Rose Hip Powder (page 359) or store-bought
- 1 to 3 tablespoons warm honey, as needed
- Pinch of sea salt

CAKES

- 1 cup pinyon pine nuts (see page 324) or other pine nuts
- 3 tablespoons honey
- ¼ teaspoon fine sea salt
- ¼ cup cassava flour
- 3 tablespoons sunflower oil

Make the jam: In a medium saucepan, cook the berries over medium heat, stirring them frequently and mashing them with a spoon, for about 5 minutes, or until they start to burst and break down. Stir in the chia seeds and rose hip powder and the jam will start to thicken quickly, as the chia seeds hydrate. Add the honey, 1 tablespoon at a time, and stir. Taste between each addition and add more as needed. Let cool. Add a pinch of salt to bring out the flavor. You'll have about 1 cup. Transfer to a bowl to serve immediately or to an airtight container and refrigerate for up to 1 week.

Make the cakes: In a food processor, combine the pinyon pine nuts, ¼ cup water, the honey, and salt and puree until smooth. Add the cassava flour and pulse to form a thick, spoonable batter. If the batter seems too thick or dry, pulse in a little more water 1 teaspoon at a time.

In a large well-seasoned cast-iron skillet, heat the oil over medium heat. For each cake, scoop about 2 tablespoons of batter into the oil, allowing them to spread and form mini pancakes. Working in batches as needed, cook them for about 3 minutes, until they're lightly browned on the bottom, then flip and cook just until the other side is browned.

Divide among plates and serve with the berry jam.

NORTHWEST COAST

WHERE THE VERDANT FOREST MEETS THE SEA

THE EXTRAORDINARY BEAUTY OF THE Northwest Coast has always beckoned to me. One of my favorite memories of this lush, plentiful place is a special meal that took place in the spring of 2017, when Muckleshoot nutritional educator and ethnobotanist Valerie Segrest invited me to the tribe's reservation just outside Seattle to help prepare their annual elders luncheon.

Val and I had become fast friends a few years earlier because our missions are so closely aligned. That wonderful spring day, we were focused on an important element of my life's work: honoring elders, without whom so much wisdom would have been lost. This act of nourishing those who have come before us is a universal Indigenous value.

Leading up to the event, a group of us—including several of Val's young mentees—spent the day harvesting wild foods in serene surroundings, engulfed in a rainforest of massive cedar and big leaf maple trees with Mount Rainier in the background. We gathered mint, Western red cedar, big leaf blossoms, cattails, horsetail shoots, miner's lettuce, purslane, lamb's ear, blackberries, morel mushrooms, and more. Those foraged ingredients made their way into dishes such as a spring greens soup and a hearty elk and vegetable stew made with meat donated by a Muckleshoot hunter. We also sourced seafood from the tribal-owned Muckleshoot Seafood Products, including crab, oysters, clams, and of course salmon, which we roasted over a huge outdoor fire atop a grate so gigantic it required a forklift to move it. That seafood bake acted as the centerpiece of the meal and was served family-style to our hundreds of guests, accompanied by beverages like dandelion root lattes and wild berry leaf tea.

A few dozen of us prepared that feast for more than a thousand elders representing tribes from across the region. Val encouraged me to bring some creative culinary takes to the table, giving these important foods a fresh taste. Just like the cuisine that Owamni diners enjoy, everything was simply but lovingly prepared. I was absolutely humbled that my dishes were so well received by our guests, who also listened intently as I spoke about my work revitalizing Indigenous foodways. It was such a beautiful moment to witness Native youth not only honoring community elders but also enthusiastically absorbing traditional ecological knowledge under Val's gentle guidance.

That lunch remains one of the most enlightening and inspiring encounters I've had along this journey. The regional ingredients that made up our menu are staples for the area's more than one hundred tribal communities (across both the United States and Canada). The long list of longtime Indigenous inhabitants includes the Burns Paiute, Chehalis, Coeur d'Alene, Colville, Coos, Coquille, Cowlitz, Ditidaht, Duwamish, Eyak, Haida, Haisla, Heiltsuk, Kalispel, Klamath, Kootenai, Kwakwaka'wakw (Kwakiutl), Lummi, Makah, Muckleshoot, Nisga'a, Nooksack, Nuxalk, Puyallup, Quinault, Samish, Siletz, Siuslaw, Skokomish, Snoqualmie, Squamish, Swinomish, Tlingit, Tulalip, Umatilla, Umpqua, Yakama, and more. Several of these tribal nations have collectively come to be known as Coast Salish due to their shared language family.

Though most people tend to think of just Washington and Oregon when they hear the term Pacific Northwest, the area spans well beyond that. Also called Cascadia, the region stretches along the coastline from Northern California through British Columbia all the way up into Southeast Alaska—which in terms of climate and culture has more commonalities with these areas than with the rest of Alaska.

There, Indigenous groups synchronized their lives with the pulse of the natural world so harmoniously that the Earth, water, and sky provided everything needed to exist for eons. Of course, colonization disrupted those balanced lifeways beginning in the late eighteenth century. Today, the many effects of human development—the extraction of natural resources, the damming of rivers, and the decline of wild foods due to habitat destruction, pollution, and climate change—can be seen all along the coast. Thankfully, land defenders and water protectors across the region are fighting to return to right relation with nature so that the foodways of the future can be as vibrant and plentiful as those of the past.

In Cordova, Alaska, situated on the Prince William Sound, Athabaskan Eyak environmentalist Dune Lankard is protecting his people's pristine homelands against oil and mining interests. Those efforts date back to 1989, when the infamous Exxon Valdez oil spill dumped upward of thirty million gallons of oil into the sound. To address the devastating effects of this catastrophe, Dune founded the Native Conservancy, which has preserved more than one million acres of wild salmon habitat along the gulf. When I visited Dune in 2022, I was totally awestruck by the area's unadulterated beauty. We sailed out onto the lake that his home sits upon, and I recall the water just wiggling with salmon—the way it should be. These days, Dune is focused on creating a kelp economy while simultaneously restoring ocean health. Demand is rising for this foundational seaweed that's being heralded as a "future-proof" food, biofuel, and consumer goods material. At the same time, kelp forests foster super-productive aquatic ecosystems where a vast variety of species can thrive.

Also hailing from that picturesque part of Alaska is determined ecologist Upingaksraq Spring Alaska Schreiner (Chugach Alaska Corporation/Valdez Native Tribe) who champions food sovereignty and security at her Sakari Farms outside Bend, Oregon. In addition to her activism and policy advocacy work, Spring teaches Native youth how to quite literally weather the storm of climate change by employing traditional ecological knowledge. For instance, amid the area's historic drought in recent years, she and her teenage helpers have been experimenting with dryland farming, which Indigenous groups in the arid Southwest have practiced for centuries (for more details, turn to Desert Lands: Southwestern United States and Northern Mexico, page 184).

Meanwhile in Vancouver, Squamish chef Paul Natrall (locally known as Mr. Bannock, for his delectable take on this frybread variation) honors his heritage with his award-winning Indigenous fusion street food—think candied-salmon power bowls, sumac-spiced duck tostadas, and bannock pizza with elk pepperoni. But his work goes far beyond the plate. He's also the director of Indigenous Culinary of Associated Nations (ICAN), aimed at uplifting chefs and entrepreneurs across the country. The organization is also striving to get culturally relevant foods into public institutions like preschools and healthcare centers, not unlike the work we're doing with our nonprofit, NATIFS (North American Traditional Indigenous Food Systems). We're lucky to have guiding lights like Dune, Spring, and Paul across the Northwest Coast reclaiming our traditional lifeways.

THE LAND

A ribbon of land tucked between the blue waters of the Pacific and the craggy peaks of the Rocky Mountains, the scenic Northwest Coast looks like it's straight off a postcard. It's made up of rugged coastlines, active volcanoes, verdant river valleys, lush temperate rainforests full of old-growth

trees, and magnificent mountains that I find so healing, having grown up in the Black Hills. As you move farther inland, the terrain gives way to boreal forest and even high desert. Like with so many places across Turtle Island, the region's borders aren't clear cut and tend to bleed into adjacent areas with similar climate and culture.

Much of that beauty is thanks to the region's ample rainfall—in some spots upward of 200 inches annually, though the major cities of Vancouver, Seattle, and Portland, Oregon, experience far less. The seasons are generally pretty mild thanks to the moderating ocean effect, but the varying geography and topography greatly impact the climate, too.

Water is very much a way of life there. The seas, rivers, and lakes have long carried with them an abundance of food, including sea vegetables, whales, marine mammals, shellfish, and cold-water fish, such as halibut, lampreys, smelt, steelhead, and the all-important salmon—a cornerstone of Coast Salish diets for millennia. Salmon also has huge spiritual significance for area tribal nations, many of which have ceremonies, traditions, and legends related to the sacred animal.

Although water is rightly the center of attention, the land also yields incredible bounty. It's rich with natural resources, one of the most important being cedar. This naturally resilient wood is incorporated into all aspects of Indigenous life, from housing and transportation to cooking and culture, including intricately woven baskets and the area's trademark totem poles. Historically, cedar provided shelter in multiple forms, including the shared post-and-beam plank houses of permanent wintertime settlements as well as more temporary summertime fishing, hunting, and gathering camps. Native communities flowed with the seasons, enjoying freshly harvested wild foods at their peak nutritional value while also saving plenty for winter stockpiles.

The dense forests foster unbelievable biodiversity, including keystone species, such as elk, deer, and bear, which Native peoples have long hunted and trapped. They also harvest fowl like ducks and grouse and collect wild plants including leafy greens, mushrooms, nuts, garlic, onions, camas, wapato (Indian potatoes), and a laundry list of berries: huckleberries, blueberries, blackberries, gooseberries, salal berries, salmonberries, and many more. Indigenous stewards cultivate all these wild foods in forest gardens and clam gardens, which have often been overlooked since they bear little resemblance to modern-day agriculture. For eons, subsistence fishing, hunting, and gathering have fed area tribal nations.

As you move up the coast to Southeast Alaska, you encounter the Tongass National Forest, the world's largest intact temperate rainforest, as well as the Alexander Archipelago, made up of about eleven hundred islands. This area—one of the wettest in North America—has a temperate marine climate thanks to the proximity to the Pacific, which creates more moderate weather than what many people expect of Alaska.

But even a place as plentiful as the Pacific Northwest can't withstand the onslaught of human development. The impacts to the water alone are extremely alarming. Seaside construction has caused shoreline erosion, while warming ocean waters are producing algae blooms and rising sea levels. Commercial fishers have decimated seafood populations, while industrial farms have drained inland waterways for agricultural irrigation. Dams have totally stifled important rivers like the Columbia and the Klamath—which is now in a period of renewal after the recent removal of its dams.

Amid the climate crisis, warmer winter temperatures mean that more winter precipitation is falling as rain instead of snow, which is hugely problematic since mountain snowpack has historically acted as a summertime water supply. More extreme weather events, like droughts, floods, wildfires, and heat waves are also occurring, while up in Southeast Alaska rising temperatures are causing glaciers to melt. These issues have such devastating effects on Indigenous lifeways that depend on the region's natural bounty—but all is not lost. Though we can't make up for what's already taken place, our conscientious choices as individuals, as societies, and as a species can prevent further damage and destruction.

THE HISTORY

Millennia ago, this region was covered in ice, with only the tallest mountain peaks poking through. As the climate warmed over time, the ice retreated to reveal deep valleys, winding rivers, and till made up of sand, silt, clay, and rocks. Melting glaciers and massive flooding shaped the area's unique landscape and caused sea levels to rise in places like Haida Gwaii (Queen Charlotte Islands), an archipelago off the coast of British Columbia that's the ancestral homelands of the Haida.

Residing in this region since time immemorial, groups including the Duwamish of what's now Seattle and the Tlingit of Southeast Alaska have legends that tell of the last Ice Age. Archeological evidence, like stone tools found in Oregon, proves that Indigenous peoples have inhabited this area for at least eighteen thousand years.

Northwest Coast tribes totally debunk anthropologists' assumption that hunters and gatherers were somehow less sophisticated than more agrarian-based communities. Because natural nourishment has always been so plentiful there, they were able to dedicate less time and energy to subsistence and therefore could develop complex societal structures.

From the very start, area tribes organized their lives around two vital resources that the Earth afforded them in abundance: salmon and cedar. Dugout canoes were the most common mode of transportation, used to facilitate hunting, gathering, trading, networking, and other activities along riverways and out on the sea. Along with countless cultural traditions, the US and Canadian governments restricted this important ritual as part of their forced assimilation policies.

The Pacific Northwest was one of the last places across Turtle Island to be hit by the colonialist machine as it rolled westward. Though voyagers had scouted the coastline in the late 1500s, it wasn't until the mid to late 1700s that Russian, Spanish, British, and American explorers invaded the region in full force. But even before then, Europeans had made their presence known, in the form of both epidemic diseases that spread across the area and word traveling from the east about the oppressive acts being waged against Indigenous groups.

Russian fur traders began making their way into present-day Alaska in the 1740s, facing fierce opposition as they encroached upon Aleut, Inuit, and Tlingit territories. They were eventually successful in establishing trading posts, and in 1784, Siberian seafarer Grigory Ivanovich Shelikhov founded the first Russian colony at Kodiak Island's Three Saints Bay. Having claimed Alaska as their own, Russian explorers moved south down the coast into British Columbia and the lower forty-eight. (For more on the colonization of Alaska, see Northern Forests: Alaska and Canadian Subarctic, page 360.)

Soon, the Northwest Coast was the site of an all-out power struggle for North American dominance. Russian presence spurred the Spanish to return to the region to reaffirm their claims of the entire Pacific coastline dating back to the 1490s. The British, meanwhile, had recently taken over Canada from France after the Seven Years' War (1756–1763). They were eager to find the Northwest Passage connecting the Pacific and Atlantic oceans and used the Hudson's Bay Company as a guise to expand their reach westward. Then in the early 1800s, the nascent US government sent Lewis and Clark to explore the new Louisiana and Oregon territories. Despite the

The canoe has come to represent Indigenous resilience and resurgence along the Northwest Coast.

lucrative maritime fur trade, colonists struggled in the rugged conditions and faced starvation, relying heavily on area tribes for food.

All of these efforts, of course, totally disregarded the First Peoples of this place and wreaked absolute havoc on the land and sea. For a time, Native and non-Native peoples coexisted somewhat amicably with a shared interest in trade, but tribal communities were constantly defending their territories against intrusion. In southeast Alaska, the Tlingit attacked settlements but were unsuccessful in staving off Russian takeover in the Battle of 1804, leading to the Sitka Kiks.ádi Survival March, in which the revered Tlingit clan was left with no choice but to flee its ancestral homelands, hiking across Baranof Island then rowing canoes across a strait to Chichagof Island. The Russian government maintained its Alaskan stronghold until signing it over to the United States in 1867.

Farther south, the Convention of 1818 authorized joint occupancy of the area west of the Rockies by both British and American interlopers. Starting in the 1840s, American pioneers infiltrated the area via the Oregon Trail, seduced by the promise of cheap land and a better life. Over the next few decades, upward of 500,000 white settlers and missionaries flooded into the region. The fur trading, lumber, and mining industries ravaged the Earth, and conflicts regularly broke out over land rights.

In 1846, the US and British governments signed the Oregon Treaty extending the international border along the 49th parallel, dividing many Coast Salish territories. Making matters worse for Indigenous groups, Congress passed the Oregon Donation Land Law in 1850, thereby legitimizing existing land grabs and encouraging even more pioneers to make their way west to claim free plots. Across the region, settlers called for the extermination of Native peoples, who were seen as an impediment to progress.

When hostilities reached a fever pitch, the US government started signing treaties with Native communities across present-day Washington and Oregon in an attempt to push them off their coastal homelands and onto reservations farther inland. Having heard of the atrocities that tribes in other regions had faced, Indigenous groups were savvy in negotiating some of the final US Indian treaties. Most Northwest Coast tribes retained their rights to fish, hunt, and gather in their usual and accustomed places.

The Makah of northwestern Washington, in particular, is the only US tribal nation whose right to whale was clearly outlined in a treaty. A court halted that subsistence right in 2000, but after years of requesting a waiver to the Marine Mammal Protection Act, the Makah tribe was finally authorized to exercise this traditional practice again in 2024. (Alaska tribal nations didn't sign treaties with the US government as Indian treaty-making was prohibited in 1871, shortly after the purchase of Alaska. For more on that, turn to Northern Forests: Alaska and Canadian Subarctic, page 360.)

Of course, tribes' allotted lands were often unfit for agriculture and cut off from important food sources, like fish-filled rivers—prompting protests against the inhospitable conditions. Skirmishes continued between Indigenous communities, citizen militias, and US forces. Native groups fought ferociously for their rights in battles such as the Puget Sound War, but ultimately were relegated to reservations.

In a mirroring situation north of the US/Canadian border, British settlers and Catholic missionaries continually intruded upon tribal territories, both before and after Indigenous communities signed treaties with the British government supposedly to safeguard them against such incursion. Many area First Nations—such as the Haida, Musqueam, Squamish, and Tsleil-Waututh—didn't sign treaties; an estimated 95 percent of British Columbia is unceded land.

Life worsened after British Columbia officially joined Canada in 1871, followed shortly by the passing of the horrendous 1876 Indian Act. Aimed at cultural genocide, the law outlined the management of First Nations reserves and prohibited important traditions such as gift-giving potlatch ceremonies (though they were still covertly practiced before the ban was lifted in 1951). In an effort toward reconciliation and healing in recent years, the Canadian government has made agreements with tribal nations reinstating their land rights, such as the 2024 returning of Haida Gwaii to the Haida people—just one of the region's many landback victories. (For more on the colonization of Canada, read Northern Forests: Alaska and Canadian Subarctic, page 360.)

In recent decades, tribal communities across the region have been actively reclaiming their food and cultural traditions. The so-called Fish Wars—1960s and 1970s civil disobedience protests from Puget Sound tribes defending their treaty rights—led to the 1974 landmark Boldt Decision that not only affirmed those rights but entitled Native Americans to half of Washington state's harvestable catch. (Unsurprisingly, that ruling was met with major backlash, but it was later upheld by the US Supreme Court.) In 1989, Coast Salish groups participated in the first intertribal canoe journey, an annual tradition recognizing the importance of this ritual that continues today. Indeed, the canoe has come to represent Indigenous resilience and resurgence along the Northwest Coast.

THE FOOD

Just as their ancestors did, contemporary Indigenous communities still rely heavily on seafood for much of their sustenance. All five types of salmon remain vital as ever, and the list of ways area groups preserve and prepare this staple is so long it sounds like Bubba's shrimp scene from *Forrest Gump*: smoked, sun-dried, wind-dried, canned, candied, barbecued, stone-baked, pit-roasted on a stick, cooked on a flavor-giving cedar plank over an open fire, mingling with other ingredients in a stew or chowder, and many other methods. For millennia, this fish has been at the center of ceremonies, feasts, and everyday meals. In the dishes that follow, I offer a few different takes on this cornerstone food, including pit-roasted and paired with quick-pickled saskatoon berries (see page 344), as roe atop a seaweed salad (see page 343), and in a seafood stew (see page 349).

But salmon isn't the only food harvested from the region's waterways. Other fish also factor heavily into Northwest Coast food systems, such as halibut, smelt, steelhead, and eulachon (also known as candlefish for its flesh, so fatty that it can be lit on fire and used as a light source). The eel-like lamprey is similarly prized for its rich, fatty meat, though the population is just now recovering under Indigenous stewardship after having its habitat destroyed. Val Segrest emphasizes the importance of rendered animal grease, which gets used as a dipping oil to coat dried fish and meats in healthy fats and other preserved nutrients. Like protein, fat plays a key role in Coast Salish diets to provide year-round energy and maintain body heat during colder months.

The ocean provides even more treasures in the form of crabs, clams, mussels, oysters, and similar shellfish. Val talks about how her ancestors smoke-dried clams, then strung them together to make a Native candy necklace of sorts, but with shellfish. Talented Tlingit chef Rob Kinneen, who also serves as NATIFS outreach director, remembers going late-night clamming with his uncles, netting fish with his dad, and endlessly savoring herring roe—a Southeast Alaska delicacy—while growing up. My West Coast Seafood Stew (page 349) is an homage to area tribes' water-centered way of life.

Because of this focus on water, Indigenous communities' reliance upon the land is often overlooked, as Val points out. All that seafood is complemented by an abundance of animal proteins, which show up in recipes for Venison Sauté with Fermented Mushrooms (page 352) and Smoked and Seared Rack of Venison or Elk with Blackberry Chutney (page 355)—because there's no better pairing than smoky venison with softly sweet berries.

Given the unreal bounty of berries, greens, and other flora found along the lush coastline, it's only fitting that we include some delectable plant-forward dishes in this chapter. For instance, springtime delights like fiddleheads, morels, wild onions, and horsetail shoots come together in a nourishing and satiating sauté (see page 340). Val also generously shares her recipe for Hazelnut Thumbprint Cookies with Rose Hip Sauce (page 359)—a sweet finish to any meal.

All of these dishes give you a taste of the elders' luncheon that we prepared on the Muckleshoot Reservation all those years ago. They also offer an opportunity to reflect upon the history that has shaped the region as well as a reminder to be a good relative and honor the First Peoples of the Northwest Coast when visiting this verdant, vibrant place tucked between the sea and the mountains. Like their ancestors, these Native communities are preserving that plentitude so that our children and our children's children can savor it, too.

ABOUT HORSETAIL

Horsetail is often brewed into tea and drunk occasionally for medicinal purposes. Rich with silica, it's believed to support bone, skin, hair, and nail health. The fertile shoots that emerge in early spring are edible as a vegetable. Most of the horsetail shoots that grow on Turtle Island tend to be thin, so by the time you peel them, you're left with not much to enjoy. In the Pacific Northwest and down the Coast, however, there's a variety known as giant horsetail (*Equisetum telmateia*) and the shoots are thick and juicy with a mild vegetal flavor. (See Spring Sauté of Fiddleheads, Horsetail Shoots, and Morels, page 340.)

Horsetail actually produces two types of shoots: one that appears earlier in spring with a bamboo-like stem, with a cone at the tip full of powdery spores. Those spores fall to the ground to help it reproduce. This is the shoot you're after. The second shoot, arriving a week or two later, has conifer-like leaves that photosynthesize and provide energy to the root system to keep it alive and thriving. You want to leave that shoot in place.

SPRING SAUTÉ OF FIDDLEHEADS, HORSETAIL SHOOTS, AND MORELS

serves 2 to 4

Several years ago, I cooked a meal for one thousand elders with ethnobotanist and nutritional educator Valerie Segrest (Muckleshoot) in the Pacific Northwest. We gathered two giant bags full of morel mushrooms as well as crisp and juicy horsetail shoots and fiddleheads, the swirly shoots from fern plants that have an asparagus-like flavor, and made something similar to this dish.

Horsetails grow widely across Turtle Island, but the variety in the Pacific Northwest is especially juicy (see About Horsetail, page 339). If you can't find them, you can make this spring sauté with asparagus.

Sea salt

1 cup lady fern fiddleheads or other edible fiddleheads (such as from ostrich ferns)

8 thick horsetail shoots

8 large morel mushrooms

2 wild onions with greens, or 1 scallion

2 tablespoons sunflower oil

Bring a large pot of water to a boil over high heat and season it generously with salt.

Meanwhile, trim and discard any dry, brown edges of the fiddleheads. Rinse the fiddleheads well under cool water.

Using your hands, peel off and discard the papery brown rings from the horsetail shoots. Cut the shoots on the diagonal into 1-inch-long pieces, keeping the spore-bearing tops intact.

Rinse the morels under cool water and halve lengthwise.

Separate the white parts of the wild onions from the green, finely chop the white parts, and cut the green parts crosswise into thin slices, keeping the white and green parts separate.

Add the fiddleheads to the boiling water and cook for 1 minute. Add the horsetail shoots and cook for 1 minute longer. Drain both the fiddleheads and horsetail shoots and run them under cold water to cool.

In a large skillet, heat 1 tablespoon of the sunflower oil over medium-high heat until shimmering. Add the morels, season with salt, and cook for about 4 minutes, stirring and tossing occasionally, until well browned. Heat the remaining 1 tablespoon of oil. Add the white parts of the onions and cook for 1 to 2 minutes, stirring, until just softened. Stir in the blanched fiddleheads and horsetail shoots and cook for about 2 minutes, just until warmed through and tender. Taste, and season with salt.

Stir in the green parts of the onion and serve.

MIXED SEAWEED SALAD
WITH PRESERVED SALMON ROE

serves 4

Indigenous peoples along the coasts have long harvested and eaten seaweeds as a nutrient-dense supplement to their diet.

Between industrial pollution, overhunting of sea otters for fur (which throws ecosystems out of balance), and climate change, colonization has wreaked havoc on local waters. Some people see regenerative seaweed farming as one way to help restore ecosystems to their former abundance, reconnect people with their traditional foods, and perhaps fight against climate change, since seaweed can help sequester carbon.

Seaweed salads found in sushi restaurants and seasoned with sesame oil are well known, but here, inspired by some of the seaweeds you can find in the region as well as other beloved local ingredients, like spruce tips and hazelnuts, I created a salad with lots of textures and a nutty, tangy vinaigrette. In the hopes that seaweed can help restore waterways for salmon and other fish, I garnished the salad with luxurious pearls of salmon roe.

- 2 cups packed fresh seaweed, such as sea lettuce, or ½ cup dried seaweed, such as Pacific dulse, sea lettuce, wakame, or a mix of all three
- 1 tablespoon Spruce Tip Vinegar (recipe below) or cider vinegar
- 2 teaspoons hazelnut oil
- Sea salt
- 2 wild onions or scallions, thinly sliced
- 2 medium carrots, scrubbed well and coarsely grated
- ¼ cup unsalted roasted hazelnuts, finely chopped
- 1 to 2 ounces salmon roe, for serving

If you're using the dried seaweed, place it in a bowl, cover it with cool water, and soak until supple, 10 to 15 minutes. Use your hands to squeeze out any excess water and transfer to a cutting board. (You can water your plants with the soaking water.)

Finely chop the rehydrated or fresh seaweed and transfer to a bowl.

Add the vinegar and oil and toss to coat evenly. Taste and season with salt. Add the onions, carrots, and hazelnuts and toss to incorporate.

Serve the salad topped with some salmon roe.

SPRUCE TIP VINEGAR

makes about 1 cup

- ½ cup spruce tips
- 1 cup cider vinegar

In a bowl, cover the spruce tips with cool water and swish gently to remove debris. Lift them out of the water, shake dry, and transfer to a 1-pint jar.

In a saucepan, bring the vinegar to a boil over high heat. Turn off the heat, let stand for 1 minute, then pour the vinegar over the spruce tips. Cool completely. Use the vinegar right away or for the best flavor, refrigerate for 1 week, shaking it every day, then strain, discarding the solids. Refrigerate for up to 1 month.

PIT-ROASTED SALMON AND PICKLED SASKATOON BERRIES

serves as many as you need

Skin-on wild salmon (8 to 12 ounces per person)

Sea salt

Maple Sugar (page 36)

Quick-Pickled Saskatoon Berries with Cedar (page 346), for serving

During salmon season, Indigenous peoples often smoke salmon in huge volumes to preserve it. To enjoy eating it right away, they'll gather to slow-roast salmon fillets on spikes set alongside a fire.

To cook the salmon this way, you'll need clean pointy wooden sticks whittled from hardwoods, such as redwood, red cedar, or ironwood. (The wood varies depending on what's available and what's traditional to each group.) Among some families, these sticks are heirlooms and passed down between generations.

Because digging the pit and heating the fire takes a few hours, this method is best used when you have a day to work with and you're serving a crowd.

I love a pickle alongside the smoky, rich salmon. Saskatoon berries have a blueberry-like sweetness with an almondy note that comes through the brine.

Dig a pit that's about 5 inches wide, 3 feet long, and 6 inches deep.

About 2 hours before you plan to cook, build a fire in the pit using seasoned alderwood (or oak, maple, or apple). Allow the fire to rise up and die down, then start adding wood as needed until you have a hot coal bed with small flames.

Meanwhile, prepare the salmon:

For large fillets (over 1½ pounds each): Slide the large sticks lengthwise through the fillet, leaving at least 10 inches clear at the bottom of the stick. Thread smaller skewers crosswise at 3-inch intervals to help keep the large fillet splayed and in place on the large stick.

For small fillets (about 8 ounces each): You can cut the salmon into 3-inch-wide pieces and thread multiple fillets onto the large stick, leaving about 10 inches clear at the bottom. Or you can thread a single fillet lengthwise on each stick.

For both sizes: Season the fish with salt and maple sugar in equal proportions.

To see if the fire is ready, place your hand approximately near where the fish will be. If you can hold your hand there for 10 seconds, the fire is ready for slow-roasting.

Plunge the sticks with the salmon next to the coals, with the flesh side facing the fire. After 15 minutes, flip so the skin side faces the fire, then flip again. Cook for 30 minutes to 1 hour, depending on the size of the fillets and flipping the direction of the fish every 15 minutes, until the salmon flesh looks richly browned on the outside, the skin feels completely dry to the touch, and the centers register 145°F on an instant-read thermometer. (If the fish was frozen and thawed before cooking, you can cook it so the fish is warm in the center for medium.)

Using fireproof gloves, remove the sticks and serve the salmon with the pickled berries.

(recipe continues)

QUICK-PICKLED SASKATOON BERRIES WITH CEDAR

makes 1 pint

Saskatoon is one name of a specific species of serviceberry known as *Amelanchier alnifolia*. The berries grow prolifically in the Pacific Northwest and across other swaths of Turtle Island. They ripen in early summer (hence, another one of their names—juneberries). If you can't find them, use blueberries instead.

- **1½ cups saskatoon berries (Pacific serviceberries)**
- **½ cup cider vinegar**
- **¼ cup honey**
- **1 tablespoon fine sea salt**
- **1 small piece Western red cedar leaf**

Pack the berries into a jar or nonreactive airtight container.

In a small saucepan, combine the vinegar, ½ cup water, the honey, salt, and cedar and bring to a boil over high heat, whisking to dissolve the salt. Turn off the heat and let stand for 1 minute.

Pour the brine over the berries and let cool to room temperature. Close the jar and refrigerate overnight for the best flavor, then pick out the cedar. Keep the berries refrigerated for up to 1 month.

SWINOMISH CLAM GARDENS

We often think of mariculture—the act of farming fish and shellfish—as more of a modern endeavor and one that sometimes deserves a bad rap for polluting waterways. But Indigenous peoples around the world have actively shaped the coastal landscape to help cultivate sea creatures and plants in ways that are beneficial to the ecosystem, too.

For millennia before colonization in the Pacific Northwest, Indigenous peoples built intertidal terraces to create what are colloquially known as clam gardens. In these sites, clams, seaweeds, and other sea life thrive, providing food for generations of families.

In 2021, the Swinomish people received a federal grant to create the first modern clam garden in Skagit Bay, Washington. Like their ancestors, they built a rock wall at the lowest tide point to form a beach optimal for clams to grow. They then tend to the garden, moving rocks and fertilizing it with ground oyster shells to help sustain more biodiversity.

The shellfish harvested at the site is used only for feeding the community and not for commercial purposes. It's an incredible food sovereignty success story that I hope inspires others.

WEST COAST SEAFOOD STEW
WITH LICORICE FERN ROOT

serves 4

The idea behind this stew is to showcase some of the aromatic plants in the region alongside local fish and shellfish—arguably some of the world's most beautiful and delicious. To first make a broth, I use the bones from a fish and shells from two crabs along with four distinctive ingredients: anise-flavored roots of the licorice fern; pungent, lightly citrusy cow parsnip seeds; pieces of Douglas fir to bring that bright conifer fragrance; and rose hips, for their citrusy tartness.

I also add these aromatics back into the stew itself, as well as a licorice fern tincture, which you can find online. This second addition lets me emphasize their flavors, but don't worry—they don't overwhelm the seafood.

STOCK

- 1 whole Pacific rockfish or other white fish (2 to 3 pounds), scaled and gutted
- 2 live or steamed Dungeness crabs
- ½ medium yellow onion, coarsely chopped
- 2 garlic cloves, smashed
- 2 tablespoons dried seedless rose hips
- 1 (2-inch) piece licorice fern root, coarsely chopped
- 1 teaspoon wild cow parsnip seeds or wild carrot seeds
- 5 small sprigs Douglas fir or other edible conifer

Make the stock: Fillet the fish, reserving the backbone and head. (You can ask a fishmonger to do this for you.) Cut the fish into 2-inch pieces, cover, and refrigerate them until ready to make the stew.

If you're using live crabs, in a very large pot, bring 10 cups water to a boil over high heat. Add the crabs, cover, and cook for 5 to 10 minutes, just until the crabs are red and stop moving. Using tongs, transfer them to a work surface and let cool to warm. Reserve the cooking liquid in the pot to make the stock.

For the crabs you just cooked or the crabs you purchased already cooked, working over the sink, pull off the flap on the undersides of the crabs. Remove the top shells and reserve. Pull out the feathery lungs and discard. Reserve the yellow tomalley (aka crab fat) and any roe that you find, if desired. (The tomalley is technically edible though it can collect environmental pollutants. If you'd like to eat the tomalley, do so with crabs from pristine waters.)

Cut the crabs into quarters so that each piece has some body and a leg. Place in a large container, cover, and refrigerate the crab pieces, roe, and tomalley, if desired, until ready to make the stew.

If you started with live crabs, set the reserved pot of cooking liquid on the stove. If you started with cooked crabs, add 10 cups water to a large pot. Add the reserved fish backbone and head, the crabs' top shells, onion, garlic, rose hips, licorice fern root, cow parsnip seeds, and Douglas fir to the pot and bring to a simmer over medium heat. Reduce the heat to medium-low or low, so the water is just below a simmer. Cook for about 1 hour to infuse the stock with flavor. Strain and discard the solids.

(recipe and ingredients continue)

Make the stew: Measure out 6 cups of the stock (reserving the rest for another use), place in a large clean pot, and set over medium heat. Add the clams and mussels, cover, and cook for about 5 minutes, stirring occasionally, just until the mussels and clams open. Using a slotted spoon, transfer all open mussels and clams to a large bowl. Discard any that do not open.

Carefully pour the cooking liquid into a large heatproof measuring cup or pitcher, stopping before you reach any grit at the bottom, or use a fine-meshed strainer lined with cheesecloth.

Clean out the pot.

Add the oil to the pot and heat over medium heat until shimmering. Add the onion, garlic, and burdock root. Season with salt and cook for about 5 minutes, stirring, until softened. Add the cow parsnip seeds and cook for about 1 minute, until fragrant. Add the licorice fern tincture and cook just until most of the liquid evaporates.

Add the reserved crab quarters and cook for about 5 minutes, stirring to coat with the aromatics, until heated through. Add the strained cooking liquid as well as any reserved tomalley and roe, if desired, and cook for 5 minutes longer. Taste and season with salt if needed.

Season the rockfish pieces with salt. Nestle the fish and smoked salmon into the stew, cover, and cook for 3 to 4 minutes, just until the white fish is opaque throughout. Carefully stir in the mussels, clams, rose hip powder, and Douglas fir tips and cook to heat through.

Break up the smoked salmon into a few pieces. Divide the stew among bowls, garnish with sliced onion greens, and serve.

Note: *When you make this stew, use the recipe as a guide but know that the seasons for fish and shellfish can vary. For example, in Northern California, Dungeness crabs are considered a winter delicacy, while farther north, people enjoy them into the summer, especially when they go out crabbing themselves. Each year, the season can change depending on water and wildlife conditions.*

STEW

- 1 pound Manila clams or Pacific littlenecks, scrubbed
- 1 pound mussels, scrubbed and debearded
- 2 tablespoons sunflower oil
- ½ yellow onion, chopped
- 2 garlic cloves, thinly sliced
- 1 thick burdock root, peeled and cut into ¼-inch pieces
- Fine sea salt
- 1 teaspoon cow parsnip seeds or wild carrot seeds
- 1 tablespoon licorice fern tincture or pastis
- 1 (8-ounce) piece hot-smoked salmon, skin removed
- 1 teaspoon Rose Hip Powder (page 359) or store-bought
- 1 teaspoon finely chopped Douglas fir tips
- 4 wild onion greens or scallion greens, sliced, for garnish

FERMENTED MUSHROOMS AND DOUGLAS FIR

makes about 1 pint

- 1 pound oyster mushrooms, cleaned and frozen overnight
- 9 grams fine sea salt (about 1½ teaspoons)
- 1 tablespoon Douglas fir needles, cleaned well and dried

Fermentation has a long history on Turtle Island. In the Northwest specifically, people historically buried fish and plants to ferment them. While some of that wisdom has been lost, people are actively working to revitalize it.

Since mushrooms are abundant in the Northwest, I thought lacto-fermenting them would be a fun and easy project for anyone new to the process. In addition to the soured mushrooms, you get a delicious, umami-rich liquid you can use in salad dressings or marinades, or as a seasoning much as you would use soy sauce, like in the venison sauté on page 352.

I developed the recipe with oyster mushrooms, but you can try it with other edible mushrooms that are safe to eat raw. Freezing the mushrooms before you ferment them helps them release lots of liquid as they thaw, forming a brine with the salt.

Toss the frozen mushrooms with the salt and Douglas fir needles in a large bowl, then transfer to a fermentation crock or large jar, making sure to scrape all of the salt from the bowl into the container. Weight down the mixture to keep the mushrooms submerged in the brine. (You can use a resealable bag filled with water.) Cover loosely with a lid or cheesecloth, so any gas is able to escape.

After a few hours, make sure the mushrooms are completely submerged in the brine.

Keep the mushrooms at a warm room temperature, about 75°F. (If any mold forms, which it shouldn't, discard the mushrooms and start again.)

After 4 days, start tasting the mushrooms and let them ferment until they taste nicely sour and funky to you.

Drain the mushrooms in a sieve set over a bowl. Reserve the juice and discard the Douglas fir needles. Refrigerate the mushrooms and juice separately in airtight containers. Use the mushrooms within 4 days. You can keep the liquid refrigerated for up to 1 month.

Note: *If you'd like to learn more about Indigenous ways of fermenting foods globally, I recommend Keith H. Steinkraus's* Handbook of Indigenous Fermented Foods. *Be warned, however—it's incredibly scientific. For more accessible texts on fermentation, I highly respect David Zilber's work, including* The Noma Guide to Fermentation, *and Pascal Bauder's* Wildcrafted Fermentation.

VENISON SAUTÉ
WITH FERMENTED MUSHROOMS

serves 2 to 4

Liquid from the home-fermented mushrooms on page 351 provides incredible umami to this otherwise simple sauté. If you have access to them, you can also serve this dish with Simply Cooked Camas (page 313) and warm them in the pan with the rest of the ingredients.

I originally developed this recipe using deer heart, which, like steaks, can be served medium-rare. But you can use any type of lean venison. For cuts that might be a little tougher, like the heart and leg steaks, you can use a meat pounder or Jaccard meat tenderizer to help tenderize them.

- 1 small yellow onion
- 3 tablespoons honey
- 3 tablespoons liquid from Fermented Mushrooms and Douglas Fir (page 351)
- 2 garlic cloves, grated
- 3 tablespoons sunflower oil
- 1½ pounds lean venison, such as backstrap, leg steaks, eye of round, or the heart
- Sea salt
- Three small sprigs Douglas fir
- 1 cup sliced Fermented Mushrooms and Douglas Fir (page 351)
- Thinly sliced wild onion greens, scallion greens, or finely chopped chives, for garnish

Grate about 1 tablespoon of the onion into a large bowl and set the rest of the onion aside. Whisk in the honey, fermented mushroom liquid, garlic, and 1 tablespoon of the oil. Transfer half of the marinade to a small bowl and reserve for the sauté.

Trim any silver skin from the meat. If you're using the heart, trim away any arteries. Cut the meat into ¼-inch-thick slices and pound them with a meat mallet to tenderize it, if desired. Then cut the slices into bite-size pieces.

Add the meat to the large bowl of marinade and toss to coat. Cover and refrigerate for 2 to 8 hours.

When you're ready to start cooking, remove the meat from the marinade and pat it dry. Discard that marinade.

Cut the remaining onion lengthwise into quarters and pull it apart into larger pieces that look like petals.

In a cast-iron skillet, heat the remaining 2 tablespoons of oil over medium-high heat until shimmering. Add the onion, season with a little salt, and cook for about 4 minutes, stirring, until the onion starts to soften but still retains its shape. Transfer everything to a plate.

Increase the heat to medium-high. Working in batches as needed, add the marinated meat in a single layer and cook for about 1 minute per side, turning once, until browned on the outside and rare within. Transfer to a plate.

Reduce the heat under the skillet to medium. Return the onion to the pan along with the reserved marinade. Cook for about 3 minutes, stirring, until the onion is tender and the sauce is thickened. Turn off the heat and stir in the venison, Douglas fir sprigs, and sliced fermented mushrooms, allowing them to just warm through. Taste and season with more salt as needed.

Serve the sauté garnished with sliced wild onion greens.

SMOKED AND SEARED RACK OF VENISON OR ELK WITH BLACKBERRY CHUTNEY

serves 4 to 8

A rack of venison (also known as a rib roast) is a dish worth serving for a celebration. To make sure it's perfectly cooked and give it a rich, complex flavor, I love to smoke it low and slow. I then sear it to give it a gorgeous crust.

The size of racks from deer and elk can vary widely depending on the size of the animal. For this reason, I recommend inserting a probe thermometer into the meat while you smoke it and take it to your desired temperature rather than relying too much on the cooking times in the recipe.

The blackberry chutney served alongside is perfectly balanced between sweet, tangy, and spiced flavors.

Coarse sea salt

2 teaspoons finely chopped Douglas fir needles or cedar

2 teaspoons garlic powder

1 (4-rib) rack of venison or elk (2 to 3 pounds), bones frenched

BLACKBERRY CHUTNEY

1 tablespoon sunflower oil

1 small yellow onion, chopped

1 tablespoon chopped wild ginger root or store-bought fresh ginger

1 tablespoon yellow mustard seeds

1-inch piece Douglas fir or cedar

3 cups fresh blackberries

½ cup honey

½ cup cider vinegar

Sea salt

FINISH

Sunflower oil, for searing

In a small bowl, stir together 1 tablespoon coarse salt, the Douglas fir needles, and garlic powder. Rub the salt all over the meat. Refrigerate for 8 hours to 24 hours.

Meanwhile, make the blackberry chutney: In a medium saucepan, heat the oil over medium heat. Add the onion and cook for about 5 minutes, stirring, until softened. Add the ginger, mustard seeds, and the piece of Douglas fir and cook for about 30 seconds, stirring, until fragrant.

Add the blackberries to the pan and use a potato masher to crush them. Add the honey and cook, stirring, until it melts into the berry juices. Add the vinegar and cook for 15 to 20 minutes, stirring frequently, until the liquid is thick and syrupy. Let cool to room temperature, allowing the chutney to thicken.

Taste and season with salt. Discard the Douglas fir. Let cool before serving.

To finish: When you're ready to cook the venison racks, preheat a smoker to 250°F (or if you don't have a smoker, see Smoking Food on a Grill, page 69).

Insert a probe thermometer into the thickest part of the meat and smoke until it registers 115°F for rare (about 40 minutes), 125°F for medium-rare (about 50 minutes), or 135°F for medium (about 1 hour). I don't recommend it past medium.

Transfer the rack to a work surface.

Heat a cast-iron skillet, grill pan, or outdoor grill over medium-high heat. If you're using a skillet or grill pan, pour in a thin layer of oil and heat until shimmering. Otherwise, oil the grates. Add the rack fat-side down and cook for 6 minutes, until nicely browned on the bottom. Flip and cook for about 4 minutes longer, until nicely seared on the other side.

Transfer the rack to a cutting board to rest for 5 to 10 minutes. Slice the rack between the bones into separate chops.

Serve the meat with the chutney.

WAPATO SALAD
WITH DUCK EGG AIOLI AND WATERCRESS

serves 4 to 6

Wapato is one name for the tubers of an aquatic plant also known as broadleaf arrowhead (*Sagittaria latifolia*). These tubers are also known as duck potatoes, because they are beloved by the water fowl. And guess what? Humans enjoy eating them, too.

Wapato grow in marshes, lakes, and along waterways in many parts of Turtle Island and other parts of the world, too. Harvesting them is a lot of fun if you don't mind digging arm-deep into the mud. They are best harvested in the fall, soon after their leaves die back.

Sometimes, you can find the same vegetable at Asian markets around Lunar New Year sold as arrowhead root.

In the kitchen, they behave a lot like potatoes but take a bit longer to cook and have a crisper texture. Because they're so much like the popular tuber, here I toss them with a duck egg aioli and pickled vegetables for an Indigenous take on potato salad.

- 1½ pounds wapato
- Sea salt
- ½ cup Duck Egg Aioli (page 36)
- 1 tablespoon cider vinegar
- 1 cup watercress, washed well and coarsely chopped
- ½ cup bite-size pieces Quick Pickles (page 37), such as burdock or carrots
- 2 scallions, white and light-green parts, thinly sliced crosswise

If the wapato are muddy, submerge them in a bowl of water to clean, and lift them out of the water (do not pour into a colander, which can reintroduce grit). Then set up a bowl of clean water. Peel the wapato and transfer them to the clean water as you work to prevent their oxidation. Cut the wapato into ½-inch pieces and place in a large pot.

Add water to cover the wapato and bring to a boil over high heat. Generously season the water with salt. Cook for 20 to 30 minutes, until tender. Drain and let cool to warm.

In a large bowl, whisk together the aioli and vinegar. Add the warm wapato and toss to coat evenly, then let cool to room temperature.

Fold in the watercress, pickled vegetables, and scallions and serve immediately.

HAZELNUT THUMBPRINT COOKIES
WITH ROSE HIP SAUCE

makes 20 cookies

My friend and colleague Valerie Segrest shared this recipe with me. To create a rich, substantial dough completely free of any grains, she blends together hazelnut flour, hazelnut butter, and hazelnut oil. She fills the lightly sweet, chewy cookies with a sweet-tart rose hip sauce that requires no cooking. You simply blend powdered rose hips with apple cider to make a spoonable sauce and after a few minutes, it sets like magic.

In addition to the sauce, you can add a roasted hazelnut to the "thumbprint" of the cookie if you'd like.

COOKIES

- 1½ cups hazelnut flour
- ¼ cup creamy hazelnut butter, well stirred
- 1 tablespoon hazelnut oil, or more as needed
- 1 tablespoon maple syrup
- ½ teaspoon baking powder
- Pinch of sea salt
- 1 teaspoon vanilla extract (optional)

SAUCE

- ⅓ cup Rose Hip Powder (recipe follows) or use store-bought
- ¼ to ½ cup unsweetened apple cider or juice
- 1 to 2 teaspoons honey (optional)
- Dried rose petals (optional), for garnish

Make the cookies: Preheat the oven to 350°F. Line a large baking sheet with parchment paper.

In a food processor, combine the hazelnut flour, hazelnut butter, hazelnut oil, maple syrup, baking powder, salt, and vanilla, if using, and pulse until a smooth, soft dough forms. If the dough is too dry, add a little more hazelnut oil or a splash of water.

Divide the dough into 20 equal portions and roll each one into a ball. Arrange them on the baking sheet so they are not touching. Press each one to flatten slightly, then use a thumb or kitchen tool to create a small, deep indentation at the center of each one. (From here, they will not spread.)

Bake for 12 to 15 minutes, until they're just set but still soft and chewy. (If the indentations fill in a bit, use a small melon baller to deepen them while the cookies are still warm.) Transfer to a wire rack to cool.

Make the sauce: Place the rose hip powder in a bowl. Stirring constantly, gradually pour in ¼ cup of the apple cider. The consistency should be on the thicker side of a sauce. Add more cider if needed. Taste the sauce and stir in a teaspoon or two of the honey, if desired.

Spoon a little of the rose hip sauce into the "thumbprint" of each cooled cookie. If desired, sprinkle some dried rose petals over the cookies before the sauce sets.

ROSE HIP POWDER

Makes ⅓ cup

If you're making a powder from rose hips you gather yourself, make absolutely sure you remove all of the seeds. They are hard enough to chip a tooth!

- ½ cup dried seedless rose hips

Put the dried seedless rose hips in a spice grinder (or a coffee grinder that isn't used for coffee, since you don't want the powder to taste like espresso) and grind them to a fine powder.

NORTHERN FORESTS

ALASKA AND CANADIAN SUBARCTIC

EVEN THOUGH ALASKA AND CANADA have distinct histories from the contiguous United States, there are so many more commonalities than there are differences. That was one of the big takeaways from my 2019 trip to Anchorage. I was there to lead a session at the Alaska Native Heritage Center's Traditional Foods Camp, but I came away from the experience with so many important lessons.

I gleaned incredible wisdom from my fellow presenters, including Lingít traditional healer Meda Dewitt, who taught a class about plant medicines, and Iñupiaq/Siberian Yupik/Tlingit culture bearer Beckie Etukeok, who showed attendees how to properly process a seal. After my presentation, we all went out to the center's traditional garden and gathered berries, greens, and other plants to be paired with locally harvested meats for the feast we'd be eating that evening.

I'd never worked with ingredients like maktak (raw whale skin and blubber) or rendered seal fat, so I loved learning from locals while also sharing some of my own culinary knowledge. Together, we made nourishing dishes such as maktak with smoked salmon head, blueberries, wild celery, cow parsnip seeds, and salmon eggs—encompassing the beautiful bounty of this place in a single bite.

Cooking with these unfamiliar foods made me think of my friend Joseph Shawana, who is an acclaimed Odawa chef and culinary educator. In 2017, he came under fire after adding seal to the menu at his buzzy Toronto spot, Kū-Kŭm Kitchen. Joseph viewed the restaurant, which has since closed, as an opportunity to introduce guests to the food of Canada's Indigenous peoples, including the First Nations, Métis (mixed Indigenous and European ancestry), and Inuit (for more on the Inuit, read Ice and Tundra: Northern Alaska and the Canadian Arctic, page 384).

Serving seal was a very purposeful decision, and Joseph knew he'd face some backlash. But it was the global scale of the vitriol that took him by surprise. Rather than deterring him, the petitions and nasty comments really underscored the need for understanding and education, causing Joseph to double down on his conviction. His explanation for keeping seal on the menu amid these attacks was simple: It's who we are. This is an animal that the Inuit have subsisted on since time immemorial. Why should we not be proud of who we are and what we eat? (If you're curious about his seal dishes, turn to page 394 for a tartare recipe.)

Subsistence hunting and fishing—upon which many Indigenous communities in the Arctic and Subarctic depend—is so misunderstood. This isn't a sport or a hobby; it's a means of survival. Like Joseph, I've always thought of food as a great educational tool. It can nourish our minds and souls at the same time that it nourishes our bodies. It can also be weaponized, as was the case with colonialism and now with profit-driven capitalism. But it's time for mankind to join arms instead of taking up arms. It feels like we've completely lost sight of our shared humanity. That 2019 Anchorage trip, for instance, reminded me just how much we all have in common. Thousands of miles away from my homelands in the Black Hills, I worked in concert with local knowledge keepers to prepare a feast that wasn't wholly *mine* or wholly *theirs*—in that moment, it was wholly *ours*. We need to rekindle our relationship with one another and with the natural world around us. Our lives quite literally depend on it.

THE LAND

Encompassing the area immediately south of the Arctic up until the humid continental climate, the enormous Subarctic zone creates a band across the entire planet. On Turtle Island, that includes much of Alaska and vast portions of Canada. In terms of climate and topography, it shares similarities with other places between 50°N and 70°N latitude, such as Northwestern Russia, Siberia, Iceland, Northern Fennoscandia, and the Cairngorms of Scotland.

The North American boreal forest (also called taiga) covering this region includes rugged mountain ranges such as the Rockies, rocky outcrops, plateaus, wetlands, lowlands, countless waterways, and the vast Canadian Shield, which is the world's largest mass of exposed Precambrian rock. Winters tend to be long and very cold with limited daylight, while summers are brief and warm with long stretches of daylight. Beneath the Earth's surface are patches of frozen permafrost, though it's not as thick or continuous as that of the Arctic. This area is experiencing climate change at an alarmingly rapid pace, which is affecting the climate, the landscape, and its inhabitants.

Most of Alaska falls within this zone, excluding the far northern Arctic area and the Southeast, which is more akin to the Pacific Northwest. (For more on that region, turn to Northwest Coast: Where the Verdant Forest Meets the Sea, page 330.) The Subarctic includes the western coastline as well as the interior taiga, which is incredibly intact compared to many other wilderness areas that have quite literally been cut down due to human development.

Spanning some 1.5 billion acres, this boreal forest pushes through the colonial borders into Canada, from the Yukon all the way to the Atlantic coast. Representing 25 percent of the world's remaining forests without any significant human footprint, it's part of the so-called Family of Five along with the Amazon, the Russian Boreal, the Congo Basin, and the tropical forests of Borneo and New Guinea. In recent decades, environmentalists have joined in the longtime Native effort to sustainably manage this important biome since it plays so many vital roles, including storing carbon and regulating climate.

The boreal forest is dominated by centuries-old cold-tolerant conifers that evolved under inhospitable conditions, such as black and white spruce, fir, pine, and tamarack. Deciduous trees like birch, aspen, and poplar are interspersed, with a thick understory of short shrubs, grasses, mosses, lichens, fungi, and berries. Understandably, there's less biodiversity than what's found in the tropical forests at the other end of the spectrum, but the boreal forest has an impressive amount of vegetation—much of it smaller in size than in other regions—considering how thin and poor the soil is.

The boreal forest is also home to an immense variety of wildlife. Mammals include bears (black, brown, and grizzly), caribou, moose, elk, deer, dall sheep, wolves, lynx, beavers, martens, minks, muskrats, rabbits, squirrels, and other game. There's also a huge population of both year-round and migratory birds, such as eagles, owls, ravens, woodpeckers, ducks, geese, osprey, herons, warblers, sparrows, and more. The freshwater sources host dozens of fish types, including keystone species like trout, perch, whitefish, walleye, northern pike, and sturgeon as well as freshwater mussels (locally called clams). And, of course, the Pacific yields salmon, halibut, cod, oysters and other mollusks, and marine mammals like whales and seals.

Though human development hasn't hit the boreal forest as hard as it has other wilderness areas, the region still faces ongoing threats from the extractive oil, gas, and logging industries. In Ontario's Far North, for instance, the so-called Ring of Fire has become a hotbed for frenzied prospectors in recent years thanks to its potential

to yield $60 billion worth of nickel, chromite, and other minerals. Reminiscent of the early days of colonialism, mining companies are making land claims left and right. It stands to become a mega-project with disastrous effects to the boreal forest as well as the animals, plants, and people who call this place home.

The overarching challenge to this area, however, is climate change. Rapidly increasing temperatures pose a threat to endemic wildlife and vegetation, at the same time increasing the likelihood of invasive species. The taiga is actually well adapted to fires, but they're now occurring more frequently. The permafrost is thawing, since it's particularly vulnerable to the region's relatively warmer temperatures as compared to the Arctic. Experts are concerned that as that frozen ground melts, the Subarctic might shift from a carbon sink to a carbon source, meaning it would emit more carbon than it stores. The impacts of these issues reach far beyond the region, and we all have a stake in preserving this hugely important place.

THE HISTORY

Like the flora and fauna there, early Subarctic Indigenous peoples adapted their ways of life to the unique and often harsh environs. They've long stewarded the taiga, which in turn has supplied sustenance, shelter, clothing, tools, and a wealth of other necessities. Early Native communities tended to be smaller in size since food was scarce; they were also pretty mobile in order to follow the bounty of the natural world. Hunting territories often overlapped between groups, who also traded extensively. Given the climate and poor soil conditions, agriculture has never really factored into these food systems, though some people do keep gardens.

While Subarctic Native communities have similar foodways based on what the natural world provides, it's crucial to recognize that they remain incredibly diverse, with distinct creation stories, cultural practices, and tribal traditions. Today, hundreds of Indigenous groups live there, including the Athabascan, Anishinaabe, Atikamekw, Cree, Dene, Gwich'in, Haida, Innu, Iñupiat, Sekani, Sugpiaq, T'atsaot'ine, Tagish, Tahltan, Tlingit, Tłıchǫ, Tr'ondëk Hwëch'in, Tutchone, Unangax̂, Yup'ik, and many more. Alaska has the most federally recognized tribal nations of any US state, while Canada's boreal forest is home to the majority of the country's First Peoples. Even so, this giant region remains relatively underpopulated in terms of density.

The Subarctic spaces of Alaska and Canada may share a landscape, but they have hugely different histories. Alaska is the only area across Turtle Island colonized by Russia, whereas Canada was colonized by the French, then the British. We'll start our history lesson in the west and work our way east.

When Russia became Europe's prevailing military force after its 1721 victory in the Great Northern War, Tsar Peter the Great looked to the east to expand the empire. In 1725, navigator Vitus Bering embarked on an expedition to determine if Asia and North America were connected and discovered the narrow waterway separating the two (the Bering Strait is now named for him). Then in a follow-up 1741 exploration, he sighted the Alaska mainland, which spurred an infiltration of Russian hunters and fur traders.

As in many other places across Turtle Island, European diseases spread throughout Alaska Native villages. At the same time, Russian Orthodox missionaries touched down in the region, determined to evangelize the Indigenous population. Russian colonizers rolled out the systemic subjugation they'd perfected in Siberia, including the twin elements of iasak (requiring tribute in the form of furs) and amanaty (holding Indigenous individuals hostage until the iasak was

The Subarctic spaces of Alaska and Canada may share a landscape, but they have hugely different histories.

fulfilled). Any initially amicable feelings between Natives and non-Natives soon become hostile. By the late 1700s, British and American fur companies established a presence in the region, but an already dwindling wildlife population due to overharvesting precipitated the industry's eventual decline.

Feeling the competition from these other European forces in the area, Russia strengthened its Alaska foothold with the founding of its first colony in 1784 at Kodiak Island's Three Saints Bay. Russian colonists struggled to survive in the challenging conditions and faced major food insecurity. To both save and expand so-called Russian America, the tsar chartered the Russian-American Company, helmed by Alexander Andreyevich Baranov. During his 28-year tenure, he established additional settlements such as Kodiak and Sitka while also sending explorers farther south into what's now Oregon and California.

In Baranov's ceaseless pursuit of Alaska's natural riches, he also oversaw the enslavement and massacre of countless Native peoples. In turn, these Indigenous fended off the intensifying encroachment and subjugation, including the Tlingit destruction of the Russian trading post at St. Michael's. That prompted the watershed Battle of Sitka (1804), in which the Russians prevailed.

But even at its peak, the Russian-America population didn't even hit one thousand people, and interest in the struggling colony waned over time. The Crimean War (1853–1856) between the Russian and Ottoman empires basically bankrupted Russia, who soon sought to offload Alaska. In 1867, they found a buyer in the United States, who purchased it for the bargain price of $7.2 million—roughly two cents per acre.

America paid little attention to its newest acquisition until gold was discovered there in the 1890s. As prospectors flooded in, so, too, did missionaries, scientists, and naturalists. Since then, there's been a steady pillage of the region's natural resources, including coal, oil, gas, silver, copper, zinc, timber, fish, and other wildlife. Alaska officially became a US territory in 1912, then a state in 1959.

American colonialism plays out in a totally different way there—without the warring, removal, and relocation to reservations that occurred in the lower forty-eight—because Congress prohibited Indian treaty-making in 1871 (shortly after the purchase of Alaska). Even so, Indigenous land rights have been an issue since the very beginning. The Organic Act of 1884 promised Native communities would be undisturbed in their occupation and use of land for hunting, fishing, and the like. Congress followed that with two land grant acts, including the 1906 Alaska Native Allotment Act and the 1926 Alaska Native Townsite Act. But the discovery of massive oil reserves along the North Slope—which required a Trans-Alaska Pipeline System that would cross over Indigenous lands—prompted a final resolution for ongoing disputes.

The 1971 Congressional passing of the Alaska Native Claims Settlement Act (ANCSA) effectively extinguished Alaska Natives' land claims as well as their hunting and fishing rights in exchange for $962.5 million (for land already lost) and 44 million acres to be held by newly established corporations owned by enrolled Native shareholders across twelve regions. Although it was heralded by some as uplifting Indigenous self-determination and economic opportunity, ANCSA has also had negative effects on tribal communities and Alaska's landscape. For instance, it effectively opened up the area to further industrial development and resource extraction by creating an incentive for Alaska Native corporations to lease the resource rights to developers, while also creating major obstacles for Indigenous groups to practice subsistence hunting and fishing. Today, Native advocates are safeguarding the land and fighting to reinstate their holistic wildlife management practices after the decimation of animal populations such as salmon due to commercial fisheries and climate change.

Moving east into Canada, explorer Jacques Cartier claimed this land in the 1530s for the French, who became an early dominant European power in North America. It wouldn't be until the 1600s that they established a more permanent presence with the founding of Quebec. Early explorations focused mainly on the eastern seaboard, but over time New France grew to encompass a massive area covering much of what's now Canada and the United States, from Hudson Bay down to the Gulf of Mexico and west almost to the Rockies.

The French were eager to assimilate Indigenous communities into their new colony via Catholicism conversion, education, and intermarriage. The first boarding school for Native children opened in 1620, setting the stage for the atrocious Indian residential school system yet to come, which the British used to force Indigenous communities to adhere to a Western lifestyle and worldview through horrifically oppressive practices. The colonists struggled amid the conditions in this new place, and quickly allied themselves with the Algonquin, Montagnais, and Huron peoples against the formidable Haudenosaunee Confederacy, consisting of the Cayuga, Mohawk, Oneida, Onondaga, and Seneca (for more on this, turn to Eastern Woodlands: The People of the First Light, page 100).

As in Alaska, the fur trade was a big economic driver for the new colony, which benefited from early joint efforts between Native and non-Native collaborators. Agriculture was also an important enterprise, and soon settlers began clearing land to grow crops as they'd done it back in Europe. Overhunting and encroachment caused tensions to flare, especially among the Haudenosaunee Confederacy (sometimes called the Iroquois), who began raiding settlements. In the 1660s, the French government stepped in to fix its floundering colony and sent armed forces to quell the conflict. In 1701, the French government and more than twenty tribal nations signed the Great Peace of Montréal, promising peaceful relations.

Then in the 1750s, the French expanded into the Ohio River Valley and challenged the British colonies, setting the stage for the Seven Years' War (1756–1763), largely centered around the two European powers' struggle for global dominance. In North America, that conflict included the French and Indian War, which pitted France and its Indigenous allies against the British and the Haudenosaunee Confederacy. When the British eventually claimed victory, they also claimed Canada through the Treaty of Paris. At the same time, King George III issued the British Royal Proclamation of 1763, which recognized Indigenous peoples' rights to hunt on unceded land and lay claim to the lands they occupied outside the colonies—while also establishing the treaty-making process.

After the American Revolutionary War (1775–1783), many British Loyalists and their Native allies fled to Canada. That influx prompted some of the earliest land surrender treaties in then Upper Canada, pushing Indigenous groups into smaller portions of their ancestral homelands. (Eventually these treaties started including reserves.) After Confederation—the official formation of the Dominion of Canada in 1867—the Crown pushed westward and signed the Numbered Treaties with the First Nations inhabiting those vast areas over the course of fifty years. In addition to relegating Indigenous communities to reserves, those unjust agreements also outlined assimilation policies that pushed for the adoption of colonial practices, such as agriculture.

In 1876, Parliament passed the horrendous Indian Act, which was essentially an all-out cultural genocide. In addition to defining who qualified as an Indian, it prohibited cultural and religious ceremonies and established the oversight of First Nations reserves by Indian Agents. (The 1885 pass system sought to further tamp down gatherings by requiring written permission for First Nations peoples to leave their reserves.) Later updates to the Indian Act also mandated that Indigenous children attend residential schools. Although amendments to the law eventually overrode its cultural bans, it wasn't until 1985 that its discriminatory clauses were removed.

The long-lasting effects of the Indian Act are still apparent today, as is the dark legacy of Canada's residential schools—the last of which only closed in 1996. It's estimated that at least 150,000 Indigenous children went through the system, enduring emotional, physical, and sexual abuse at the hands of Catholic priests and nuns. The Truth and Reconciliation Commission of Canada helped bring much of that horror to light.

But for me, watching the 2024 award-winning documentary film *Sugarcane* really drove home the anguish and intergenerational trauma caused by the residential schools. Directed by and starring Julian Brave NoiseCat of the Canim Lake Band Tsq'secen of the Secwepemc Nation, it delves into his own family's history and that of others. It's an absolute must-watch to better understand the aftershocks of Canada's oppressive policies against Indigenous peoples.

THE FOOD

Although there's a clear delineation between the Arctic and Subarctic zones, many Native communities inhabit both areas. For that reason, I highly suggest reading Ice and Tundra: Northern Alaska and the Canadian Arctic (page 384) to get a fuller picture of the Indigenous lifeways of Turtle Island's northernmost areas.

The recipes in this chapter are my modern interpretations of Subarctic dishes utilizing key ingredients and are by no means meant to be all-encompassing. If you're yearning to dig deeper into the rich foodways of this region, my friends who grew up there have you covered. Tlingit chef Rob Kinneen's *Fresh Alaska Cookbook* and Enoch Cree chef Shane Chartrand's *Tawâw* welcome readers into the worlds of Indigenous Alaska and Canadian cuisine, respectively, with plenty of storytelling along the way.

For Native communities living in the Subarctic, caribou has been a staple for eons, providing not only nutrient-dense nourishment but also clothing and tools. Here, I pair this important game meat—browned in animal fat to stay true to the area's culinary techniques—with mushrooms and red currants in a hearty stew (see page 378). Berries also show up atop a moose meatloaf made in a cast-iron skillet (see page 377), lending moisture to this lean meat.

Fish from the area's abundant freshwater sources also plays such an important role. Chef Shane, who grew up in central Alberta, shares a recipe for charred trout (see page 373) that's served on a pillow of honeyed carrot puree and grilled ramps, topped with cattail shoots. In case the boreal forest feels far away, this dish reminds us just how closely connected our world really is, with familiar ingredients that can be found across much of Turtle Island.

Indigenous cooks in this region often preserve animal proteins via smoking and drying to ensure harvested bounty lasts throughout the cold winter months. Flavorful smoked whitefish—which frequently makes its way onto our menu at Owamni—enriches a simple soup (see page 381) made from earthy, slightly nutty sunchokes.

Preservation takes on another form in an easy Duck Jerky (see page 370) employing just three ingredients: duck breast, maple sugar, and salt. If you're looking for a bit more variety, many communities also make a pemmican with tallow and dried berries, not unlike the wasná that I grew up eating on the Great Plains (see Pápa and Wasná: A Great Plains Tradition, page 51). Though meat tends to factor more heavily into Subarctic foodways, plants still play an important role. This duck jerky is also delicious atop a salad of cattail shoots and wild greens dressed in maple vinegar (see page 370).

Of course, this chapter would be incomplete without one of the most quintessential boreal forest offerings: teas made from foraged superfoods like spruce tips, rose hips, fireweed, chaga, and leaves of the Labrador tea plant (a slightly confusing name for the evergreen shrubs found in the area). On pages 368–369, I showcase a trio of these healing beverages, which offer medicinal properties as well as an authentic taste of this place with every sip.

BOREAL FOREST TEAS

Indigenous peoples throughout Turtle Island brew medicinal teas and infusions for overall enjoyment and wellness or for medicinal purposes. I wanted to spotlight some of the aromatic plants and fungi from the Northern Forests because many of them are so powerful—not to mention delicious and warming. It's incredible that a place that's so frozen for much of the year can have this kind of biodiversity.

Drying plants for tea is also a resourceful way to preserve seasonal abundance. If you harvest wild plants or grow herbs in your garden, I encourage you to try it!

To do so, you can use a dehydrator, of course. You can also arrange the leaves, flowers, or other plant parts on wire racks in a dry room and set up fans to help speed along the process. Check on them every day or so until it seems like no moisture remains. To store, transfer the herbs to a paper bag, which will allow them to breathe and help any excess moisture evaporate. Shake the bag every few days. When you are sure they are totally dry, after a week or more, you can transfer them to jars and store in a dry place. Most herbs stay flavorful and potent for at least one year.

If you are pregnant or breastfeeding, taking medication, or living with any chronic health issues, be sure to consult a healthcare provider before trying any new herb.

SPRUCE AND ROSE HIP TEA

Serves 1

Bright with the tangy flavor of rose hips and citrusy notes of the spruce, this tea will lift your spirits on a cold day.

In the spring, spruce and other conifers push out new growth and have tender tips, which are especially aromatic. You can dry them, but they retain more of their flavors and aromatics if you keep them in the freezer.

Rose hips, however, ripen in the fall. You can spot the bright orangey-red beads growing on rose plants along clearings of the forest and dry them for long-term storage.

Both rose hips and spruce are high in vitamin C, so this tea is a good one for overall wellness. (If you are pregnant, however, it's generally a good idea to avoid food and beverages made with conifers.)

¼ cup fresh or frozen spruce tips or needles or 2 tablespoons dried spruce tips
1 tablespoon dried seedless rose hips
Birch syrup or honey (optional), for sweetening

In a small saucepan, bring 1 cup water to a boil over high heat. Turn off the heat, add the spruce tips and rose hips, and let steep for 10 minutes.

Strain the tea into a cup, discarding the solids, then stir in a little birch syrup to sweeten, if desired.

FIREWEED AND CHAGA TEA

Serves 1

In the summer, swaths of showy pinkish-purple flowers appear on roadsides, mountains, and meadows throughout the North, including in the Yukon and Alaska. The fireweed plant—which will even grow on tundra—tends to colonize areas after a fire, which is how it gets its name.

Indigenous peoples have long valued fireweed for food and medicine, harvesting the shoots in spring to enjoy as a vegetable, the flowers to eat raw or dry for tea, and the leaves for delicately sweet tea.

Chaga is a fungus that grows on birch trees that has been used by Indigenous peoples in the North for centuries as a medicine. In modern parlance, chaga is known as an adaptogen, meaning it can help the body adapt to stressors. It's also valued for its antioxidant properties. Its rich but slightly bitter flavor also makes it a good coffee substitute.

1 tablespoon ground chaga
1 teaspoon dried fireweed flowers or leaves
Fireweed honey or wildflower honey (optional), for sweetening

In a small saucepan, bring 1½ cups water just to a simmer (about 175°F) over medium heat. Turn off the heat, add the chaga and fireweed flowers, and let steep for 45 minutes.

Strain the tea into a cup, discarding the solids, and sweeten with honey if desired. (If you prefer a warm tea, gently heat the tea once more before straining, stopping before the water simmers.)

LABRADOR AND ROSE HIP TEA

Serves 1

Labrador tea is the English name for three species of evergreen shrubs: *Rhododendron tomentosum* (previously *Ledum palustre*), *Rhododendron groenlandicum* (previously *Ledum groenlandicum*), and *Rhododendron neoglandulosum* (previously *Ledum glandulosum*). They grow throughout the northern climes, including the boreal forests, swamps, and tundra in Canada, Alaska, and even parts of the Lower 48 in the United States.

The leathery leaves are harvested and brewed into a tea that's seen as a cure-all of sorts. People drink it if they feel a cold coming on, if they have a headache, and when they have digestive distress. Some people use the leaves for smudging to help cleanse the body, spirit, and spaces.

While this tea is high in vitamin C, and some people drink it for overall wellness, most herbal medicine practitioners recommend consuming no more than 1 cup per day. Too much can cause digestive upset and cramping.

When brewed, the tea tastes a little smoky with a honeyed wintergreen-like flavor. It can get a bit tannic when steeped for more than 10 minutes.

You can also use the leaves in your cooking as you would rosemary. (Again, do so in moderation.)

When foraging for Labrador tea, work with someone who knows the plant well, as there are lookalikes that can be toxic. You can also find it for sale from spice and tea vendors.

1 heaping tablespoon dried labrador tea leaves (about 30 leaves)
1 tablespoon dried seedless rose hips
Birch syrup or honey (optional), for sweetening

In a small saucepan, bring 1 cup water to a boil over high heat. Turn off the heat, add the labrador leaves and rose hips, and let steep for 10 minutes.

Strain into a cup, discarding the solids, then stir in a little birch syrup to sweeten, if desired.

CATTAIL SHOOT SALAD WITH DUCK JERKY

serves 4 to 6

The flavor of cattail shoots (see About Cattails, page 374) reminds me of cucumbers, so I like them served in a salad with a simple vinegar dressing. You can keep the salad vegetarian, but it's also delicious with the little bits of sweet-and-salty duck jerky on top.

- 10 young cattail shoots
- 1 wild spring onion or scallion, thinly sliced
- 2 tablespoons maple vinegar (or 1½ tablespoons cider vinegar and 1½ teaspoons maple syrup)
- Fine sea salt
- 8 cups wild greens, such as dandelion, plantain, pennycress, lamb's quarters, wild celery, chickweed, and fireweed leaves
- 3 tablespoons sunflower oil
- 1 ounce Duck Jerky (recipe follows) or store-bought

Discard the outer layers of the cattails until you reach their tender inner cores. Rinse them well, then cut the cattail cores on the diagonal into ½-inch slices and place them in a bowl. Cover with water and swish to clean one more time, then drain and pat dry. (Or clean and dry them in a salad spinner.)

In a bowl, combine the cattail shoots, onion, vinegar, and ½ teaspoon salt and toss to combine. Let stand for 10 minutes. Taste and season with more salt as needed.

In a large bowl, toss the greens with the oil and season with salt.

Transfer the greens to serving bowls and arrange some of the marinated cattails on top. Tear up or use scissors to snip the duck jerky into small pieces. Sprinkle over the salad and serve.

DUCK JERKY

Makes about 2 ounces

- 2 tablespoons Maple Sugar (page 36) or store-bought
- 2 teaspoons coarse sea salt
- 1 boneless duck breast (about 8 ounces)

In a small bowl, stir together the maple sugar and salt.

Carefully remove all of the skin and the fat from the duck breast, cutting close to, but not into the meat. Reserve the trimmings for another use.

Cut the duck breast into long thin slices along the grain. Rub both sides of the duck strips with the salt and sugar mixture.

If you have a food dehydrator, follow its instructions for making jerky. (You might need to cook the meat first.) Alternatively, to dry the duck in the oven, preheat the oven to the lowest setting (170°F or lower). Arrange the slices on a wire rack set over a sheet pan and let dry for 5 to 8 hours, until the meat is dried but still pliable. Cool completely.

Refrigerate in an airtight container for up to 2 weeks.

CHARRED RAINBOW TROUT WITH GRILLED RAMPS, CATTAILS, AND CARROT-HONEY PUREE

serves 2 to 4

Chef Shane Chartrand of the maskêkosak (Enoch Cree Nation) grew up in central Alberta with two adopted parents—his father, of the Métis Nation, and his mother, a member of the Mi'kmaq Nation and of Irish-Canadian descent. When he was a kid, his family ate the birds they raised, the moose meat his dad hunted, and trout, like this, that they fished together.

Like me, he worked his way up through restaurants that had nothing to do with his Indigenous heritage. Over time, however, he started looking to his roots and overall Indigenous history for inspiration to start cooking what he called progressive Indigenous cuisine.

To read more about his story and try his recipes, check out his book, *Tawâw*. I'm thrilled he shared this recipe for a crispy-skinned trout served over a luscious honeyed carrot puree and simply cooked seasonal vegetables. It's a taste of the Northern Forests in spring. As always, when handling nettles, wear gloves until after they are cooked. Otherwise, the leaves and stems can sting.

- 2 cups vegetable broth
- 4 large carrots, peeled or scrubbed well and cut crosswise into ½-inch-thick rounds
- 2 tablespoons honey
- Fine sea salt
- 4 ounces nettles
- 4 thin cattail shoots (see About Cattails, page 374)
- 4 ramps, young spring onions, or scallions
- 3 tablespoons sunflower oil
- 2 skin-on trout fillets (about 8 ounces each), halved crosswise to serve 4
- 1 teaspoon cider vinegar
- Flaky sea salt, for sprinkling

In a deep saucepan, bring the broth to a boil over high heat. Reduce the heat to medium, add the carrots, cover, and cook for 10 to 12 minutes, until very tender. Turn off the heat.

Using a slotted spoon, transfer the carrots to a blender (reserve the broth). Let cool until warm. Start pureeing the carrots while slowly adding some of the broth from the saucepan, blending just until you have a nice, smooth puree. Add the honey and season with fine sea salt. Pour the puree into a clean medium saucepan and keep warm.

Set up a large bowl of ice and water and place near the stove. Pour the broth remaining in the deep saucepan into a container and save for another use. Rinse out the saucepan, fill with salted water, and bring to a boil.

While wearing gloves, pull the nettle leaves from the stems. Using tongs, add the leaves to the boiling water and cook for 10 seconds, then transfer to the ice bath. Drain and squeeze the nettles dry.

Discard the outer layers of the cattails until you reach their tender inner cores. (See About Cattails, page 374, for more instructions.) Rinse them well.

Preheat an outdoor grill to medium-high or a cast-iron skillet or grill pan over medium-high heat.

In a bowl, toss together the cattails, ramps, and 1 tablespoon of the oil and season with fine sea salt. Add to the grill grates or skillet and sear for about 2 minutes, turning frequently, until charred on both sides. Set aside.

(recipe continues)

If you're using a grill, heat a cast-iron skillet on the grates. Otherwise, continue using your skillet or grill pan on the stove over medium-high heat. Add 1 tablespoon of the oil. When it's just starting to shimmer, season both sides of the fresh trout with fine sea salt.

Add the fish skin-side down to the skillet and cook for about 3 minutes, or until the skin is crisp and well charred. If, after the skin is charred, the flesh is warm all the way throughout, you won't need to flip it. But if it's still cool in the center or if you prefer more well-done fish, flip the fillets and cook until opaque throughout.

Spoon the warm carrot puree onto plates. Add the grilled ramps and then arrange the fish on top. Top with the cattails.

Gently toss the nettles with the vinegar and the remaining 1 tablespoon of oil. Divide the nettles among the plates. Season everything with flaky sea salt and serve.

ABOUT CATTAILS

If you live anywhere near fresh water, you've probably seen seven-foot-tall cattails (*Typha latifolia* and *Typha angustifolia*) growing with their signature brown fluffy seed heads. They grow widely all over Turtle Island in and alongside ponds, streams, marshes, and swamps. Many parts of the plant are edible, including the roots, pollen, and (my favorite part) the tender, crisp shoots. You can also use the dried leaves for weaving.

In spring, after the new cattails push through the mud but before their flowers form, their inner stems are wonderfully crisp-tender with a flavor reminiscent of cucumber. If you go out to harvest them, practice good foraging tactics, as always. Look for cattails growing in or near water that's free from extensive human traffic and various forms of pollution, including runoff from pesticide-treated fields. Also, make sure you're definitely harvesting cattail shoots, which might look like other shoots in the spring. (If you're not sure, ask an expert.)

To harvest the shoots, you want to try to pull off the bottom part of the plant as close to the ground as possible without disturbing the roots. To do so, push back any outer papery leaves if you can and grip the tender inner core where the plant meets the ground. Give it a twist and it should detach from the plant.

Or you can simply cut the plant at its base with sharp scissors.

After you clean the cattail shoots well, you can eat them raw. Some people find raw cattails give them a fuzzy feeling in their throat, so before you make the salad on page 370, taste a bite to see how you feel. If you get that fuzzy feeling, then give them a quick sauté, which will deactivate the compound that causes that reaction.

SKILLET MOOSE MEATLOAF
WITH LINGONBERRY GLAZE

serves 6

I like meatloaf cooked in a 10-inch cast-iron skillet because you get more surface area of glaze per piece, and nicely browned edges. Because ground moose is so lean, I bring in moisture by adding half the glaze to the meat as well as a cooked onion and a rich duck egg. (You can also make sure your meat mixture has at least 10 percent fat—20 percent is even better.) If you don't have access to moose, you can absolutely substitute ground venison, elk, or bison here. Dried mushrooms add a rich, earthy flavor to the meatloaf and balance the tart glaze.

GLAZE

- 2 cups lingonberries or cranberries, fresh or thawed frozen
- ½ cup Maple Sugar (page 36) or store-bought
- 2 teaspoons cider vinegar
- ¼ teaspoon fine sea salt

MEATLOAF

- 2 tablespoons moose fat, other animal fat, or sunflower oil, plus more for the pan
- ½ ounce dried oyster mushrooms or other dried mushrooms
- 1 small yellow onion, finely chopped
- 3 garlic cloves, minced
- 1 teaspoon dried wild bergamot (bee balm)
- 1 teaspoon garlic powder
- 1 teaspoon mustard powder
- 2 teaspoons fine sea salt
- 1 duck egg
- 2 pounds ground moose, venison, elk, or bison
- ½ cup fine cornmeal

Make the glaze: In a large saucepan, combine the berries, maple sugar, and 2 cups water and bring to a simmer over medium heat. Cook for 5 to 7 minutes, stirring, until the sugar has dissolved and the berries burst and release their liquid.

Pour the berry liquid into a fine-mesh sieve set over a clean saucepan, pressing on the berries. Discard the solids. Bring to a simmer over medium heat and cook for about 5 minutes, or until it has reduced enough to coat the back of a spoon. Stir in the vinegar and salt. Set aside.

Cook the meatloaf: Preheat the oven to 350°F. Lightly grease a 10-inch cast-iron skillet with a little fat.

Place the dried mushrooms in a spice grinder or mini food processor and process to a powder.

In a large skillet, warm the 2 tablespoons fat over medium heat. Add the onion and garlic and cook for about 5 minutes, stirring, until softened. Stir in the bergamot, garlic powder, mustard powder, and 1 teaspoon of the salt until evenly distributed. Let cool to warm.

In a large bowl, whisk together the egg, mushroom powder, half the glaze, and the remaining 1 teaspoon of salt. Add the ground meat, cornmeal, and the warm onion/garlic mixture and stir to incorporate. Press the meatloaf mixture into the prepared skillet and transfer to the oven.

Bake for 45 minutes to 1 hour, until an instant-read thermometer inserted in the center registers 140°F.

Brush the remaining glaze over the meatloaf and bake for 6 to 10 minutes longer, or until the internal temperature (taken the same way) registers 160°F.

Let it rest for 5 minutes before serving.

CARIBOU STEW
WITH MUSHROOMS AND RED CURRANTS

serves 4 to 6

Caribou roam the entire Arctic and Subarctic, providing food, clothing, and tool materials for people in the North. (The word "caribou" comes from the Mi'kmaq word *qalipu*.) In Europe, the same animal is called a reindeer.

Both dried and fresh mushrooms bring a savory depth of flavor to this stew and the berry garnish brightens it all up. You can serve it with a mash or puree made from Alpine sweet vetch roots (see About Alpine Sweet Vetch, page 381) or other root vegetables.

If you don't have access to caribou, you can substitute venison or elk here.

- 2 ounces dried wild mushrooms
- 2 cups boiling water
- 2 pounds caribou, venison, or elk stew meat, cut into 1-inch pieces
- Sea salt
- 5 tablespoons animal fat or sunflower oil
- 1 medium yellow onion, finely chopped
- 2 quarts Rich Bison or Other Game Stock (page 41)
- 1 tablespoon cider vinegar
- 5 juniper berries, lightly crushed
- 1 tablespoon birch syrup or maple syrup
- 8 ounces fresh wild mushrooms
- ¼ cup red currants, fresh or frozen, for garnish

In a heatproof bowl, combine the dried mushrooms and boiling water and let stand for at least 15 minutes to rehydrate.

Season the meat well all over with salt. In a large heavy pot or Dutch oven, heat 2 tablespoons of the fat over medium-high heat until shimmering. Working in batches to avoid overcrowding, add the meat pieces in a single layer so they're not touching and cook for about 8 minutes, flipping occasionally, until they're browned all over. Transfer to a plate.

Heat 2 more tablespoons of the fat over medium heat. Add the onion and cook for about 5 minutes, or until softened.

Scoop out the rehydrated mushrooms and set aside. Strain the mushroom-soaking liquid into the pan, stopping before you reach any grit at the bottom. Add the game stock, vinegar, juniper berries, and birch syrup to the pan and bring to a simmer over medium heat. Return the meat to the pan. Reduce the heat to medium-low, cover, and cook for 2 to 2½ hours, until the meat is tender.

Using a slotted spoon, transfer the meat to a plate and bring the cooking liquid to a boil over medium-high heat. Cook for about 20 minutes, or until it's thickened and glossy. Taste and season with salt as needed.

Meanwhile, in a skillet, heat the remaining 1 tablespoon of fat over medium heat until shimmering. Add the fresh mushrooms, season with salt, and cook for about 2 minutes, stirring, until they start to release their liquids. Increase the heat to medium-high and cook for about 7 minutes, or until the liquid evaporates and the mushrooms start to brown.

Add the fresh mushrooms and the rehydrated mushrooms to the reduced cooking liquid. Return the meat to the pot and cook over medium heat, stirring, just until everything is heated through. Taste and season with salt as needed.

Serve the stew garnished with the currants.

SUNCHOKE SOUP WITH SMOKED WHITEFISH

serves 4

In this region, it's common to preserve freshwater fish through smoking, drying, and sometimes pickling. The smoked fish can then provide a delicious depth of flavor with a simple soup, like this one, which is reminiscent of creamy potato-leek soup but uses sweet sunchokes and hazelnut milk instead. Sunchokes are native to Turtle Island but only grow in parts of the Northern Forests. If you like, you can try replacing the sunchokes with other roots, like burdock, Alpine sweet vetch (see below), or parsnips, which are not native but do grow well in cold climes.

- 1 large leek, white and light-green parts only, cut crosswise into thin slices
- 2 tablespoons cider vinegar, plus more for the sunchokes
- 1 pound sunchokes or other local roots
- 2 tablespoons sunflower oil
- Sea salt
- 1 quart hazelnut or wild rice milk (see Seed, Nut, and Grain Milks, page 35)
- 8 to 10 ounces smoked whitefish, skin and bones removed, flesh flaked
- Sliced wild onion greens or chives, for garnish

Fill a large bowl with cool water and add the leeks. Gently swish around and let sit for a few minutes so that any grit falls to the bottom. Lift the leeks out of the water, shaking off excess water, and transfer to a separate bowl.

Rinse out the empty bowl and fill it with fresh water. Add a few tablespoons of vinegar. Peel the sunchokes as much as you can without stressing about getting every last bit of skin. Cut the sunchokes into 1-inch pieces and add to the vinegared water. This will prevent them from oxidizing too much.

In a large saucepan, heat the oil over medium heat. Add the cleaned leeks and 1 teaspoon salt and cook for 4 to 5 minutes, stirring, until the leeks are wilted and tender.

Add the sunchokes and hazelnut milk and bring to a simmer over medium heat. Cook for 30 to 40 minutes, until the sunchokes can be mashed with a fork. Remove from the heat and cool to warm.

Working in batches as needed, transfer the soup to a blender and puree until very smooth. Pulse in the 2 tablespoons cider vinegar. Taste and season with salt. Reheat the pureed soup over medium-low heat.

Ladle the soup into bowls and garnish with the flaked whitefish and onion greens.

ABOUT ALPINE SWEET VETCH

Alpine sweet vetch (*Hedysarum alpinum*) grows wild in some northern parts of the United States, as well as central Canada all the way up to parts of the Arctic tundra. It's part of the legume family and has pretty pink and purple blooms, but the roots are what people (as well as bears) dig up and eat. Colloquially in English, they've become known as "Eskimo potatoes." (Many Indigenous peoples now consider "Eskimo" to be a slur, though some still embrace the term.) But there are many Native names for this plant, including marralaq or masru (Yup'ik), masu (Iñupiaq), and k'tl'ila (Dena'ina).

While the roots taste extra sweet in the spring and are easier to dig then, too, sometimes people will build a fire to thaw the ground in winter to dig them out.

To enjoy their flavor, which is similar to a cross between parsnips and carrots, they're best served simply.

MAPLE-CHAGA MUFFINS
WITH SASKATOON BERRIES

makes 12 muffins

Chaga is traditionally made into a tea (see Fireweed and Chaga Tea, page 369) or burned for incense. In small amounts, its natural vanilla-like flavor can also complement baked goods, such as these muffins made of wild rice and cassava flour. Wild rice grows sporadically in the Northern Forests. While cassava is not a regional ingredient, people all over Turtle Island have traditionally made flours out of wild root vegetables. Cassava flour is one common root vegetable–based flour that's easy to access, so I call for that here.

- **3 tablespoons sunflower oil, plus more for the muffin tin**
- **¾ cup wild rice flour (see Note)**
- **¼ cup cassava flour**
- **½ teaspoon baking soda**
- **1 tablespoon chaga powder**
- **¾ teaspoon fine sea salt**
- **1 duck egg**
- **¾ cup maple syrup**
- **½ cup wild rice milk (see Seed, Nut, and Grain Milks, page 35) or other nondairy milk**
- **2 cups saskatoon berries or blueberries, fresh or frozen**

Preheat the oven to 350°F. Line 12 cups of a standard muffin tin with paper liners or lightly grease the wells with a little oil.

In a medium bowl, whisk together the wild rice flour, cassava flour, baking soda, chaga powder, and salt.

In a second bowl, using a whisk, lightly beat the egg, then whisk in the maple syrup, the 3 tablespoons oil, the wild rice milk, and ¼ cup water. Stir the flour mixture into the milk mixture until well incorporated to form a thin batter. Fold in 1 cup of the berries.

Fill each muffin cup so it's about two-thirds full (or about 5 tablespoons of batter per cup). Divide the remaining 1 cup of berries among the muffins.

Bake for about 18 minutes, or until a tester inserted in the center comes out clean and the muffins spring back when you touch them.

Transfer the muffin tin to a rack to cool for a few minutes before lifting the muffins out of the pan to serve.

Note: *While you can purchase wild rice flour, you can also make your own. Place 1 cup wild rice in a food processor or a high-powered blender and pulse to finely chop. Then let the machine run until the rice is ground to a flour-like consistency. Sift the wild rice flour through a fine-mesh sieve to remove any large pieces before using. Refrigerate or freeze the flour for up to 1 month.*

ICE AND TUNDRA

NORTHERN ALASKA AND THE CANADIAN ARCTIC

I FEEL SO FORTUNATE THAT MY WORK has taken me so many places to meet with Indigenous communities across the world, but I haven't yet journeyed up to the Arctic. To introduce us to this region, I'm handing things off to my collaborator, Tlingit writer Kate Nelson, who recently embarked on an adventure much farther north than I've been, to the Canadian territory of Nunavut. I'll let her take it from here.

You know you've officially crossed into the Arctic when you hit the tree line, a somewhat fuzzy boundary beyond which major vegetation can't grow. I was on the final leg of my trip to Iqaluit—Canada's northernmost city and the capital of Nunavut territory, where the majority of residents are Inuit—when all the passengers started pointing out the plane windows. Sure enough, we'd just flown over the point where the coniferous trees of the Subarctic give way to a white abyss stretching as far as the eye can see.

As soon as I set foot in the Iqaluit airport, I was surrounded by Inuit culture. I stopped to admire the beautiful textiles adorning the walls; a placard explained they were larger-than-life replicas of Indigenous artworks. Once outside, I noticed all the signage on the city's colorful buildings was in Inuktitut first, English second.

On an initial drive through town, I spotted an archway of bowhead whale jaw bones standing tall in the municipal cemetery. Those burial grounds sit outside the city center in Apex (traditionally known as Niaqunngut), which is where the Inuit were relegated when a now-closed US Air Force base was established in Iqaluit (previously called Frobisher Bay) during World War II. Not far away is a string of historic buildings, one of them bearing the name Hudson's Bay Company, the fur trading business that served as a front for British imperialism.

Iqaluit bears all sorts of scars from its painful past, juxtaposed with countless instances of the Inuit culture that colonialism couldn't kill. The city's striking balance of tradition and modernity reflects the challenge many Indigenous communities face in trying to simultaneously honor their past and forge their future. This is particularly pronounced in the Arctic, which was hit by colonialism later but is now being hugely impacted by both climate change and an influx of interest from the mining, oil and gas, tourism, and transportation industries. Some experts predict we're on the brink of a Cold Rush.

All those enterprises will have to contend with the Inuit in Iqaluit and beyond, who for eons have safeguarded the land, water, and ice there—the three components that make up Inuit Nunangat. Meaning "homeland" in Inuktitut, that term refers to their four land claims, which account for more than a third of Canada's land mass and half of its coastline.

In the Arctic, carrying on ancestral traditions isn't just about maintaining a sense of pride; it's about staying alive. Though they've been modernized over time, Inuit lifeways still very much revolve around subsistence hunting and fishing. These communities' resilience and resourcefulness—developed from adapting to the ever-changing and oft-harsh natural environment for eons—has allowed them to thrive in a way few of us can understand, living relatively plush lives so far from the Arctic Circle. There remains a mysticism about this place and major misconceptions about its inhabitants, likely because so few people have ventured there.

During my time in Iqaluit, I witnessed so much Indigenous joy and vibrancy. Locals were eager to guide me through quintessential Inuit experiences, like a snowmobiling excursion out across the frozen bay, where I spied caribou and ptarmigan along the way. I also noshed on dishes like char and caribou Wellington, ptarmigan soup, and a scrumptious salad made with maktak (raw whale skin and blubber). I reveled at the endless late-spring daylight. Most of all, in this place that's so closely associated with cold, I felt such an overwhelming warmth from my new friends, who proudly and openly shared their culture with me.

THE LAND

Despite its name, the Arctic zone extends beyond the bounds of the Arctic Circle. Most ecologists define the region as where the average July temperature doesn't break 50°F (10°C), which roughly corresponds with that tree line where the boreal forest ends. Thanks to its extreme cold and extensive sea ice, the Arctic is known as the Earth's icebox. It provides a cooling effect for the entire planet and shapes jet streams, influencing the climate and weather in places much farther south.

The area closest to the North Pole is actually classified as desert given the dry conditions; it receives just 10 inches of annual precipitation—akin to that of the Sahara Desert. That's because the air is too cold to hold much moisture, and this polar desert is largely barren due to its extreme environs. As you move farther south, the conditions become slightly more hospitable, giving way to Arctic tundra. This ecosystem is still arid but overall milder (especially in the summer), which allows the biome to sustain life.

The entire region is underlain by permafrost, a thick frozen layer of soil, sand, and sediment bound together by ice that's been in place for at least two years straight. In most cases, it's thousands of years old, and in spots like Siberia, it descends some five thousand feet below the surface. It stores an immense amount of carbon, which scientists fear could be released into the atmosphere as climate change causes it to melt.

Winters there are long and cold, while summers are short and cool. This area also experiences polar night and day, where the sun doesn't rise above the horizon for months at a time in the winter, or alternatively remains above the horizon for 24 hours in the summer. All that sunlight causes seasonal warming and ice melting.

The freezing and thawing of ice has shaped the topography over time, yielding pits, valleys, and even caves. The landscape is dotted with pingos—dome-shaped hills that emerge when the pressure of freezing groundwater pushes up frozen ground—as well as polygons, the quilt-like patterns caused by the freeze-thaw cycle of subterranean ice wedges.

The tundra also has countless lakes, ponds, and rivers, which shape-shift due to natural forces and, more recently, climate change. They are paramount to the Arctic ecosystem, providing important wildlife habitat and serving as a vital water source for area Indigenous communities. The glaciers and icebergs of the Arctic Ocean, meanwhile, make up about 20 percent of the planet's freshwater supply.

The arid environs and frigid temperatures mean that only the hardiest flora and fauna can survive there. The regional vegetation has evolved to handle the short growing season (just fifty to sixty days), limited drainage, sweeping winds, soil disturbances, and permafrost that doesn't allow for deep root systems. Even so, the area has an estimated seventeen hundred plant varieties, including flowering plants, low shrubs, sedges, mosses, lichens, liverworts, and grasses, which tend to stay short in stature and group together for greater protection from the elements.

Animals are similarly well adapted to the environs. On land, that includes polar bears, wolves, caribou, moose, musk oxen, dall sheep, wolverines, foxes, hares, and smaller species like ermine, lemmings, and squirrels. The surrounding ocean and interspersed waterways, meanwhile, host marine mammals including walruses, seals, and whales—ranging from beluga to narwhal to massive bowhead—as well as char, salmon, cod, grayling, flatfish, shrimp, clams, mussels, and more. There are also plenty of birds, like puffins, ravens, terns, eagles, ducks, snow geese, and snowy owls. Many of these animals migrate or hibernate during the winter, though some tough it out throughout the cold season.

As Europeans infiltrated the region, they overhunted and overharvested wildlife populations, especially whales and Arctic foxes. They also began pillaging natural resources like gold, silver, nickel, copper, zinc, lead, diamonds, and natural gas and oil through extractive mining operations.

Today, the beautiful natural balance of this place is in peril due to climate change, which is hugely affecting both this region and the Subarctic zone just to the south. The Arctic is warming about three times faster than anywhere else on Earth, with dire consequences for all of us.

Summer sea ice is shrinking at a rapid rate of about 13 percent per decade, and some climatologists think the Arctic could be ice-free by 2040 if human emissions continue to go unchecked. That's a major problem since this zone's albedo effect—how the snow and ice reflect the sunlight back into space—balances out the heat-absorbing areas of the planet.

Additionally, the global sea level has risen upward of eight inches since 1900 (with three of those inches occurring since 1993), thereby putting coastal and island communities at risk. The one-two punch of receding ice and melting permafrost is threatening animals like polar bears, walruses, narwhals, and caribou—and the Indigenous groups that depend on them for sustenance. It's affecting fish, too, with Subarctic species like orcas, cod, beaked redfish, and long rough dab making their way farther north and disrupting the delicate aquatic ecosystem.

The region's rapidly changing climate has far-reaching reverberations, because what happens in the Arctic doesn't stay in the Arctic. For the Native peoples on the front lines of this crisis whose lifeways are being threatened, there's no pretending that climate change isn't happening.

THE HISTORY

The resilience and resourcefulness of Arctic Indigenous communities date back millennia. The early Thule culture—thought to be the predecessors of modern Inuit—migrated across much of the region, likely from Alaska's northwest coast into Canada and onward to Greenland. They evolved along with, and in response to, the land, designing highly sophisticated technology to ensure their survival in this challenging environment.

Their winter villages typically consisted of partially subterranean shelters built from stones, sod, and whale bones, with a tent-like animal skin cover stretched atop. Wisely, they arranged entrances as narrow underground passages and connected these homes by a tunnel system in order to minimize exposure to the elements. Similarly constructed summer camps were often set along the coastline. It's an outdated stereotype that Arctic peoples lived in—or continue to live in—igloos; these dome-shaped snow huts generally served as temporary hunting shelters.

For food, the Thule depended hugely on marine mammals, such as bowhead whales, then available in abundance. They developed innovations like bows and arrows, drag floats, dog sleds, kayaks, and umiaks (large open boats) to ensure their hunting success. Other inventions such as qulliq (stone lamps), knives, and cooking pots showcase their ingenuity, as does their carved wood and stone art.

After the Little Ice Age in 1400 CE caused a climate shift, the Thule began hunting land animals like caribou and musk oxen as well as fishing for char and other species. Around that time, they also started migrating south beyond the Arctic Circle, potentially in search of new food sources.

Modern Arctic Indigenous communities still practice that same level of resourcefulness and carry on many of those early traditions. Today, the region boasts more than sixty Indigenous communities, home to the Gwich'in, Igluingmiut, Inuinnait, Iñupiat, Inuvialuit, Kivallirmiut, Labradormiut, Netsilingmiut, Nunavimmiut, Siberian Yupik, and more. In many places, the broad term Inuit is used to describe most of these peoples, though every community should be referred to by the name of their choosing. It should also be noted that Inuit live beyond the Arctic; after all, they aren't bound there.

Arctic peoples remain intimately and inextricably connected to the land, which provides food, clothing, shelter, tools, and most of all, a sense of identity. Their deeply embedded understanding of the science of this place—its climate, its weather, its wildlife, its cycles—has been passed down from one generation to the next. It's not a stretch to say it's in their DNA.

Though these Native communities sporadically traded with Europeans leading up to this time, they first felt the impacts of qallunaat (non-Inuit) in the 1500s. That's when European and Asian explorers chartered into Arctic waters in search of the Northwest Passage, thought to connect the Atlantic and Pacific oceans. Most expeditions were woefully unprepared for the harsh environs.

Then starting in the early 1700s, the Dutch came for one of the most valued regional resources: whales. Over the course of the next century, they developed settlements in places like Cumberland Sound. They introduced European diseases, which wiped out as much as two-thirds of the Indigenous population. Before long, they had overfished the whale population, causing further hardships for the Inuit. As conflict grew between Natives and non-Natives, the British in the 1770s sent in Moravian Protestant missionaries to convert the Inuit to Christianity as well as provide education and health services.

When the whaling industry declined in the late 1800s, Europeans began trapping Arctic foxes, then engaging Inuit in this enterprise. As the white pelts became all the rage, companies like Hudson's Bay Company developed regional posts. Around the same time, the first residential schools were established in the Arctic. Through this sustained contact, Inuit started to depart from their ancestral subsistence traditions, causing growing dependency on the European interlopers and their capitalist economy.

Up until the early 1900s, the Canadian government had little to do with the Arctic. Then in 1939, in the so-called Eskimo Decision, the Supreme Court determined that Inuit were not citizens but Indians and therefore wards of the state. Because Europeans couldn't pronounce Inuit names, the government in the early 1940s implemented the disc system, giving each person a small identification tag used to track any and all interactions, such as accessing basic services. A shining example of Indigenous erasure, this racist practice was in place until 1978.

World War II and the Cold War brought further changes to the region, which soon became home to US military outposts that pushed Inuit off their ancestral homelands. As American presence in the area grew and Soviet threat loomed, Canada asserted its Arctic claims by using Indigenous people as pawns. In the 1950s in an absolutely egregious act known as the High Arctic relocation, the government displaced nearly one hundred Inuit from Inukjuak, Quebec, up to the uninhabited Ellesmere and Cornwallis islands—some two thousand kilometers away—to establish the towns of Grise Fiord and Qausuittuq (also known as Resolute).

Brought there under false pretenses and on empty promises, the Inuit suffered greatly in these unfamiliar places where many natural resources had already been depleted, causing major food insecurity. They had been promised return to Inukjuak after two years, but that didn't actually happen until the late 1980s. In 1996, the government passed the Reconciliation Agreement with a dedicated fund for the relocated Inuit (though payment stopped in 2009 during the stock market crash).

The 1950s also saw the growth of the residential school system across the Arctic as well as the development of government-operated high schools. Given the low population across the vast area, the latter brought together Indigenous teens from around the region in a rare positive effect of these education systems, who for the first time learned about civil and human rights in Canada—giving rise to a young generation of activists in the 1960s and 1970s. They helped develop the political organization Inuit Tapiriit Kanatami (ITK) to uphold Inuit culture and rights; by the 1980s, the group represented Inuit across the country.

The 1982 Constitution Act recognized Inuit as Aboriginal peoples (along with First Nations and Métis peoples) and upheld their cultural, land, hunting, fishing, and self-governing rights. That set the stage for the creation of Nunavut. Established in 1999, it's not only the youngest and largest Canadian territory but also the first to institute Indigenous self-governance. This and other autonomous communities, such as the North Slope Borough of Alaska, serve as strong symbols of Native sovereignty.

As Russians encroached upon other parts of Alaska in the 1700s, they largely ignored the North Slope, a horizontal strip at the northernmost part of the state that falls within the Arctic zone. In many ways, the colonization of this area echoes that of the Canadian Arctic. In the mid-1800s, Europeans depleted the whale population, then moved onto trapping fur-bearing land animals, along the way spreading epidemic diseases across the region. Presbyterian missionaries also began infiltrating the area to evangelize the Iñupiat. They tested out assimilation tactics like attempting to convert these Native groups to a sedentary lifestyle through a caribou herding experiment, which failed miserably.

But it was the discovery of oil at Prudhoe Bay in 1968—less than a decade after Alaska statehood—that dramatically changed life in the Far North. That prompted the Alaska Native Claims Settlement Act (ANCSA) to resolve ongoing land disputes in order to clear the way for the Trans-Alaska Pipeline System. It would take another decade for companies to totally transform the landscape into a massive oil field, which remains the largest in North America.

Upon that oil discovery, the area Indigenous communities rallied to form the self-governing North Slope Borough in order to maintain greater control over the region's resources. Unsurprisingly, the oil industry fought that, but the Alaska Supreme Court ruled in favor of its creation in 1972. Since then, the borough has implemented major infrastructure improvements and advocated on behalf of its constituents.

Even with this development, the North Slope remains relatively cut off from the rest of Alaska, with only the Dalton Highway connecting Fairbanks to Prudhoe Bay. That relative isolation has helped Native groups there maintain their cultures. So too have international efforts at upholding Indigenous self-determination, such as the 1977 establishment of the Inuit Circumpolar Council (ICC). In 2009, ICC leaders developed the Circumpolar Inuit Launch Declaration on Arctic Sovereignty, which reaffirms Inuit self-determination and reminds the world that they're the longtime stewards of this region during a time when everyone seems to want a piece of it.

THE FOOD

Arctic food systems are some of the most maligned culinary traditions of Turtle Island, probably because they don't resemble the way most of us feed ourselves. That largely stems from a major misunderstanding about this way of life, which has a deep connection to place. People like award-winning Inuk chef Trudy Metcalfe-Coe are introducing the world to these unique tastes through her "country food" catering (a term often used to describe Inuit cuisine).

For many Inuit, subsistence harvesting still accounts for the majority of their diet. Some towns do have grocery stores, but food prices are ridiculously high since it costs so much to transport these goods that far north. Hunting and fishing are communal activities with elaborate customs and ceremonies to honor the animal that has given itself. Out of respect and necessity, absolutely every part of a harvested animal is utilized, right down to the sinew, which is used to make nets and skin boats. When a group of hunters brings in a massive bowhead—which can feed an entire village for several months—it's call for celebration.

Everyone plays a role in animal processing, including hooking, cutting, and preparing for storage in underground ice cellars (known as sigluaqs in Iñupiaq). Home cooks prepare whale meat countless ways, such as boiling the organ meats, fermenting it to make mikigaq, and using an ulu knife to cut up cubes of maktak (raw whale skin and blubber). See page 394 for a recipe featuring this Far North delicacy. Whale is also served in more familiar fashions, like steak or stir-fry.

Of course, few people outside the Arctic have the opportunity to taste these foods, especially since these animals are protected by laws like the Marine Mammal Protection Act. Over the decades, Indigenous communities have fought hard to maintain their subsistence rights to sustainably harvest these animals in accordance with guidelines from conservation groups like the International Whaling Commission.

Though whales are the most prized catches, other marine mammals like walruses and seals supplement that bounty. Odawa chef Joseph Shawana caught heat for serving seal at his Toronto restaurant but chose to keep it on the menu as a way to educate people about Indigenous foodways. Here, he shares the recipe that caused both rants and rave reviews, a delectable Seal Tartare (page 391) with a rich duck egg yolk.

After Inuit families process a harvested seal, they then render down the fat to make nutrient-rich seal oil. A staple in Far-North households, this liquid gold is used as a flavoring agent, dipping sauce, and fuel for traditional qulliq lamps. Although it's not commercially available, we wanted to highlight seal oil in this chapter given its importance in Arctic foodways. One beloved way to savor it is in Akutaq (page 405), a traditional dessert made from animal fat, berries, and snow. It also adds some fat and flavor to Simplest Summer Greens with Seal Oil (page 393).

We also offer recipes utilizing ingredients that are at home in the Arctic but that cooks far from the region can also access. For example, on page 397, char gets wrapped in kelp, baked, and topped with a duck egg aioli. Duck or goose breasts—flavored with white spruce and angelica seed—are smoked, seared, and served alongside a sweet yet tart cranberry sauce (see page 398).

Caribou, another cornerstone, is skewered and grilled on page 402 with onions and sweet gale nutlets (bog myrtle), paired with quick-pickled blackberries (see page 402), a sweet and savory take on a beloved foraged food. Even if you never get a chance to travel there, we hope these recipes give you a better understanding of the Arctic and the people who live off the land, water, and ice of the Far North.

SEAL TARTARE

serves 1 or 2

"This Seal Tartare Might Be the Most Controversial Dish in North America," wrote *Maxim* magazine in 2017. Similar headlines blared across the Internet. Chef Joseph Shawana, who grew up on the Wikwemikong Unceded Indian Reserve on Manitoulin Island in Northern Ontario, served this dish for a while at his restaurant Kū-Kŭm in Toronto to honor the way people in northern Canada live and eat.

The dish received overwhelming amounts of backlash from animal rights activists, inspiring petitions and counter petitions. Through the controversy, Joseph maintained a simple position: This is a food Indigenous people depend on, so why should he hide this culture?

I'm grateful Joseph agreed to share his recipe for his famous seal tartare. His preparation showcases the minerally flavor of seal so beautifully.

I know that the reality is most people reading this book won't get to try this dish.

In the United States, hunting seal is legal only for Indigenous people for personal subsistence use. In Canada, seal hunting for commercial use is legal but heavily managed. If you do have access to seal loin, I encourage you to try this preparation!

- 4 ounces frozen seal loin
- 2 ramps or scallions, thinly sliced
- 1 wild onion with greens, thinly sliced
- 1 small shallot, finely chopped
- 2 tablespoons wild mustard flowers
- Sea salt
- 1 tablespoon sunflower oil
- 1 duck egg yolk
- Wild flowers, for garnish

Thaw the seal loin in the refrigerator just until it's sliceable, then finely dice it and transfer to a small bowl. Add the ramps, wild onion, shallots, and mustard flowers. Season with salt, stir in the oil, and mix well.

Cover and refrigerate for 3 hours so the tartare mixture is well chilled.

Transfer to a plate. (You can mold it using a ring mold or biscuit cutter if you like.) Set a duck egg yolk on top and garnish with wildflowers.

SIMPLEST SUMMER GREENS
WITH SEAL OIL

serves 4

In the summer, people gather wild greens and enjoy them raw or simply served with seal oil, sometimes tossed with seal meat, dry fish, or whale meat. Different people harvest different greens, depending on what's available where they live. For example, in the Arctic, you'll find saltwater-loving plants, like sweet, lightly bitter beach peas and oyster leaves, which taste remarkably like its namesake bivalve, without the salinity, as well as hardy plants like sourdock, which has a rhubarb-like sourness. A bit farther south in the Subarctic, you might find earthy nettles at the edge of the forests and bitter marsh marigold in cold, freshwater streams and other wet areas.

As always when harvesting and handling wild foods, use caution and work with an expert. If you have any doubt about an ingredient, do not eat it.

To round out this Arctic snacking plate, of sorts, we recommend serving the greens and seal oil with Hot-Smoked Salmon (page 281) and pickled sea vegetables. You can purchase pickled sea vegetables from the region online or make your own using the brine from Quick Pickles (page 37).

- Sea salt
- 8 ounces summer greens, such as beach greens, sorrel, dock, willow, marsh marigold, nettles, or dandelion (see Note), rinsed well
- ¼ cup seal oil (see Why Seal Oil?)
- Pickled sea vegetables (optional), such as bull kelp and sea beans, for serving
- 8 ounces smoked salmon (optional), for serving

Bring a large pot of water to a boil and season with salt. Add the greens. (Use tongs to add the nettles so you don't get stung!) Boil for about 10 seconds for the nettles and beach greens to turn bright green. For the marsh marigold, boil for about 3 minutes, until tender.

Drain and spin the greens in a salad spinner until dry. Transfer to a platter.

Serve the greens with the seal oil, for dipping, and with pickled sea vegetables and smoked salmon, if desired.

Note: *You need to harvest marsh marigold (*Caltha palustris*) before it blooms; do not eat it raw. Toxins in the plant must be destroyed through cooking before you consume it. (Sound scary? It's the same for potatoes.) Nettles are best when harvested when they're under 2 feet tall. Be sure to wear gloves when harvesting and handling as they sting.*

WHY SEAL OIL?

Seal oil, a golden fat rendered from seal blubber, is one of the most important ingredients in the North, including the Arctic and coastal Subarctic. People who eat seal oil regularly generally find the flavor mild. Others find it a bit fishy.

Seal oil is rich in omega-3 fatty acids and provides many vitamins and minerals.

Traditionally, seal oil was collected simply by hanging the blubber and allowing the oil to drop into a container. Today, many people use heat to render it, first boiling the blubber to help remove some impurities, then chopping it up and slowly cooking it to allow the fat to release.

To store the oil long-term, it's important to boil it first to remove moisture or freeze it.

Most of us will likely never be fortunate enough to try seal oil, because it is not available commercially for culinary use. It's crucial, however, that Indigenous people retain access to this precious fat.

MAKTAK WITH BLUEBERRIES AND COW PARSNIP

serves 2 to 4

Maktak is the Indigenous name for the skin and blubber of a whale, typically a bowhead, beluga, or narwhal. Soon after a whale is caught, the maktak is separated from the meat, cut into squares about the size of fish fillets, and hung outside to dry and drain for a few days. It's then boiled for about an hour at the camp so it softens. After it's distributed to families, people freeze it for long-term keeping. People eat maktak throughout the year as part of their meal or as a snack; it's incredibly calorie-rich in a place where high-protein diets are common, and the fat supports many important functions in the body.

When cooking at an event in Alaska several years ago, I was inspired to dice the maktak small and toss it with what was growing around me: wild blueberries and citrus-y cow parsnip seeds.

Maktak is one of those foods that unless you are Indigenous to the North or are friendly with someone who is, you will likely not have a chance to try. But I wanted to share this recipe to honor the tradition of processing maktak.

- 8 ounces maktak, cut into ¼-inch dice
- Flaky sea salt
- 1 teaspoon cow parsnip seeds, lightly crushed
- 1 cup blueberries, fresh or thawed frozen
- Salmon roe (optional), for garnish

In a bowl, toss the maktak with a few pinches of flaky salt. Add the crushed cow parsnip seeds and blueberries and gently toss. Divide among small bowls and garnish each portion with a small spoonful of salmon roe, if desired.

PRESERVING FISH AND SEA MAMMALS THE NORTHERN WAY

During fishing and hunting seasons, many Native Alaskan and northern Canadian communities are all hands on deck. For a few weeks, families who live a partially or fully subsistence lifestyle gather to pull fish from the water or hunt seal and whale and preserve them for months to come.

The fish and meat are often cut, then hung outside to dry. In some communities, they're also smoked in a smokehouse.

People—typically women and older children—cut the animals in different ways using an ulu, a curved metal cutting blade designed specifically for women to use (and is considered "a women's knife"). Each method exposes more or less of the surface area of the flesh to the air and smoke, changing the shelf life of each type.

Traditionally, the fish and meat, as well as other foods, were stored in pits dug below the permafrost. Now people will sometimes pressure-can their bounty or vacuum-seal it for freezing.

HOUSEHOLD TRASH ONLY!
SAVE THE WHALES...
FOR DINNER
CAUTION

KELP-WRAPPED ARCTIC CHAR
WITH SMOKED SALT

serves 2 to 4

In the Arctic, as well as the northern Atlantic and Pacific, underground forests of kelp historically thrived, providing Indigenous people with essential minerals, supporting an ecosystem of traditional foods, and sequestering carbon from the atmosphere.

Climate change and other horrors of colonialism have threatened the abundance, but regenerative kelp farming is now on the rise, with some projects led by Indigenous people. In addition to its culinary uses on its own, it makes a beautiful wrapper for cooking fish, lightly seasoning it, and imparting its depth of umami flavor, while keeping the fish moist at the same time. While people traditionally smoke and otherwise preserve their fish in the Arctic, I picture this being a dish people could make at the fish camp with freshly caught fillets pulled right from the water.

While you could nestle the kelp-wrapped fish over a fire or grill to cook it, here, it's seasoned with a little smoked salt and roasted in the oven.

- 2 ounces dried kelp or kombu
- 1 tablespoon sunflower oil, plus more for the pan
- 2 skin-on wild Arctic char or thin salmon fillets (8 ounces each)
- Smoked salt
- Seaweed flakes, for serving
- Duck Egg Aioli (page 36), for serving

Preheat the oven to 400°F.

Place the kelp in a large bowl and cover with 4 cups cool water. Let stand for about 5 minutes, until softened.

Use a little oil to lightly grease a sheet pan. Using half the softened kelp, create two separate beds of it about the size of each fish fillet, spreading out the pieces in a single layer but slightly overlapping. Arrange a piece of fish skin-side down on top of each bed.

Rub the top of the fish fillets with the 1 tablespoon oil and sprinkle generously with smoked salt. Bring up the sides of the kelp to enclose the fish as much as possible, then cover the fish with the remaining kelp.

Roast the fish for 10 to 15 minutes, until an instant-read thermometer registers 145°F when inserted into the center of the fish. If the fish has been frozen and thawed first, you can cook until a knife inserted into the center comes out warm for medium to medium-rare fish.

Unwrap the fillets and sprinkle with seaweed flakes. Serve with the aioli.

SMOKED AND SEARED DUCK OR GOOSE BREASTS

WITH SPRUCE AND CRANBERRY

serves 4 to 6

The breasts of waterfowl like duck and goose are best enjoyed when cooked to medium-rare. Otherwise, they can taste dry and leathery. To add layers of flavor, I enjoy smoking the breasts after they're rubbed with an aromatic salt flavored with citrusy white spruce needles and angelica seed, which is a bit licorice-y with a celery-like edge. These two hardy plants grow in and near the Arctic.

Because duck and goose breasts can vary in size, their cooking time can also vary. To make sure they're perfectly cooked, it's best to use a probe thermometer when smoking them to monitor their temperature.

- 2 tablespoons fresh white spruce needles or 1 tablespoon dried (or use another edible conifer), coarsely chopped
- 1 teaspoon angelica seeds
- 2 tablespoons coarse sea salt
- 4 small boneless duck breast halves (about 7 ounces each) or 2 large boneless duck or goose breast halves (12 to 16 ounces each), preferably skin-on
- 2 cups cranberries, fresh or frozen
- ½ cup Maple Sugar (page 36) or store-bought
- 1 teaspoon Rose Hip Powder (page 359) or store-bought
- 2 tablespoons duck or goose fat

In a mortar, combine the spruce needles, angelica seeds, and coarse salt and pound with a pestle until you have what looks like a green salt with tiny flecks of conifer.

Season the breasts all over with some of this spruce salt and refrigerate them for 1 hour or up to 4 hours. Reserve the remaining spruce salt.

Remove the meat from the refrigerator, pat dry, and let sit at room temperature while you preheat a smoker.

Preheat a smoker to 200°F (or if you don't have a smoker, see Smoking Food on a Grill, page 69, or see Note).

Insert a probe thermometer into one of the breasts (choose a part that's medium thickness). Cook in the smoker until the small duck registers 125°F, 25 to 30 minutes; or the large duck or goose registers 130°F, 35 to 45 minutes.

Meanwhile, in a medium saucepan, combine the cranberries, maple sugar, ½ cup water, and the rose hip powder. Cook over medium-high heat for about 5 minutes, or until the cranberries just start to burst and turn into a chunky sauce.

When the meat reaches the correct temperature, let it cool for a bit, then use the tip of a sharp knife to score the skin if it's still on the breast.

In a cast-iron skillet, heat the duck or goose fat over medium-high heat until nearly smoking. Add the breasts with the skin- or skinned-side down. Sear for 1 to 3 minutes, pressing them, until beautifully browned.

Transfer the meat to a carving board, skin- or skinned-side up, and let them rest for 1 to 3 minutes. Thinly slice the breasts crosswise, then serve with the cranberry sauce and the remaining spruce salt on the side.

Note: *If you don't have a smoker or a grill, you can season the breasts with smoked salt and slow-roast them in a 200°F oven before searing them.*

STUFFED EGGS WITH ARCTIC GARNISHES

serves 4 to 8

What do deviled eggs look like in a place that's so far north? They might look like these stuffed eggs, with a filling made extra silky from a rich duck egg aioli, then served with toppings that reflect a sense of place. Below, you'll see a range of options, from tart rose hips (which bring a floral aroma and lemon-like acidity) to dried seaweed for crisp briny depth, to cooked shrimp or rich salmon roe. I also enjoy a sprinkle of either angelica seeds, which are commonly used in vermouth and have a licorice-y, celeryish flavor, or cow parsnip seeds, which have citrus peel notes and create a Sichuan peppercorn–like buzz on the tongue. Both seeds come from plants in the carrot family.

Some Indigenous peoples in the North gather eggs from wild birds in the spring, when shorebirds return to breed and build their nests. They're careful to always leave behind some eggs as they gather, so that generations of birds can thrive, and they never harvest eggs from endangered birds.

The practice of egging is generally illegal in the lower forty-eight states and Canada, but in Alaska and on Indigenous-managed land in Canada, the tradition is protected for Indigenous people. Indigenous leaders also work with biologists and regulatory agencies to make sure the bird populations stay healthy.

EGGS

- 4 eggs from wild birds, such as duck, goose, or gull
- 5 tablespoons Duck Egg Aioli (page 36)
- 1 teaspoon cider vinegar
- Sea salt

TOPPINGS (CHOOSE WHAT YOU LIKE)

- Smashed cow parsnip seeds or angelica seeds
- Crushed seedless rose hips
- Dried seaweed flakes
- Salmon roe
- Cooked Northern shrimp

Cook the eggs: Bring a medium saucepan of water to a boil over high heat. Set up a bowl of ice water.

Reduce the heat to medium so the water is simmering and carefully add the eggs. Cook for 10 minutes (see Note), then transfer the eggs to the ice water to cool completely.

Gently crack and peel the eggs. Cut them in half lengthwise. Scoop out the yolks and set aside. Arrange the egg white halves on a platter.

In a mini food processor, combine the aioli, vinegar, and ¼ teaspoon salt and pulse to incorporate. Add the egg yolks and puree until smooth. Taste and season with more salt as needed.

Transfer the yolk mixture to a piping bag and pipe it into the egg whites, or simply use a spoon to fill them. Add the toppings of your choice.

Note: *Ten minutes is the ideal cooking time to make hard-boiled duck eggs. For other eggs, you will have to play around to find the best time.*

CARIBOU SKEWERS WITH ARCTIC SALT AND QUICK-PICKLED BERRIES

serves 4 to 8

As with other game meats, a lot of the cuts of caribou are ground, or need to be stewed to become tender. But some cuts, like the backstrap, loin, and leg, can be enjoyed medium-rare. Here, the meat gets sprinkled with a fragrant salt that includes sweet gale, which is also known as bog myrtle. This bog-loving plant grows prolifically in the northern reaches of Turtle Island, including occasionally in the Arctic regions. It produces resinous little cones known as nutlets. When lightly ground, the nutlets have a bright, citrusy, almost Sichuan peppercorn–like aroma that is excellent with game meats.

The sweet gale nutlets as well as other spices in the salt get added to the brine for pickled berries, served with the dish. The little bit of brine in the duck egg aioli helps bring all the flavors together.

- 2 teaspoons coarse sea salt
- 4 juniper berries
- 2 teaspoons angelica seeds
- 1 teaspoon sweet gale nutlets (bog myrtle)
- 1 large onion, preferably sweet, cut into 12 equal wedges
- 2 pounds caribou, elk, or venison loin or leg steak, cut into 24 pieces (each about 1½ inches)
- Sunflower oil, for brushing
- 1 cup Duck Egg Aioli (page 36), for serving
- Quick-Pickled Berries with Arctic Spices (recipe follows), for serving, plus 1 tablespoon of their brine

In a mortar, combine the salt, juniper berries, angelica seeds, and sweet gale nutlets and pound the mixture with a pestle to form a seasoned salt.

Pull apart each onion wedge into halves so you have 24 pieces of onion, each with 2 or 3 layers.

Preheat a grill to medium-high heat.

Pat the meat dry. Use all the meat and onion pieces to thread onto 8 metal skewers in an alternating pattern.

Lightly brush them with oil and sprinkle with some of the seasoned salt. Grill for 3 to 5 minutes (medium-rare), turning frequently, until you start to see grill marks form and the onion is charred at the edges and slightly softened. Transfer the skewers to a platter to rest for a few minutes.

Meanwhile, whisk together the aioli with the tablespoon of berry brine in a medium bowl.

Serve the skewers with the aioli and pickled berries.

QUICK-PICKLED BERRIES WITH ARCTIC SPICES

makes about 2 cups

- ½ teaspoon sweet gale nutlets (bog myrtle)
- 2 juniper berries
- 1 cup cider vinegar
- ¼ cup birch syrup, maple syrup, or fireweed honey
- 1 teaspoon sea salt
- 1 small shallot, quartered lengthwise
- 2 cups fresh berries, such as crowberries or blackberries

In a mortar, combine the sweet gale nutlets and juniper berries and lightly crush them with the pestle.

In a saucepan, combine the spices, vinegar, 1 cup water, the syrup, salt, and shallot. Bring just to a simmer over medium heat, then turn off the heat and let cool.

Pack the berries into a jar. Strain the cooled brine over the top, seal, and refrigerate for 1 to 5 days.

AKUTAQ WITH ARCTIC BERRIES

serves 4 to 6

Akutaq (pronounced ah-GOO-duck) is a Yup'ik word that means "mix them together." (You'll also see other spellings, like agudak.) The dish is sometimes colloquially known as "Eskimo ice cream." (Note that many Inuit and Inupiaq people find the word "Eskimo" offensive, although there are some regions in Alaska and some elders who still embrace this term.)

Traditionally, it's made by whipping animal fat with fallen snow to create an emulsion. People would then add berries, dried meat, dried fish, wild greens, or really anything that's special and in season. (The type of fat used and other inclusions varied regionally and seasonally.)

With colonialism, people started making akutaq using the Crisco that came in their boxes of government rations and adding refined white sugar to make it sweeter. Some people continue to add savory ingredients, like cooked or smoked fish, while others keep it entirely sweet, just adding berries.

This very simple version is more modern, in that it's sweetened, but it's re-Indigenized by using animal fat and maple sugar. However akutaq is made, know that it's still common throughout northern Turtle Island, making frequent appearances on the table at weddings, birthdays, and potluck celebrations.

If you're using frozen berries, pulse any large ones in a food processor until chopped into smaller pieces.

- **½ cup rendered and cooled animal fat, such as duck fat, moose fat, or seal fat**
- **½ cup Maple Sugar (page 36) or store-bought**
- **¼ cup ice-cold water**
- **2 cups fresh or frozen sweet berries, such as cloudberries, blueberries, or other berries**

In a stand mixer fitted with the whisk (or in a bowl using a hand mixer), beat the fat on medium speed until it starts to become aerated. Add the maple sugar and continue mixing until it's fluffy, like frosting. Add the ice water and whip it until emulsified and even fluffier.

If you prefer an akutaq in which the berries are suspended in the creamy fat, gently fold them in by hand. If you prefer some of the berries to break down and stain the fat, mash some of them lightly and add them as you beat the fat and maple sugar. (You could always mix in some with the mixer and some by hand if you want a varied texture.)

Transfer to a large bowl and serve right away or freeze first to allow it to set and become scoopable. You can refrigerate akutaq for up to 2 days or freeze in an airtight container for up to 1 month.

ACKNOWLEDGMENTS

It's been an incredible honor to share some of the stories behind the foods of Turtle Island, and of course, there is no way I could have ever done it by myself.

Special thanks to those who have shared recipes with me: Sherry Pocknett, Crystal Wahpepah, Mariah Gladstone, Valerie Segrest, Shane Chartrand, and Joseph Shawana.

Thank you to Linda Black Elk for sharing your ethnobotanical knowledge with the world, and with me, and for bringing so many plants you gathered over multiple seasons to our photo shoots. I am also so deeply appreciative to Claudia Serrato for bringing your expert eye to the chapters about Mexico and Mesoamerica in general.

Thank you to my agent, Jonah Straus, for believing not only in this book, but also in me from the earliest days and helping guide its way to publication.

To Kristin Donnelly, thank you for bringing your deep knowledge, steady organization, and generous spirit to this project. Your talent for shaping recipes and wrangling the beautiful chaos of my mind and my schedule, along with building a cookbook with such a large scope, is unmatched. Working alongside you was not only a gift but a master class in how to bring something this complex and meaningful to life.

And to Kate Nelson, whose journalistic heart and thoughtful storytelling helped this book find its voice. Your ability to connect with the powerful diverse voices across Turtle Island and hold space for their stories brought depth and resonance to these pages. Thank you for listening so carefully, writing so truthfully, and helping shape something that speaks beyond the ingredients and into our shared passion for promoting Indigenous foodways.

Thank you to Clarkson Potter, especially editor Francis Lam in the United States and Andrea Magyar in Canada, for embracing this book wholeheartedly and encouraging me to tell these stories in the way that felt most authentic and natural.

Also on the Clarkson Potter team, thank you to art director Stephanie Huntwork for your guiding hand with the photography, design, and cover. Thank you to Darian Keels for all you have done behind the scenes to make this project a success. To Bonnie Benwick and Kate Slate, thank you for your care as you worked through the text in the book.

Thank you to Brianne Sperber, Felix Cruz, David Hawk, Adria Iwasutiak, and Kelly Albert for helping spread the word about Turtle Island!

Thank you to Jimmy Dean for your artwork, helping us create a meaningful cover for this book.

We photographed this book over several different shoots in multiple locations, and there are so many people to whom we are grateful. To David Alvarado—thank you for leading the way! To Jaida Grey Eagle—thank you for being part of the photography process and serving as another set of eyes to ensure cultural sensitivity was at the forefront of our imagery.

Thank you to the styling team in Minnesota, including food stylist Lara Miklasevics and prop stylist Alison Hoekstra. I know sourcing ingredients and props for these photos required some Herculean efforts, and I am forever grateful! Thank you to the kitchen team, Tess Bouska and Susan Barrientos, for bringing your skills to the photo shoot. (Thank you as well to Tess for being a careful and thoughtful recipe tester!)

Thank you to Steelite and Eighth Generation for providing us with stunning wares we could use as props. Thank you to the folks and businesses who provided some ingredients we needed at the last minute for photo shoots and testing, including Sean Lenihan of The Honest Bison, Mill Valley Markets, Clancey's Butcher Shop, Derek Nichols, Hank Shaw, Samuel Thayer, Tim Clemens, Valerie Segrest, and my brother, Ben Sherman.

Thank you to grower Jessi Peine for nurturing plants—including Devil's Claw, Lakota Squash, and so many more—over multiple seasons so we could have them to showcase in the book.

Thank you Chanelle Gallagher of Waabigan Clay for lending us some truly beautiful pieces to use for our shoots. And to April Stone for sharing your handcrafted baskets.

Thank you to the Guthrie Theater, including MJ Kedrowski, Olivia Smith, Diana Brown, and Trisha Kirk, for letting us take over the kitchen and restaurant for five days so we could shoot.

Thank you to Perry Hanson of Studio 8900 for having one of the most beautiful studios around and letting us spend a wonderful week there.

In Mexico, I was privileged to work with another incredible team on the photography, including food and prop stylist Vega Hernando, chef Ricardo Garrido, kitchen producer Alisa Bartels, production assistant Natalia Reca, and kitchen assistant Thania Rodriguez.

Thank you as well to Dennis Lazarus for sharing your space at Colonia Bar & Meadery in Mexico City. (You'll recognize some of its beautiful textured walls in the photos!)

And of course I must thank all of the experts and knowledge keepers who contributed their wisdom to help me showcase the diversity of this beautiful place we call home, including Jody Eddy, Nancy J. Turner, Roxanne Dubar-Ortiz, Tricia Alexander, Jacobo and María Ángeles, Jessie Bergren, Taelor Barton, Tawnya Brant, Marcus Briggs-Cloud, Janice Brown, Twila Cassadore, Larry Cesspooch, Jennifer Cockrall, Nephi Craig, Pyet DeSpain, Jeffery Darensbourg, Hugo Duran, Neftalí Durán, Bradley Dry, Angie Ferguson, Amyrose Foll, Nora Frank-Buckner, Ben Jacobs, Thalía Barrios García, Michial Graywolf Garvin, Ciarra Greene,Lilian Hill, Elizabeth Hoover, Dune Lankard, Jenni Lessard, Melissa Lewis, Timara Lotah Link, Mezcal Macurichos, José Bautista Maldonado, Trudy Metcalfe-Coe, Nicole Myers-Lim, Stephen McComber, Sara Calvosa Olson, Roxanne Dunbar Ortiz, Paul Natrall, Marie-Cecile "Cezin" Kakgoosh Nottaway-Wawatie, Loretta Barrett Oden, Abra Nungasuk Patkotak, Tia Quintanilla Pioche, Darren Parry, Kelly Pingree, Sherry Pocknett, Odilia Romero, Felicia Cocotzin Ruiz, Richard Sherman, Bruce Savage, Spring Alaska Schreiner, Valerie Segrest, Simone Senogles, Brittny Seowtewa, Neely Snyder, Kimberly Tilsen-Brave Heart, Alejandra Treviño, Ian Thompson, Rowen White, and Troy Wiipongwii.

Thank you to my executive assistant, Jo Boyer, for everything you do to keep me on track and for all the work you do for NATIFS.

To the passionate, hardworking teams at both NATIFS and Owamni, thank you for helping bring this vision to life each and every day. Special thanks to Owamni's executive chef, Lee Garman, leading an amazing culinary team, and also Tom Peterson, Tara Mostrom, and Alexa Wyatt for all of your amazing hard work!

To my father, Gerald Sherman, who has created such a beautiful legacy to follow and taught me to return energy and opportunity back into Indian Country, and to my stepmother, Jael Kampfe, for being such an energetic force to make the world a better place!

To my mother, Joan Conroy, who has always been there for me, your laugh, your heart, and your caring for others have always been an inspiration.

To my sister Kelly Conroy, for always being willing to help, even though I fully embrace my role as the teasing older brother. And to all my siblings: Sarabeth, Ben, Luke, and Bekkah, thank you for your love and support!

I'm also so grateful for my son, Phoenix Danger, and his journey into culinary school at Saint Paul College. We've been through so much together, and I'm excited to see the world through your eyes as you find your own path in life.

And last but not least, my love, my partner, my adventure buddy, and my soulmate, Mecca Bos. From kicking off the recipe testing to navigating the steady stream of strange ingredients taking over our kitchen, you've been there through it all. Thank you for your patience, your sharp eye, your laughter, and your honesty. For grounding me when things felt overwhelming, and for reminding me why this work matters. This book wouldn't be what it is without your presence, your perspective, and the life we've built together, side by side, one meal, one moment, and one travel adventure at a time.

INDEX

Note: Page references in *italics* indicate photographs.

T

Clarkson Potter/Publishers
An imprint of the Crown Publishing Group
A division of Penguin Random House LLC
1745 Broadway
New York, NY 10019
clarksonpotter.com
penguinrandomhouse.com

Photos by Sean Sherman: pages 12 (upper left), 103, 363, and 367.

Photos by Jaida Grey Eagle: pages 19 (bottom), 56, 73, 80, 83, 120, 127, 160, 169, 296, 314–315, 334, 345, 347, and 357.

Photo by Cody Hammer: page 159

Photos by Kari Rowe: pages 187, 275, 277, and 333

Photo by Sara Calvosa Olson: page 288

Photo by Brian Adams: page 395

Library of Congress Cataloging-in-Publication Data is available upon request.

ISBN 978-0-593-57923-7
Ebook ISBN 978-0-593-57924-4

Editor: Francis Lam | Editorial assistant: Darian Keels
Art director and Designer: Stephanie Huntwork | Production designer: Christina Self
Illustrator: Jimmy Dean Horn Jr.
Production editor: Abby Oladipo
Production: Phil Leung
Compositors: Merri Ann Morrell and Hannah Hunt
Food stylists: Lara Miklasevics and Vega Hernando | Food stylists assistants: Tess Bouska, Susan Barrientos, Ricardo Garrido, Alisa Bartels, and Thania Rodriguez
Prop stylists: Alison Hoekstra and Vega Hernando
Photo assistant: Natalia Reca
Recipe testers: Mecca Bos and Tess Bouska
Copyeditor: Kate Slate
Proofreaders: Penelope Haynes, Rachel Holzman, Diana Drew, and Andrea Peabbles
Indexer: Elizabeth Parson
Publicists: Felix Cruz and David Hawk | Marketer: Brianne Sperber

Manufactured in China

10 9 8 7 6 5 4 3 2

First Edition

The authorized representative in the EU for product safety and compliance is Penguin Random House Ireland, Morrison Chambers, 32 Nassau Street, Dublin D02 YH68, Ireland, https://eu-contact.penguin.ie.

SEAN SHERMAN, Oglala Lakota, born on South Dakota's Pine Ridge Indian Reservation, is a chef and leader who has been cooking across the United States and the world for the past thirty years. His main culinary focus has been to raise awareness of and revitalize Native food systems in a modern culinary context. In 2014, he founded The Sioux Chef, a food education and catering project, in the Minneapolis–Saint Paul area. His first book, *The Sioux Chef's Indigenous Kitchen,* was published in 2017 and won a James Beard Award for Best Book in American Cooking. His restaurant Owamni opened in Minneapolis in 2021 and was honored on many best new restaurant lists, winning the James Beard Award for Best New Restaurant. In 2023, Sean was named on *Time* magazine's list of 100 most influential people.